French

FOR

DUMMIES®

2ND EDITION

by Dodi-Katrin Schmidt, Michelle M. Williams, Dominique Wenzel, and Zoe Erotopoulos

WILEY

John Wiley & Sons, Inc.

French For Dummies®, 2nd Edition

Published by
John Wiley & Sons, Inc.
111 River St.
Hoboken, NJ 07030-5774
www.wiley.com

Copyright © 2011 by John Wiley & Sons, Inc.

Published by John Wiley & Sons, Inc., Hoboken, NJ

Published simultaneously in Canada

For general information on our other products and services, please contact our Customer Care Department within the U.S. at 877-762-2974, outside the U.S. at 317-572-3993, or fax 317-572-4002.

For technical support, please visit www.wiley.com/techsupport.

Wiley also publishes its books in a variety of electronic formats and by print-on-demand. Not all content that is available in standard print versions of this book may appear or be packaged in all book formats. If you have purchased a version of this book that did not include media that is referenced by or accompanies a standard print version, you may request this media by visiting http://booksupport.wiley.com. For more information about Wiley products, visit us at www.wiley.com.

Library of Congress Control Number: 2011932271

ISBN 978-1-118-00464-7 (pbk); ISBN 978-1-118-13864-9 (ebk); ISBN 978-1-118-13865-6 (ebk); ISBN 978-1-118-13866-3 (ebk)

Manufactured in the United States of America

10 9 8 7 6 5 4 3 2 1

WILEY

About the Authors

Dodi-Katrin Schmidt has been a writer, translator, and editor for over a decade. Aside from translating German, French, and English texts of various kinds, including linguistic handbooks, film reviews, travel guides, and children's books, she has also been involved in developing language textbooks, language courses, teachers' handbooks, and grammar companions for video language courses. Dodi has been teaching for more than two decades at high school, adult education, and college levels in Europe as well as the United States. She also writes test items for various national language tests and recorded textbook and test material. Together with her husband, she travels a great deal, and they continually house and entertain foreign students and former students in their home in Princeton, NJ.

Michelle M. Williams is an editor at a major educational publisher. A former French teacher, she has taught students ranging from 2-years old to adults in both the public and private sectors. She is a firm believer in making the language fun and accessible to all who want to learn. Her most rewarding experience, however, is in watching and listening to her son Nathaniel learn to speak and sing in French.

Dominique Wenzel has been a freelance teacher of French and a translator for 15 years. Born and raised in France, she received a Master's degree from the University of Paris-Sorbonne and studied at the University of Chicago on a postgraduate Fulbright scholarship. Her students include business professionals, children, and adults of all levels and interests. She travels regularly to France. Dominique raised two bicultural, bilingual children who are both active in the international field.

Dr. Zoe Erotopoulos was born in Greece and immigrated to the United States at a young age. Her love of the French language, literature, and culture inspired her to pursue her academic studies in these areas. She holds an MA, MPhil, and PhD in French and Romance Philology from Columbia University in New York, NY. Dr. Erotopoulos has also studied in Aix-en-Provence, at the Sorbonne, and at the École Normale Supérieure in Paris.

Her teaching experience in French ranges from elementary to advanced level courses, including literature and theater. Dr. Erotopoulos's area of expertise is 17th-century French theater. Throughout her academic career, she has taught at a number of institutions, including Columbia University, Reid Hall in Paris, and Trinity College in Hartford, Connecticut. She is presently teaching in the Department of Modern Languages and Literatures at Fairfield University in Fairfield, Connecticut. Dr. Erotopoulos is the author of *French Verbs For Dummies* and *French For Dummies,* Audio Set. She lives in Connecticut with her husband, Steve, and three children, Despina, Olga, and Stathi.

Dedication

Zoe: To my family.

Acknowledgments

Zoe: I am very grateful to my family for their unwavering love and support, especially to my children who are my personal cheering squad. I would like to wholeheartedly thank my editor, Tracy Barr, for her professionalism, her insightful comments and suggestions, and her expertise. A special thank you goes to Michael Lewis for entrusting me with this project and to the technical reviewers, Eric Laird and Lydia de Faveri, for their expertise and careful attention to detail. I must also thank Dodi Schmidt, Michelle Williams, and Dominique Wenzel, who put so much time, effort, and knowledge into the first edition of this book. Last, but certainly not least, a heartfelt thank you to my colleagues in the Department of Modern Languages and Literatures at Fairfield University and Cynthia Nadal for their friendship, encouragement, and sound advice.

Publisher's Acknowledgments

We're proud of this book; please send us your comments at http://dummies.custhelp.com. For other comments, please contact our Customer Care Department within the U.S. at 877-762-2974, outside the U.S. at 317-572-3993, or fax 317-572-4002.

Some of the people who helped bring this book to market include the following:

Acquisitions, Editorial, and Vertical Websites

Editor: Tracy L. Barr

Acquisitions Editor: Michael Lewis

Assistant Editor: David Lutton

Editorial Program Coordinator: Joe Niesen

Technical Editors: Eric H. Laird, Lydia de Faveri Spiegel

Associate Producer: Josh Frank

Supervising Producer: Richard Graves

CD Producer: Her Voice Unlimited, LLC

Senior Editorial Manager: Jennifer Ehrlich

Editorial Supervisor and Reprint Editor: Carmen Krikorian

Editorial Assistant: Rachelle Amick

Art Coordinator: Alicia B. South

Cover Photos: ©iStockphoto.com/Lisa F. Young

Cartoons: Rich Tennant (www.the5thwave.com)

Composition Services

Project Coordinator: Nikki Gee

Layout and Graphics: Timothy C. Detrick, Joyce Haugey, Corrie Socolovitch, Christin Swinford, Laura Westhuis

Proofreaders: Rebecca Denoncour, Susan Moritz, Nancy L. Reinhardt

Indexer: Potomac Indexing, LLC

Illustrator: Elizabeth Kurtzman

Publishing and Editorial for Consumer Dummies

Kathleen Nebenhaus, Vice President and Executive Publisher

Kristin Ferguson-Wagstaffe, Product Development Director

Ensley Eikenburg, Associate Publisher, Travel

Kelly Regan, Editorial Director, Travel

Publishing for Technology Dummies

Andy Cummings, Vice President and Publisher

Composition Services

Debbie Stailey, Director of Composition Services

Contents at a Glance

Table of Contents

Introduction

As society becomes increasingly more international and as we seek to become global citizens, knowing how to say at least a few words in other languages becomes more and more useful. The European Union is a great example of global citizenry as borders between the member countries become easier to cross. Furthermore, global business environments necessitate overseas travel. Thanks to numerous travel websites, finding a package deal for airfare and hotel stays makes travel abroad easier and more convenient than ever before. Moreover, the Internet allows us to have contact with people all over the world, making learning a foreign language a great asset.

Whether you are traveling overseas on business, exploring a different culture, or even connecting with your heritage, learning a little bit of the language has many advantages. Whatever your reason for wanting to learn some French, *French For Dummies,* 2nd Edition, can help. It gives you the skills you need for basic communication in French. We're not promising fluency here, but if you need to greet someone, purchase a ticket, ask for directions, make a hotel reservation, or order off a menu in French, you need look no further than this book.

Remember that everyday French is like everyday English. It makes use of simplified lingual forms which, although perfectly correct, avoid and ignore certain complicated verb tenses and moods such as, say, the future perfect or the subjunctive. In everyday French, you can express yourself adequately by following just a few easy-to-understand grammar rules and by knowing a minimum number of words. So you should find the lessons in this book to be fun and not the least bit overwhelming.

Now is playtime: **C'est la récréation** (seh lah rey-krey-ah-syohN).

About This Book

French For Dummies, 2nd Edition, isn't like a class that you have to drag yourself to twice a week for a specified period of time. You can use this book however you want to, whether your goal is to learn some words and phrases to help you get around when you visit France or a francophone country, or you just want to be able to say "Hello, how are you?" to your French-speaking neighbor. Go through this book at your own pace, reading as much or as little at a time as you like. You don't have to trudge through the chapters in sequential order, either; just read the sections that interest you.

Conventions Used in This Book

To make this book easy to navigate, we've set up some conventions:

- French terms are set in **boldface** to make them stand out.

- Pronunciation, set in parentheses, follows the French terms. Hyphens connect syllables in the same word as well as words that are linked by the French liaison (which you can find out all about in Chapter 3).

- Translation of the French terms is set in *italic* and follows the pronunciation.

- Because French nouns are typically preceded by an article, we include those articles in the word lists throughout this book, even though the English translation may not use the article. Furthermore, because articles indicate a noun's gender, they're helpful bits of information when you're learning a language. When the article is abbreviated (l'), however, you can't tell the gender. In those instances, we add a gender designation: (m) for masculine and (f) for feminine.

- Verb conjugations (lists that show you the forms of a verb) are given in tables in this order:

  - The "I" form
  - The "you" (singular, informal) form
  - The "he/she/it/one" form
  - The "we" form
  - The "you" (plural, and singular, formal) form
  - The "they" form.

Pronunciations follow in the second column. The example shown uses the verb **parler** (pahr-ley) (*to speak*). The conjugation starts with the French equivalent of *I speak* or *I am speaking*; *you speak,* or *you are speaking,* and so on.

Conjugation	*Pronunciation*
je parle	zhuh pahrl
tu parles	tew pahrl
il/elle/on parle	eel/ehl/ohN pahrl
nous parlons	nooh parh-lohN
vous parlez	vooh parh-ley
ils/elles parlent	eel/ehl parhl

So that you can make fast progress in French, this book includes a few elements to help you along:

- ✔ **Talkin' the Talk dialogues:** The best way to learn a language is to see and hear how it's used in conversation, so we include dialogues throughout the book. The dialogues come under the heading "Talkin' the Talk" and show you the French words, the pronunciation, and the English translation.

- ✔ **Words to Know blackboards:** Memorizing key words and phrases is also important in language learning, so we collect the important words in a chapter (or section within a chapter) in a chalkboard, with the heading "Words to Know."

- ✔ **Fun & Games activities:** If you don't have actual French speakers to practice your new language skills on, you can use the Fun & Games activities to reinforce what you learn. These games are fun ways to gauge your progress.

Also note that, because each language has its own way of expressing ideas, the English translations that we provide for the French terms may not be exactly literal. We want you to know the gist of what's being said, not just the words that are being said. For example, the phrase **C'est normal** (seh nohr-mahl) can be translated literally as *It's normal,* but the phrase really means *It's no big deal.* This book gives the second translation.

Foolish Assumptions

To write this book, we had to make some assumptions about who you are and what you want from a book called *French For Dummies.* Here are the assumptions that we've made about you:

- ✔ You know no or very little French — or if you took French back in school, you don't remember much of it.

- ✔ You're not looking for a book that will make you fluent in French; you just want to know some words, phrases, and sentence constructions so that you can communicate basic information in French.

- ✔ You don't want to have to memorize long lists of vocabulary words or a bunch of boring grammar rules.

- ✔ You want to have fun and learn a little bit of French at the same time.

If these statements apply to you, you've found the right book!

How This Book Is Organized

This book is divided by topic into parts and then into chapters. The following sections tell you what types of information you can find in each part.

Part 1: Getting Started

This part lets you get your feet wet by giving you some French basics: how to pronounce words, what the accents mean, and so on. We even boost your confidence by reintroducing you to some French words that you probably already know. Finally, we outline the basics of French grammar that you may need to know when you work through later chapters in the book.

Part II: French in Action

In this part, you begin learning and using French. Instead of focusing on grammar points as many language textbooks do, this part focuses on everyday situations, such as asking for directions, shopping, dining, going out on the town, and making small talk.

Part III: French on the Go

This part gives you the tools you need to take your French on the road, whether you're going to a local French restaurant or to a museum in France. This part covers all aspects of travel in French-speaking parts of the world, and it even has a chapter on how to handle emergencies.

Part IV: The Part of Tens

If you're looking for small, easily digestible pieces of information about French, this part is for you. Here you can find ten ways to learn French quickly, ten useful French expressions to know, ten things never to say in French, and more.

Part V: Appendixes

This part of the book includes important information that you can use for reference. Appendix A is a mini-dictionary in both French-to-English and English-to-French formats. If you encounter a French word that you don't understand or you need to say something in French that you can't find quickly elsewhere in the book, you can look it up here. Appendix B features verb tables, which show you how to conjugate regular verbs and then how to conjugate those verbs that stubbornly don't fit the pattern. Appendix C gives you the answer keys to all of the Fun & Games activities that appear in the book, and Appendix D lists the tracks that appear on the audio CD that comes with this book so that you can find the dialogues easily and follow along.

Icons Used in This Book

You may be looking for particular information while reading this book. To make certain types of information easier to find, we've placed the following icons in the left-hand margins throughout the book:

This icon highlights tips that can make learning French easier.

This icon points out interesting information that you ought not forget.

To help you avoid linguistic, grammatical, and cultural faux pas, we use this icon.

Languages are full of quirks that may trip you up if you're not prepared for them. This icon points to discussions of these peculiar grammar rules.

If you're looking for information and advice about culture and travel, look for this icon. It draws your attention to interesting tidbits about the countries in which French is spoken.

The audio CD that comes with this book gives you the opportunity to listen to real French speakers so that you can get a better understanding of what French sounds like. This icon marks the Talkin' the Talk dialogues that you can find on the CD.

Where to Go from Here

Learning a language is all about jumping in and giving it a try (no matter how bad your pronunciation is at first). So make the leap! Start at the beginning, pick a chapter that interests you, or listen to a few dialogues on the CD. Before long, you'll be able to respond **Oui!** (wee!) (*Yes!*) when people ask **Parlez-vous français?** (pahr-ley vooh frahN-seh?) (*Do you speak French?*).

Note: If you've never been exposed to French before, you may want to read the chapters in Part I before you tackle the later chapters. Part I gives you some of the basics that you need to know about the language, such as how to pronounce the various sounds, some basic expressions and words, and the fundamentals of French sentence structure.

Part I
Getting Started

The 5th Wave   By Rich Tennant

"There are many French phrases that we all use every day. You're no doubt familiar with the term 'à la mode.'"

In this part . . .

You have to start somewhere, but we bet that you know a lot more French than you think. Don't think so? Then check out Chapter 1 and see how many French words and idioms you already use. Chapters 2 and 3 provide some basic background on French grammar and pronunciation, while Chapters 4 and 5 get you talking about yourself and your family. So get started and don't worry — We make it fun!

Chapter 1

The French You Already Know

In This Chapter

▶ French words that are identical or similar to their English counterparts

▶ French words to watch out for

▶ Idioms and popular expressions you may already know

*L*earning a new language can be challenging. Not only do you need to know a whole new vocabulary, but you also need to twist your head around different grammar rules and your tongue around different pronunciation rules. But here's a little news that may make the task seem a little less daunting: You already know quite a few French words and expressions. How? Because the English language, being the borrower that it is, contains many French words and expressions, and French has absorbed some English words, too.

In this chapter, you get to explore some French words and phrases without having to know pronunciation or grammar rules (that info comes in Chapters 2 and 3). Here, we include French words that are spelled the same and mean the same as their English counterparts, as well as words that are close in meaning and spelling. But because not every French word that resembles an English word shares its meaning, we also tell you what words to watch out for. In addition, we include some French expressions that you probably already know and understand. By the end of this chapter, you may discover that you actually know more French than you previously thought.

The French You're Familiar With

With just a narrow stretch of water between them, the English and the French have historically been pretty close, even if they haven't always been the friendly allies they are today. In fact, French was the language of the English court for a very long time — a fact that many people tend to forget. (The Normans who invaded England in 1066 with William the Conqueror were French, as were some of the most prominent people in English history).

What does this have to do with your learning French? Well today, about 35 percent of English vocabulary is of French origin. That being the case, you already know an impressive amount of French, whether you realize it or not. The only pitfall you have to watch out for is that sometimes the English words have a different meaning from their French counterparts, and they almost certainly have a different pronunciation.

French nouns are preceded by either definite or indefinite articles. The definite articles are **le** (masculine), **la** (feminine), **l'** (an abbreviation of either **le** or **la**), and **les** (plural); these are the equivalent to the English word *the.* The indefinite articles are **un** (masculine)**, une** (feminine)**, des** (plural); these are all equivalent to the English words *a, an,* or *some.* As you learn French, knowing which articles go with what nouns helps you identify the noun's gender; that's why we include the articles with the nouns in the lists throughout this book. Because the abbreviated article **l'** obscures the noun's gender, we added the gender in parentheses. Finally, because the articles are not always used in English translations, we don't include them in the translations of the word lists: **l'université** (f) (lew-nee-vehr-see-tey) (*university*) and **le kiosque** (luh kyohhsk) (*kiosk*), for example.

Friendly allies — bons alliés

Several French words are spelled the same and have the same meaning as their English counterparts. The only thing that may be different is the pronunciation (for more on pronunciation guidelines, head to Chapter 3). Take a look at these **bons alliés** (bohN-zah-lyey) (*friendly allies*):

- **l'art** (m) (lahr)
- **brave** (brahv)
- **le bureau** (luh bew-roh)
- **le client** (luh klee-yahN)
- **le concert** (luh kohN-sehr)
- **la condition** (lah kohN-dee-syohN)
- **content** (kohN-tahN)
- **le courage** (luh kooh-rahzh)
- **le cousin** (luh kooh-zaN)
- **la culture** (lah kewl-tewr)
- **différent** (dee-fey-rahN)

- **excellent** (ehk-seh-lahN)
- **le garage** (luh gah-rahzh)
- **le guide** (luh geed)
- **important** (aN-pohr-tahN)
- **le journal** (luh zhoohr-nahl)
- **la machine** (lah mah-sheen)
- **le message** (luh mey-sahzh)
- **le moment** (luh moh-mahN)
- **la nation** (lah nah-syohN)
- **la nièce** (lah nyehs)
- **l'orange** (f) (loh-rahNzh)
- **le parent** (luh pah-rahN)

- **possible** (poh-see-bluh)
- **principal** (praN-see-pahl)
- **probable** (proh-bah-bluh)
- **la question** (lah kehs-tyohN)
- **la radio** (lah rah-dyoh)
- **le restaurant** (luh rehs-toh-rahN)
- **la rose** (lah rohz)
- **rouge** (roohzh)
- **la route** (lah rooht)
- **la science** (lah syahNs)
- **le secret** (luh suh-kreh)
- **le service** (luh sehr-vees)
- **le signal** (luh see-nyahl)
- **le silence** (luh see-lahNs)
- **la solitude** (lah soh-lee-tewd)
- **le sport** (luh spohr)
- **la station** (lah stah-syohN)
- **la statue** (lah stah-tew)
- **la suggestion** (lah sewg-zheh-styohN)
- **la surprise** (lah sewr-preez)
- **la table** (lah tah-bluh)
- **le taxi** (luh tah-ksee)
- **le tennis** (luh tey-nees)
- **le train** (luh traN)
- **urgent** (ewr-zhahN)
- **violet** (vyoh-leh)
- **le voyage** (luh voh-yahzh)
- **le zoo** (luh zooh)

Kissing cousins

Some French words, while not identical in spelling to their English counterparts, look very similar. These words also have similar meanings. Table 1-1 shows words that fit into this category.

Table 1-1	Words Similar in Meaning, Slightly Different in Spelling		
French	*English*	*French*	*English*
l' acteur (m) (lahk-tuhr)	actor	**l' hôtel (m)** (loh-tehl)	hotel
l'adresse (f) (lah-drehs)	address	**le kiosque** (luh kyohhsk)	kiosk
l'aéroport (m) (lah-eyr-oh-pohr)	airport	**la lampe** (lah lahmp)	lamp
l'allée (f) (lah-ley)	alley	**la lettre** (lah leh-truh)	letter

(continued)

Table 1-1 *(continued)*

French	English	French	English
l'Américain (m)/**l'Américaine** (f) (lah-mey-ree-kaN/ lah-mey-ree-kehn)	*American*	**la mémoire** (lah mey-mwahr)	*memory*
l'âge (m) (lahzh)	*age*	**le miroir** (luh mee-rwahr)	*mirror*
l'artiste (m/f) (lahr-teest)	*artist*	**la musique** (lah mew-zeek)	*music*
la banque (lah bahNk)	*bank*	**la nationalité** (lah nah-syoh-nah-lee-tey)	*nationality*
la cathédrale (lah kah-tey-drahl)	*cathedral*	**nécessaire** (ney-sey-sehr)	*necessary*
le chèque (luh shehk)	*check*	**ordinaire** (ohr-dee-nehr)	*ordinary*
la classe (lah klahs)	*class*	**le papier** (luh pah-pyey)	*paper*
la chambre (lah shahN-bruh)	*chamber, bedroom*	**le poème** (luh poh-ehm)	*poem*
la comédie (lah koh-mey-dee)	*comedy*	**potentiel** (poh-tahN-syehl)	*potential*
le congrès (luh kohN-greh)	*congress*	**le problème** (luh proh-blehm)	*problem*
la crème (lah krehm)	*cream*	**le professeur** (luh proh-feh-suhr)	*teacher/ professor*
la démocratie (lah dey-moh-krah-see)	*democracy*	**le sénateur** (luh sey-nah-tuhr)	*senator*
le développement (luh dey-vlohp-mahN)	*development*	**le succès** (luh sew-kseh)	*success*
la famille (lah fah-meey)	*family*	**la terrasse** (lah teh-rahs)	*terrace*
la géographie (lah zhey-oh-grah-fee)	*geography*	**la tragédie** (lah trah-zhey-dee)	*tragedy*
le gouvernement (luh gooh-vehr-nuh-mahN)	*government*	**l'université** (f) (lew-nee-vehr-see-tey)	*university*
l'histoire (f) (lee-stwahr)	*history*	**la visite** (lah vee-zeet)	*visit*

False friends — faux amis

Some French words are **faux amis** (foh-zah-mee) (*false friends*). They look similar to English words, but they don't have the same meaning. Misusing these words can be quite confusing. For example, if you tell someone that your young adult son or daughter is in a **collège** (koh-lehzh), they'd probably look at you — or your child — strangely because the French word **collège** means *middle school*, not *university*. The following list shows some of these easy-to-confuse words:

- ✔ **actuellement** (ahk-tew-ehl-mahN): This word means *now*, not *actually*. The French word for *actually* is **en fait** (ahN feht).

- ✔ **assister à** (ah-sees-tey ah): This word means *to attend*, not *to assist*. The French word for *to assist* is **aider** (ey-dey).

- ✔ **attendre** (ah-tahN-druh): This word means *to wait for*, not *to attend*. The French word for *to attend* is **assister à** (ah-sees-tey ah).

- ✔ **la bague** (lah bahg): This word means *ring* (the kind you wear on your finger), not *bag*. The French word for *bag* is **le sac** (luh sahk).

- ✔ **blesser** (bleh-sey): This word means *to wound* or *to hurt*. The French word for *to bless* is **bénir** (bey-neer).

- ✔ **la cave** (lah kahv): The French word **cave** means *cellar* in French. The word for *cave* is **la grotte** (lah grohht) in French.

- ✔ **le collège** (luh koh-lehzh) means *middle school*; use the French word **l'université** (f) (lew-nee-vehr-see-tey) when you want to say *college*.

- ✔ **formidable** (fohr-mee-dah-bluh): This word means *wonderful* or *tremendous*, not *fearsome* or *daunting*. To say *formidable* in French, you use the word **redoutable** (ruh-dooh-tah-bluh).

- ✔ **la lecture** (lah leh-ktewr): This word means *a reading*, as in a reading of Balzac's novels. The word for *lecture* is **la conférence** (lah kohN-fey-rahNs).

- ✔ **la librairie** (lah lee-brey-ree): This word means *bookstore*, not *library*. The French word for *library* is **la bibliothèque** (lah bee-blee-oh-tehk).

- ✔ **la place** (lah plahs): This word means *square*, *seat at the theater,* or *seat on the bus*, not *place*. The French word for *place* is **le lieu** (luh lyuh) or **l'endroit** (m) (lahN-drwah).

- ✔ **rester** (rehs-tey): This word means *to stay* or *to remain*, not *to rest*. The French word for *to rest* is **se reposer** (suh-ruh-poh-zey).

- ✔ **sympathique** (saN-pah-teek): This word means *nice*. To say *sympathetic* in French, you say **compatissant(e)** (kohN-pah-tee-sahN[t]).

- ✔ **la veste** (lah vehst): This word means *jacket* in French, not *vest* or *waistcoat*. The French word for *vest* is **le gilet** (luh zhee-leh).

Borrowed English words

The preceding sections note quite a few English words that have been borrowed from French and that have retained their French meaning, even though the pronunciation is different.

But English isn't the only language that's nicked a few words. French has also borrowed many words from English and continues to do so in spite of the loud protest by purists who condemn this trend as a sign of cultural contamination and name it **franglais** (frahN-gleh): Here is a list of some of the terms borrowed from English and absorbed into the French language. Note the different pronunciation:

- **le budget** (luh bewd-zheh)
- **le business** (luh beez-nehs)
- **le camping** (luh kahN-peeng)
- **le chewing-gum** (luh shweeng-gohhm)
- **les chips** (ley sheep[s])
- **le coca** (luh koh-kah)
- **cool** (koohl)
- **le fast food** (luh fahst foohd)
- **le hamburger** (luh ahm-boohr-guhr)

- **le jet set** (luh jeht seht)
- **le manager** (luh mah-nah-jehr)
- **le marketing** (luh mahr-kuh-teeng)
- **le parking** (luh pahr-keen)
- **le rock** (luh rohk) (as in rock music)
- **le shopping** (luh shoh-peeng)
- **le steak** (luh stehk)
- **le chat** (luh chaht)
- **le tunnel** (luh tew-nehl)
- **le week-end** (luh wee-kehnd)

Talkin' the Talk

Take a look at this conversation between two young French people making plans for their weekend. They're using several words borrowed from English.

Thomas: **Sylvie, qu'est-ce que tu fais ce week-end?**
seel-vee, kehs-kuh tew feh suh wee-kehnd?
Sylvie, what are you doing this weekend?

Sylvie: **Oh, du shopping probablement. Tu veux venir avec moi?**
oh, dew shoh-peeng proh-bah-bluh-mahN. tew vuh vuh-nee-rah-vehk mwah?
Oh, I'll probably go shopping. Do you want to come with me?

Thomas: **OK, cool, et après, on va aller manger dans un fast food.**
oh-keh, kooh-ley-ah-preh, ohN vah ah-ley mahN-zhey dahN-zuhN fahst foohd.
OK, cool, and afterwards, we'll go eat in a fast food place.

Sylvie: **J'espère qu'on va trouver un parking!**
zhehs-pehr kohN vah trooh-vey uhN pahr-keeng!
I hope we'll be able to find a parking space!

Quebec is pure French

The rules of good and pure French speech are especially enforced in Quebec. People in Quebec will easily understand your **franglais**, but you may be taken aback when you hear Quebeckers talk about the following, where the French use the English word:

✔ **la fin de semaine** (lah faN duh suh-mehn) (*weekend*)

✔ **un hambourgeois** (uhN ahN-boohr-zhwah) (*hamburger*)

✔ **le magasinage** (luh mah-gah-zee-nazh) (*shopping*)

✔ **la mise en marché** (lah mee-zahN mahr-shey) (*marketing*)

✔ **le stationnement** (luh stah-syoh-nuh-mahN) (*parking*)

Quebec's purism is easily explained:

✔ The proximity of the United States south of its border, plus the English-speaking majority in Canada threatens the French cultural identity of Quebec's 7.5 million inhabitants. For Quebeckers, their language constitutes a rampart against the all-powerful presence of the English — spoken by 300 million people — surrounding them.

✔ People who lived mostly in rural isolation for 300 years are now living in modern cities like Montreal, Quebec, Sherbrooke, and a few others where cable TV is constantly bombarding them with American commercials, movies, and a variety of shows. These people are trying to preserve the French lanuage.

Although protective of their language, French-Canadians are an extremely friendly people who welcome their southern neighbors.

Idioms and Popular Expressions

French, like English, has many *idioms* (unusual ways of expressing feelings and ideas). You may find the meaning of these expressions puzzling if you try to translate them word for word.

These fixed forms of expression belong specifically to the language in question. If you walk up to a French person and say **Il pleut des chats et des chiens** (eel pluh dey shah ey dey shyaN) (*It's raining cats and dogs*), he or she would question your sanity. On the other hand, you may find yourself wondering what a French speaker means when she says **Il tombe des cordes** (eel tohNb dey kohrd), whose literal translation is *Ropes are falling,* but it's roughly equivalent to *It's raining cats and dogs.*

Apart from those idioms, which take a long time to comprehend and belong specifically to a culture, every language has many expressions and phrases that, although they cannot be translated word for word, can easily be learned and used. Here are a few of the useful expressions you frequently hear in French:

- ✔ **À la vôtre!** (ah lah voh-truh!) (*Cheers!*)

- ✔ **À mon avis** (ah mohN-nah-vee) (*in my opinion*)

- ✔ **À tes/vos souhaits!** (ah tey/voh sweh!) (*Bless you!/Gesundheit!*)

- ✔ **Allez! Un petit effort!** (ah-ley! uhN puh-tee-teh-fohr!) (*Come on! Try a little!*)

- ✔ **Bien sûr.** (byaN sewr.) (*Of course.*)

- ✔ **Bon appétit!** (bohN-nah-pey-tee!) (*Enjoy your meal!*)

- ✔ **Ça vaut la peine/le coup.** (sah voh lah pehn/luh kooh.) (*It's worth it.*)

- ✔ **D'accord.** (dah-kohr.) (*Okay.*)

- ✔ **De rien.** (duh ryaN.) (*Don't mention it.*)

- ✔ **Jamais de la vie!** (zhah-meh duh lah vee!) or **Pas question!** (pah kehs-tyohN!) (*No way!*)

- ✔ **Revenons à nos moutons.** (ruh-vuh-nohN ah noh mooh-tohN.) (*Let's get back to the subject at hand.*)

- ✔ **Tant mieux.** (tahN myuh.) (*So much the better.*)

- ✔ **Tant pis.** (tahN pee.) (*Too bad.*)

- ✔ **Tout à fait.** (tooh-tah feh.) (*Quite.*)

- ✔ **Un coup d'oeil** (uhN kooh duhy) (*a glance, a quick look*)

Chapter 2

Laying the Foundation: Basic French Grammar

*I*n your native language, you instinctively know how to form sentences and ask questions that make sense. However, when learning a new language, you need to learn that language's grammar because it lays the foundation for communicating correctly and effectively. This chapter simplifies French grammar, introducing you to the parts of speech and telling you how to construct grammatically correct sentences and questions. As you read this material, you'll be amazed to discover that learning basic French grammar is easy and completely painless. The key to success is to remain cool and patient. Little by little — and before you know it — you'll be able to speak French.

Key Parts of Speech

Words are classified based on their part of speech — verbs, nouns, pronouns, adjectives, adverbs, prepositions, conjunctions, and interjections — depending on how they are used. In this section, we concentrate on a few key parts of speech you need to know in order to form and understand basic French sentences: nouns, articles, pronouns, adjectives, and adverbs. You can check out verbs in the later section "Cavorting with Verbs."

Naming things with nouns

Nouns name things: people, objects, places, concepts, and so on. *House* is a noun. So is *Mary* or *truth* or *Sandusky*. There are a few key differences between French and English nouns, however, as the next sections explain.

That whole gender thing

Unlike English nouns, all French nouns have a gender: They are either grammatically masculine or feminine. Knowing whether a noun is masculine or feminine is very important because it has an impact on the sentence construction. For example, if the noun is feminine, the articles and adjectives that modify that noun must also be feminine.

But how do you know whether a noun is masculine or feminine? Of course, if you are talking about the sex of a person or an animal, the gender is obvious. But if the noun is a thing or an idea, how do you determine its gender? For the most part, just look at the word's ending. With a few exceptions, the ending of a noun is a rather good indication of its gender. Table 2-1 shows common masculine and feminine endings.

Table 2-1 Common Masculine and Feminine Noun Endings

Masculine Endings	Example	Feminine Endings	Example
–eur (uhr)	l'auteur (loh-tuhr) (*author*); le bonheur (luh boh-nuhr) (*happiness*)	–ade (ahd)	la promenade (lah prohm-nahd) (*walk*); la limonade (lah lee-moh-nahd) (*lemonade*)
–eau (oh)	le chapeau (luh shah-poh) (*hat*); le manteau (luh mahN-toh) (*coat*)	–ance/–ence (ahNs)	la naissance (lah neh-sahNs) (*birth*); la différence (lah dee-fey-*rahNs*) (*difference*)
–isme (eez-muh)	le capitalisme (luh kah-pee-tah-leez-muh) (*capitalism*); le féminisme (luh fey-mee-neez-muh) (*feminism*)	–oire (wahr)	la mémoire (lah mey-mwahr) (*memory*); la victoire (lah veek-twahr) (*victory*)

Masculine Endings	Example	Feminine Endings	Example
–ment (mahN)	l'appartement (lah-pahr-tuh-mahN) (*apartment*); le logement (luh lohzh-mahN) (*lodging, place of residence*)	–sion/tion (syohN)	l'impression (laN-prey-syohN) (*impression*); la condition (lah kohN-dee-syohN) (*condition*)
–ail (ahy)	le travail (luh trah-vahy) (*work*); le détail (luh dey-tahy) (*detail*)	–son (zohN)	la saison (lah seh-zohN) (*season*); la maison (lah meh-zohN) (*house*)
Final vowels other than –e	le cinéma (luh see-ney-mah) (*movies*); le piano (luh pyah-noh) (*piano*); le genou (lee zhuh-nooh) (*knee*)	–té, –ée (tey, ey)	la liberté (lah lee-behr-tey) (*freedom*); l'égalité (ley-gah-lee-tey) (*equality*); l'idée (lee-dey) (*idea*); la pensée (lah pahN-sey) (*thought*)
-al (ahl)	le journal (luh zhoohr-nahl) (*newspaper*); le festival (luh feh-stee-vahl) (*festival*)	–ie (ee)	la boulangerie (lah booh-lahN-zhree) (*bakery*); l'épicerie (ley-pees-ree) (*grocery store*)

In addition, certain occupations are always masculine in French, even though both men and women work in them. Some examples include

- **un professeur** (uhN proh-feh-suhr) (*teacher, professor*)
- **un architecte** (uhN-nahr-shee-tehkt) (*architect*)
- **un chef** (uhN shehf) (*chef*)
- **un ingénieur** (uhN-naN-zhey-nyuhr) (*engineer*)
- **un agent** (uhN-nah-zhahN) (*agent*)
- **un médecin** (uhN meyd-saN) (*doctor*)
- **un auteur** (uhN-noh-tuhr) (*author*)

Similarly, some nouns are always feminine, even when they refer to a male. Here they are:

- ✔ **une vedette** (ewn veh-deht) (*movie star*)
- ✔ **une personne** (ewn pehr-sohhn) (*person*)
- ✔ **une victime** (ewn veek-teem) (*victim*)

If you come across a noun that does not follow any of these patterns, simply consult Appendix A in the back of this book or a French dictionary.

Making singular nouns plural

In French, as in English, nouns are either singular or plural. The French say they have a *number*. To make nouns plural, you simply add an *s* to most of them, just like in English. **La maison** (lah meh-zohN) (*house*) is singular while **les maisons** (ley meh-zohN) (*houses)* is plural.

However, if a noun ends in **–ou**, **–eu**, or **–eau**, you add an *x* instead of an *s* to make it plural: The singular **le bureau** (luh bew-roh) (*office, desk)* becomes the plural **les bureaux** (ley bew-roh) (*offices, desks*).

If a noun already ends in an **–s**, **–z**, or **–x,** you don't add anything to it. In these instances, the article (and the context) makes clear that the noun is plural):

Singular	Plural
un fils (uhN fees) (*son*)	**des fils** (dey fees) (*sons*)
un nez (uhN ney) (*nose*)	**des nez** (dey ney) (*noses*)
un époux (uhN-ney-pooh) (*spouse*)	**des époux** (dey-zey-pooh) (*spouses*)

Keeping an eye on articles

Unlike English nouns, which don't necessarily need articles (the words *the, a,* and *an*), French nouns are almost always preceded by articles. In English, for example, you say *France,* but in French, you say **la France** (lah frahNs) (*France*). The same convention applies to plural nouns: *mountains* in English becomes **les montagnes** (ley mohN-tah-nyuh) (*mountains*) in French. Another difference between English and French articles is that French articles mark the gender and the number of nouns.

When you learn the gender of a noun, try to learn the article that goes with it. Instead of memorizing **table** (tah-bluh) (*table*), for example, memorize **la table** (lah tah-bluh) (*the table*) or **une table** (ewn tah-bluh) (*a table*). Instead of **livre** (lee-vruh) (*book*), think **le livre** (luh lee-vruh) (*the book*) or **un livre** (uhN lee-vruh) (*a book*).

Table 2-2 lists the variations of definite, indefinite, and partitive articles in French. For details on how these articles are used, keep reading.

Table 2-2	Definite, Indefinite, and Partitive French Articles			
Type of Article	Masculine	Feminine	Preceding a Vowel or Mute H	Masculine and Feminine Plural
Definite (*the*)	le (luh)	la (lah)	l' (see note)	les (ley)
Indefinite (*a, an, some*)	un (uhN)	une (ewn)	un (uhN), une (ewn)	des (dey)
Partitive (*some, any*)	du (dew)	de la (duh lah)	de l' (see note)	des (dey)

Note: L' (ehl ah-pohs-trohf) means *l apostrophe* and **de l'** (duh ehl ah-pohs-trohf) means *de l apostrophe*. These abbreviations are used when these articles are followed by a vowel or a mute h.)

Defining definite articles

The definite article refers to a specific noun and has only one form in English, even when used in the plural: *the*. In French, because nouns have a gender, the article has to take the gender of the noun as well as its number, singular or plural. Here are the definite articles in French:

- ✔ **le** (luh) (*the*) — masculine definite article, singular

- ✔ **la** (lah) (*the*) — feminine definite article, singular

- ✔ **l'** (ehl ah-pohs-trohf) (*the*) — masculine and feminine definite article, singular, used in front of nouns that start with a vowel or mute h.

- ✔ **les** (ley) (*the*) — masculine and feminine definite article, plural

For example, the word **nuage** is masculine singular; therefore, you add a masculine, singular article in front of it: **le nuage** (luh new-ahzh) (*the cloud*). You follow the same pattern for a feminine singular noun: Simply add the feminine singular article **la** in front of **maison,** for example, and you have **la maison** (lah meh-zohN) (*the house*). If the noun is plural, regardless of whether it's masculine or feminine, the article is always **les**. For example, **les nuages** (ley new-ahzh) (*the clouds*) or **les maisons** (ley meh-zohN) (*the houses*).

If a masculine or feminine noun begins with a vowel or a mute h (more on the mute h in Chapter 3), then you drop the *e* in **le** and the *a* in **la** and you add an apostrophe, **l'**. If nouns beginning with a vowel or a mute h are plural, just use **les** (ley). Here are some examples:

> **l'idée** (f) (lee-dey) (*idea*)
>
> **les idées** (ley-zee-dey) (*ideas*)
>
> **l'hôtel** (m) (loh-tehl) (*hotel*)
>
> **les hôtels** (ley-zoh-tehl) (*hotels*)

French also uses definite articles after verbs of preference, such as **aimer** (eh-mey) (*to like, to love*), **détester** (dey-tehs-tey) (*to hate*), and **préférer** (prey-fey-rey) (*to prefer*). (You can check verbs of preference out in Chapter 6). For example: **J'aime le café** (zhehm luh kah-fey) (*I like coffee*).

Using the indefinite article

When referring to undetermined objects, you use indefinite articles, equivalent to the English words *a* and *an*. In French, the indefinite articles are

- ✔ **un** (uhN) (*a, an*) — masculine indefinite article, singular
- ✔ **une** (ewn) (*a, an*) — feminine indefinite article, singular
- ✔ **des** (dey) (*some, any*) — masculine and feminine indefinite article, plural

You use French indefinite articles the same way you use English indefinite articles. Check out the following examples:

- ✔ **Paris est une grande ville.** (pah-ree eh-tewn grahNd veel.) (*Paris is a big city.*)
- ✔ **Je voudrais un café.** (zhuh vooh-dreh-zuhN kah-fey.) (*I would like a coffee.*)
- ✔ **Il y a des maisons dans la rue.** (eel ee ah dey meh-zohN dahN lah rew.) (*There are houses on the street.*)

Choosing the partitive

The French language has a specific article that refers to a part of something as opposed to the whole. You can sometimes translate this article as *some* or *any*, but it is frequently omitted in English.

As you may guess, the article has a masculine form, **du** (dew); a feminine form, **de la** (duh lah); and a plural form, **des** (dey). There is also a singular form when the noun that follows starts with a vowel or a mute h, **de l'** (duh ehl ah-pohs-trohf). Here are a few examples:

> **Je voudrais du pain et du fromage.** (zhuh vooh-dreh dew paN ey dew froh-mahzh.) (*I would like [some] bread and [some] cheese.*)
>
> **Si tu as soif, bois de l'eau!** (see tew ah swahf, bwah duh loh!) (*If you are thirsty, drink [some] water!*)
>
> **Il mange souvent de la salade.** (eel mahNzh sooh-vahN duh lah sah-lahd.) (*He often eats [some] salad.*)

Meeting subject pronouns face to face

Pronouns replace nouns, enabling you to avoid clumsy repetition when you write or speak. In French, pronouns change, depending on their role (subject, direct object, indirect object, or to show possession) in a sentence. Fortunately, you don't need to worry about all those different forms at this point. Instead, this section focuses on French *subject pronouns,* those that function as subjects. (The other pronouns are covered in various chapters throughout the book.)

In a sentence, the *subject* indicates who or what is performing the action. In the sentence "John plays tennis," *John* is the subject. You can replace *John* with the pronoun *he,* and the sentence becomes "He plays tennis." In this case, the pronoun *he* is the subject. Here are the French subject pronouns with their English translations:

Singular	*Plural*
je (zhuh) (*I*)	nous (nooh) (*we*)
tu (tew) (*you*)	vous (vooh) (*you*)
il/elle/on (eel/ehl/ohN) (*he/she/it, one*)	ils/elles (eel/ehl) (*they*)

Taking a closer look at "je"

Unlike the English *I,* **je** is not capitalized in French, unless it begins the sentence. Also, if the verb that follows **je** begins with a vowel or a mute h (head to Chapter 3 for more on the mute h), the **–e** is dropped and an apostrophe added. This doesn't happen with any other subject pronoun. Here's an example:

> **J'aime le français.** (zhehm luh frahN-seh.) (*I like French.*)

More on "il," "elle," "ils," and "elles"

As mentioned previously, French nouns are either feminine or masculine. The same is true of French pronouns. Therefore, **il** refers not only to a person, meaning *he,* but also to a masculine singular object, meaning *it.* For example, **il siffle** (eel see-fluh) could mean *he is whistling* or *it is whistling,* depending on the context of the sentence. The same thing applies to **elle. Elle est belle** (ehl eh behl) could mean *she is beautiful* or *it is beautiful.* Of course, **ils** and **elles,** the masculine and feminine third person plurals, have only one meaning, *they,* regardless of whether they refer to people or things.

It's "you," you know: The tu/vous issue

Both **tu** and **vous** mean *you,* but you need to be aware of a fundamental difference between them. **Tu** is always singular, whereas **vous** can be singular or plural.

Vous is both singular and plural, yet even when it refers to one person, you always conjugate the verb in the plural. So start practicing your greetings using **vous** and the corresponding verb form ending **–ez** (except for three irregular verbs), whether you're addressing one person or more.

How you address someone in French depends on how well you know them. If the person is a family member, a peer, or a child, you use **tu**, which is an informal way of speaking to someone. You need to use the more polite and respectful form of the English *you*, **vous**, in these situations:

- ✔ When you meet someone for the first time (unless that person is a child)
- ✔ When you're talking to someone older than yourself
- ✔ When you're talking with someone with authority, like your teacher or your supervisor
- ✔ When you are referring to two or more people

Go to Chapter 3 for more information about using **tu** and **vous**.

In France, using **tu** to address a stranger or a new acquaintance would sound strange at best and impolite at worst. However, if you go to Quebec, you may soon discover that the familiar **tu** is much more liberally used at all times.

Using "on" for all

On, a very versatile subject pronoun, has several meanings: *one, we, they,* and *people.* The sentence **On parle français au Québec** (ohN pahrl frahN-seh oh key-behk), for example, can mean *One speaks French in Quebec* or *We/ they/people speak French in Quebec.*

On can also be used when you want to repeat something that you heard without revealing your source: **On m'a dit qu'on vous a renvoyé.** (ohN mah dee kohN vooh-zah rahN-vwah-ey.) (*Someone told me that you got fired.*)

Pretty handy pronoun, right? Remember that whether **on** refers to a singular or a plural subject, its verb conjugation is always third person singular. (See the verb conjugations later on in this chapter)

Getting descriptive with adjectives

Adjectives describe nouns. Because French nouns have both gender and number, any adjectives have to match the nouns they modify in gender and number.

Changing adjective endings to specify gender

You can change the ending of an adjective so that it agrees in gender and number with the noun. Table 2-3 shows the masculine and feminine singular and plural forms, as well as examples using these endings.

Table 2-3	Endings of French Adjectives		
Masc., Sing	*Fem. Sing.*	*Masc. Plural*	*Fem. Plural*
–e: calme (kahlm) (*calm*)	**–e: calme** (kahlm)	**–es: calmes** (kahlm)	**–es: calmes** (kahlm)
–é: fatigué (fah-tee-gey) (*tired*)	**–ée: fatiguée** (fah-tee-gey)	**–és: fatigués** (fah-tee-gey)	**–ées: fatiguées** (fah-tee-gey)
–consonant: **grand** (grahN) (*big, tall*)	–consonant + **e: grande** (grahNd)	–consonant + **s: grands** (grahN)	–consonant + **es: grandes** (grahNd)
–eux: heureux (uh-ruh) (*happy*)	**–euse: heureuse** (uh-ruhz)	**–eux: heureux** (uh-ruh)	**–euses: heureuses** (uh-ruhz)
–eur: travailleur (trah-vah-yuhr) (*hard working*)	**–euse: travailleuse** (trah-vah-yuhz)	**–eurs: travailleurs** (trah-vah-yuhr)	**–euses: travailleuses** (trah-vah-yuhz)
–teur: conservateur (kohN-sehr-vah-tuhr) (*conservative*)	**–trice: conservatrice** (kohN-sehr-vah-trees)	**–teurs: conservateurs** (kohN-sehr-vah-tuhr)	**–trices: conservatrices** (kohN-sehr-vah-trees)
–f: sportif (spohr-teef) (*athletic*)	**–ve: sportive** (spohr-teev)	**–fs: sportifs** (spohr-teef)	**–ves: sportives** (spohr-teev)
–ien: canadien (kah-nah-dyaN) (*Canadian*)	**–ienne: canadienne** (kah-nah-dyehn)	**–iens: canadiens** (kah-nah-dyaN)	**–iennes: canadiennes** (kah-nah-dyehn)
–on: bon (bohN) (*good*)	**–onne: bonne** (bohhn)	**–ons: bons** (bohN)	**–onnes: bonnes** (bohhn)
–er: fier (fyehr) (*proud*)	**–ère: fière** (fyehr)	**–ers: fiers** (fyehr)	**–ères: fières** (fyehr)

A few adjectives have very irregular forms in the feminine singular:

- ✔ **beau/belle** (boh/behl) (*beautiful*): **un beau garçon** (uhN boh gahr-sohN) (*a beautiful [handsome] boy*) and **une belle fille** (ewn behl feey) (*a beautiful girl*)

- ✔ **nouveau/nouvelle** (nooh-voh/nooh-vehl) (*new*): **un nouveau manteau** (uhN nooh-voh mahN-toh) (*a new coat*) and **une nouvelle robe** (ewn nooh-vehl rohhb) (*a new dress*)

- ✔ **vieux/vieille** (vyuh/vyehy) (*old*): **un vieux bureau** (uhN vyuh bew-roh) (*an old desk*) and **une vieille maison** (ewn vyehy meh-zohN) (*an old house*)

Putting the adjective in the right place

Most French adjectives are placed after the noun they describe, which is the opposite from English. Whereas in English you say *an interesting trip*, for example, in French you say **un voyage intéressant** (uhN voh-yahzh aN-tey-reh-sahN). However, this rule changes when the adjectives relate to any of the following. In these cases, the adjective goes in front of the noun:

- ✔ **Beauty**: Adjectives in this category include **beau/belle** (boh/behl) (*beautiful*) and **joli/jolie** (zhoh-lee) (*pretty*)

- ✔ **Age:** The category includes words like **jeune** (zhuhn) (*young*), **vieux/vieille** (vyuh/vyehy) (*old*), and **nouveau/nouvelle** (nooh-voh/nooh-vehl) (*new*).

- ✔ **Numbers**: Words in this group include **premier/première** (pruh-myey/pruh-myehr) (*first, premiere*), **dernier/dernière** (dehr-nyey/dehr-nyehr) (*last*), **deux** (duh) (*two*), **trois** (trwah) (*three*), and so forth.

- ✔ **Goodness (or lack of it):** Words like **bon/bonne** (bohN/bohhn) (*good*), **mauvais/mauvaise** (moh-veh/moh-vehz) (*bad*), and **gentil/gentille** (zhahN-tee/zhahN-teey) *(nice)* are in this group.

- ✔ **Size:** This category includes words like **grand/grande** (grahN/grahNd) (*big, tall*), **petit/petite** (puh-tee/puh-teet) (*small, little*), and **gros/grosse** (groh/grohs) (*large, fat, thick*).

To help you remember that these categories of words precede the noun, think **B-A-N-G-S: B**eauty, **A**ge, **N**umbers, **G**oodness, **S**ize).

Some adjectives are a little tricky because they can change meaning according to whether they are placed before or after the noun. Check out the following list:

- ✔ **ancien/ancienne** (ahN-syaN/ahN-syehn): Before the noun, it means *former*; after the noun it means *ancient* or *old*.

- ✔ **cher/chère** (shehr/shehr): Before the noun, it means *dear*; after the noun, it means *expensive*.

- ✔ **pauvre** (poh-vruh): Before the noun, it means *unfortunate*, and after, it means *penniless*.

> ✔ **propre** (proh-pruh): Before the noun, it means *own;* after the noun, it means *clean.*

Here's a way to remember the different meanings of these adjectives: When placed before the noun, the meaning is figurative. When placed after the noun, the meaning is literal. Here are some examples:

un ancien collègue (uhN-nahN-syaN koh-lehg) (*a former colleague*) versus **un bâtiment ancien** (uhN bah-tee-mahN ahN-syaN) (*an old building*)

un pauvre garçon (uhN poh-vruh gahr-sohN) (*an unfortunate boy*) versus **un enfant pauvre** (uhN-nahN-fahN poh-vruh) (*a poor or impoverished child*)

Getting creative with adverbs

An adverb is a word that modifies (describes) a verb, an adjective, or another adverb. In English, many adverbs end with *–ly: quickly, nervously, slowly,* and so on. In French, most adverbs end in **–ment,** and they usually follow the verb. Here are the rules:

- ✔ To the feminine form of an adjective, add **–ment: lente** (lahNt) (*slow*) becomes **lentement** (lahNt-mahN) (*slowly*), and **active** (ahk-teev) (*active*) becomes **activement** (ack-teev-mahN) (*actively*).

- ✔ To the masculine form of an adjective that ends in a vowel, add **–ment: vrai** (vreh) (*true*) becomes **vraiment** (vreh-mahN) (*truly, really*), and **absolu** (ahb-soh-lew) (*absolute*) becomes **absolument** (ahb-soh-lew-mahN) (*absolutely*).

- ✔ To the masculine form of an adjective that ends in **–ent** or **–ant**, drop the **nt** and add **–mment: constant** (kohN-stahN) (*constant*) becomes **constamment** (kohN-stahN-mahN) (*constantly*), and **évident** (ey-vee-dahN) (*evident*) becomes **évidemment** (ey-vee-dah-mahN) (*evidently, obviously*).

The adverbial forms of good and bad are irregular in French. The adjective *good* — **bon** (bohN) — becomes the adverb **bien** (byaN) (*well*) and **mauvais** (moh-veh) (*bad*) becomes **mal** (mahl) (*badly*).

Most adverbs in French come right after the verb:

Parlez lentement, s'il vous plaît. (pahr-ley lahNt-mahN, seel-vooh-pleh.) (*Speak slowly, please.*)

Les petits oiseaux chantent joyeusement. (ley puh-tee-zwah-zoh shahNt zhwah-yuhz-mahN.) (*The little birds sing happily.*)

Cavorting with Verbs

A verb expresses an action or a state of being. In French as in English, the verb form that is not conjugated and has no marking to indicate a subject or a tense (past, present, future) for the action is called the *infinitive form*. English infinitives begin with *to*, as in *to go* or *to speak*. In French, infinitives have special endings, such as **–er**, **–ir**, or **–re**:

- **aller** (ah-ley) (*to go*)
- **parler** (pahr-ley) (*to speak*)
- **finir** (fee-neer) (*to finish*)
- **être** (eh-truh) (*to be*)

In addition, verbs can be regular or irregular. Regular verbs have the same stem throughout the conjugation, while the stems on irregular verbs change. (The *stem* is the main part of the verb before you add the endings.) For example, in English, the verb *to love* is a regular verb because it has the same stem whoever the subject is: I love, you love, he/she/it love**s**, we love, you love, they love. But the verb *to be* is irregular because it doesn't have a common stem throughout the conjugation. The form of the verb depends on the subject: I am, you are, he/she/it is, we are, you are, they are.

Just as in English, French verbs must match the subject (you don't say, for example, "The children sings"). In French, the verb has a special ending for each subject (*I, you, she, we,* and so on). The following sections have the details.

Regular verbs

In French, regular verbs — those that follow a set pattern — belong to three large groups, which are determined by the ending of the verb's infinitive:

- The largest group whose infinitive ends with **–er:** Examples include **chanter** (shahN-tey) (*to sing*), **parler** (pahr-ley) (*to speak*), and **donner** (dohh-ney) (*to give*).

  A simple way to conjugate this category is to first drop the **–er** from the infinitive and add the following endings: **–e**, **–es**, **–e**, **–ons**, **–ez**, and **–ent**. Here is the present tense conjugation of **parler**:

Conjugation	Pronunciation
je parle	zhuh pahrl
tu parles	tew pahrl
il/elle/on parle	eel/ehl/ohN pahrl
nous parlons	nooh parh-lohN
vous parlez	vooh parh-ley
ils/elles parlent	eel/ehl parhl

Don't be lulled into thinking that all verbs ending in **–er** are regular. **Aller** (ah-ley) (*to go*), for example, is an irregular verb.

✔ The group whose infinitive ends in **–ir,** such as **finir** (fee-neer) (*to finish*) and **choisir** (shwah-zeer) (*to choose*).

To conjugate these verbs, first drop the **–r** from the infinitive and add the following endings: **–s**, **–s**, **–t**, **–ssons**, **–ssez**, and **–ssent**. Here is the present tense conjugation of **finir** (fee-neer) (*to finish*):

Conjugation	Pronunciation
je finis	zhuh fee-nee
tu finis	tew fee-nee
Il/elle/on finit	eel/ehl/ohN fee-nee
nous finissons	nooh fee-nee-sohN
vous finissez	vooh fee-nee-sey
ils/elles finissent	eel/ehl fee-nees

✔ The smaller but important group whose infinitive ends in **–re,** such as **attendre** (ah-tahN-druh) (*to wait*) and **vendre** (vahN-druh) (*to sell*).

To conjugate this category of verbs, just drop the **–re** from the infinitive and add **–s**, **–s**, nothing, **–ons**, **–ez**, and **–ent**. Consider the present tense conjugation of **vendre**:

Conjugation	Pronunciation
je vends	zhuh vahN
tu vends	tew vahN
il/elle/on vend	eel/ehl/ohN vahN
nous vendons	nooh vahN-dohN
vous vendez	vooh vahN-dey
ils/elles vendent	eel/ehl vahNd

Irregular verbs

Irregular verbs are verbs that don't follow a regular pattern throughout the conjugation. Although the irregular verbs can present a bit of a challenge, you can master them with some practice and a little memorization. The most important ones are the following:

✔ **être** (eh-truh) (*to be*)

The following table shows the present tense conjugation of **être:**

Conjugation	*Pronunciation*
je suis	zhuh swee
tu es	tew eh
il/elle/on est	eel/ehl/ohN eh
nous sommes	nooh sohm
vous êtes	vooh-zeht
ils/elles sont	eel/ehl sohN

✔ **avoir** (ah-vwahr) (*to have*)

The following table shows the present tense conjugation of **avoir:**

Conjugation	*Pronunciation*
j'ai	zhey
tu as	tew ah
il/elle/on a	eel/ehl/ohN ah
nous avons	nooh-zah-vohN
vous avez	vooh-zah-vey
ils/elles ont	eel-/ehl-zohN

Not only are **être** and **avoir** used in many expressions, but they also serve as helping verbs or auxiliaries in making up past compound tenses as we explain in Chapter 11.

✔ **faire** (fehr) (*to do, to make*)

The following table shows the present tense conjugation of **faire:**

Conjugation	Pronunciation
je fais	zhuh feh
tu fais	tew feh
il/elle/on fait	eel/ehl/ohN feh
nous faisons	nooh fuh-zohN
vous faites	vooh feht
ils/elles font	eel/ehl fohN

 ✔ **aller** (ah-ley) (*to go*)

The following table shows the present tense conjugation of **aller:**

Conjugation	Pronunciation
je vais	zhuh veh
tu vas	tew vah
il/elle/on va	eel/ehl/ohN vah
nous allons	nooh-zah-lohN
vous allez	vooh-zah-ley
ils/elles vont	eel/ehl vohN

For more irregular verbs, refer to Appendix B.

Verbs tenses

Verb tense simply means time. To express an action or a state of being taking place in the present, you use the present tense. If the action hasn't happened yet, you use the future tense. And if it took place in the past, you use a past tense.

Speaking in the present

When something is happening now, use the present tense. Here's what a simple sentence in the present looks like in French: **Les enfants chantent.** (ley-zahN-fahN shahNt.) (*The children sing/are singing/do sing*).

The French present tense can be translated in three different ways, as the preceding example shows. Although you can use these translations interchangeably, you need to decide which is the better translation for the context of the sentence. For the conjugation of the present tense of regular and irregular verbs, refer to the preceding two sections.

A quick look at past tense

You can express past tense in French in several ways, but the simplest and the most common is **le passé composé** (luh pah-sey kohN-poh-zey) (*the compound past*). This tense is made up of more than one component: an auxiliary verb (**avoir** or **être**) conjugated in the present tense and the past participle of the desired verb (the form which in English would often end with *–ed*). Here are some examples:

> **J'ai travaillé.** (zhey trah-vah-yey.) (*I worked.*)
>
> **Il est entré.** (eel eh-tahN-trey.) (*He entered.*)

To give you an idea of what a regular verb looks like in past tense, here's how you conjugate the verb **parler** (pahr-ley) (*to speak*):

Conjugation	*Pronunciation*
j'ai parlé	zhey pahr-ley
tu as parlé	tew ah pahr-ley
il/elle/on a parlé	eel/ehl/ohN ah pahr-ley
nous avons parlé	nooh-zah-vohN pahr-ley
vous avez parlé	vooh-zah-vey pahr-ley
ils/elles ont parlé	eel-/ehl-zohN pahr-ley

Chapter 11 covers the past tense in more detail.

Peeking into the future

To make the future tense, you use the present tense conjugation of **aller** followed by an infinitive. Here's an example: **Demain, Sylvie va voyager** (duh-maN, seel-vee vah voh-yah-zhey) (*Tomorrow, Sylvie is going to travel.*)

This future form — **aller** (ah-ley) + the infinitive — is called the *immediate* or *near future* because it expresses events that will take place soon or fairly soon. French has another future tense, called the *simple future,* which translates to *will* in the English. The simple future and immediate future are often interchangeable. For example, you can say *Sylvie will travel* (simple future) or *Sylvie is going to travel* (immediate future). To find out more about the simple future tense, head to Chapter 13.

To get an idea of how to construct the immediate future with all the subject pronouns, look at the following example that uses the verb **parler** (pahr-ley) (*to speak*):

Conjugation	*Pronunciation*
je vais parler	zhuh veh pahr-ley
tu vas parler	tew vah pahr-ley
Il/elle/on va parler	eel/ehl/ohN vah pahr-ley
nous allons parler	nooh-zah-lohN pahr-ley
vous allez parler	vooh-zah-ley pahr-ley
ils/elles vont parler	eel/ehl vohN pahr-ley

Forming Sentences and Questions

A simple sentence construction (in French or in English) consists of at least a subject and a verb. Beyond that, it may include an object noun, an adjective, and an adverb. The sentence **Elle porte une jolie robe** (ehl pohr-tewn zhoh-lee rohhb) (*She is wearing a pretty dress*) has a subject (**elle**), a verb (**porte**), a feminine singular indefinite article (**une**), an adjective (**jolie,** in its feminine form), and an object noun (**robe**).

The English translation of a French sentence may not follow the same order of the sentence components because, as mentioned earlier, French adjectives can go before or after the noun. In the sentence, **Charles est un garçon intelligent** (shahrl eh-tuhN gahr-sohN aN-teh-lee-zhahN) is translated as *Charles is an intelligent boy,* even though the adjective (**intelligent**) comes after the noun (**garçon**) in the original sentence.

Believe it or not, some grammar issues in French are easier than in English. A good example of this is the way you can form questions:

- ✔ Use intonation by raising your voice at the end of your statement: **Vous avez un ticket?** (vooh-zah-vey-zuhN tee-keh?) (*Do you have a ticket?*)

- ✔ Add **est-ce que** (ehs-kuh) to the beginning of the phrase: **Est-ce que vous avez un ticket?** (ehs-kuh vooh-zah-vey-zuhN tee-keh?) (*Do you have a ticket?*)

   If a word beginning with a vowel follows **est-ce que** (ehs-kuh), it becomes **est-ce qu'** (ehs-kuh). For example: **Est-ce qu'elle a un ticket?** (ehs-kehl-ah uhN tee-keh) (*Does she have a ticket?*)

These easy forms of questioning are valid no matter what the tense of the verb is: present, past, or future.

Chapter 3

Getting Started with Pronunciation and Basic Expressions

*W*henever anyone hears a foreign language spoken or sung at normal speed, the words — which don't make sense to begin with — create a muddle of sounds impossible to reproduce. So one of the hardest parts of learning any language — including French — is overcoming your fear of not sounding French. Once you overcome this fear of sounding "funny," however, everything else is fun and easy. To that end, this chapter includes all the information you need to know to pronounce French correctly.

The world has over 200 million *francophones* (people who speak French), and as you can imagine, the French accent varies in the different parts of the world. This book concentrates on the Parisian accent, which is considered the standard French accent.

The French Alphabet

The French alphabet has the same 26 letters that the English alphabet does. Of course, some of the letters are pronounced differently. Table 3-1 lists the letters and gives you their names in French, which you may find useful if, for example, you have to spell your name on the phone or write down an address. You can hear the French alphabet on Track 1 on the CD.

Table 3-1	The French Alphabet		
Letter	*Pronunciation*	*Letter*	*Pronunciation*
A	ah	N	ehn
B	bey	O	oh
C	sey	P	pey
D	dey	Q	kew
E	uh	R	ehr
F	ehf	S	ehs
G	zhey	T	tey
H	ahsh	U	ew
I	ee	V	vey
J	zhee	W	dooh-bluh-vey
K	kah	X	eeks
L	ehl	Y	ee-grehk
M	ehm	Z	zehd

Uttering Vowel and Consonant Sounds

French is a romance language. Romance languages — which also include Spanish, Italian, Romanian, and Portuguese — share the same origin and thus the same characteristics. One of the most important characteristics of the romance languages is that their sound is mostly based on vowels, unlike the Anglo-Saxon languages — English and German — which are based on consonants. The emphasis on vowels gives French its soft, smooth, even, and musical character. French words certainly contain consonants, but compared to the consonants in English, French consonants are much softer. Read on to find out how to pronounce French vowels and consonants.

The tables in the following sections help you with the pronunciation of French sounds, and they include English words where the French and English pronunciation is the same. However, French also includes sounds that don't exist in the English language. In those cases, we give you tips on how you can pronounce that particular sound.

The vowel sounds

Vowel sounds, listed in Table 3-2, are the most difficult to pronounce in French. They are shorter than in English and usually end a syllable. Almost all of them have an equivalent in English.

Table 3-2		French Vowel Sounds	
French	*Symbol*	*As in English*	*French Word*
a â à	ah	c<u>ar</u>d	**la tasse** (lah tahs) (*cup*); **la pâtis-serie** (lah pah-tees-ree) (*pastry shop*); **là-bas** (lah-bah) (*over there*)
e eu	uh	d<u>u</u>ll (approximate)	**le petit** (luh puh-tee) (*little one*); **la fleur** (lah fluhr) (*flower*)
é ez er	ey	m<u>ay</u>	**les cafés** (ley kah-fey) (*coffee houses*); **le nez** (luh ney) (*nose*); **parler** (pahr-ley) (*to speak*)
è ê ai ei et	eh	s<u>e</u>t	**la mère** (lah mehr) (*mother*); **la fenêtre** (lah fuh-neh-truh) (*window*); **clair** (klehr) (*clean, light-colored*); **la neige** (lah nehzh) (*snow*); **le secret** (luh suh-kreh) (*secret*)
i î y	ee	f<u>ee</u>t	**vite** (veet) (*quickly*); **la gîte** (lah zheet) (*shelter*); **le/les pays** (luh/ley pey-ee) (*country/countries*)
o ô au eau	oh	b<u>oa</u>t	**le mot** (luh moh) (*word*); **les côtes** (ley koht) (*ribs*); **aujourd'hui** (oh-zhoohr-dwee) (*today*); **l'eau** (f) (loh) (*water*)
o	ohh	l<u>o</u>ve	**la pomme** (lah pohhm) (*apple*); **les bottes** (ley bohht) (*boots*)
ou où	ooh	y<u>ou</u>	**l'amour** (m) (lah-moohr) (*love*); **où** (ooh) (*where*)
oi oy	wah	<u>w</u>atch	**la soie** (lah swah) (*silk*); **moyen** (mwah-yaN (*average*)
u	ew	No English equivalent	**salut** (sah-lew) (*hello*)

Represented in French by the letter **u,** the *ew* sound does not exist in English, and it takes a little practice to get it right. Here is a little trick to help you: Say *ee* with the tip of your tongue against your front bottom teeth; then keeping your tongue against your bottom teeth, round your lips. The sound coming out of your mouth is . . . the French *ew*.

The mute e

When the letter **e** appears at the end of a word or between two consonants, it is usually not pronounced; it is *mute.* For example, you don't pronounce the **e** at the end of **grande** (grahNd) (*tall*) or in the middle of **samedi** (sahm-dee) (*Saturday*).

The nasal sounds

The nasal sound, which is very common in French but does not exist in English, is fairly easy to pronounce. Imagine you have a cold and pronounce the sounds *ah, oh,* and *un* (without the *n*) through your nose. They come out nasalized. Here's a phrase that contains all the nasal sounds in French: **un bon vin blanc** (uhN bohN vaN blahN) (*a good white wine*).

Table 3-3 lists the nasal sounds. Although English has no true equivalent for the French nasal sounds, we include some words in English that come close. When you read these "equivalents," don't focus on the word itself: focus on how the vowel sound changes ever so slightly as your mouth prepares to make the *n* or *ng* sound that follows.

Table 3-3		French Nasal Sounds	
French	*Symbol*	*Approximate English Equivalent*	*French Word*
an **am** **en** **em**	ahN	f<u>o</u>nd	**grand** (grahN) (*big, large*); **ambitieux** (ahN-bee-syuh) (*ambitious*); **l'enfant** (m/f) (lahN-fahN) (*child*); **l'employé/e** (m/f)(lahN-plwah-yey) (*employee*)
un	uhN	<u>u</u>ncle	**brun** (bruhN) (*brown*)
ain **in** **aim** **im**	aN	sl<u>a</u>ng	**le pain** (luh paN) (*bread*); **le matin** (luh mah-taN) (*morning*); **la faim** (lah faN) (*hunger*); **impossible** (aN-poh-see-bluh) (*impossible*)
oin	waN	w<u>a</u>ng	**loin** (lwaN) (*far*)
ien	yaN	<u>Ya</u>nkee	**le chien** (luh shyaN) (*dog*)
on **om**	ohN	wr<u>o</u>ng	**bon** (bohN) (*good*); **le nom** (luh nohN) (*name*)

Consonants

French consonants are pronounced almost like in English, except that you don't linger on them; let them explode and move on to the vowel that follows. Because the consonants are said so quickly, it's important that you articulate them clearly; otherwise, they get lost, and the word is hard to understand.

The French **r** often scares foreigners. No need to be scared. You just have to pronounce it with your throat. Imagine that you've got something stuck in your throat and you're trying to get it out, but make the sound as soft and gentle as you can.

Another thing you need to know about French consonants is that the consonants at the end of a word are not usually pronounced. Consider these examples: **l'argent** (m)(lahr-zhahN) (*money*), **vingt** (vaN) (*twenty*), and **les fruits** (ley frwee) (*fruit*). Of course, this rule has some exceptions. The consonants **c, r, f,** or **l** (think of the consonants in the word *careful* to help you remember) at the end of a word *are* usually pronounced. Here are some examples of these consonants: **chic** (sheek) (*chic, stylish*), **neuf** (nuhf) (*nine, new*), **cher** (shehr) (*dear, expensive*), and **avril** (ah-vreel) (*April*).

Table 3-4 lists the consonants whose sounds in French may change depending on the vowel or the consonant that follows. Note that the letter **s** is pronounced as an **s** when it starts a word, but when it's within a word, you pronounce it as you do the letter **z**.

Table 3-4		Tricky French Consonants	
French Letter	*Symbol*	*As in English*	*French Word*
c (in front of **a, o, u**)	k	<u>c</u>ollege	**le collège** (luh koh-lehzh) (*middle school*)
ç (in front of **a, o, u**)	s	<u>s</u>ole	**le garçon** (luh gahr-sohN) (*boy*)
c (in front of **e** and **i**)	s	<u>s</u>ole	**le ciel** (luh syehl) (*sky*)
ch	sh	<u>sh</u>ip	**le chapeau** (luh shah-poh) (*hat*)
g (in front of **a, o, u**)	g	<u>g</u>reed	**le gâteau** (luh gah-toh) (*cake*)
gn	ny	ca<u>ny</u>on	**la montagne** (lah mohN-tah-nyuh) (*mountain*)
gu (in front of **e** and **i**)	g	<u>g</u>reed	**la guerre** (lah gehr) (*war*); **la guitare** (lah gee-tahr) (*guitar*)

(continued)

Table 3-4 (continued)

French Letter	Symbol	As in English	French Word
j, g (in front of **e** and **i**)	zh	lei<u>s</u>ure	**le jour** (luh zhoohr) (*day*), **le genou** (luh zhuh-nooh) (*knee*)
s (at the beginning of word)	s	<u>s</u>ole	**le soleil** (luh soh-lehy) (*sun*)
s (between two vowels)	z	civili<u>z</u>ation	**la civilisation** (lah see-vee-lee -zah-syohN) (*civilization*)
ss (between two vowels)	s	<u>s</u>ole	**le poisson** (luh pwah-sohN) (*fish*)

The mute h and the aspirate h

French has two different *h*'s: the *mute h* and the *aspirate h* — neither of which you pronounce. So why know the difference? For the following reasons:

- With the mute h, you drop the vowel of the definite singular article, **le** or **la,** and add an apostrophe before the mute h. For example, to say *the man* in French, you say **l'homme** (m) (lohhm), essentially turning two words into one.

- With the aspirate h, you don't drop the vowel of the definite article. The words remain separate. Here's an example: **le hockey** (luh oh-keh (*hockey*).

In the plural, a liaison (check out the later section on the liaison) appears between the articles and the mute h. For example, to say *the men,* you say **les hommes** (ley-zohhm) as though it were one word. However, no liaison appears between the article and words that begin with an aspirate h, like in the word **les héros** (ley ey-roh) (*the heroes*). If the liaison were permitted here, the word would have been **les zéros** (ley-zey-roh) (*the zeros*) — not *the heroes*.

Here is a list of some common words, besides **le hockey** and **le héros,** that begin with an aspirate h in French: **le homard** (luh oh-marh) (*lobster*), **le handicapé/la handicapée** (lah ahn-dee-kah-pey) (*handicapped*), **les haricots** (ley ah-ree-koh) (*beans*), **les hors-d'oeuvre** (ley orh-duh-vruh) (*hors d'oeuvres, appetizers*).

With a mute h, there is elision and liaison. With an aspirate h, there is no elision or liaison.

Don't stress; intone instead

In French, every syllable is of equal importance in volume and stress (hence, the absence of stressed syllables in the pronunciations in this book). The emphasis in French words of two or more syllables is on the last one, but it is one of duration rather than intensity. For example, in the English word *photography*, the stress is on the second syllable. In the French word **la photographie** (lah foh-toh-grah-fee) (*photography*), you don't stress any one particular syllable. Instead, French speakers use intonation: they raise or lower their voices in multi-syllable words, phrases, and sentences. For example, to ask a question, the French speakers raise their voices at the end of a statement.

Remembering to "unstress" the syllable you're used to pronouncing in those words that have similar spellings in French and in English may take quite a bit of practice. It's like ironing the stubborn pleat out of a pair of trousers!

Getting Clear on Accents, Liaisons, and Elisions

French has five accents, or *diacritical marks,* as grammarians like to call them. It is important to note that the accent over a vowel in French does not indicate that that syllable is stressed. The accent only affects the letter on which it stands, and even then, it doesn't change the pronunciation of that letter unless the letter is an **e** or a **c** (refer to Table 3-2). In addition to recognizing the five French accents, you also need to know how liaisons and elisions work. The following sections have the details.

The five French accents

The accent can either change the pronunciation of the letter or distinguish one word from another. In both cases, omitting an accent is like misspelling a word. The following list explains each of the five accents:

✔ **l'accent aigu** (lah-ksahN-tey-gew) (*the sharp accent*). This accent appears only over the **e** (**é**), and its sound closely resembles the *a* in the word *take*: **le café** (luh kah-fey) (*coffee, café*).

✔ **l'accent grave** (lah-ksahN grahv) (*the grave accent*). This accent appears over the letters **e** (**è**), **a** (**à**), and **u** (**ù**), but it only affects the sound of the letter **e**. The **è** is an open *eh* sound, as in the English word *set* or in the French word **la mère** (lah mehr) (*mother*). Over the letters **a** and **u**, this accent distinguishes between two words otherwise spelled the same. With **l'accent grave**, for example, **à** is a preposition meaning *to, in,* or *at.* Without the accent, **a** is the third person singular present tense of the verb **avoir** (ah-vwahr), which means *has.* The same goes for the letter **u.** The word **où** (ooh) means *where,* but the word **ou** (ooh) means *or.*

✔ **l'accent circonflexe** (lah-ksahN seehr-kohN-flehks) (*circumflex accent*). When this accent (^) appears over the vowels **a, e, i, o,** and **u,** it represents a letter (usually an **s**) that was dropped from the French word centuries ago but that may still remain in the related English word. Here are some examples: **l'hôpital** (m)(loh-pee-tahl) (*hospital*), **le château** (luh shah-toh) (*castle, chateau*), **la forêt** (lah foh-reh) (*forest*), and **l'arrêt** (m) (lah-reh) (*arrest*).

✔ **la cédille** (lah sey-deey) (*the cedilla*) or **c cédille** (sey sey-deey) (*c cedilla*).This accent appears only under the letter **c** (**ç**). The cedilla indicates that you pronounce the **c** as an **s.** If the letter **c** does not have the cedilla under it and it is followed by **a, o,** or **u,** then you pronounce it as you would the letter **k,** as in the English words *can* or *kite.* Check out this French command: **Commençons** (koh-mahN-sohN) (*Let's begin*).

✔ **le tréma** (luh trey-mah) (*dieresis*). This accent (¨) indicates that each vowel in a word is pronounced separately. Check out the following words: **naïf** (nah-eef) (*naïve*), **Noël** (noh-ehl) (*Christmas*).

The liaison

Have you ever thought, when listening to a French conversation, that it sounded like a great big, long word? Probably. That's because of a French phenomenon called the *liaison.* **Faire la liaison** (fehr lah lyey-zohN) (*to make a liaison*) means that the last consonant of a word is linked with the vowel that begins the following word. A liaison affects any final consonant when linked with the vowel of the following word. Check out these examples.

> **C'est un petit appartement.** (seh-tuhN puh-tee-tah-pahr-tuh-mahN.) (*It's a small apartment.*)

> **Vous êtes mon ami depuis six ans.** (vooh-zeht moh-nah-mee duh-pwee see-zahN.) (*You have been my friend for six years.*)

Besides the aspirate h (explained in the earlier section), a liaison never appears with the conjunction **et** (ey) (*and*): **un livre et un crayon** (uhN lee-vruh ey uhN kreh-yohN) (*a book and a pencil*), for example.

Using gestures

French people express themselves with hand and body gestures to a greater extent than English speakers do. The actual expression or word doesn't have to accompany these gestures, although it often does. Following are some examples of some common French gestures:

✔ Pulling on your eye as if to open it with your finger and saying **Mon oeil!** (mohN nuhy!) means *No way! You're pulling my leg!* (Literally: *my eye*).

✔ Raising your thumb, demonstratively shaking it in front of someone means *Perfect!*

✔ Scratching your cheek with the back of your hand and saying **Ah! la barbe!** (ah! lah bahrb!) means *What a pain!* (literally: *the beard*). Using the same scratching gesture and saying **Une vraie barbe!** (ewn vreh bahrb!) about something or someone means *A real bore!* (literally: *a real beard*).

✔ Extending both arms on each side of your hips and shrugging your shoulders means *There's nothing I can do about it!* This gesture is so commonly associated with the French that it is often referred to in the U.S. as the Gallic shrug.

You'll no doubt come across other gestures, many of which are not appropriate for a family book. We trust that you can use your own, ample wits to make sense out of them.

The elision

When a word ending with an **e** or an **a** (usually an article or a pronoun) is followed by a word starting with a vowel or a mute h, the first **e** or **a** disappears and is replaced by an apostrophe. This rule, like the liaison, contributes to the easy flow of the French language. Here are some examples:

> **la** + **école** = **l'école** (ley-kohl) (*the school*)
>
> **je** + **aime** = **j'aime** (zhehm) (*I like*)
>
> **le** or **la** + **enfant** = **l'enfant** (lahN-fahN) (*the child*)
>
> **la** + **histoire** = **l'histoire** (lee-stwarh) (*the story, history*)

Note that the elision does not occur with the aspirate h: **le homard** (luh oh-mahr) (*lobster*), for example.

Greetings: Formal and Friendly

Greetings are the first steps in establishing contact with someone, whatever the language. In many cases, a smile does the job, and you just have to wait for the other person to greet you and repeat what he or she just said. However, this section presents plenty of very simple French greetings that you may use on different occasions to help you meet people.

Addressing someone formally or informally

In French, you can vary the level of formality in your speech by how you say the word *you*. Depending on whom you are addressing, you can use the informal **tu** (tew) or the more formal **vous** (vooh). It's important to know when one or the other is appropriate because if you say the wrong thing, at best, you sound a little funny; at worst, you offend someone.

In general, use the formal **vous** when you address somebody you have never met, a superior, or an older person. As you get to know that person better, you may both switch to **tu**. Use the less formal **tu** when you speak to a friend, a child, or an animal. In addition, members of the same family, whatever their age, use the **tu** form.

The environment in which you find yourself also determines the correct form of address. For example, if you're a young person traveling on the train in France and you meet other young people, you would address one another as **tu**. On the other hand, if you're in a store, you'd address the clerk with **vous**, even if she looks a lot younger than you. Also keep in mind that the **vous** form is used to address one person on a formal level, but it is also a plural form used to address any number of people formally or informally.

If you are not sure what to do, use the **vous** form until the person you are addressing asks you to use the **tu** form. Then you avoid any **faux pas** (foh pah) (*social blunder* [literally, *false step*]).

In French, in a formal situation, it is more polite to add **monsieur** (muh-syuh) (*mister, sir*) to address a man, **madame** (mah-dahm) (*ma'am, missus*) to address a married woman, and **mademoiselle** (mahd-mwah-zehl) (*miss*) to address an unmarried woman, after even the simplest of expressions like **bonjour** (bohN-zhoohr) (*good day, hello*) and **merci** (mehr-see) (*thank you*). (The English Ms. has no equivalent in French.) If you don't know whether a woman is married or not, to be on the safe side, use **madame**. Remember also that **monsieur, madame,** and **mademoiselle** can be used on their own and are, most of the time.

Saying hello and good-bye

Nothing is easier than saying hello in a foreign language. Actually, the French language has a saying, when referring to something that is really a cinch: **C'est simple comme bonjour** (seh saN-pluh kohm bohN-zhoohr) (*It's as easy as saying hello*). So go ahead and practice these greetings and farewells:

- **Bonjour!** (bohN-zhoohr!) literally means *Good day!*, but you can use it when first greeting someone in the morning or afternoon, as long as the sun is shining.

    In Québec, people also say **Bonjour** when leaving, giving it the true meaning of *good day*.

- **Bonsoir!** (bohN-swahr!*) (Good evening!*).You use this greeting in the late afternoon and the evening to say hello or good-bye.

- **Salut!** (sah-lew!) (*Hi! Bye!*). This is the most informal of all hellos and is also a way of saying good-bye. Although you can use it at any time of day, you can't use it with just anybody. Use this word only with children and people you're familiar with.

- **Au revoir!** (ohr-vwahr!) (*Good-bye!*). Like its English counterpart, you can use this term any time of day or night.

- **Bonne nuit!** (bohhn nwee!) (*Good night!*). Say this only when you're retiring for the night or when you're putting a child to bed. It essentially means *sleep well*.

- **A bientôt!** (ah byaN-toh!) (*See you soon!*). Say this when you expect to see the person again in the near future.

- **A tout à l'heure!** (ah tooh-tah luhr!) (*See you later!*). Use this phrase only when you'll see the person the same day.

- **A demain!** (ah duh-maN!) (*See you tomorrow!*)

- **Bonne journée!** (bohhn zhoohr-ney!) (*Have a nice day!*)

Introducing yourself and others

It is not enough to greet people and ask how they are; you also need to introduce yourself and find out what their names are. The purpose of this section is to help you do just that.

In French, when you want to say *My name is. . .*, you use a reflexive form of the verb **appeler** (ahp-ley) (*to call*). Thus, **je m'appelle** (zhuh mah-pehl) literally means *I call myself.* The following table shows all the forms of **appeler** in the present tense. (Refer to Chapter 2 for general information on French verbs.)

Conjugation	Pronunciation
je m'appelle	zhuh mah-pehl
tu t'appelles	tew tah-pehl
il/elle/on s'appelle	eel/ehl/ohN sah-pehl
nous nous appelons	nooh nooh-zah-plohN
vous vous appelez	vooh vooh-zah-pley
ils/elles s'appellent	eel/ehl sah-pehl

You may use either of these phrases:

- **Je m'appelle . . . .** (zhuh mah-pehl. . . .) (*My name is . . . .*)
- **Je suis . . . .** (zhuh swee. . . .) (*I am . . . .*)

If you want to know who that person over there is, you ask **Qui est-ce?** (kee ehs?) (*Who is that?*). And you receive the answer **C'est . . .** (seh. . .) (*That is . . .*). To introduce someone, you say any of the following:

- **Je vous présente . . . .** (zhuh vooh prey-zahNt. . . .) (*Let me introduce . . . to you.*) (formal)
- **Je te présente . . . .** (zhuh tuh prey-zahNt. . . .) (*Let me introduce . . . to you.*) (informal)
- **Voici . . . ./Voilà . . . .** (vwah-see. . . ./vwah-lah. . . .) (*Here is . . . ./There is . . . .*)

After you introduce yourself or someone else, the other person, if a man, typically says **Enchanté!** (ahN-shahN-tey!) or, if a woman, **Enchantée!** (pronounced the same). In either case, the meaning is the same: *Delighted!* Of course, on the playground or at a gathering of young people, you may hear these expressions instead:

Comment tu t'appelles?/Comment t'appelles-tu? (koh-mahN tew-tah-pehl?/koh-mahN tah-pehl-tew?) (*What's your name?*)

Et lui, qui est-ce? (ey lwee kee ehs?) (*And who is he?*), or **Et elle, qui est-ce?** (ey ehl kee ehs?) (*And who is she?*)

Talkin' the Talk

Marc Sauval and his wife Christine, entrepreneurs from Québec, are meeting their French counterpart, Claire Rivet for the first time. (Track 2)

Marc:	**Bonjour, madame. Je m'appelle Marc Sauval.** bohN-zhoohr, mah-dahm. zhuh mah-pehl mahrk soh-vahl. *Hello, ma'am. My name is Marc Sauval.*
Claire:	**Ah, monsieur Sauval. Je suis Claire Rivet. Enchantée!** ah, muh-syuh soh-vahl. zhuh swee klehr ree-vey. ahN-shahN-tey. *Ah, Mr. Sauval. I am Claire Rivet. Delighted to meet you!*
Marc:	**Madame Rivet, je vous présente ma femme, Christine.** mah-dahm ree-vey, zhuh vooh prey-zahNt mah fahm, krees-teen. *Mrs Rivet, let me introduce you to my wife, Christine.*
Claire:	**Enchantée, madame!** ahN-shahN-tey, mah-dahm! *Delighted, ma'am!*
Christine:	**Enchantée!** ahN-shahN-tey *Delighted!*

Asking Questions to Get to Know People

One of the ways to get information is by asking questions. You may want to ask, for example, whether the bistro around the corner is good, whether the banks are open on Mondays, or whether the train is running on schedule. And what about asking how someone is? Well, you can ask all these questions simply by following the guidelines explained in the following sections.

Informal and formal ways to ask questions

You can form a yes or no question in French in four ways. The first three are very informal, and the last is more formal.

Using intonation

To ask a question using intonation, simply raise your voice at the end of a statement: **Vous parlez français?** (vooh parh-ley frahN-seh?) (*Do you speak French?*)

Using "n'est-ce pas"

One way to form a question is to add **n'est-ce pas** (nehs pah) to the end of the sentence. This expression takes on the translation of whatever the question is. It could mean *isn't it, don't you, doesn't she,* and so on.) This type of question anticipates a yes answer: **Vous parlez français, n'est-ce pas?** (vooh parh-ley frahN-seh, nehs pah?) (*You speak French, don't you?*)

Using "est-ce que"

You can form a question by adding **est-ce que** (ehs-kuh) to the front of the statement. The statement **Paris est une grande ville** (pah-ree eht-ewn grahNd veel) (*Paris is a big city*) becomes **Est-ce que Paris est une grande ville?** (ehs-kuh pah-ree eht-ewn grahNd veel?) (*Is Paris a big city?*). Note that the final **e** in **Est-ce que** is dropped when it comes before a vowel: **Est-ce qu'il parle français?** (ehs-keel parhl frahN-seh?) (*Does he speak French?*)

Using inversion

In this method, you switch the places of the verb and the subject pronoun and add a hyphen between them. Consider these examples:

> **Vous parlez français** (vooh parh-ley frahN-seh) (*You speak French*) becomes **Parlez-vous français?** (parh-ley vooh frahN-seh?) (*Do you speak French?*)

> **Tu aimes la musique** (tew ehm lah mew-zeek) (*You like music*) becomes **Aimes-tu la musique?** (ehm-tew lah mew-zeek?) (*Do you like music?*)

To use inversion correctly, when the verb ends in a vowel and the subject pronoun begins with a vowel — mainly **il** (eel) (*he, it*), **elle** (ehl) (*she, it*), **on** (ohN) (*one*) — you add the letter *t* in between them and place hyphens on both sides: **Il parle français** (eel parhl frahN-seh (*He speaks French*) becomes **Parle-t-il français?** (parhl-teel frahN-seh?) (*Does he speak French?*)

Asking and replying to "How are you?"

Most of the time, when you meet someone, especially someone you already know, your greeting is followed by the question "How are you?" French has several different ways of asking the question, depending on the level of formality between the two speakers:

> Formal: **Comment allez-vous?** (koh-mahN-tah-ley-vooh?) (*How are you?*) and **Vous allez bien?** (vooh-zah-ley byaN?) (*Are you well?*)

> Informal: **Comment vas-tu?** (koh-mahN vah-tew?) (*How are you?*), **Comment ça va?** (koh-mahN sah vah?) (*How is it going?*), and **Ça va?** (sah vah?) (*Is it going?*, meaning *Are you okay?*).

Of course, others may well want to know how you are. In those cases, they naturally expect you to reply, albeit without going into lengthy details about your health, your work, or your private life. A short phrase will do, such as the following:

- ✔ **Ça va!** (sah vah!) (*I'm okay!*)

- ✔ **Ça va bien!/Ça va très bien!** (sah vah byaN!/sah vah treh byaN!) (*I'm fine!/I'm very well!*)

- ✔ **Bien, merci!/Très bien, merci!** (byaN, mehr-see!/treh byaN, mehr-see!) (*Fine, thank you!/Very well, thank you!*)

- ✔ **Je vais bien, merci.** (zhuh veh byaN, mehr-see.) (*I am well, thank you.*) This is a more formal response.

- ✔ **Pas mal!** (pah mahl!) (*Not bad!*)

Of course, you can also answer negatively. You can say, for example, **Je ne vais pas très bien aujourd'hui** (zhuhn veh pah treh byaN oh-zhoohr-dwee) (*I am not very well today*).

The negative in French has two parts: **ne** (nuh) which you place in front of the conjugated verb and **pas** (pah) (*not*), which you place after the conjugated verb. If the verb begins with a vowel or a mute h, then you drop the **e** from **ne** and you add an apostrophe: **n'**. For example, **Il n'est pas fatigué** (eel neh pah fah-tee-gey) (*He is not tired*).

Whenever you answer a "How are you?" question, you probably want to follow it up with an inquiry about the well-being of the other person. To do so, you simply follow your answer with either the formal **Et vous?** (ey vooh?) or the informal **Et toi?** (ey twah?). Both mean *And you*?

Revisiting the verb "aller"

Aller (ah-ley) (*to go*) is a very useful and multifunctional verb in French. As Chapter 2 explains, **aller** is an irregular verb, which means that the stem is different throughout its conjugation:

Conjugation	*Pronunciation*
je vais	zhuh veh
tu vas	tew vah
Il/elle/on va	eel/ehl/ohN vah
nous allons	nooh-zah-lohN
vous allez	vooh-zah-ley
ils/elles vont	eel/ehl vohN

You use the verb **aller** when you want to say you're going to the store or to the movies, but you also use this verb when you want to talk about how you or someone else is, which makes it a vital verb when you're making introductions and want to ask *How are you?* in French. To do so, you use the interrogative adverb **comment** (koh-mahN) (*how*) in the following ways:

> **Comment est-ce que vous allez?/Comment est-ce que tu vas?** (koh-mahN ehs-kuh vooh-zah-ley?/koh-mahN ehs-kuh tew vah?) (*How are you?*)

> **Comment allez-vous?/Comment vas-tu**? (koh-mahN-tah-ley-vooh?/koh-mahN vah-tew?) (*How are you?*) — This construction is more common.

Talkin' the Talk

Madame Leblanc is doing her daily food shopping and goes into Monsieur Martin's butcher shop.

M. Martin: **Bonjour, Madame Leblanc. Comment allez-vous?**
                 bohN-zhoor, mah-dahm luh-blahN koh-mahN-tah-ley-vooh?
                 Hello, Mrs Leblanc. How are you?

Mme. Leblanc: **Très bien, merci, et vous?**
                 treh byaN, mehr-see, ey vooh?
                 Very well, thank you, and you?

M. Martin: **Ça va bien, merci.**
                 sah vah byaN, mehr-see.
                 I'm fine, thank you.

Later, after Madame Leblanc has made her purchases, she prepares to leave the store.

M. Martin: **Au revoir, Madame Leblanc. Bonne journée.**
                 ohr-vwahr, mah-dahm luh-blahN. bohhn zhoohr-ney.
                 Good-bye, Mrs Leblanc. Have a nice day.

Mme. Leblanc: **Au revoir, monsieur.**
                 ohr-vwahr, muh-syuh.
                 Good-bye, sir.

As Madame Leblanc leaves the shop, she overhears two teenagers who have just met on the street.

Girl:
Salut, Michel. Comment ça va?
sah-lew, mee-shehl. koh-mahN sah vah?
Hi, Michel. How are you doing?

Boy:
Pas mal. Et toi?
pah mahl. ey twah?
Not too bad, How about you?

Girl:
Oh, ça va. Et lui, qui est-ce?
oh, sah vah. ey lwee, kee ehs?
Oh, I'm okay. And who is he?

Boy:
C'est mon frère. Il s'appelle Thomas.
seh mohN frehr. eel sah-pehl toh-mah.
He's my brother. His name is Thomas.

Girl:
Salut, Thomas!
sah-lew, toh-mah!
Hi, Thomas!

CULTURAL WISDOM

Friendly greetings

The French touch a lot more than the Anglo-Saxons do in greeting others. The handshake is not restricted to the first meeting between two persons, for example. Instead, most people in an office shake hands every morning when they get to work and every evening when they leave the office. On a more informal level, women friends kiss lightly on each cheek when they greet each other or say good-bye. A man and a woman meeting or saying good-bye do the same. Male family members may kiss one another, too. If you travel to different parts of France, you may be surprised to discover that in some areas people kiss not twice but three times, and sometimes up to four times! You even see a large amount of cheek-pecking between high school students arriving at school in the morning!

Say you're invited to a dinner party by a French family with children and the parents introduce their children to you before they are sent to bed. They may tell the children **Dites bonsoir à tout le monde** (deet bohN-swahr ah tooh luh mohNd) *(Say good evening to everyone).* Immediately, the little ones might go around the dinner table giving a kiss to all the guests and expecting a kiss back.

Fun & Games

Here is a list of words that got loose. See whether you can put them back where they belong in the dialog below.

elle   je   m'appelle   l'anglais   grande   femme

Bonjour, je (1)_____ Pierre Lanvin. (2)_____ suis de Marseille. C'est une (3)_____ ville française. Ma (4)_____ s'appelle Monique et (5)_____ est canadienne. Je parle le français, bien sûr et aussi un peu (6)_____.

Now fill in the missing words in this dialog between an elderly woman and a teenage boy with a teenage girl.

voici   bien   ça va   parles   toi

Bonjour, madame Legrand. Comment (7)_____?

Ça va bien, merci Denis. Et (8)_____, comment vas-tu?

Ça va, merci. Madame Legrand, (9)_____ Lucy. Elle vient des Etats-Unis.

Oh, bonjour Lucy. Alors tu (10)_____ français?

Pas très (11)_____, madame

Chapter 4

Getting Your Numbers, Dates, and Times Straight

In This Chapter

▶ Discovering cardinal and ordinal numbers

▶ Using the calendar and dates

▶ Telling time

Counting and being able to express and understand numbers is an indispensable part of everyday life. You need numbers when you reveal your age, when you are making the perfect soufflé, or when you're trying to find your favorite TV program. One of the most important uses of numbers is to tell time. How else can you keep track of appointments or plan trips? In this chapter, we show you how to do all of that — use numbers, dates, and time — one step at a time.

Counting Your Lucky Stars: Numbers

You don't need to juggle numbers like a mathematician: Most of the time, you can use plain old cardinal numbers from 0 to around 100 to express the number of units of anything: how much money you have in your wallet, how many sheep you have to count before you fall asleep, how many hours you have to wait before your plane takes off, and so on. Fortunately, French numbers follow a pattern, much like numbers in English.

Counting up to 20

The following list shows the numbers **un** (uhN) (*one*) through **vingt** (vaN) (*twenty*):

- 1 **un** (uhN)
- 2 **deux** (duh)
- 3 **trois** (trwah)
- 4 **quatre** (kah-truh)
- 5 **cinq** (saNk)
- 6 **six** (sees)
- 7 **sept** (seht)
- 8 **huit** (weet)
- 9 **neuf** (nuhf)
- 10 **dix** (dees)
- 11 **onze** (ohNz)
- 12 **douze** (doohz)
- 13 **treize** (trehz)
- 14 **quatorze** (kah-tohrz)
- 15 **quinze** (kaNz)
- 16 **seize** (sehz)
- 17 **dix-sept** (dee-seht)
- 18 **dix-huit** (deez-weet)
- 19 **dix-neuf** (deez-nuhf)
- 20 **vingt** (vaN)

The pronunciation of some numbers changes when the number is followed by a vowel, a mute h (check out the mute h in Chapter 3), or a consonant. The following list explains:

- When a number ending in **–s** or **–x** is followed by a vowel: In these instances, the final **s** and **x** make a *z* sound: **deux enfants** (duhz-ahN-fahN) (*two children*) and **trois enfants** (trwahz-ahN-fahN) (*three children*), for example.

- When the numbers **neuf** (nuhf) (*nine*) and **dix-neuf** (dees-nuhf) (*nineteen*) are followed by a vowel: In these cases, the final **f** makes the *v* sound: **neuf artistes** (nuhv arh-teest) (*nine artists*), for example.

- When the numbers **six** (sees) (*six*), **huit** (weet) (*eight*), **dix** (dees) (*ten*) are followed by a consonant: The final consonants of these numbers are not pronounced: **six livres** (see lee-vruh) (*six books*), **huit personnes** (wee pehr-sohhn) (*eight people*), and **dix films** (dee feelm) (*ten films*), for example.

Counting higher

After you count to **vingt**, you're ready to go higher. After all, if you want to make a special purchase like an exceptional bottle of wine, for example, it will surely cost more than 20 euros! With what follows, you can handle almost everything number-related.

For numbers 20 through 69

You form the numbers 20 through 69 in French much as you do in English, counting up from each tens number, until you hit the next tens number and then starting over.

- ✔ 21 **vingt et un** (vaN-tey-uhN)
- ✔ 22 **vingt-deux** (vahNt-duh)
- ✔ 23 **vingt-trois** (vahNt-trwah)

   and so on

- ✔ 30 **trente** (trahNt)
- ✔ 31 **trente et un** (trahN-tey-uhN)
- ✔ 32 **trente-deux** (trahN-duh)

   and so on

- ✔ 40 **quarante** (kah-rahNt)
- ✔ 41 **quarante et un** (kah-rahN-tey uhN)
- ✔ 42 **quarante-deux** (kah-rahN-duh)

   and so on

- ✔ 50 **cinquante** (saN-kahNt)
- ✔ 51 **cinquante et un** (saN-kahN-tey uhN)
- ✔ 52 **cinquante-deux** (saN-kahNt-duh)

   and so on

- ✔ 60 **soixante** (swah-sahNt)
- ✔ 61 **soixante et un** (swah-sahN-tey uhN)
- ✔ 62 **soixante-deux** (swah-sahNt-duh)

   and so on

For numbers 70 through 99

The number 70 in French is 60 + 10. The number 71 is 60 + 11, 72 is 60 + 12, and so on until you get to 80. For example:

- ✔ 70 **soixante-dix** (swah-sahNt-dees)
- ✔ 71 **soixante et onze** (swah-sahN-tey ohNz)
- ✔ 72 **soixante- douze** (swah-sahNt-doohz)

   and so on

The number 80 is 4×20, although the word "times" isn't used. The number 81 is $4 \times 20 + 1$, 82 is $4 \times 20 + 2$ and so on, until you get to 90, which is $4 \times 20 + 10$. The number 91 is $4 \times 20 + 11$. (Notice that you don't use the conjunction **et** in the number 81 and higher. Also when another number follows 80, the **s** in **vingt** is dropped.) Here are some examples:

- 80 **quatre-vingts** (kah-truh-vaN)
- 81 **quatre-vingt-un** (kah-truh-vaN-uhN)
- 82 **quatre-vingt-deux** (kah-truh-vaN-duh)

  and so on

- 90 **quatre-vingt-dix** (kah-truh-vaN-dees)
- 91 **quatre-vingt-onze** (kah-truh-vaNt-ohNz)
- 92 **quatre-vingt-douze** (kah-truh-vaN-doohz)

  and so on

If you travel to Switzerland or to Belgium, you may be happy to know that the old — and easier — forms of **septante** (sehp-tahNt) (70) and **nonante** (noh-naNt) (90) are commonly used instead of the French **soixante-dix** and **quatre-vingt-dix**. Some parts of Switzerland use the forms **huitante** (wee-tahNt) or **octante** (ohk-tahNt) for 80.

For the numbers 100 and up

After you hit 100, counting to a thousand or even hundreds of thousands is a breeze. Just indicate the number of hundreds or thousands and count up as you do in English. For example:

- 100 **cent** (sahN)
- 101 **cent-un** (sahN-uhN)
- 102 **cent-deux** (sahN-duh)

  and so on

- 200 **deux cents** (duh sahN)
- 201 **deux cent un** (duh sahN uhN)
- 202 **deux cent deux** (duh sahN duh)

  and so on

- 1,000 **mille** (meel)
- 2,000 **deux mille** (duh meel)
- 3,000 **trois mille** (trwah meel)

  and so on

- 1,000,000 **un million** (uhN mee-lyohN)
- 1,000,000,000 **un milliard** (uhN mee-lyahr)

In the preceding list, notice that you drop the **s** in **cents** when another number follows it. Also, the number **mille** doesn't use an **s**, even when it refers to several thousands. Finally, **un** does not precede **cent** or **mille** when you say *one hundred* or *one thousand*.

Discovering ordinal numbers

Ordinal numbers are important when you need to give or follow directions. (Go to Chapter 7 for info on giving and getting directions in French.) To recognize ordinal numbers, remember that, except for **premiere** (pruh-myey) (*first*), they all have **–ième** (ee-ehm) after the number (just like the *-th* ending in English). Also, whereas English uses the superscript *th* (or *st* or *rd*) to indicate ordinal numbers (5th, for example), in French, the superscript is the letter **e**: 9e, 4e, and so on. Table 4-1 lists the ordinal numbers from first through twentieth, but you can go as high as you like. Here are the rules for forming ordinal numbers:

- If the cardinal number ends in an **–e**, the **–e** is dropped: For example, **quatre** (kah-truh) (*four*) becomes **quatrième** (kah-tree-ehm) (*fourth*), **seize** (sehz) (*sixteen*) becomes **seizième** (seh-zee-ehm) (*sixteenth*).

- For the number **cinq** (saNk) (*five*), add a **u** before **–ième**: **cinquième** (sahN-kee-ehm) (*fifth*).

- For the number 9, **neuf** (nuhf), the **f** changes to **v**: **neuvième** (nuh-vee-ehm) (*ninth*).

Table 4-1		Ordinal Numbers, from 1er through 20[e]			
Abbrev.	*French*	*Pronunciation*	*Abbrev.*	*French*	*Pronunciation*
1[e]	**premiere**	(pruh-myey)	11[e]	**onzième**	(ohN-zee-ehm)
2[e]	**deuxième**	(duh-zee-ehm)	12[e]	**douzième**	(dooh-zee-ehm)
3[e]	**troisième**	(trwah-zee-ehm)	13[e]	**treizième**	(treh-zee-ehm)
4[e]	**quatrième**	(kah-tree-ehm)	14[e]	**quatorzième**	(kah-tohr-zee-ehm)
5[e]	**cinquième**	(sahN-kee-ehm)	15[e]	**quinzième**	(kahN-zee-ehm)
6[e]	**sixième**	(see-zee-ehm)	16[e]	**seizième**	(seh-zee-ehm)
7[e]	**septième**	(seh-tee-ehm)	17[e]	**dix-septième**	(dee-seh-tee-ehm)
8[e]	**huitième**	(wee-tee-ehm)	18[e]	**dix-huitième**	(dee-zwee-tee-ehm)
9[e]	**neuvième**	(nuh-vee-ehm)	19[e]	**dix-neuvième**	(deez-nuh-vee-ehm)
10[e]	**dixième**	(dee-zee-ehm)	20[e]	**vingtième**	(vaN-tee-ehm)

Approximating quantities

Sometimes you want to approximate the numbers instead of being very exact. If you were speculating on someone's age, for example, you may say in English that she is or looks about 40. You can do the same in French by adding the suffix **–aine** (ehn) to the cardinal numbers. Here are some examples:

- ✔ **une dizaine** (ewn deez-ehn) (*about 10*)
- ✔ **une vingtaine** (ewn vaN-tehn) (*about 20*)

If a noun follows the approximate quantity, then add the preposition **de** (duh) or **d'** if the noun begins with a vowel or a mute h, as these examples show:

> **Je voudrais une dizaine de croissants.** (zhuh vooh-dreh ewn deez-ehn duh krwah-sahN.) (*I would like about 10 croissants.*)

> **Il y a une vingtaine d'étudiants dans la classe.** (eel ee ah ewn vahN-tehn dey-tew-dyahN dahN lah klahs.) (*There are about 20 students in the class.*)

You can refer to approximate numbers by using the words **à peu près** (ah puh preh) or **environ** (ahN-vee-rohN), both of which mean *approximately*. For example, **J'ai environ quatre-vingts livres dans mon bureau** (zhey ahN-vee-rohN kah-truh-vaN lee-vruh dahN mohN bew-roh) (*I have approximately 80 books in my office*).

Using the Calendar and Dates

France, the United States, and many other countries around the world use a similar calendar, one that has seven days and twelve months. Yet countries differ in how the date is presented. In English, the month comes first, followed by the day of the month, followed by the year. In French, the day of the month comes first, followed by the month, followed by the year. For example, the date *May 8, 2011* is presented like this in French: **le 8 mai, 2011** (luh wee meh duh-meel-ohNz), and it's written 8-5-2011. Imagine how funny (or embarrassing) it would be if you were invited to an important event on 8-5-2011 and you showed up on 5-8-2011 (August 5, 2011)!

Even though a week has seven days, the French refer to a week as **huit jours** (wee zhoohr) (*8 days*) and to two weeks as **quinze jours** (kaNz zhoohr) (*15 days*). The reason is that if you count from Monday to Monday and you include both Mondays, then you have 8 days, and if you continue counting to the following Monday (the third Monday), you have 15 days.

Recounting the days of the week

The French calendar begins on a Monday as the first day of the week. Unlike English, the days of the week are not capitalized in French:

- ✔ **lundi** (luhN-dee) (*Monday*)
- ✔ **mardi** (mahr-dee) (*Tuesday*)
- ✔ **mercredi** (mehr-kruh-dee) (*Wednesday*)
- ✔ **jeudi** (zhuh-dee) (*Thursday*)
- ✔ **vendredi** (vahN-druh-dee) (*Friday*)
- ✔ **samedi** (sahm-dee) (*Saturday*)
- ✔ **dimanche** (dee-mahNnsh) (*Sunday*)

When referring to a particular day, state the day without an article: **je travaille samedi** (zhuh trah-vahy sahm-dee) (*I work [on] Saturday*). But if you want to say *I work on Saturdays*, you have to place the definite article **le** (luh) (*the*) in front of the day of the week, like this: **je travaille le samedi** (zhuh trah-vahy luh sahm-dee) (*I work on Saturdays*). Placing the definite article **le** in front of the day(s) of the week is like adding an *s* to the day(s) of the week in English.

Knowing the names of the months

Just like the days of the week, the months of the year are not capitalized in French. Here are the months in French:

- ✔ **janvier** (zhahN-vyey) (*January*)
- ✔ **février** (fey-vryey) (*February*)
- ✔ **mars** (mahrs) (*March*)
- ✔ **avril** (ah-vreel) (*April*)
- ✔ **mai** (meh) (*May*)
- ✔ **juin** (zhwaN) (*June*)
- ✔ **juillet** (zhwee-yeh) (*July*)

- ✔ **août** (ooht) (*August*)
- ✔ **septembre** (sehp-tahN-bruh) (*September*)
- ✔ **octobre** (ohk-toh-bruh) (*October*)
- ✔ **novembre** (noh-vahN-bruh) (*November*)
- ✔ **décembre** (dey-sahN-bruh) (*December*)

To say that something is happening in a certain month, you use the preposition **en** (ahN) (*in*) in front of the month. Here are some examples:

Mon anniversaire est en décembre. (mohN-nah-nee-vehr-sehr eht-ahN dey-sahN-bruh.)(*My birthday is in December.*)

En janvier, je pars pour la Martinique. (ahN zhaN-vyey, zhuh pahr poohr lah mahr-tee-neek.) (*In January, I leave for Martinique.*)

Je reviens en avril. (zhuh ruh-vyaN ahN-nah-vreel). (*I am coming back in April.*)

Setting specific dates

When expressing a specific date, use the following construction:

> **Le** + cardinal number + month + year

You use this formula to express all dates, except for the first of the month, when you use the ordinal number. Here are a couple of examples:

C'est le 6 avril 2000. (seh luh see-zah-vreel duh meel.) (*It's the sixth of April 2000.*)

C'est le premier mai. (seh luh pruh-myey meh.) (*It's the first of May.*)

The following are some important dates in some French-speaking countries:

- ✔ **le 14 juillet** (luh kah-tohrz zhwee-yeh) (*July14*): The French national holiday
- ✔ **le premier août** (luh pruh-myey ooht) (*August 1*): The Swiss national holiday
- ✔ **le 17 juillet** (luh dee-seht zhwee-yeh) (*July 17*): The Belgian national holiday
- ✔ **le premier juillet** (luh pruh-myey zhwee-yeh) (*July 1*): The Canadian national holiday

Remembering the seasons

The seasons in French are masculine and, unlike in English, require the definite article:

- ✔ **le printemps** (luh praN-tahN) (*spring*)
- ✔ **l'été** (ley-tey) (*summer*)
- ✔ **l'automne** (loh-tohn) (*fall*)
- ✔ **l'hiver** (lee-vehr) (*winter*)

To express *in the spring,* for example, use **au** (oh) before a consonant sound and use **en** (ahN) before a vowel sound: **au printemps** (oh praN-tahN) (*in the spring*), **en été** (ahN-ney-tey) (*in the summer*), **en automne** (ahN-noh-tohn) (*in the fall*), and **en hiver** (ahN-nee-vehr) (*in the winter*).

Talkin' the Talk

Juliette is talking to her friend Corinne about her sister's upcoming wedding.

Juliette:	**Ma soeur va se marier au printemps.** mah suhr vah suh mah-ryey oh praN-tahN. *My sister is getting married in the spring.*
Corinne:	**Ah oui. Quand exactement?** ah wee. kahN-tehg-zah-ktuh-mahN? *Oh yes. When exactly?*
Juliette:	**Le 6 avril.** luh see-zah-vreel. *April 6.*
Corinne:	**C'est quel jour?** seh kehl zhoohr? *What day is it?*
Juliette:	**C'est un samedi.** seh-tuhN sahm-dee. *It's a Saturday.*
Corinne:	**À quelle heure est la cérémonie?** ah kehl uhr eh lah sey-rey-moh-nee? *What time is the ceremony?*
Juliette:	**À 11 heures.** ah ohNz uhr. *At 11:00 a.m.*
Corinne:	**Combien de personnes avez-vous invitées?** kohN-byaN duh pehr-sohhn ah-vey-vooh-zaN-vee-tey? *How many people did you invite?*
Juliette:	**Une centaine de personnes.** ewn sahN-tehn duh pehr-sohhn. *About a hundred people.*

Words to Know

ma soeur	mah suhr	my sister
se marier	suh mah-ryey	to get married
Quand exactement?	kahN-tehg-zah-ktuh-mahN	When exactly?
Quel jour?	kehl zhoohr	What day?
À quelle heure est. . . ?	ah kehl uhr eh. . . ?	What time is. . . ?
la cérémonie	lah sey-rey-moh-nee	the ceremony

Telling Time in French

One of the most important and frequent uses of numbers is, of course, to tell time. The French use both the familiar 12-hour clock and the official 24-hour clock to tell time.

Using the 12-hour clock

To express the time in French using the 12-hour system, you begin with **il est** (eel eh) (*it is*) and add a number representing the hour and then the word **heure(s)** (uhr) (*time, o'clock*). Use the singular **heure** when it's 1:00; use the plural **heures** for all other hours. Here are some examples:

> **Il est huit heures.** (eel eh weet-uhr.) (*It's 8 o'clock.*)
>
> **Il est neuf heures.** (eel eh nuhv-uhr.) (*It's 9 o'clock.*)
>
> **Il est une heure.** (eel eh ewn-uhr.) (*It's 1 o'clock.*)

Of course, the time isn't always exactly on the hour. Therefore, you need a way to indicate time past and before the hour, too. To indicate time past the hour, you can simply follow the phrase **il est. . .heure(s)** with the number of minutes it is past the hour. To express time before the hour (10 minutes to

2:00, for example), you add the word **moins** (mwaN), which means *minus*. Consider these examples:

> **Il est huit heures dix.** (eel eh weet-uhr dees.) (*It's 8:10* or *It's 10 past 8.*)

> **Il est huit heures moins dix.** (eel eh weet-uhr mwaN dees.) (*It's 7:50.* [Literally: *It's 8:00 minus 10.*])

> **Il est dix heures moins vingt-cinq.** (eel eh deez-uhr mwaN vahN-saNk.) (*It's 9:35* or *It's 25 to 10:00.* [Literally: *It's 10:00 minus 25 minutes.*])

Alternatively, you can use these French phrases:

> ✔ **et quart** (ey kahr) (*quarter after*). For example: **Il est neuf heures et quart.** (eel eh nuh-vuhr ey kahr.) (*It's 9:15* or *It's quarter past nine.*)

> ✔ **et demi** (e) (ey duh-mee) (*half-past*). For example: **Il est huit heures et demie.** (eel eh weet-uhr ey duh-mee.) (*It's half past 8:00.*)

> ✔ **moins le quart** (mwaN luh kahr) (*quarter till*). For example: **Il est neuf heures moins le quart.** (eel eh nuhv-uhr mwaN luh kahr.) (*It's quarter to 9:00.*)

To distinguish between a.m. and p.m. in the 12-hour clock, use these phrases after the time:

> ✔ **du matin** (dew mah-taN) (*in the morning*)

> ✔ **de l'après-midi** (duh lah-preh-mee-dee) (*in the afternoon*)

> ✔ **du soir** (dew swahr) (*in the evening*)

> ✔ **midi** (mee-dee) (*noon*)

> ✔ **minuit** (mee-nwee) (*midnight*)

Here are a couple of examples:

> **Il est 10 heures du matin.** (eel eh deez-uhr dew mah-taN.) (*It is 10:00 in the morning [a.m.]*)

> **Il est 10 heures du soir.** (eel eh deez-uhr dew swahr.) (*It is 10:00 in the evening [p.m.]*)

Both **midi** and **minuit** are masculine, so when you say *half past noon* or *half past midnight*, you don't add an **e** to the word **demi**: **Il est midi et demi** (eel eh mee-dee ey duh-mee) (*It's half past noon*).

In North America, we abbreviate time in the *hour:minute* format: 12:15 for example, or 3:35. In France, time is abbreviated differently. Instead of using a colon to separate the hour from the minutes, you use a lowercase *h*. For example, 11:30 becomes 11h30. You abbreviate in the same way whether you're using the 12-hour system or the 24-hour system. For example, 10h30 means 10:30 a.m. and 22h30 means 10:30 p.m.

Using the 24-hour routine

In Europe, as well as French-speaking Canada, the use of the 24-hour clock, or military time, is very common. It's used for all transportation schedules, concert times, store hours, appointment times, and any other scheduled events. When you use the 24-hour clock, you don't need to distinguish between a.m. or p.m.

If you're accustomed to the 12-hour system, telling time by the 24-hour clock may be a little confusing. Here's what you need to know: You count up from 1:00 a.m. to 12:00 noon just as you're used to, but instead of starting over again at 1, you keep counting up: 13:00, 14:00, and so on until you hit 24:00, which is midnight. So 13:00 is 1:00 p.m., 14:00 is 2:00 p.m. and so on.

To say what time it is in the 24-hour system, simply add the number of minutes to the hour. Here are some examples:

Il est 11h15 [onze heures quinze]. (eel eh ohNz uhr kaNz.) (*It's 11:15 [a.m.].*)

Il est 16h10 [seize heures dix]. (eel eh sehz uhr dees.) (*It's 4:10 [p.m.].*)

Talkin' the Talk

 Pierre and Claire are running late. (Track 3)

Pierre: **Claire, quelle heure est-il?**
klehr, kehl uhr eh-teel?
Claire, what time is it?

Claire: **Il est 10h10 (dix heures dix).**
eel eh deez-uhr dees.
It's 10:10 am.

Pierre: **Il est 10h10 (dix heures dix)?**
eel eh deez-uhr dees?
It's 10:10 am?

Claire: **Oui, nous sommes en retard.**
wee, nooh-sohmz-ahN ruh-tahr.
Yes, we're late.

Pierre: **Oh non! Allons-y! Dépêchons-nous!**
oh nohN! ahl-ohN-zee! dey-pehsh-ohN-nooh!
Oh no! Let's go! Hurry up!

Words to Know

Il est. . . heures	eel eh. . . uhr	It's. . . o'clock
et quart	ey kahr	quarter past
et demi(e)	ey duh-mee	half past
moins. . .	mwaN. . .	(minus) to. . .
moins le quart. . .	mwaN luh kahr. . .	quarter to. . .
Quelle heure est-il?	kehl uhr eht-eel?	What time is it?
être en retard	eh-truh ahN reh-tahr	to be late
Allons-y!	ahl-ohN-zee!	Let's go!
Dépêchons-nous!	dey-pehsh-ohN-nooh!	Let's hurry up!

Fun & Games

Write the time in 12-hour format and 24-hour format for each of the following clocks.

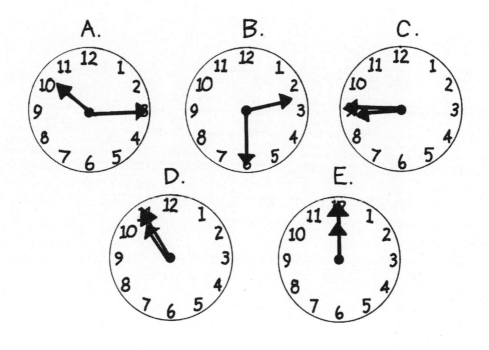

	In 12-hour format	In 24-hour format
A.	_____	_____
B.	_____	_____
C.	_____	_____
D.	_____	_____
E.	_____	_____

Chapter 5

Talking about Your Home, Family, and Daily Routine

. . . .

In This Chapter

▶ Talking about where you live and the rooms in your house

▶ Using the reflexive verb form to talk about your daily routine

▶ Discussing meals with the verbs **manger**, **prendre**, and **boire**

▶ Introducing family members with possessive adjectives

. . . .

*I*f you're like most people, home and family are at the center of your life, and they provide numerous topics of daily conversation. Just try counting the number of times a day you mention your home and family to your coworkers or friends. The same is true of people everywhere, which is why these topics are often the first you tackle when you learn a new language. Furthermore, these topics of conversation are often the first things people who don't know you ask about. They may ask you where you live, whether you have siblings, whether you're married or single, and so on. With the vocabulary and information in this chapter, you'll be ready to answer these questions and perhaps even ask a few of your own.

Discussing Where You Live with the Verb "Habiter"

In French, two verbs correspond to the English *to live*: **habiter** (ah-bee-tey) and **vivre** (vee-vruh). Most of the time, these verbs are interchangeable, but **habiter** refers to space, whereas **vivre** refers to time as well as space. For example, to say *We live in the 21st century*, you use **vivre**: **Nous vivons au vingt-et-unième siècle** (nooh vee-vohN oh vaN-tey-ew-nee-ehm syeh-kluh). But when you talk about where you live, you use the verb **habiter**, as these examples show:

J'habite dans une maison. (zhah-beet dahN-zewn meh-zohN.) (*I live in a house.*)

J'habite dans un appartement. (zhah-beet dahN-zuhN-nah-pahr-tuh-mahN.) (*I live in an apartment.*)

Nous habitons à la campagne/en ville. (nooh-zah-bee-tohN ah lah kahN-pah-nyuh/ahN veel.) (*We live in the country/city.*)

Nous habitons en banlieue. (nooh-zah-bee-tohN ahN bahN-lyuh.) (*We live in the suburbs.*)

Vivre is an irregular verb, so when you talk about space, stick to **habiter** for now because it is regular and easy to use.

Regardless of whether you live in a private house or an apartment, various rooms have a special and particular function. The following list introduces **les pièces de la maison** (ley pyehs duh lah meh-zohN) (*the rooms of a house*):

- **le salon** (luh sah-lohN) (*living room*)
- **la cuisine** (lah kwee-zeen) (*kitchen*)
- **la chambre** (lah shahN-bruh) (*bedroom*)
- **la salle de bains** (lah sahl duh baN) (*bathroom*)

The following sections introduce the basic rooms of a house or apartment and list the furniture and appliances each may contain.

In France, the stories of a house or an apartment are counted differently than in the United States. The French consider the first floor as the ground floor, **le rez-de-chaussée** (luh reyd-shoh-sey) (*street level*), and start counting after that. Therefore, what we would consider to be the *second floor* is actually the first floor — **le premier étage** (luh pruh-myey-rey-tahzh) — in France; the *third floor* is **le deuxième étage** (luh duh-zee-ehm ey-tahzh), and so forth.

In "le salon" (the living room)

The French have two names for the living room: **le salon,** which is a more formal living room, and **la salle de séjour** (lah sahl duh sey-zhoohr) — **le séjour** (luh sey-zhoohr) for short — meaning a casual *family room*. The French also use the Anglicism **le living** (luh lee-veeng). Here is a list of furniture that you'd normally find in a living room:

- **un sofa/un canapé** (uhN soh-fah/uhN kah-nah-pey) (*sofa/couch*)
- **un fauteuil** (uhN foh-tohy) (*arm chair*)
- **un tapis** (uhN tah-pee) (*rug*)
- **une moquette** (ewn moh-keht) (*wall-to-wall carpet*)

- ✔ **une table de salon** (ewn tah-bluh duh sah-lohN) (*coffee table*)
- ✔ **une lampe** (ewn lahmp) (*lamp*)
- ✔ **des rideaux** (dey ree-doh) (*curtains, drapes*)
- ✔ **une télévision/une télé** (ewn tey-ley-vee-zyohN/ewn tey-ley) (*TV*)

In "la cuisine" (the kitchen)

The kitchen is the heart of many homes. Not only is it the place to prepare and eat home cooked meals, but it is also the place where family and friends gather to discuss their day, to make plans for the weekend, or to talk about the weather. Here is a list of what you may find in a typical kitchen:

- ✔ **une cuisinière** (ewn kwee-zee-nyehr) (*stove*)
- ✔ **un réfrigérateur/un frigo** (uhN rey-free-zhey-rah-tuhr/uhN free-goh) (*refrigerator/fridge*)
- ✔ **un évier** (uhN-ney-vyey) (*kitchen sink*)
- ✔ **un comptoir** (uhN kohN-twahr) (*counter*)
- ✔ **un four à micro-ondes** (uhN foohr ah mee-kroh-ohNd) (*microwave oven*)
- ✔ **un lave-vaisselle** (uhN lahv-veh-sehl) (*dishwasher*)
- ✔ **une table de cuisine** (ewn tah-bluh duh kwee-zeen) (*kitchen table*)
- ✔ **des chaises** (dey shehz) (*chairs*)

In France, the kitchen is not usually counted as part of the rooms of the house. If you're looking in the French classifieds to rent an apartment or a house, for example, and see **un appartement à trois pièces** (uhN-nah-pahr-tuh-mahN ah trwah pyehs), it means *a 3-room apartment*, indicating a living room and two bedrooms.

In "la chambre" (the bedroom)

Your bedroom is your own personal space that reflects your personality and taste. It's also the place you can go when you need some privacy. Here is a list of some of the things you may find in a bedroom:

- ✔ **un lit** (uhN lee) (*bed*)
- ✔ **des lits jumeaux** (dey lee zhew-moh) (*twin beds*)
- ✔ **un lit d'une personne** (uhN lee dewn pehr-sohhn) (*single bed*)
- ✔ **un lit de deux personnes** (uhN lee duh duh pehr-sohhn) (*double bed*)
- ✔ **une commode** (ewn koh-mohhd) (*dresser*)

✔ **une armoire** (ewn ahr-mwahr) (*armoire*)

✔ **une table de nuit** (ewn tah-bluh duh nwee) (*nightstand*)

✔ **un réveil** (uhN rey-vehy) (*alarm clock*)

✔ **une couverture** (ewn kooh-vehr-tewr) (*blanket*)

✔ **un oreiller** (uhN-noh-rey-yey) (*pillow*)

✔ **des draps** (dey drah) (*sheets*)

In "la salle de bains" (the bathroom)

In French, there's a difference between **la salle de bains** and **les toilettes** (ley twah-leht) (*toilet*). **La salle de bains** literally means *bathroom,* or a place to bathe. It does not necessarily have a toilet. If you are looking for the restroom, be sure to ask for either **les toilettes** or **les W.C.** (ley vey sey) (*water closet*). Here are some things commonly found in **la salle de bains**:

✔ **une baignoire** (ewn beh-nywahr) (*bathtub*)

✔ **une douche** (ewn doohsh) (*shower*)

✔ **un lavabo** (uhN lah-vah-boh) (*sink*)

✔ **une serviette** (ewn sehr-vyeht) (*towel*)

✔ **un miroir** (uhN mee-rwahr) (*mirror*)

✔ **une brosse** (ewn brohs) (*hairbrush*)

✔ **un peigne** (uhN peh-nyuh) (*comb*)

✔ **un rasoir** (uhN rah-zwahr) (*razor*)

✔ **une brosse à dents** (ewn brohs ah dahN) (*toothbrush*)

✔ **du dentifrice** (dew dahN-tee-frees) (*toothpaste*)

✔ **du savon** (dew sah-vohN) (*soap*)

You also often find **un bidet** (uhN bee-deh) (*a bidet*) in French bathrooms.

Talkin' the Talk

Suzanne, a student at the Sorbonne, is looking for a roommate to share her rent and other expenses. She has posted an ad and found another student who is interested in sharing the apartment. The two meet to discuss the situation. (Track 4)

Suzanne: **Où habites-tu maintenant?**
ooh ah-beet-tew maN-tuh-nahN?
Where do you live now?

Agnès: **J'habite en banlieue mais je voudrais être plus près de l'université. Où se trouve l'appartement?**
zhah-beet ahN bahN-lyuh meh zhuh vooh-dreh eh-truh plew preh duh lew-nee-vehr-see-tey. ooh suh troohv lah-pahr-tuh-mahN?
I live in the suburbs, but I would like to be closer to the university. Where is the apartment located?

Suzanne: **L'appartement se trouve dans le 5e arrondissement, près de la Sorbonne.**
lah-pahr-tuh-mahN suh troohv dahN luh saNk-ee-ehm ah-rohN-dees-mahN, preh duh lah sohr-bohhn.
The apartment is in the 5th district, near the Sorbonne.

Agnès : **Combien de pièces y a-t-il?**
kohN-byaN duh pyehs ee ah-teel?
How many rooms are there?

Suzanne: **Il y a trois pièces: un séjour, deux chambres et la cuisine.**
eel ee ah trwah pyehs: uhN sey-zhoohr, duh shahN-bruh ey lah kwee-zeen.
There are three rooms: a living room, two bedrooms and the kitchen.

Agnès: **Est-ce que l'appartement est meublé?**
ehs-kuh lah-pahr-tuh-mahN eh muh-bley?
Is the apartment furnished?

Suzanne : **Oui, il y a un canapé, un fauteuil, une table de salon et une télévision dans le séjour et un lit, une armoire et une table de nuit dans la chambre.**
wee, eel ee ah uhN kah-nah-pey, uhN foh-tohy, ewn tah-bluh duh sah-lohN ey ewn tey-ley-vee-zyohN dahN luh sey-zhoohr ey uhN lee, ewn ahr-mwahr ey ewn tah-bluh duh nwee dahN lah shahN-bruh.
Yes, there is a sofa, a chair, a coffee table and a television in the living room and a bed, an armoire, and a nightstand in the bedroom.

Agnès: **Est-ce que la cuisine est aménagée?**
ehs-kuh lah kwee-zeen eh-tah-mey-nah-zhey?
Is the kitchen equipped?

Suzanne:	**Oui, il y a un frigo, une cuisinière et un four à micro-ondes.**	
	wee, eel ee ah uhN free-goh, ewn kwee-zee-nyehr ey uhN foohr ah mee-kroh-ohNd.	
	Yes, there is a fridge, a stove, and a microwave.	
Agnès:	**Combien est le loyer?**	
	kohN-byaN eh luh lwah-yey?	
	How much is the rent?	
Suzanne:	**550 euros par mois.**	
	saNk sahN saNk-ahNt uh-roh pahr mwah.	
	550 euros a month.	
Agnès:	**C'est parfait!**	
	seh pahr-feh!	
	It's perfect!	

Words to Know

la banlieue	lah bahN-lyuh	the suburbs
près de	preh duh	near, close to
combien de	kohN-byaN duh	how many
meublé	muh-bley	furnished
aménagé	ah-mey-nah-zhey	equipped
le loyer	luh lwah-yey	the rent
par mois	pahr mwah	per month

Il y a means both *there is* or *there are,* depending on context. Whatever the meaning, however, the verb is always in the third person singular: **a.**

Discussing Daily Routine with Reflexive Verbs

A reflexive verb is one where the subject performs the action on itself. For example, in the English sentence *I cut myself,* the subject (*I*) is performing an action (*cut*) and the receiver of that action is *myself*, which refers back to the subject. Reflexive verbs are much more common in French than they are in English. In particular, you use them when you want to describe what you do in the morning to get yourself ready for the day. For example, in French you say **je me réveille** (zhuh muh rey-vey) (*I wake up* [Literally: *I wake up myself*]).

Reflexive verbs are regular verbs (check out Chapter 2 for the conjugation of regular verbs), except that they have an added pronoun — the reflexive pronoun — before the verb.

In the infinitive form, the sign of a reflexive verb is the pronoun **se** (suh), which means *oneself*, but can also mean *myself, yourself,* and so on, depending on the pronoun in the conjugation. Here is the conjugation of the reflexive verb **se réveiller** (suh rey-vey-ey) (*to wake up*):

Conjugation	*Pronunciation*
je me réveille	zhuh muh rey-vey
tu te réveilles	tew tuh rey-vey
il/elle/on se réveille	eel/ehl/ohN suh rey-vey
nous nous réveillons	nooh nooh rey-vey-ohN
vous vous réveillez	vooh vooh rey-vey-ey
ils/elles se réveillent	eel/ehl suh rey-vey

After you wake up, you have to get out of bed. In French, you use the reflexive verb **se lever** (suh luh-vey) (*to get up*). This verb requires an accent grave on the first **e** in the first (**je**), second (**tu**), and third (**il/elle/on**) person singular, as well as in the third person plural (**ils/elles**) for pronunciation purposes. The accent grave on the **e** makes it sound like (*eh*) rather than (*uh*) without the accent. Here is the conjugation of **se lever**:

Conjugation	*Pronunciation*
je me lève	zhuh muh lehv
tu te lèves	tew tuh lehv
il/elle/on se lève	eel/ehl/ohN suh lehv
nous nous levons	nooh nooh luh-vohN
vous vous levez	vooh vooh luh-vey
ils/elles se lèvent	eel/ehl suh lehv

In addition to **se réveiller** and **se lever,** you need the following reflexive verbs to describe your morning routine:

- ✔ **se laver** (suh lah-vey) (*to wash*)

- ✔ **se doucher** (suh dooh-shey) (*to shower*)

- ✔ **se baigner** (suh bey-nyey) (*to bathe*)

- ✔ **se raser** (suh rah-zey) (*to shave*)

- ✔ **se brosser les dents** (suh broh-sey ley dahN) (*to brush your teeth*)

- ✔ **se brosser les cheveux** (suh broh-sey ley shuh-vuh) (*to brush your hair*)

- ✔ **se peigner (les cheveux)** (suh pey-nyey [ley shuh-vuh]) (*to comb [your hair]*)

- ✔ **s'habiller** (sah-bee-yey) (*to get dressed*)

- ✔ **s'en aller** (sah-nah-ley) (*to leave*)

You can use a number of these reflexive verbs to describe your daily routine or someone else's. For example, you can say

Je me réveille à huit heures. (zhuh muh rey-vey ah weet-uhr.) (*I wake up at 8 o'clock.*)

Il se douche. (eel suh doohsh.) (*He takes a shower.*)

Nous nous brossons les dents. (nooh nooh broh-sohN ley dahN.) (*We brush our teeth.*)

Elle s'habille. (ehl sah-beey.) (*She is getting dressed.*)

Appendix B has verb tables you can use for easy reference. For a complete explanation of all types of verbs and tenses, check out the book *French Verbs For Dummies* (John Wiley & Sons, Inc.).

Three squares a day, French-style

In the United States, people eat breakfast, lunch, and dinner. Wouldn't it be simple if only three words designated **les repas** (ley ruh-pah) (*the meals*) in all French-speaking countries? Well, it simply isn't so. Québec has kept some of the 17th-century French its first settlers used, and people in some parts of the French countryside also use terms from that era. The following sections explain the proper term and the kinds of foods eaten during a typical meal in France. Of course, not all meals are eaten at home. You can find information about dining out in Chapter 8.

A bounty for breakfast

The word for *breakfast* is **le petit déjeuner** (luh puh-tee dey-zhuh-ney) in France and **le déjeuner** (luh dey-zhuh-ney) in Québec. The traditional French breakfast is usually made up of the following:

- ✔ **le café** (luh kah-fey) (*coffee*). If you don't like your coffee black, you can choose **le café au lait** (luh kah-fey oh leh) (*coffee with hot milk*) or **le café crème** (luh kah-fey krehm) (*coffee with a little milk*).

- ✔ **le thé nature** (luh tey nah-tewr) (*plain tea*). If plain tea isn't your cup of tea, opt for **le thé au lait** (luh tey oh leh) (*tea with milk*), **le thé au citron/le thé citron** (luh tey oh see-trohN/luh tey see-trohN) (*tea with lemon*), or **la tisane** (lah tee-zahn) (*herbal tea*).

- ✔ **le pain** (luh paN) (*bread*) or **le pain grillé** (luh paN gree-yey) (*toast*). You can also get **les tartines** (ley tahr-teen) (*slices of bread with some kind of spread*), like **le beurre** (luh buhr) (*butter*) or **la confiture** (lah kohN-fee-tewr) (*jam*).

- ✔ **un croissant** (uhN krwah-sahN) (*a croissant*). A traditional French breakfast may include pastries like **le pain au chocolat** (luh paN oh shoh-koh-lah) (*a chocolate croissant*), **le chausson aux pommes** (luh shoh-sohN oh pohhm) (*applesauce-filled danish*), or **le pain aux raisins** (luh paN oh reh-zaN) (*raisin bread*).

You can find all of these mouth-watering goodies in any **pâtisserie** (pah-tees-ree) (*confectioner's shop*) or **boulangerie** (booh-lahN-zhree) (*bakery*) throughout France. If you aren't sure what something is, you can always simply point to it in the window and be delightfully surprised at whatever delicious confection you discover! Go to Chapter 8 for more on selecting items at a market or café.

Eating lunch

The word for *lunch* is **le déjeuner** (luh dey-zhuh-ney) in France and **le dîner** (luh dee-ney) in Québec and other francophone countries. Common lunch items include

> ✔ **un sandwich** (uhN sahN-dweesh) (*a sandwich*)
>
> ✔ **une salade** (ewn sah-lahd) (*a salad*)
>
> ✔ **une soupe** (ewn soohp) (*soup*)
>
> ✔ **une omelette** (ewn-ohm-leht) (*an omelet*)

Dinner time!

The word for *dinner* is **le dîner** (luh dee-ney) in France and **le souper** (luh sooh-pey) in Québec and other francophone countries. As in North America, the biggest meal of the day in most French homes nowadays is dinner. French families usually eat dinner around 7:30 or 8:00 p.m. The French are more formal when sitting down to dinner, and even on a weekday, the dinner consists of at least an appetizer, a main dish, and a cheese platter.

L'entrée (lahN-trey) (*the appetizer*) begins the meal and can be anything from soup to pâté to a tomato salad. The *main dish*, or **le plat principal** (luh plah praN-see-pahl), usually consist of **de la viande** (duh lah vyahNd) (*meat*), **de la volaille** (duh lah voh-lahy) (*poultry*), or **du poisson** (dew pwah-sohN) (*fish*), and **des légumes** (dey ley-gewm) (*vegetables*). **Le plat principal** is usually followed by a salad, a cheese platter, and a dessert.

Snacking between meals

After coming home from school, children enjoy **le goûter** (luh gooh-tey) (*mid-afternoon snack*), which usually consists of bread and butter, jam, or chocolate. If you suddenly find yourself hungry between meals, you can always have **un casse-croûte** (uhN kahs-krooht) (*a snack*, literally: *break the crust*), like a crêpe, at a stand in Paris, a hot dog sold by a street vendor in Montreal, or anything in between.

Setting the table

If you take the trouble to plan and prepare a home-cooked meal, you want to sit down at a properly set table so that you can enjoy it. To set the table, you use the expression **mettre le couvert/la table** (meh-truh luh kooh-vehr/lah tah-bluh) (*to set the table*). Check out the conjugation of the verb **mettre:**

Conjugation	Pronunciation
je mets	zhuh meh
tu mets	tew meh
il/elle/on met	eel/ehl/ohN meh
nous mettons	nooh meh-tohN
vous mettez	vooh meh-tey
ils/elles mettent	eel/ehl meht

For example, you can say **ils mettent le couvert** (eel meht luh kooh-vehr) (*they are setting the table*). And just what do you set on the table? These items:

- ✔ **une nappe** (ewn nahp) (*a tablecloth*)
- ✔ **une assiette** (ewn ah-syeht) (*a plate*)
- ✔ **les couverts** (ley kooh-vehr) (*silverware*)
- ✔ **un verre** (uhN vehr) (*a glass*)
- ✔ **une fourchette** (ewn foohr-sheht) (*a fork*)
- ✔ **une cuillère** (ewn kwee-yehr) (*a spoon*)
- ✔ **un couteau** (uhN kooh-toh) (*a knife*)
- ✔ **une serviette** (ewn sehr-vyeht) (*a napkin*)
- ✔ **le sel et le poivre** (luh sehl ey luh pwah-vruh) (*salt and pepper*)

Eating and drinking with the verbs "manger," "prendre," and "boire"

When you're talking about eating and drinking in French, you need to know the verbs **manger** (mahN-zhey) (*to eat*), **prendre** (prahN-druh) (*to take*), and **boire** *(bwahr)* (to drink). The verb **manger** is a regular **–er** verb except for the first person plural (**nous**) form. (Chapter 2 shows you how to conjugate regular verbs.) Check out the conjugation:

Conjugation	Pronunciation
je mange	zhuh mahNzh
tu manges	tew mahNzh
il/elle/on mange	eel/ehl/ohN mahNzh
nous mangeons	nooh mahN-zhohN
vous mangez	vooh mahN-zhey
ils/elles mangent	eel/ehl mahNzh

Although **manger** is a regular **–er** verb, **boire** is another matter. The following table shows you how to conjugate this irregular verb:

Conjugation	Pronunciation
je bois	zhuh bwah
tu bois	tew bwah
il/elle/on boit	eel/ehl/ohN bwah
nous buvons	nooh bew-vohN
vous buvez	vooh bew-vey
ils/elles boivent	eel/ehl bwahv

Here are some examples of **manger** and **boire** in action:

> **Nous mangeons des légumes tous les jours.** (nooh mahN-zhohN dey ley-gewm tooh ley zhoohr.) (*We eat vegetables every day.*)

> **Je bois du café le matin.** (zhuh bwah dew kah-fey luh mah-taN.) (*I drink coffee in the morning.*)

In English, when you talk about what's on the menu at mealtime, you use the verb *to have*: "We're having soup and sandwiches," for example, or "They're having salad." In French, however, you use the verb **prendre,** which means *to take,* rather than the verb **avoir** (ah-vwahr) (*to have*). Following are a couple of examples:

> **Pour le petit déjeuner, je prends du pain et de la confiture.** (poohr luh puh-tee dey-zhuh-ney, zhuh prahN dew paN ey duh lah kohN-fee-tewr.) (*For breakfast, I have bread and jam.* [Literally: *For breakfast, I take bread and jam.*])

> **Je prends le steak frites.** (zhuh prahN luh stehk freet.) (*I'll have the steak with French fries.*)

Prendre is an irregular verb and can be used instead of **manger** and **boire**. Here's the conjugation of **prendre**:

Conjugation	Pronunciation
je prends	zhuh prahN
tu prends	tew prahN
il/elle/on prend	eel/ehl/ohN prahN
nous prenons	nooh pruh-nohN
vous prenez	vooh pruh-ney
ils/elles prennent	eel/ehl prehn

Using "faire," "passer," and other verbs to take charge of chores

In French, you can do any number of household chores with the verb **faire** (fehr) (*to do, to make*). **Faire** is an irregular verb (refer to Chapter 2 for more on irregular verbs). Here's its conjugation:

Conjugation	Pronunciation
je fais	zhuh feh
tu fais	tew feh
il/elle/on fait	eel/ehl/ohN feh
nous faisons	nooh fuh-zohN
vous faites	vooh feht
ils/elles font	eel/ehl fohN

Faire is a handy verb because you use it in many expressions. It's sometimes used in place of **jouer** (zhooh-ey) (*to play*) when talking about sports and instruments. You also use it when talking about the weather (Chapter 6), travel (Chapter 13), and other things. Here is a list of household chores and errands that you use **faire** with:

- **faire le lit** (fehr luh lee) (*to make the bed*)
- **faire le café** (fehr luh kah-fey) (*to make [the] coffee*)
- **faire le ménage** (fehr luh mey-nahzh) (*to do the housework*)

✔ **faire la cuisine** (fehr lah kwee-zeen) (*to cook*)

✔ **faire la vaisselle** (fehr lah veh-sehl) (*to do the dishes*)

✔ **faire la lessive** (fehr lah leh-seev) (*to do the laundry*)

✔ **faire les courses** (fehr ley koohrs) (*to do errands*)

As handy as **faire** is, it can't do everything. For things like vacuuming and cleaning the bathroom, you need a few other verbs: To say *vacuum* in French, use the verb **passer** (pah-sey) (*to pass*), which is a regular **–er** verb, followed by the word for *vacuum cleaner*, **l'aspirateur** (m) (lahs-pee-rah-tuhr): **Il passe l'aspirateur** (eel pahs lahs-pee-rah-tuhr) (*He is vacuuming*). Check out the conjugation of the regular verbs in Chapter 2.

Another regular verb associated with cleaning is the verb **ranger** (rahN-zhey) (*to arrange, to straighten up, to tidy up*): **Je range ma chambre** (zhuh rahNzh mah shahN-bruh) (*I tidy up my room*).

The ultimate verb for *to clean* in French is **nettoyer** (neh-twah-yey). This is a stem-changing verb because, although the endings are regular, like those of **parler**, the **y** changes to an **i** in all forms except for the **nous** (nooh) (*we*) and **vous** (vooh) (*you*) forms. Check out its conjugation:

Conjugation	*Pronunciation*
je nettoie	zhuh neh-twah
tu nettoies	tew neh-twah
il/elle/on nettoie	eel/ehl/ohN neh-twah
nous nettoyons	nooh neh-twah-yohN
vous nettoyez	vooh neh-twah-yey
ils/elles nettoient	eel/ehl neh-twah

For example, you can say, **Je nettoie la salle de bains** (zhuh neh-twah lah sahl duh baN) (*I am cleaning the bathroom*).

Taking command of commands

When you say "Sit" to your dog, "Do your homework" to your children, or "Let's eat" to your family, you're using the imperative form. The *imperative form* is simply a command, even when it's phrased politely, as in "Please do your homework." When you give a command, you don't use the subject pronoun. For example, you don't say "You sit" to your dog or "You do your homework" to your children. Instead, the subject — *you* — is understood.

In French, to make the imperative, or command, form of a verb, you use only the **tu** (*you* [informal, singular]), **vous** (*you* [formal singular, plural]), and **nous** (*we*) forms of the verb. Table 5-1 shows examples of **–er, –ir** and **–re** verbs in the imperative form.

Notice that you drop the final **s** of the **tu** form of all **–er** verbs in the command form. For example, **tu parles** (tew pahrl) (*you speak*) becomes **parle** (pahrl) (*speak*). This is not the case for **–ir** or **–re** verbs.

Table 5-1	Examples of –er, –ir and –re Verbs, in the Imperative Form	
Type of Verb	**Declarative Sentence**	**Imperative Sentence**
–er	**Tu restes ici.** (tew rehst ee-see.)(*You stay here.*)	**Reste ici!** (rehst ee-see!) (*Stay here!*)
–er	**Vous parlez français.** (vooh pahr-ley frahN-seh!) (*You speak French.*)	**Parlez français!** (pahr-ley frahN-seh!) (*Speak French!*)
–er	**Nous mangeons des frites.** (nooh mahN-zhoN dey freet.) (*We are eating [some] fries.*)	**Mangeons des frites!** (mahN-zhohN dey freet!) (*Let's eat [some] fries!*)
–ir	**Tu finis ton lait.** (tew fee-nee tohN leh.) (*You finish your milk.*)	**Finis ton lait!** (*fee-nee tohN leh!*) (*Finish your milk!*)
–re (irregular verb)	**Nous faisons le ménage.** (nooh fuh-zohN luh mey-nahzh.) (*We are doing housework.*)	**Faisons le ménage!** (fuh-zohN luh mey-nahzh!) (*Let's do housework!*)
–re (irregular verb)	**Tu fais la vaisselle.** (tew feh lah veh-sehl.) (*You are doing the dishes.*)	**Fais la vaisselle!** (feh lah veh-sehl!) (*Do the dishes!*)
–ir	**Tu choisis un CD.** (tew shwah-zee uhN sey-dey.) (*You are choosing a CD.*)	**Choisis un CD!** (shwah-zee uhN sey dey!) (*Choose a CD!*)
–re	**Tu rends les livres.** (tew rahN ley lee-vruh.) (*You give back the books.*)	**Rends les livres!** (rahN ley lee-vruh!) (*Give back the books!*)

For negative commands — "Don't hit your brother!" for example — you "wrap" the **ne. . . pas** (nuh pah) (*not*) that you use for straightforward negations around the conjugated verb (refer to Chapter 3 for more details on the negative); remember, if the verb begins with a vowel or a mute h, **ne** becomes or **n':**

N'attendez pas Paul. *(*nah-tahN-dey pah pohl.) (*Don't wait for Paul.*)

Ne fais pas la cuisine, sortons! (nuh feh pah lah kwee-zeen, sohr-tohN!) (*Don't cook, let's go out!*)

Talkin' the Talk

M. Seiffert has just called his wife, Élise, and informed her that he's bringing home his business associate, M. Morrissette, for dinner. Madame Seiffert is talking to her two teenage children, Charles and Josephine, to organize the work to be done.

Élise:	**Charles! Joséphine! Vite! Aidez-moi à faire le ménage.**
	shahrl! zhoh-zey-feen! veet! ey-dey-mwah ah fehr luh mey-nahzh.
	Charles! Josephine! Quickly! Help me clean the house.
Charles:	**Pourquoi, maman?**
	poohr-kwah, mah-mahN?
	Why, Mom?
Élise:	**Monsieur Morrissette va venir dîner ce soir.**
	muh-syuh moh-ree-seht vah vuh-neer dee-ney suh swahr.
	Mr. Morrissette is coming to dinner this evening.
Joséphine:	**Charles, range la salle de séjour.**
	shahrl, rahNzh lah sahl duh sey-zhoohr.
	Charles, clean up the living room.
Charles:	**Joséphine, fais la vaisselle.**
	zhoh-zey feen, feh lah veh-sehl.
	Josephine, do the dishes.
Élise:	**Charles, passe l'aspirateur dans la salle de séjour. Joséphine, nettoie la salle de bains et les toilettes.**
	shahrl, pahs lahs-pee-rah-tuhr dahN lah sahl duh sey-zhoohr. zhoh-zey-feen, neht-wah lah sahl duh baN ey ley twah-leht.
	Charles, vaccuum the living room. Josephine, clean the bathroom and the toilet.
Joséphine:	**Et quoi d'autre, maman?**
	ey kwah doh-truh mah-mahN?
	And what else, Mama?
Élise:	**Mettez la table.**
	meh-tey lah tah-bluh.
	(You two) Set the table.
Charles:	**Et toi maman, fais la cuisine.**
	ey twah mah-mahN, feh lah kwee-zeen.
	And you, Mom, cook!

Words to Know

faire le/la/les. . .	fehr luh/lah/ley. . .	to do the. . .
faire le ménage	fehr luh mey-nahzh	to clean the house, to do housework
fais la vaisselle	fey lah veh-sehl	do the dishes
Vite!	veet!	Quickly!

Using Possessive Adjectives to Introduce Your Family Members

Family is at the center of French life. No matter where you go, one of the topics of conversation is about family. People may ask you whether you have brothers and sisters, grandparents, cousins, children, and so on. Therefore, you're going to talk about your family, which you can do very easily with these words for your immediate family:

- ✔ **le mari** (luh mah-ree) (*husband*)
- ✔ **la femme** (lah fahm) (*wife*)
- ✔ **le père** (luh pehr) (*father*)
- ✔ **la mère** (lah mehr) (*mother*)
- ✔ **les parents** (ley pah-rahN) (*parents*)
- ✔ **le fils** (luh fees) (*son*)
- ✔ **la fille** (lah feey) (*daughter*)
- ✔ **les enfants** (ley-zahN-fahN) (*children*)
- ✔ **le frère** (luh frehr) (*brother*)
- ✔ **la soeur** (lah suhr) (*sister*)

Of course, many families go beyond immediate family members to include the extended family. When you talk about aunts, uncles, grandparents, and others beyond mom and dad and brother and sister, use these words:

- **les grands-parents** (ley grahN-pah-rahN) (*grandparents*)

- **le grand-père** (luh grahN-pehr) (*grandfather*)

- **la grand-mère** (lah grahN-mehr) (*grandmother*)

- **les petits-enfants** (ley puh-tee-zahN-fahN) (*grandchildren*)

- **le neveu** (luh nuh-vuh) (*nephew*)

- **la nièce** (lah nyehs) (*niece*)

- **le cousin/la cousine** (luh kooh-zaN/lah kooh-zeen) (*cousin*)

- **l'oncle** (m) (lohN-kluh) (*uncle*)

- **la tante** (lah tahNt) (*aunt*)

When you talk about your family members, you undoubtedly have to use possessive adjectives, like *my*, *our*, *your*, and so on. For example, when you say "My brother lives in Boston, and my grandparents in Vermont," or "Our house is near the school," you're using possessive adjectives.

You use possessive adjectives the same way in French as you do in English. Here's an important difference, however. In French, because nouns have a gender, the possessive adjectives change to agree with the gender (masculine or feminine) and number (singular or plural) of the noun, just as the articles **le/la/les** (luh/lah/ley) (*the*) do (refer to Chapter 2 for more on agreement). Because the possessive adjective agrees with the noun and not with the person, there is no difference between the French words for *his* and *her*. Table 5-2 lists the possessive adjectives.

In English, you can refer to a whole family by making the last name plural: the Millers or the Whites, for example. In French, however, you can't add a *s* to a proper name. So **Monsieur et Madame Texier** (muh-syuh ey mah-dahm tehk-syey) (*Mr. and Mrs. Texier*) are **Les Texier** (ley tehk-syey).

Table 5-2	Possessive Adjectives		
In English	*Masculine Singular*	*Feminine Singular*	*Masc. / Feminine Plural*
my	**mon** (mohN)	**ma** (mah)	**mes** (mey)
your (singular)	**ton** (tohN)	**ta** (tah)	**tes** (tey)
his/her	**son** (sohN)	**sa** (sah)	**ses** (sey)
our	**notre** (nohh-truh)	**notre** (nohh-truh)	**nos** (noh)
your (formal singular/ plural)	**votre** (vohh-truh)	**votre** (vohh-truh)	**vos** (voh)
their	**leur** (luhr)	**leur** (luhr)	**leurs** (luhr)

Here are some examples using the masculine, singular noun **le frère**:

mon/ton/son frère (mohN/tohN/sohN frehr) (*my/your/his, her brother*)

notre/votre/leur frère (nohh-truh/vohh-truh/luhr frehr) (*our/your/ their brother*)

These examples use the feminine, singular noun **la soeur**:

ma/ta/sa soeur (mah/tah/sah suhr) (*my/your/his, her sister*)

notre/votre/leur soeur (nohh-truh/vohh-truh/luhr suhr) (*our/your/ their sister*)

Finally, here are some examples using the plural noun **les grands-parents**:

mes/tes/ses grands-parents (mey/tey/sey grahN-pah-rahN) (*my/your/ his, her grandparents*)

nos/vos/leurs grands-parents (noh/voh/luhr grahN-pah-rahN) (*our/your/ their grandparents*)

Although you should remember that you use **mon** (mohN) for the masculine version of *my* and **ma** (mah) for the feminine, there is an exception: When a feminine singular noun begins with a vowel or a mute h, you use the masculine singular possessive adjective **mon, ton,** or **son**. Take the masculine singular word **ami** (ah-mee) (friend) and the feminine singular **amie** (ah-mee) (friend), for example. To say *my* friend, regardless whether that friend is male or female, you use **mon** for both the masculine and the feminine form — **mon ami** and **mon amie** — because the word **amie** starts with a vowel.

Whenever a word starts with a vowel or a mute h in French, an alarm should go off in your head, alerting you that funny things may be happening. This is one of them. (Check out Chapters 2 and 3 for more on nouns that start with a vowel or mute h.)

Fun & Games

Using the illustration, first identify the rooms (A, B, C, D) and then the items (1, 2, and 3) that are pointed out in each room.

A. _____ 1) _____ 2)_____

B. _____ 1) _____ 2)_____

C. _____ 1) _____ 2)_____ 3)_____

D. _____ 1) _____ 2)_____ 3)_____

Part II
French in Action

The 5th Wave   By Rich Tennant

"I practice my French with the owner. So far I've learned how to say, 'Leave me alone', 'Not you again?', and 'Buy something or get out.'"

In this part . . .

We present French in the context of daily life. We show you how to ask key questions, keep up in casual conversations, order in a French restaurant, request assistance and identify items you want while shopping, ask for directions, make plans for nights out, communicate with coworkers, and much, much more. Along the way, you'll discover some key grammatical constructions that enable you to express yourself, share your likes and dislikes, make comparisons, and talk about the weather, your profession, and your hobbies.

Chapter 6

Getting to Know You: Making Small Talk

Whether you're conversing with someone you just met or chatting with an old acquaintance, small talk is a key part of many conversations. Although it can lead to more serious discussions, small talk generally deals with innocent subjects such as what you do for a living, your likes and dislikes, the weather, and so on. It's a wonderful way to get acquainted with someone and allows you to decide whether you want to pursue a conversation with the stranger next to you on the plane or bus or go back to the book you're reading. After reading this chapter, you'll have the information you need to **parler de tout et de rien** (pahr-ley duh tooh ey duh ryahN) (*talk about everything and nothing*).

Basic Questions and Polite Expressions

As Chapter 3 explains, you can ask a yes-or-no question in French in numerous ways: make your voice rise at the end of a sentence, place **est-ce que** (ehs-kuh) in front of the sentence, or invert the subject and the verb. When you make small talk, however, you want to ask questions that elicit more than a yes-or-no answer. With the information in the following sections, you'll be able to ask basic questions and use expressions that are an important part of every conversation.

Using key question words

To get specific information, you need to know these key question words:

- **à quelle heure** (ah kehl uhr) (*at what time*)
- **combien de** (kohN-byaN duh) (*how many*)
- **combien** (kohN-byaN) (*how much*)
- **comment** (koh-mahN) (*how*)
- **où** (ooh) (*where*)
- **pourquoi** (poohr-kwah) (*why*)
- **qu'est-ce que** (kehs-kuh) (*what*)
- **quand** (kahN) (*when*)
- **quel(s)/quelle(s)** (kehl) (*which, what*)
- **qui** (kee) (*who*)

You can use these question words on their own, just as in English, or you can use them in sentences. For example, to find out someone's name or to ask who someone is, you can ask these questions:

Qui est-ce? (kee ehs?) (*Who is it?*)

Comment vous appelez-vous? (koh-mahN vooh-zah-pley-vooh?) (*What's your name?*)

Comment s'appelle . . . ? (koh-mahN sah-pehl. . . ?) (*What's . . . name?*)

Quel est son prénom? (kehl-eh sohN prey-nohN?) (*What's his/her first name?*)

You can also ask about where someone lives and someone's age with these questions:

Où habitez-vous? (ooh ah-bee-tey-vooh?) (*Where do you live?* [formal or plural])

Quel âge avez-vous? (kehl-ahzh ah-vey-vooh?) (*How old are you?* [formal or plural])

The question **Quel âge avez-vous** uses the verb **avoir** (ah-vwahr) (*to have*) instead of **être** (eh-truh) (*to be*), so the literal translation is *What age do you have?* The logical answer uses the verb **avoir,** as well: **J'ai douze ans** (zhey dooh-zahN) (*I am 12* [Literally: *I have 12 years*]).

Saying the magic words: Polite expressions

Your mother was right: A kind word goes a long way. Saying *please*, *thank you*, and *excuse me*, as well as a few other universal phrases, mark you as a considerate person and one worth getting to know. So use these following expressions liberally:

- ✔ **Pardon/Excusez-moi.** (pahr-dohN/eks-kew-zey-mwah.) (*Excuse me.*)
- ✔ **Je suis désolé/désolée.** (zhuh swee dey-zoh-ley.) (*I am sorry.*)
- ✔ **Ce n'est pas grave!** (suh neh pah grahv!) (*That's okay!*)
- ✔ **De rien.** (duh ryahN.) (*You're welcome.* [Literally: *It's nothing.*])
- ✔ **Je vous en prie.** (zhuh vooh-zahN pree.) (*You are welcome.*)
- ✔ **S'il vous plaît.** (seel vooh pleh.) (*Please.*)

When you're just learning a foreign language, you may need to let the person speaking to you know that you're having a little difficulty understanding or responding. Instead of saying "Huh?" try out these expressions:

Je ne comprends pas. (zhuhn kohN-prahN pah.) (*I don't understand.*)

Je ne sais pas. (zhuhn seh pah.) (*I don't know.*)

Pouvez-vous parler plus lentement, s'il vous plaît? (pooh-vey-vooh pahr-ley plew lahNt-mahN, seel vooh pleh?) (*Can you speak more slowly, please?*)

Pouvez-vous répéter, s'il vous plaît? (pooh-vey-vooh rey-pey-tey seel vooh pleh?) (*Can you repeat, please?*)

Un moment, s'il vous plaît. (uhN moh-mahN, seel vooh pleh.) (*One moment, please.*)

Talkin' the Talk

After arriving in Paris from New York on an all-night flight, Amanda gets on her connecting flight to Nice. Exhausted, she collapses in her seat and is about to fall asleep when a young man addresses her. (Track 5)

Patrick: **Pardon, madame, quel est le numéro de votre place?**
pahr-dohN, mah-dahm, kehl eh luh new-mey-roh duh vohh-truh plahs?
Excuse me, ma'am. What is your seat number?

Amanda: **Je ne sais pas. Attendez! Oh, c'est le 24B; excusez-moi. Je suis désolée.**
zhuhn seh pah. ah-tahN-dey! oh, seh luh vaNt-kah-truh bey; eks-kew-zey-mwah. zhuh swee dey-zoh-ley.
I don't know. Wait! Oh, it's number 24B. Excuse me. I am sorry.

After Amanda moves to her assigned seat, their conversation continues.

Patrick: **Ce n'est pas grave! Je m'appelle Patrick, et vous?**
suh neh pah grahv! Zhuh-mah-pehl pah-treek, ey vooh?
That's okay! My name is Patrick, and you?

Amanda: **Enchantée monsieur. Je m'appelle Amanda.**
ahN-shahN-tey muh-syuh. zhuh-mah-pehl ah-mahn-dah.
Delighted sir. My name is Amanda.

Patrick: **Enchanté madame. Où allez-vous?**
ahN-shahN-tey mah-dahm. ooh ah-ley-vooh?
Delighted, ma'am. Where are you going?

Amanda: **Je vais d'abord à Nice, puis à Toulon voir ma fille.**
zhuh veh dah-boh-rah nees, pwee ah tooh-lohN vwahr mah feey.
I am going to Nice first, then to Toulon to see my daughter.

Patrick: **Vous venez souvent en France?**
vooh vuh-ney sooh-vahN ahN frahNs?
Do you often come to France?

Amanda: **Oh oui, j'adore la France.**
oh wee, zhah-dohr lah frahNs.
Oh yes, I love France.

Patrick: **Combien de temps restez-vous en France?**
kohN-byaN duh tahN reh-stey-vooh ahN frahNs?
How long are you staying in France?

Amanda: **Un mois. Et vous, pourquoi allez-vous à Nice?**
uhN mwah. ey vooh, poohr-kwah ah-ley-vooh-zah nees?
A month. And you, why are you going to Nice?

Patrick: **Pour le travail.**
poohr luh trah-vahy.
For work.

Pay attention to two little words that you see over and over again in French: **et** (ey) (*and*) and **dans** (dahN) (*in*). To use them correctly, remember these rules:

- ✔ **et:** Never link **et** with the next word (in other words, don't make the liaison, explained in Chapter 3). For example, to say *He is handsome and intelligent,* say **Il est beau et intélligent** (ee-leh boh ey aN-tey-lee-zhahN).

- ✔ **dans:** Use **dans** for time and space (location). Notice that it can have slightly different meanings depending on the context. Here are some examples: **dans un mois** (dahN-zuhN mwah) (*in a month*) and **dans l'avion** (dahN lah-vyohN) (*on/in the plane*).

Words to Know

Quel est le numéro?	kehl eh luh new-mey-roh?	What is the number?
attendez	ah-tahN-dey	wait
je vais/vous allez	zhuh veh-/vooh-zah-ley	I go/you go
souvent	sooh-vahN	often
j'adore	zhah-dohr	I love, adore
le travail	luh trah-vahy	work

Stating Your Preferences

One of the ways in which you get to know someone or they get to know you is by expressing likes and dislikes. When you say in French that you like to travel, that you hate waiting in line, or even that you love a certain film, you use *verbs of preference.* These verbs include

✔ **aimer** (eh-mey) (*to like, to love*)

✔ **aimer mieux** (eh-mey myuh) (*to like better, to prefer*)

✔ **adorer** (ah-doh-rey) (*to adore*)

✔ **préférer** (prey-fey-rey) (*to prefer*)

✔ **détester** (dey-teh-stey) (*to hate*)

Aimer, adorer, and **détester** are all regular **–er** verbs; go to Chapter 2 for information on conjugating regular verbs. The verb **préférer,** however, has a stem change: The accent on the second **e** changes from an **aigu** (**é**) to a **grave** (**è**), except for the **nous** and **vous** forms. Check out the conjugation of **préférer:**

Conjugation	Pronunciation
je préfère	zhuh prey-fehr
tu préfères	tew prey-fehr
il/elle/on préfère	eel/ehl/ohN prey-fehr
nous préférons	nooh prey-fey-rohN
vous préférez	vooh prey-fey-rey
ils/elles préfèrent	eel/ehl prey-fehr

To say that you like or hate something in French, you use the definite article *the* — **le** (luh), **la** (lah), and **les** (ley) — even though the article may not be necessary in English. Check out these examples:

J'aime le café au lait. (zhehm luh kah-fey oh leh.) (*I like coffee with milk.*)

Nous préférons les films étrangers. (nooh prey-fey-rohN ley feelm ey-trahN-zhey.) (*We prefer foreign films.*)

Ils détestent le bruit. (eel dey-tehst luh brwee.) (*They hate noise.*)

Talking about Your Livelihood

In French, when you state your profession, you just say **Je suis. . .** (zhuh swee) (*I am. . .*) and then name the profession. For example, **Je suis professeur** (zhuh swee proh-feh-suhr) means *I am a teacher, professor.* To identify someone else's profession, use the construction **Il/Elle est. . .** (eel/ehl eh) (*He/She is. . .*). **Il est ingénieur** (ee-leh-tahN-zhey-nyuhr), for example, means *He is an engineer.* Notice that in these constructions, you don't use the article **un** (uhN) (*a, an*), as you do in English (I am *a* teacher, for example, or he is *an* engineer).

You use the same construction to describe yourself or someone else: **Je suis optimiste** (zhuh swee-zohp-tee-meest) (*I am optimistic*), for example, or **Il est intelligent** (ee-leh-taN-teh-lee-zhahN) (*He is intelligent*).

Although not exhaustive by any means, this list includes many common occupations.

- ✔ **professeur** (proh-feh-suhr) (*high school teacher, college professor*)
- ✔ **informaticien/informaticienne** (aN-fohr-mah-tee-syaN/aN-fohr-mah-tee-syehn) (*computer scientist*)
- ✔ **secrétaire** (suh-krey-tehr) (*secretary*)
- ✔ **médecin** (meyd-saN) (*physician*)
- ✔ **infirmier/infirmière** (aN-feer-myey/aN-feer-myehr) (*nurse*)
- ✔ **avocat/avocate** (ah-voh-kah/ah-voh-kaht) (*lawyer*)
- ✔ **ingénieur** (aN-zhey-nyuhr) (*engineer*)
- ✔ **serveur/serveuse** (sehr-vuhr/sehr-vuhz) (*waiter/waitress*)
- ✔ **dentiste** (dahN-teest) (*dentist*)
- ✔ **retraité/retraitée** (ruh-treh-tey) (*retired*)
- ✔ **homme d'affaires/femme d'affaires** (ohhm dah-fehr/fahm dah-fehr) (*business man/business woman*)
- ✔ **architecte** (ahr-shee-tehkt) (*architect*)
- ✔ **PDG** (pey dey zhey) (*CEO* [**Note:** This acronym stands for **Président Directeur Général**])

Notice that some professions have only one form for the masculine and the feminine. As a rule, nouns and adjectives that end with an *e,* for example — **dentiste** — are the same regardless of gender. (Check out Chapter 2 for more on the transformation of nouns and adjectives.) Some professions on the preceding list do not have a feminine form because the gender designation is a remnant of the (sexist) days when certain professions were mostly filled by men, which is no longer the case in the 21st century.

The following are some useful job-related expressions:

Quel est votre métier? (kehl eh vohh-truh mey-tyey?) (*What is your profession?*)

Qu'est-ce que vous faites dans la vie? (kehs-kuh vooh feht dahN lah vee?) (*What do you do for a living?*)

Pour quelle entreprise/compagnie travaillez-vous? (poohr kehl ahN-truh-preez/kohN-pah-nyee trah-vah-yey-vooh?) (*What company do you work for?*)

Voyagez-vous souvent pour votre travail? (voh-yah-zhey-vooh sooh-vahN poohr vohh-truh trah-vahy?) (*Do you travel often for your job/work?*)

Votre métier est intéressant. (vohh-truh mey-tyey eh-taN-tey-reh-sahN.) (*Your profession is interesting.*)

Talkin' the Talk

On the flight to Nice, newly acquainted Amanda and Patrick talk about work.

Amanda: **Où travaillez-vous?**
ooh trah-vah-yey-vooh?
Where do you work?

Patrick: **Mon bureau est à Paris, mais je vais souvent à Nice en voyage d'affaires.**
mohN bew-roh eh-tah pah-ree, meh zhuh veh sooh-vahN ah nees ahN voh-yahzh dah-fehr.
My office is in Paris, but I often go to Nice on business trips.

Amanda: **Quel est votre métier?**
kehl eh vohh-truh mey-tyey?
What is your profession?

Patrick: **Je suis informaticien. Je travaille pour une compagnie d'informatique.**
zhuh swee-zaN-fohr-mah-tee-syaN. zhuh trah-vahy pooh-rewn kohN-pah-nyee daN-fohr-mah-teek.
I am a computer scientist. I work for a computer science company.

Amanda: **C'est une grande compagnie?**
seh-tewn grahNd kohN-pah-nyee?
Is it a large company?

Patrick: **Non, elle est très petite. Il y a seulement dix employés.**
nohN, ehl eh treh puh-teet. eel ee ah suhl-mahN dee-zahN-plwah-yey.
No, it is very small. There are only ten employees.

Words to Know

le voyage d'affaires	luh voh-yahzh dah-fehr	business trip
mon bureau	mohN bew-roh	my office
une compagnie	ewn kohN-pah-nyee	a company
un employé/ une employée	uhN-nahN-plwah-yey/ ew-nahN-plwah-yey	an employee
un collègue/une collègue	uhN koh-lehg/ewn koh-lehg	coworker

Chatting about the Weather

Another great topic for small talk is, of course, **le temps** (luh tahN) (*the weather*). As a matter of fact, one way to designate small talk in French is with the phrase **parler de la pluie et du beau temps** (pahr-ley duh lah plwee ey dew boh tahN) (Literally: *to talk about the rain and the nice weather*). In countries of great weather contrasts, like Canada, weather is a constant topic of conversation. Under more temperate climates, like that of France, the weather is still a favorite topic, especially if you want to complain about it.

Of course, you cannot talk about the weather without knowing the names of the seasons; **le printemps** (luh praN-tahN) (*spring*), **l'été** (m) (ley-tey) (*summer*), **l'automne (m)** (loh-tohn) (*fall*), and **l'hiver (m)** (lee-vehr) (*winter*). Check out Chapter 4 for more details on the seasons. You can also ask about the weather with the question **Quel temps fait-il?** (kehl tahN feh-teel) (*What is the weather like?*). To answer this question, you use **Il fait. . . .** (eel feh . . .) (*It's. . . .*) and plug in any of the following phrases:

- ✔ **chaud** (shoh) (*warm, hot*)
- ✔ **froid** (frwah) (*cold*)

✔ **frais** (freh) (*cool*)

✔ **doux** (dooh) (*mild*)

✔ **beau** (boh) (*nice*)

✔ **mauvais** (moh-veh) (*bad*)

✔ **du vent** (dew vahN) (*windy*)

✔ **du soleil** (dew soh-lehy) (*sunny*)

To indicate that it's raining or snowing, you say **Il pleut** (eel pluh) (*It's raining*) or **Il neige** (eel nehzh) (*It's snowing*).

You can also say what the temperature is: **La température est de 20 degrés** (lah tahN-pey-rah-tewr eh duh vaN duh-grey) (*It is 20 degrees* [*Celsius*]); just substitute the current temperature for the 20.

Throughout the world, the temperature is not stated in Fahrenheit but in Celsius (centigrades). So when you hear **La température est de 25 degrés** (lah tahN-pey-rah-tewr eh duh vaN saNk duh-grey) (*The temperature is 25 degrees*), it means 25 degrees Celcius.

Notice that all the weather phrases start with **il.** While you may be familiar with **il** as the masculine singular pronoun — **il s'appelle** (eel sah-pehl) (*his name is*) or **il habite** (eel ah-beet) (*he lives*), for example — this **il** doesn't refer to a male person or a masculine object. Instead, it's impersonal, like the English *it.* Using **il** in this context isn't difficult: As far as conjugation and verb agreement go, the verb form that follows is third person singular (just as it is for any **il** and **elle**).

Talkin' the Talk

The captain of the plane Patrick and Amanda are on makes an announcement about the weather in Nice, prompting a conversation between the two acquaintances. (Track 6)

Captain: **A Nice, il fait beau et chaud et la température est de 30 degrés.**
ah nees, eel feh boh ey shoh ey lah tahN-pey-rah-tewr eh duh trahNt duh-grey.
In Nice, the weather is nice and warm, and the temperature is 30 degrees.

Patrick: **A Nice, il fait toujours beau!**
ah nees, eel feh tooh-zhoohr boh!
In Nice, the weather is always nice!

Amanda:	**Même en hiver?**
	meh-mahN-nee-vehr?
	Even in winter?

Patrick:	**En hiver, il pleut un peu, mais il fait doux. Et à New York?**
	ahN-nee-vehr, eel pluh uhN puh, meh-zeel feh dooh. ey ah New York?
	In winter, it rains a little, but it is mild. And in New York?

Amanda:	**En hiver, il fait très froid et il neige, et en été il fait très chaud et humide.**
	ahN-nee-vehr, eel feh treh frwah ey eel nehzh, ey ahN-ney-tey eel feh treh shoh ey ew-meed.
	In winter, it is very cold and it snows, and in summer, it is very hot and humid.

Patrick:	**Et au printemps et en automne?**
	ey oh praN-tahN ey ahN-noh-tohn?
	What about spring and fall?

Amanda:	**Le temps est agréable.**
	luh tahN eh-tah-grey-ah-bluh.
	The weather is pleasant.

Words to Know

d'abord	dah-bohr	first
puis	pwee	then
toujours	tooh-zhoohr	always
même	mehm	even
un peu	uhN puh	a little
agréable	ah-grey-ah-bluh	pleasant

In every language, the weather is the source of many proverbs. Here is one of those French proverbs: **Une hirondelle ne fait pas le printemps** (ew-nee-rohN-dehl nuh feh pah luh praN-tahN) (*One swallow does not make the spring*). In France, you can expect cold weather soon when the swallows start gathering on the electric wires, ready to take off to warmer climates; when you see them coming back, you know that spring is close, but it hasn't quite arrived.

Deciding to Keep in Touch

As you get to know your new acquaintances better, you may want to exchange addresses or phone numbers. To trade contact information, you can use these phrases:

- ✔ **Où habitez-vous?** (ooh ah-bee-tey-vooh?) (*Where do you live?*)

- ✔ **Quelle est votre adresse?** (kehl eh vohh-trah-drehs?) (*What is your address?*)

- ✔ **Donnez-moi votre numéro de téléphone.** (dohh-ney-mwah vohh-truh new-mey-roh duh tey-ley-fohhn.) (*Give me your phone number.*)

In this day and age, you are likely to want and give an e-mail address. The French language has a word for it: **l'adresse électronique** (lah-dreh-sey-lehk-troh-neek), but saying **e-mail** (ee-mehl) is so much more convenient; it's even been french-ified as **le mél** (luh meyl)! Of course, French also has a word for the @ sign: **arobas** (ah-roh-bah) or, more commonly, **à** (ah) (*at*); the dot is **point** (pwaN), which means, among many other things, *the period at the end of a sentence.*

Canada has the same telephone system as the United States: a local area code — **l'indicatif** (m) (laN-dee-kah-teef) — followed by the seven digits of a personal phone number. In France, each time you make a call, even locally, you have to dial the two-digit area code (which begins with a zero, like 01 or 02) followed by eight numbers that are stated in groups of two (04 94 37 08 56, for example). To call a French number from the United States, dial 011, the code for France (33) and then the number directly, skipping the 0 of the area code (011 33 4 94 37 08 56, for example).

Fun & Games

In the blanks provided, identify the seasons shown in the illustrations.

le printemps   l'été   l'automne   l'hiver

A._____

B._____

C._____

D._____

Now, identify the weather conditions shown in these images, using the provided word bank.

il neige   il fait du vent   il pleut   il fait chaud

E._____

F._____

G._____

H._____

Chapter 7

Asking Directions and Finding Your Way

*W*hen you set out for a trip, you probably have a pretty good idea of all the things you want to do and the places you want to see. You figure out beforehand how you'll manage to get there, what type of transportation you need, and how to arrange for it. After you arrive, however, you'll probably discover that you don't quite know where the nearest bus stop or bank is or how to find the restroom or telephone. And if your plans change, all your previous preparation won't be enough to get you where you want to go. In those situations, you need to know how to ask for directions. Where do you go for the phrases and questions that let you get to where you want to be? Right here.

Asking and Answering "Where?" Questions

The most common question when you are traveling is probably *Where is. . . ?* You make *where* questions the same way in French as you do in English: You follow the question word **où** *(ooh)* *(where)* with the verb **être** *(eh-truh)* *(to be)* or the verb **se trouver** *(suh trooh-vey)* *(to be located)*.

Asking questions with "où," plus the verbs "être" and "se trouver"

The verb **être** is the verb most often connected with **où**, as these examples show (check out Chapter 2 for the complete conjugation of the verb **être**):

> **Où est le Louvre?** (ooh eh luh looh-vruh?) (*Where is the Louvre?*)
>
> **Où est la place Victor Hugo?** (ooh eh lah plahs veek-tohr ew-goh?) (*Where is the Victor Hugo Square?*)
>
> **Où sont les toilettes?** (ooh sohN ley twah-leht?) (*Where is the bathroom?*)

But, as mentioned previously, another verb, **se trouver**, is also very frequently used to ask *where* questions:

> **Où se trouve le Louvre?** (ooh suh troohv luh looh-vruh?) (*Where is the Louvre [located]?*)
>
> **Où se trouve la place Victor Hugo?** (ooh suh troohv lah plahs veek-tohr ew-goh?) (*Where is the Victor Hugo Square?*)
>
> **Où se trouvent les toilettes?** (ooh suh troohv ley twah-leht?) (*Where is the bathroom?*)

As all the preceding examples show, *where* questions follow this construction:

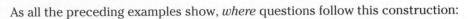

> **où** + verb + subject

In fact, you use this sentence structure for all other verbs you choose to connect with **où**:

> **Où va ce bus?** (ooh vah suh bews?) (*Where is this bus going?*)
>
> **Où mène cette rue?** (ooh mehn seht rew?) (*Where does this road lead?*)

Answering questions with "à"

Prepositions are (often) little words, like *to*, *in*, and *at*, that indicate a relationship between one thing and another in a sentence. They're also a key element in answering *where* questions: Where are you going? To the zoo. Where is the concert? In the park. Where's Alice? At the museum.

Fortunately, rather than remember three French prepositions, you only have to remember one, **à** (ah), which means *to*, *in*, or *at* (consider it a three-fer). How you use **à**, though, depends on the context of the answer.

As a rule, you use the preposition **à** when you want to say that you are going to or staying in a city or town. For example:

> **Je vais à Lille.** (zhuh veh-zah leel.) (*I am going to Lille.*)

> **Ils sont à Montréal.** (eel sohN-tah mohN-rey-ahl.) (*They are in Montreal.*)

However, when you want to talk about going to or staying at places in general, such as museums, cathedrals, or churches, you need to add the definite article — **le** (luh), **la** (lah), or **les** (ley), all of which mean *the* — after **à**. Note that **à** contracts with the masculine, singular **le** and the plural **les**. The following list shows these combinations and provides a sample sentence using that construction:

- ✔ **à** + **le** = **au** — Example: **Sylvie va au musée.** (seel-vee vah oh mew-zey.) (*Sylvie is going to the museum.*)

- ✔ **à** + **la** = **à la** — Example: **Guy veut aller à la cathédrale.** (gee vuh-tah-ley ah lah kah-tey-drahl.) (*Guy wants to go to the cathedral.*)

- ✔ **à** + **l'** = **à l'** — Example: **Les Martin vont à l'église St. Paul.** (ley mahr-taN vohN-tah ley-gleez saN pohl.) (*The Martins go to St. Paul's church.*)

- ✔ **à** + **les** = **aux** — Example: **Allez aux feux!** (ah-ley oh fuh!) (*Go to the traffic lights!*)

Using "voici" and "voilà"

Occasionally, the place you're looking for (or being asked about) is right in front of you (or close enough to point to). After all, if you've never been to a particular location before, you may not know quite what you're looking for or you may not recognize that you've already arrived! Similarly, if you're giving directions to your companion as you go along, you'll very likely announce your arrival with *Here is the. . .* or a similar expression. To create these expressions, you use the words **voici** (vwah-see) (*here*) and **voilà** (vwah-lah) (*there*):

> **Voici la poste/le musée/l'université!** (vwah-see lah pohst/luh mew-zey/lew-nee-vehr-see-tey!) (*Here is the post office/the museum/the university!*)

> **Voilà les bureaux!** (vwah-lah ley bew-roh!) (*There are the offices!*)

The difference between **voici** and **voilà** is that **voici** refers to something very close to you (*here*), and **voilà** refers to something farther away from you (*there*).

Of course, people are always using expressions that convey the same meaning but with fewer words. To do that with these answers, you simply eliminate the noun (**le musée, l'université,** and so on) and use a pronoun in its place (**le, la,** or **les**) in front of **voici** or **voilà,** as shown in the following answers:

Question	*Answer*
Où est le musée? (ooh eh luh mew-zey?) (*Where is the museum?*)	**Le voici!** (luh vwah-see!) (*Here it is!*)
Où est l'université? (ooh eh lew-nee-vehr-see-tey?) (*Where is the university?*)	**La voilà!** (lah vwah-lah!) (*There it is!*)
Où sont les bureaux? (ooh sohN ley bew-roh?) (*Where are the offices?*)	**Les voilà!** (ley vwah-lah!) (*There they are!*)

Getting specific with prepositions

French has many more prepositions than **à**. And you need to know these other prepositions when someone is giving you directions or when you want to give more specific directions to others. With the prepositions in the following list, you'll know, for example, whether the restaurant you are looking for is next to the cathedral, across from the mall, or in front of the square:

- **à côté de** (ah koh-tey duh) (*next to*)
- **à gauche de** (ah gohsh duh) (*to the left of*)
- **à droite de** (ah drwaht duh) (*to the right of*)
- **en face de** (ahN fahs-duh) (*across from, in front of*)
- **près (de)** (preh [duh]) (*near [to], close [to]*)
- **loin (de)** (lwaN [duh]) (*far [from]*)
- **devant** (duh-vahN) (*in front of*)
- **derrière** (deh-ryehr) (*behind*)
- **entre** (ahN-truh) (*between*)
- **dans** (dahN) (*in, inside*)
- **sur** (sewr) (*on, on top of*)
- **sous** (sooh) (*under, underneath*)

Here are some example sentences using these prepositions:

Le restaurant est entre la poste et l'hôtel de ville. (luh reh-stoh-rahN eh-tahN-truh lah pohst ey loh-tehl duh veel.) (*The restaurant is between the post office and town hall.*)

Le cinéma est en face de l'hôtel. (luh see-ney-mah eh-tahN fahs duh loh-tehl.) (*The movie theater is across from the hotel.*)

La boulangerie se trouve à côté du musée. (lah booh-lahN-zhree suh troohv ah koh-tey dew mew-zey.) (*The bakery is next to the museum.*)

Talkin' the Talk

John and Ann are in their hotel lobby inquiring about directions to go to the Cathedral of Notre Dame. The desk clerk, **le réception-niste** (luh rey-seh-psyoh-neest), helps them.

Le réceptionniste:	**Bonjour, monsieur. Je peux vous aider?** bohN-zhoohr, muh-syuh. Zhuh puh vooh-zey-dey? *Hello, sir. Can I help you?*
John:	**Nous voulons savoir où se trouve la cathédrale Notre-Dame.** nooh vooh-lohN sah-vwahr ooh suh troohv lah kah-tey-drahl nohh-truh dahm. *We want to know where the Cathedral of Notre Dame is.*
Le réceptionniste:	**Notre-Dame se trouve à l'Ile de la Cité.** nohh-truh dahm suh troohv ah leel duh lah see-tey. *Notre Dame is on the Ile de la Cité.*
John:	**Est-ce que c'est loin d'ici? Nous voulons aller à pied.** ehs-kuh seh lwaN dee-see? nooh vooh-lohN-zah-ley ah pyey. *Is it far from here? We want to walk.*
Le réceptionniste:	**Non, c'est à 15 minutes peut-être. Sortez de l'hôtel, tournez à gauche et continuez tout droit.** nohN, seh-tah kahNz mee-newt puh-teh-truh. sohr-tey duh loh-tehl, toohr-ney ah gohsh ey kohN-tee-new-ey tooh drwah. *No, it's 15 minutes maybe. Leave the hotel, turn left, and keep going straight ahead.*
John:	**Et ensuite?** ey ahN-sweet? *And then?*
Le réceptionniste:	**Traversez le Pont Neuf et la cathédrale est à gauche.** trah-vehr-sey luh pohN nuhf ey lah kah-tey-drahl eh-tah gohsh. *Cross the Pont Neuf, and the Cathedral is on the left.*

John:	**Merci beaucoup.**
	mehr-see boh-kooh.
	Thank you very much.
Le réceptionniste:	**Je vous en prie.**
	zhuh vooh-zahN pree.
	You are welcome.

Words to Know

Je peux vous aider?	zhuh puh vooh-zey-dey?	Can I help you?
Nous voulons savoir . . .	nooh vooh-lohN sah-vwahr . . .	We want to know . . .
C'est loin?	seh lwaN?	Is it far?
aller à pied	ah-ley ah pyey	to walk, to go on foot
peut-être	puh-teh-truh	perhaps, maybe
continuez tout droit	kohN-tee-new-ey tooh drwah	continue straight ahead
Et ensuite?	ey ahN-sweet?	And then?

Getting Direction about Directions

Whenever and wherever you travel, you are bound to need directions at some point. Understanding a few basic expressions can enable you to get the general idea or direction of where to go. The following sections have the details. You can also find information that tells you what to do if you find yourself having difficulty catching everything you're told.

Using direct commands to give directions

When someone directs you to a location, that person is giving you a command. In a command, it's understood that you're being addressed, but French has two ways to say *you* — the familiar **tu** (tew) and the polite **vous** (vooh).

As discussed in Chapter 5, to form the command, you just omit the **tu, nous** (nooh) (*we*)**, or vous** in front of the verb (just as you drop the *you* and *we* in English):

> **Va au centre.** (vah oh sahN-truh.) (*Go to the center.*)
>
> **Allez tout droit.** (ah-ley tooh drwah.) (*Go straight ahead.*)
>
> **Traversons le pont.** (trah-vehr-sohN luh pohN.) (*Let's cross the bridge.*)

For **–er** verbs only, drop the final **–s** from the **tu** form in all commands, as in these examples:

Infinitive (-er)	*Tu form*	*Command form*
aller (ah-ley) (*to go*)	**tu vas** (tew vah) (*you go*)	**va!** (vah) (*go!*)
continuer (kohN-tee-new-ey) (*to continue*)	**tu continues** (tew kohN-tee-new) (*you continue*)	**continue!** (kohN-tee-new!) (*continue!*)

However, when you ask directions from people you don't know or don't know well, you'll probably find that they address you with the polite **vous**. In such a case, remember that the ending of most verbs in the **vous** form is **–ez**. Here are some verbs in the **vous** form that will come in very handy:

- ✔ **Tournez. . . .** (toohr-ney. . . .) (*turn. . . .*) as in **Tournez à droite/à gauche/à la rue....** (toohr-ney ah drwaht/ah gohsh/ah lah rew. . . .) (*Turn right/left/on. . . street.*)

- ✔ **Prenez. . . .** (pruh-ney. . . .) (*take. . . .*) as in **Prenez la deuxième rue à droite/à gauche.** (pruh-ney lah duh-zee-ehm rew ah drwaht/ah gohsh.) (*Take the second street on the right/on the left.*)

- ✔ **Montez. . . .** (mohN-tey. . . .) (*go up. . . .*) as in **Montez la rue. . . /le boulevard. . . /l'avenue. . . .** (mohN-tey lah rew. . . /luh boohl-vahr. . . / lahv-new. . . .) (*Go up. . . street/. . . boulevard/. . . avenue.*)

- ✔ **Descendez. . . .** (dey-sahN-dey. . . .) (*go down. . . .*) as in **Descendez la rue. . . /le boulevard. . . ./l'avenue. . . .** (dey-sahN-dey lah rew. . . ./ luh boohl-vahr. . . ./lahv-new. . . .) (*Go down. . . street/. . . boulevard/. . . avenue.*)

- ✔ **Suivez. . . .** (swee-vey) (*follow. . . .*) as in **Suivez la rue. . . ./le boulevard. . . ./ l'avenue. . . .** (swee-vey lah rew. . . ./luh boohl-vahr. . . ./ lahv-new. . . .) (*Follow. . . street/. . . boulevard/. . . avenue.*)

- ✔ **Continuez à. . . .** (kohN-tee-new-ey ah. . . .) (*continue on. . . .*) as in **Continuez à la rue. . . ./au boulevard. . . ./à l'avenue. . . .** (kohN-tee-new-ey ah lah rew. . . ./oh boohl-vahr. . . ./ah lahv-new. . . .) (*Continue on. . . street/. . . boulevard/. . . avenue.*)

- ✔ **Allez tout droit.** (ah-ley tooh drwah.) (*Go straight.*)

✔ **Traversez. . . .** (trah-vehr-sey. . . .) (*cross. . . .*) as in **Traversez la rue. . . ./ le boulevard. . . ./l'avenue. . . ./le pont.** (trah-vehr-sey lah rew. . . ./luh boohl-vahr. . . ./lahv-new. . . ./luh pohN.) (*Cross. . . street/. . .boulevard/. . . avenue/the bridge.*)

Softening commands with "il faut"

Commands tend to sound a bit bossy. So in French, you have a way out of this. You can use just one form for everybody — **il faut** (eel foh) (*one has to*). This impersonal form exists only in the **il** (eel) (*it*) form. When you use **il faut** in commands, the form **il faut** never changes. Simply put the infinitive of any verb after it, as these examples show. Whether the sentence is translated with *I, you,* or *we* depends on the context:

✔ **Il faut retourner à l'hôtel.** (eel foh ruh-toohr-ney ah loh-tehl.) (*I/you/ we have to go back to the hotel.*)

✔ **Il faut aller au centre-ville.** (eel foh-tah-ley oh sahNn-truh veel.) (*I/you/ we have to go downtown.*)

✔ **Il faut prendre un taxi.** (eel foh prahN-druhN tah-ksee.) (*I/you/we have to take a cab.*)

For information on using **il faut** with indirect pronouns, refer to Chapter 16.

Expressing distances in time and space

As Chapter 3 explains, you can use the preposition **à** for time expressions such as **à demain** (ah duh-mahN) (*see you tomorrow*), **à bientôt** (ah byaN-toh) (*see you soon*), and even **à la semaine prochaine** (ah lah suh-mehn proh-shehn) (*see you next week*), but you can also use **à** for distance away from you, as in the following:

À deux minutes. (ah duh mee-newt.) (*It takes only two minutes, It's two minutes away.*)

À cent mètres. (ah sahN meh-truh.) (*Only 100 meters farther, It's in about 100 meters.*)

C'est à cent mètres (d'ici). (seh-tah sahN meh-truh [dee-see].) (*It's 100 meters [from here].*)

C'est à deux kilomètres. (seh-tah duh kee-loh-meh-truh.) (*It's 2 kilometers away, It's 2 kilometers from here.*)

Paris has 20 districts called **arrondissements** (ah-rohN-dees-mahN) (see Figure 7-1), numbered in a clockwise spiral pattern. The first district is in the heart of Paris and includes the Louvre. The higher the number, the farther from the center the district is; the smaller the number, the closer to the center it is. When you speak with people who live in Paris, you often hear them use ordinal numbers to indicate what section of the city a particular location is. For example, if someone says **Dans quel arrondissement est le restaurant?** (dahN kehl ah-rohN-dees-mahN eh luh reh-stoh-rahN?) (*In which district is the restaurant?*), the response may be **Il est dans le deuxième** (eel eh dahN luh duh-zee-ehm) (*It is in the second* [*district*]).

If you're going to give or follow directions, you need to know your ordinal numbers so that you know where to turn: at the first, second, or third street or traffic light, for example. Check out the ordinal numbers in Chapter 4.

Going north, south, east, and west

If you're unfamiliar with a place, the directions that use local landmarks (which may only be known by the locals!) aren't going to do you much good. And when the person giving you directions doesn't know *your* exact location (if you're asking for directions over the phone, for example), he or she can't very well tell whether you need to turn right or left to get to your destination. In those cases, it's easier to use cardinal points: north, south, east, and west. What's an added bonus of using cardinal directions? It makes taking unplanned side trips — exploring the French countryside, for example — that much easier.

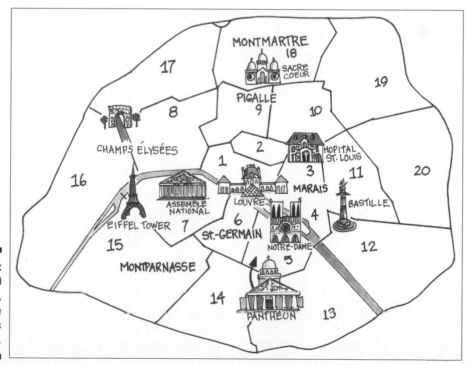

Figure 7-1:
Paris's 20 districts, with some landmarks identified.

- ✔ **nord** (nohr) (*north*), **nord-est** (nohr-ehst) (*northeast*), and **nord-ouest** (nohr-wehst) (*northwest*)

- ✔ **sud** (sewd) (*south*), **sud-est** (sew-dehst) (*southeast*), and **sud-ouest** (sew-dwehst) (*southwest*)

- ✔ **est** (ehst) (*east*)

- ✔ **ouest** (wehst) (*west*)

When you ask for or give directions by using cardinal points, always place **au** (oh) (*to the*) in front of a cardinal point that begins with a consonant and **à l'** (ahl) (*to the*) in front of a cardinal point that begins with a vowel. Here are some examples:

> **Paris est au nord de Nice.** (pah-ree eh-toh nohr duh nees.) (*Paris is north of Nice.*)

> **La Suisse est à l'est de la France.** (lah swees eh-tah lehst duh lah frahNs.) (*Switzerland is east of France.*)

Talkin' the Talk

Julie asks her French friend Cécile about the location of the Versailles castle. (Track 7)

Julie:	**Cécile, où est le château de Versailles?**
	sey-seel, ooh eh luh shah-toh duh vehr-sahy?
	Cécile, where is the palace of Versailles?

Cécile:	**Il se trouve au sud-ouest de Paris.**
	eel suh troohv oh sew-dwehst duh pah-ree.
	It's southwest of Paris.

Julie:	**C'est loin?**
	seh lwaN?
	Is it far?

Cécile:	**Ton hôtel est à l'est, n'est-ce pas? C'est à une heure en voiture, à peu près. Allons ensemble samedi.**
	tohN-noh-tehl eh-tah lehst, nehs pah? seh-tah ewn uhr ahN vwah-tewr, ah puh preh. ah-lohN ahN-sahN-bluh sahm-dee.
	Your hotel is in the east, right? It's one hour by car, roughly. Let's go together on Saturday.

Julie: **Très bonne idée!**
treh bohhn ee-dey!
That's a very good idea!

Cécile: **OK. Il faut se téléphoner avant samedi.**
oh-keh. eel foh suh tey-ley-fohh-ney ah-vahN
sahm-dee.
*Okay. We have to telephone each other before
Saturday.*

Julie: **Très bien. Au revoir, Cécile.**
treh byaN. ohr-vwahr, sey-seel.
Great. Bye, Cécile.

Words to Know

le château	luh shah-toh	castle, palace
N'est-ce pas?	nehs pah?	Isn't that so?
en voiture	ahN vwah-tewr	by car
à peu près	ah puh preh	roughly
Allons ensemble	ah-lohN ahN-sahN-bluh	Let's go together
Il faut se téléphoner	eel foh suh tey-ley-fohh-ney	We have to tele-phone each other
avant	ah-vahN	before

Checking directions or your location

What if you get lost on your way to Versailles? Or maybe you just want to make sure that you're on the right track, wherever you may be going. Here are some helpful questions that you can ask:

Est-ce que c'est la bonne route pour. . . ? (ehs-kuh seh lah bohhn rooht poohr. . . ?) (*Is this the right way to. . . ?*)

Où va cette rue? (ooh vah seht rew?) (*Where does this street go?*)

Comment s'appelle cette ville? (koh-mahN sah-pehl seht veel?) (*What's the name of this town?*)

Pourriez-vous m'indiquer comment aller. . . ? (pooh-ree-ey-vooh maN-dee-key koh-mahN-tah-ley. . . ?) (*Could you indicate. point out [to me] how to get to. . . ?*)

What to do when you don't understand

What do you do if you don't understand the directions just because the person to whom you are speaking is talking too fast, mumbling, or has a pronounced accent? Well, don't give up! Instead, say that you don't understand and ask the person to repeat the information more slowly. That's when the following phrases can help you:

- ✔ **Pardon. Je ne comprends pas.** (pahr-dohN. zhuh nuh kohN-prahN pah.) (*Pardon. I don't understand.*)

- ✔ **Excusez-moi! Est-ce que vous pouvez répéter, s'il vous plaît?** (ehks-kew-zey-mwah! ehs-kuh vooh pooh-vey rey-pey-tey, seel vooh pleh?) (*Excuse me. Can you repeat that, please?*)

- ✔ **(Parlez) plus lentement.** ([pahr-ley] plew lahNt-mahN.) ([*Speak*] *more slowly.*)

- ✔ **Qu'est-ce que vous avez dit?** (kehs-kuh vooh-zah-vey dee?) (*What did you say?*)

Of course, it's always handy to know how to say *thank you*, or *thank you very much*, which in French is **merci** (mehr-see) or **merci beaucoup** (mehr-see boh-kooh). In reply, you may hear **De rien** (duh ryaN) (*It's nothing*) or **Je vous en prie** (zhuh vooh-zahN pree) (*You are welcome*).

Talkin' the Talk

Vivianne is looking for **Le Panthéon** (luh pahN-tey-ohN) (*the Pantheon*). She asks **un agent de police** (uhN-nah-zhahN duh poh-lees) (*a police officer*) for directions.

Vivianne: **Excusez-moi, s'il vous plaît. Pour aller au Panthéon?**
ehks-kew-zey-mwah, seel vooh pleh. poohr ah-ley oh pahN-tey-ohN?
Excuse me, please. To get to the Pantheon?

Agent
de Police:

Montez la rue Saint-Jacques et prenez la troisième rue à droite.
mohN-tey lah rew saN zhahk ey pruh-ney lah trwah-zee-ehm rew ah drwaht.
Go up St. Jacques Street and take the third street on the right.

Vivianne:

Bon. La troisième à droite. Elle s'appelle comment, cette rue?
bohN. lah trwah-zee-ehm ah drwaht. ehl sah-pehl koh-mahN, seht rew?
Okay. The third on the right. What's the name of that street?

Agent
de Police:

C'est la rue Pierre et Marie Curie. Tournez à gauche à la rue d'Ulm et continuez tout droit. Le Panthéon est à votre droite.
seh lah rew pyehr ey mah-ree kew-ree. toohr-ney ah gohsh ah lah rew dewlm ey kohN-tee-new-ey tooh drwah. luh pahN-tey-ohN eh-tah vohh-truh drwaht.
It's Pierre and Marie Curie Street. Turn left on Ulm Street and continue straight. The Pantheon is on your right.

Vivianne:

Je ne comprends pas. Pouvez-vous répéter, s'il vous plaît?
zhuh nuh kohN-prahN pah. pooh-vey-vooh rey-pey-tey, seel vooh pleh?
I don't understand. Could you please repeat?

Agent
de Police:

Tournez à gauche à la rue d'Ulm et continuez tout droit. Le Panthéon est à votre droite.
toohr-ney ah gohsh ah lah rew dewlm ey kohN-tee-new-ey tooh drwah. luh pahN-tey-ohN eh-tah vohh-truh drwaht.
Turn left on Ulm Street and continue straight. The Pantheon is on your right.

Vivianne:

Merci beaucoup.
mehr-see boh-kooh.
Thank you very much.

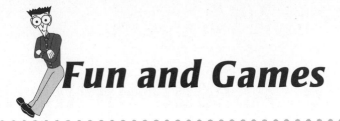

Fun and Games

You need to explain to a friend how to go from point A to point B on the map following the arrows.

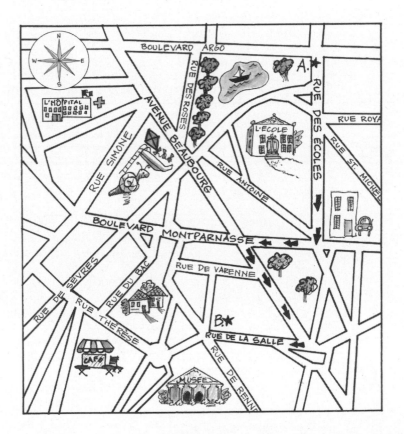

Using the vocabulary in this chapter, fill in the blanks.

(A) _____ (*Go down* or *Take*) la Rue des Écoles. (B) _____ (*Turn right*) au Boulevard Montparnasse. (C) _____ (*Take*) le Boulevard Montparnasse à l'Avenue Beaubourg et (D)_____ (*turn southwest*). (E) _____ (*Turn right*) à la Rue de La Salle et (F) _____ (*Follow*) la Rue de La Salle et votre destination est à droite (to your destination on the right).

Chapter 8

Bon Appétit! Dining Out and Going to the Market

....

In This Chapter

▶ Making restaurant reservations, ordering, and paying the check

▶ Using the conditional tense of **vouloir** and **pouvoir**

▶ Going to the market with the verbs **acheter** and **vendre**

....

*E*xploring the food and eating habits of people in another country is one of the most pleasant ways to discover their culture. When the subject is French food and restaurants, the exploration is especially enjoyable. This chapter is undoubtedly the most appetizing and probably one of the most useful if you are planning to visit a French-speaking country or if you just want to impress your date by ordering in French at the hot, new bistro in your town. Whether you want to eat in a fancy two- or three-star restaurant or eat bread and cheese sitting on a park bench, you need to know how to select, order, and then enjoy (which we promise will be easy)! Of course, not every meal is eaten out, so this chapter also explains what kinds of items you can find at the local outdoor markets and the specialty shops.

Dining Out

What better way to enjoy what you're eating than to start with an empty stomach? Then you can say **J'ai faim** (zhey faN) (*I'm hungry*) or **J'ai soif** (zhey swahf) (*I'm thirsty*), and the glorious world of French gastronomy is yours!

French-speaking people like to emphasize the way they feel. So instead of simply saying *I am very hungry* or *I am very thirsty*, a French person tells you **Je meurs de faim** (zhuh muhr duh faN) (*I am dying of hunger*) or **Je meurs de soif** (zhuh muhr duh swahf) (*I am dying of thirst*).

French food is probably one of the most famous and the most praised in the world. And you don't have to go to Paris to enjoy it. You can find French restaurants and specialty food shops in many of the larger metropolitan areas in the United States, although they are often expensive. But just across the border, you can find total satisfaction at reasonable prices in Montreal, Québec's largest city.

French law requires that all restaurants post their menus — with prices — outside, so you won't have any costly surprises when you get in. Some restaurants provide **un menu à prix fixe** (uhN muh-new ah pree feeks) (*a fixed price menu*) that includes an entrée, main dish, and dessert for a reasonable price.

Making a restaurant reservation

In most big cities like Paris or Montreal, many popular or well-known restaurants require a reservation — as much as two months in advance in some cases! For that reason, whenever you plan to dine out casually with friends or go to a fancy restaurant, phone ahead and reserve a table. To do so politely, you have to use the conditional conjugation of verbs. These verbs express a wish, possibility, and supposition. Best of all, the conditional is used to make polite requests, such as *I would like some water, please* or *Could you please pass the salt?*

One verb you use quite often in the conditional is **vouloir** (vooh-lwahr) (*to want*). In its conditional form, its translation is *would like*. You use this verb to make a reservation, for example: **Je voudrais faire une réservation** (zhuh vooh-dreh fehr ewn rey-zehr-vah-syohN) (*I would like to make a reservation*) or **Je voudrais réserver une table** (zhuh vooh-dreh rey-zehr-vey ewn tah-bluh) (*I would like to reserve a table*). The following table shows how to conjugate the conditional tense for **vouloir**:

Conjugation	Pronunciation
je voudrais	zhuh vooh-dreh
tu voudrais	tew vooh-dreh
il/elle/on voudrait	eel/ehl/ohN vooh-dreh
nous voudrions	nooh vooh-dree-ohN
vous voudriez	vooh vooh-dree-ey
ils/elles voudraient	eel/ehl vooh-dreh

Pouvoir (pooh-vwahr) (*to be able to*) is another very important verb you use to make polite requests. In its conditional tense, this verb means *may* or *could*, as in *Could you please recommend a good restaurant?* For example, you would say **Pourriez-vous (me/nous) recommander un bon restaurant, s'il vous plaît?** (pooh-ree-ey vooh [muh/nooh] ruh-kohh-mahN-dey uhN bohN reh-stoh-rahN, seel vooh pleh?) (*Could you recommend a good restaurant [to me/to us], please?*). The following table shows the conditional tense for the verb **pouvoir**:

Conjugation	Pronunciation
je pourrais	zhuh pooh-reh
tu pourrais	tew pooh-reh
il/elle/on pourrait	eel/ehl/ohN pooh-reh
nous pourrions	nooh pooh-ree-ohN
vous pourriez	vooh pooh-ree-ey
ils/elles pourraient	eel/ehl pooh-reh

You may be asked to spell your name when you make any kind of reservation, so be sure to check the letters of the alphabet and their pronunciations in Chapter 3.

Talkin' the Talk

Mr. Miller is visiting Paris with his wife, and they've decided to dine at a very nice restaurant. Mr. Miller gets on the phone and talks to **la réceptionniste** (lah rey-sehp-syoh-neest) (*the receptionist*) to reserve a table.

Mr. Miller:	**Bonjour, je voudrais réserver une table.** bohN-zhoohr, zhuh vooh-dreh rey-zehr-vey ewn tah-bluh. *Hello, I would like to reserve a table.*
La réceptionniste:	**Bien sûr monsieur, pour quand?** byaN sewr muh-syuh, poohr kahN? *Of course, sir, for when?*
Mr. Miller:	**Pour lundi prochain.** poohr luhN-dee proh-shaN. *For next Monday.*
La réceptionniste:	**Ah je suis désolée, monsieur, nous sommes fermés le lundi.** ah zhuh swee dey-zoh-ley, muh-syuh, nooh sohm fehr-mey luh luhN-dee. *Oh, I'm sorry, sir, we're closed on Mondays.*
Mr. Miller:	**Alors mardi.** ah-lohr mahr-dee. *Tuesday, then.*

La réceptionniste:	**D'accord, pour déjeuner ou pour dîner?** dah-kohr, poohr dey-zhuh-ney ooh poohr dee-ney? *Very well, for lunch or dinner?*
Mr. Miller:	**Pour dîner.** poohr dee-ney. *For dinner.*
La réceptionniste:	**Pour combien de personnes?** poohr kohN-byaN duh pehr-sohhn? *For how many (people)?*
Mr. Miller:	**Pour deux personnes.** poohr duh pehr-sohhn. *For two people.*
La réceptionniste:	**Et à quelle heure?** ey ah-kehl uhr? *And at what time?*
Mr. Miller:	**À vingt heures.** ah-vaN-tuhr. *At eight o'clock (p.m.).*
La réceptionniste:	**C'est à quel nom?** seh-tah kehl nohN? *What is the name?*
Mr. Miller:	**Miller, M-I-L-L-E-R.** mee-lehr, ehm-ee-ehl-ehl-uh-ehr. *Miller, M-I-L-L-E-R.*
La réceptionniste:	**Très bien monsieur, une table pour deux personnes mardi 16 à 20 heures. A bientôt.** treh byaN muh-syuh, ewn tah-bluh poohr duh pehr-sohhn mahr-dee seh-zah vaN-tuhr. ah byaN-toh. *Very well, sir, a table for two Tuesday the 16th, at 8:00 p.m. See you soon.*

To find a restaurant in Paris, you can consult the **Guide Michelin** (geed meesh-laN) (*The Michelin Guide*). This guide is the restaurant lover's bible. A new edition of this internationally known red book — the one with stars for food quality and forks for the level of formality — is published annually and can make or break a restaurant overnight.

Words to Know

Pour quand?	poohr kahN	For when?
Nous sommes fermés	nooh sohm fehr-mey	We're closed
lundi prochain	luhN-dee proh-shaN	next Monday
Je suis désolé(e)	zhuh swee dey-zoh-ley	I am sorry
d'accord	dah-kohr	okay, all right
C'est à quel nom?	seh-tah kehl nohN?	What's the name?

Perusing the menu

In most restaurants in France, you can order from a **menu à prix fixe** (muh-new ah pree feeks) (*set-price menu*). The **prix fixe** menu generally costs less and often offers several set menus, each with a selection of an appetizer, a main dish, and cheese and/or dessert. Alternatively, you can order **à la carte** (ah lah kahrt) (*a la carte*), with a stated price for each dish. When you order **à la carte**, you can choose anything on the menu. Following is a sample of some of the menu items you may find in a French restaurant. Remember, different restaurants may give these things different names, so if you're unsure, ask the waiter or waitress.

Appetizers to get the meal started

Here are **les entrées** (ley-zahN-trey) (*appetizers*) you may find on a French menu:

- **le pâté/la terrine** (luh pah-tey/lah teh-reen) (*pâtés, meat paste*)
- **le saumon fumé** (luh soh-mohN few-mey*) (*smoked salmon*)
- **la salade verte** (lah sah-lahd vehrt) (Literally: *green salad, salad with lettuce only*)
- **les crudités** (ley krew-dee-tey) (*mixed raw vegetables, crudités*)

The French word **entrée** (ahN-trey) (*entrance, way in*) is a false friend (refer to Chapter 1). Because it leads in to the meal, the **entrée** of a French meal is the first course, not the main course, as it is in the United States. What Americans call the entree, the French call **le plat principal** (luh plah praN-see-pahl) (*the main course*).

Meat and poultry

The French menu may contain any — or all — of these varieties of **les viandes** (ley vyahNd) (*meats*) and **volaille** (voh-lahy) (*poultry*):

- ✔ **le boeuf** (luh buhf) (*beef*). You can order your steak **saignant** (seh-nyahN) (*rare*), **à point** (ah pwaN) (*medium*), or **bien cuit** (byaN kwee) (*well done*).

- ✔ **le veau** (luh voh) (*veal*). **La côte de veau** (lah koht duh voh) is a *veal chop.*

- ✔ **l'agneau** (m) (lah-nyoh) (*lamb*). Selections often include **la côte d'agneau** (lah koht dah-nyoh) (*lamb chop*) or **un gigot** (uhN zhee-goh) (*leg of lamb*).

- ✔ **le porc** (luh pohr) (*pork*). **La côte de porc** (lah koht duh pohr) (*pork chop*) and **le jambon** (luh zhahN-bohN) (*ham*) are popular items.

- ✔ **la volaille** (lah voh-lahy) (*poultry*). Your poultry selections can include **le poulet** (luh pooh-leh) (*chicken*), **la dinde** (lah daNd) (*turkey*), and **le canard** (luh kah-nahr) (*duck*).

What a difference an accent can make! **Le pâté** (luh pah-tey) is a meat paste, usually made from pork meat and spices, which is eaten as an appetizer with bread. Of course, there is also the famous **pâté de foie gras d'oie** (pah-tey duh fwah grah dwah) (*goose liver pâté*), which is more expensive. On the other hand, **les pâtes** (ley paht) are the familiar pastas. So watch out for that accent when you order, or you may be surprised by what you receive!

Seafood

Following are a variety of **les fruits de mer** (ley frwee duh mehr) (*seafood*) selections that commonly appear on French menus:

- ✔ **les poissons** (ley pwah-sohN) (*fish*), such as **le saumon** (luh soh-mohN) (*salmon*), **le thon** (luh tohN) (*tuna*), **l'espadon** (m) (leh-spah-dohN) (*swordfish*), and **la truite** (lah trweet) (*trout*)

- ✔ **les crevettes** (ley kruh-veht) (*shrimp*)

- ✔ **les huitres** (ley wee-truh) (*oysters*)

- ✔ **le homard** (luh oh-mahr) (*lobster*)

- ✔ **les coquilles Saint-Jacques** (ley koh-keey saN zhahk) (*scallops*)

Le riz (luh ree) (*rice*), **les pâtes** (ley paht) (*pasta*), or **les pommes de terre** (ley pohhm duh tehr) (*potatoes*) are often served with all of the above.

Vegetables

Your mother always said, "Eat your vegetables!" With the selection you find on French menus, doing so isn't a problem at all:

- ✔ **les légumes** (ley ley-gewm) (*vegetables*)
- ✔ **les pommes de terre** (ley pohhm duh tehr) (*potatoes*)
- ✔ **les haricots verts** (ley ah-ree-koh vehr) (*green beans*)
- ✔ **les petits pois** (ley puh-tee pwah) (*peas*)
- ✔ **les épinards** (ley-zey-pee-nahr) (*spinach*)
- ✔ **les asperges** (ley-zah-spehrzh) (*asparagus*)
- ✔ **le chou** (luh shooh) (*cabbage*)
- ✔ **le chou-fleur** (luh shooh-fluhr) (*cauliflower*)
- ✔ **les choux de Bruxelles** (ley shooh duh brewk-sehl) (*Brussels sprouts*)
- ✔ **les poireaux** (ley pwah-roh) (*leaks*)
- ✔ **les champignons** (ley shahN-pee-nyohN) (*mushrooms*)

Cheeses

France is known for its wonderfully delicious **fromages** (froh-mahzh) (*cheeses*), and most French people eat **le fromage** with every meal. France is said to have a different cheese for each day of the year. In fact, France has many sayings about the importance of cheese, such as this one: **Un repas sans fromage est comme une journée sans soleil** (uhN ruh-pah sahN froh-mahzh eh kohm ewn zhoohr-ney sahN soh-lehy) (*A meal without cheese is like a day without sun*).

Cheeses you commonly see on a French menu may include **le chèvre** (luh shehv-ruh) (*goat cheese*), **le camembert** (luh kah-mahN-behr) (*Camembert*), and **le brie** (luh bree) (*brie*).

Desserts

Here are **les desserts** (ley deh-sehr) (*desserts*) you often see on French menus.

- ✔ **la glace** (lah glahs) (*ice cream*)
- ✔ **la crème** (lah krehm) (*pudding*)
- ✔ **la crème brulée** (lah krehm brew-ley) (*crème brulée*)
- ✔ **le gâteau au chocolat** (luh gah-toh oh shoh-koh-lah) (*chocolate cake*)
- ✔ **la tarte aux pommes** (lah tahr-toh-pohhm) (*apple tart*)

The French eat ice cream and apple pie, but they don't eat them together, which is funny, considering that the phrase **à la mode** (ah lah mohhd) (*in fashion*), which is often used in the U.S. to indicate pie with a scoop of ice cream, is a French phrase! French apple pies are also very different from their American counterpart. They are very thin and do not have a top crust. They look more like what Americans would call a tart.

Beverages

You surely want to compliment your delicious meal with a drink. Of course, the drink of choice in France is **le vin** (luh vaN) (*wine*). If you are in **une brasserie** (ewn brah-sree) (*a pub*), you may even want to try **une bière à la pression** (ewn byehr ah lah preh-syohN) (*a draught beer*). Of course, not all drinks have to be alcoholic. Here is a list of possible drinks that you can order at the local café or at any restaurant:

- ✔ **le jus d'orange** (luh zhew doh-rahNzh) (*orange juice*)
- ✔ **le jus de pomme** (luh zhew duh pohhm) (*apple juice*)
- ✔ **le jus de fruit** (luh zhew duh frwee) (*fruit juice*)
- ✔ **le lait** (luh leh) (*milk*)
- ✔ **l'eau minérale/gazeuse** (loh mee-ney-rahl/gah-zuhz) (*mineral, sparkling water*)
- ✔ **la boisson gazeuse** (lah bwah-sohN gah-zuhz) (*soda*)
- ✔ **le thé** (luh tey) (*tea*)
- ✔ **le café** (luh kah-fey) (*coffee*)
- ✔ **le chocolat chaud** (luh shoh-koh-lah shoh) (*hot chocolate*)

Un apéritif (uhN-nah-pey-ree-teef) (*an aperitif*) is not just any drink, but more specifically a drink before the meal. Its purpose is to open the meal and the appetite. As an **apéritif**, the French like fairly mild alcoholic drinks like **kir** (keer), which consists of white wine or champagne with **crème de cassis** (krehm duh kah-sees) (*blackcurrant liqueur*); sweet wines like sherry or port, and so on; and they drink regular wine during the meal. **Un digestif** (uhN dee-zheh-steef) is an *after-dinner drink,* usually cognac or brandy, which, as the name indicates, is supposed to aid digestion. In general, **un apéritif** and **un digestif** are reserved for special occasions like family gatherings or dinner parties.

When you want to order specific quantities of a beverage, use these phrases:

- ✔ **un verre de. . .** (uhN vehr duh. . .) (*a glass of. . .*)
- ✔ **une bouteille de. . .** (ewn booh-tehy duh . . .) (*a bottle of. . .*)
- ✔ **une carafe de** . . . (ewn kah-rahf duh . . .) (*a carafe of . . .*)
- ✔ **une tasse de** (ewn tahs duh . . .) (*a cup of . . .*)

Coffee break

When you order coffee from a café or a restaurant in France, you get **un express** (uhN-nehk-sprehs) (*an espresso*) in a small cup. Only at breakfast do you get a medium-size pot of *coffee with hot milk* on the side, **un café au lait** (uhN kah-fey oh leh). At home, the French drink **café au lait** in a large bowl in the morning rather than in a cup. If you want milk in your coffee at any other time of the day, you have to order **un café crème** (uhN kah-fey krehm) (*coffee with milk*). Of course, you can also order one of the following:

✔ **un double express** (uhN dooh-blehk-sprehs) (*a double espresso*)

✔ **un grand crème** (uhN grahN krehm) (*a large coffee with milk*)

Note: Large doesn't mean large in the American sense, but more exactly double, which is the equivalent of two small espresso cups.

✔ **un déca/un décaféiné** (uhN dey-kah/uhN dey-kaf-fey-ee-ney) (*a decaf coffee*)

If you're really desperate for those gallons of weak coffee, many large hotels in Paris do offer **un café américain** (uhN kah-fey ah-mey-ree-kaN) (*American coffee*). You can also ask anywhere for **de l'eau chaude** (duh loh shohd) (*hot water*) and carry your instant coffee powder with you.

People seldom order wine by the glass in France. More often they order wine as **un quart** (uhN kahr*) (a quarter of a liter*), **une demi-bouteille** (ewn duh-mee-booh-tehy*) (a half a bottle*), or **une bouteille** (ewn booh-tehy) (*a bottle*). They order the house wine in **une carafe** (ewn kah-rahf) (*a carafe*) or **un pichet** (uhN pee-sheh) (*a jug*). In addition, you usually don't have water on the table unless you say **une carafe d'eau, s'il vous plaît** (ewn kah-rahf doh, seel vooh pleh) (*a pitcher of water, please*).

Placing your order

You may want to ask the waiter a few questions about the dishes on the menu. Actually, the more sophisticated the restaurant, the less likely you are to understand its menu! The art of giving unusual names to dishes is almost as elaborate as the art of actually preparing them. And don't think that you're the only one who doesn't understand. The average French restaurant-goer doesn't either. Your best bet is to ask the waiter. You can also ask for the waiter's recommendation by saying **Qu'est-ce que vous recommandez/suggérez?** (kehs-kuh vooh ruh-kohh-mahN-dey/sewg-zhey-rey?) (*What do you recommend/suggest?*)

When it's time to order, the waiter will ask you these kinds of questions:

Qu'est-ce que vous voulez boire? (kehs-kuh vooh vooh-ley bwahr?) (*What do you want to drink?*). Or you may hear **Qu'est-ce que vous voulez comme boisson?** (kehs-kuh vooh vooh-ley kohhm bwah-sohN?), which more literally translates *What do you want as a drink?*

Avez-vous choisi? (ah-vey-vooh shwah-zee?) (*Have you decided?*)

Qu'est-ce que vous voulez prendre? (kehs-kuh vooh vooh-ley prahN-druh?) (*What do you want to have [to eat/to drink]?*)

Que prenez-vous comme plat principal? (kuh pruh-ney-vooh kohhm plah praN-see-pahl?) or **Qu'est-ce que vous prenez comme plat principal?** (kehs-kuh vooh pruh-ney kohhm plah praN-see-pahl?), both of which mean *What will you have as a main course?*

The phrase consisting of **comme** (kohhm) (*as*) followed by a noun is very commonly used in French, not only for food and drink items, but also each time you are asked to express a preference. For example, you may ask a friend **Qu'est-ce que vous aimez comme films?** (kehs-kuh vooh-zehm-ey kohhm feelm?) (*What kind of movies do you like?*)

If you want to ask the waiter what kinds of selections are available, you use the question **Qu'est-ce que vous avez comme. . . ?** (kehs-kuh vooh-zah-vey kohhm . . . ?) (*What do you have as. . .?*). Take a look at these examples:

Qu'est-ce que vous avez comme boisson? (kehs-kuh vooh-zah-vey kohhm bwah-sohN?) (*What do you have as a drink?*). Alternatively, you can say **Qu'est-ce qu'il y a comme boisson?** (kehs-keel ee ah kohhm bwah-sohN?) (*What is there as a drink?*)

Qu'est-ce que vous avez comme vin? (kehs-kuh vooh-zah-vey kohhm vaN?) (Literally: *What do you have as wine?* or *What kind of wine do you have?*)

Qu'est-ce que vous avez comme entrée? (kehs-kuh vooh-zah-vey kohhm ahN-trey?) (*What do you have as an appetizer?*)

Qu'est-ce que vous avez comme fromage? (kehs-kuh vooh-zah-vey kohhm froh-mahzh?) (*What do you have as cheese?*)

When you're all set and ready to order, you need to have these phrases handy:

✔ **Comme entrée, je prends. . . .** (kohhm-ahN-trey, zhuh prahN. . . .) (*For the first course [appetizer], I'll have. . . .*)

✔ **Je voudrais . . . .** (zhuh vooh-dreh. . . .) (*I would like. . . .*)

- ✔ **Pour moi. . . .** (poohr mwah. . . .) (Literally: *For me. . . .*)

- ✔ **Et ensuite. . . .** (ey ahN-sweet. . . .) (*And then. . . .*)

- ✔ **Et comme boisson. . . .** (ey kohm bwah-sohN. . . .) (*And to drink. . . .*)

- ✔ **Et comme dessert. . . .** (ey kohm deh-sehr. . . .) (*And for dessert. . . .*)

You no longer address the waiter as **garçon** (gahr-sohN), which is considered condescending because it means *boy*. Use **monsieur** (muh-syuh) (*sir*), instead. In case your server is **une serveuse** (ewn sehr-vuhz) (*a waitress*), you say **madame** (mah-dahm) (*ma'am*) or, if she is very young, **mademoiselle** (mahd-mwah-zehl) (*miss*).

Talkin' the Talk

Julie, a young woman from Québec, and her friend Mike, visiting from the United States, have spent a long morning sightseeing in **le vieux Montréal** (luh vyuh mohN-rey-ahl) (*the old Montreal*). They're getting hungry, and the street is lined with restaurants.

Julie: **Je meurs de faim, pas toi?**
           zhuh muhr duh faN, pah twah?
           I'm starving, aren't you?

Mike: **Moi aussi! Tu veux un sandwich?**
           mwah oh-see! tew vuh uhN sahN-dweesh?
           Me too! Do you want a sandwich?

Julie: **Oh non, il y a un tas de bons petits restaurants pas chers ici. Et puis je suis fatiguée.**
           oh nohN, eel ee ah uhN tah duh bohN puh-tee rehs-toh-rahN pah shehr ee-see. ey pwee zhuh swee fah-tee-gey.
           Oh no, there are plenty of inexpensive little restaurants here. And I am tired.

Mike: **Bon, d'accord. Alors, on mange dehors!**
           bohN, dah-kohr. ah-lohr, ohN mahNzh duh-ohr!
           Well, okay. Let's eat outside then!

After looking at a few places, they settle on a little bistro with a lovely terrace. They sit down and **le serveur** (luh sehr-vuhr) (*the waiter*) brings them the menu.

Le serveur:	**Vous voulez boire quelque chose?**
	vooh vooh-ley bwahr kehl-kuh shohz?
	Would you like something to drink?

Julie:	**Un verre de vin blanc, s'il vous plaît.**
	uhN vehr duh vaN blahN, seel vooh pleh.
	A glass of white wine, please.

Mike:	**Et pour moi, une bière.**
	ey poohr mwah, ewn byehr.
	And for me, a beer.

A few minutes later, the waiter comes back with the drinks.

Le serveur:	**Voilà vos boissons. Vous avez choisi?**
	vwah-lah voh bwah-sohN. vooh-zah-vey shwah-zee?
	Here are your drinks. Have you decided?

Julie:	**Oui, je voudrais le poulet avec des pommes de terre et une salade verte.**
	wee, zhuh vooh-dreh luh pooh-leh ah-vehk dey pohhm duh tehr ey ewn sah-lahd vehrt.
	Yes, I would like the chicken with potatoes and a green salad.

Mike:	**Moi, je prends le steak-frites.**
	mwah, zhuh prahN luh stehk-freet.
	Me, I'll have the steak with fries.

Le serveur:	**Et comme boisson, la même chose?**
	ey kohhm bwah-sohN, lah mehm shohz?
	Would you like the same thing to drink?

Mike:	**Oui, merci.**
	wee, mehr-see.
	Yes, thank you.

Words to Know

moi aussi	mwah oh-see	me too
un tas de	uhN tah duh	lot's of, plenty of
cher/pas cher	shehr/pah shehr	expensive/ inexpensive
dehors	duh-ohr	outside
Avez-vous choisi?	Ah-vey vooh shwah-zee?	Have you decided (chosen)?
la même chose	lah mehm shohz	the same thing

Paying the bill

After you finish your lovely meal, it's time to pay the bill. But don't expect a waiter in France to bring you the check before you ask for it. (That's considered pushy and impolite.) To get your check, call the waiter and say **L'addition, s'il vous plaît** (lah-dee-syohN, seel vooh pleh) (*Check, please*).

In France, the tax and a 15 percent tip are included in the price list: **le pourboire est compris** (luh poohr-bwahr eh kohN-pree) or **le service est compris** (luh sehr-vees eh kohN-pree) (*the tip is included*). What you see is what you get. Of course, you may tip extra if you so desire, especially in a very good restaurant, but in cafés and ordinary restaurants, you don't have to. In Canada, a tax is added to your check, and the waiter expects to be tipped in addition (about 15 percent).

Le pourboire (luh poohr-bwahr) (*the tip*) is a funny word in French. It literally means *in order to drink*. This very old word dates back to the 17th century when it was customary to give a tip so the recipient could go and buy himself a drink (alcoholic supposedly). The name has remained, but its function has changed; today many waiters and theater ushers are paid only with tips.

Talkin' the Talk

 Julie and Mike are thoroughly enjoying their meal and relaxing when the waiter comes along. (Track 8)

Le serveur: **Vous voulez un dessert?**
              vooh vooh-ley uhN deh-sehr?
              Would you like dessert?

Julie: **Non, merci. Deux cafés seulement et l'addition.**
              nohN, mehr-see. duh kah-fey suhl-mahN ey
              lah-dee-syohN.
              No, thank you, just two coffees and the check.

The waiter comes back with the check, and Mike takes out his credit card.

Mike: **Vous prenez les cartes de crédit?**
              vooh pruh-ney ley kahrt duh krey-dee?
              Do you take credit cards?

Le serveur: **Bien sûr, monsieur.**
              byaN sewr, muh-syuh.
              Of course, sir.

Finding the restrooms

Before leaving the restaurant, you may want to visit the restroom, in which case you ask **Où sont les toilettes, s'il vous plaît?** (ooh sohN ley twah-leht, seel vooh pleh?) (*Where are the restrooms?*). In French restaurants, the restrooms are usually located **en bas** (ahN bah) (*downstairs*). Don't forget to take some change along with you; you often have to pay to get in! In most places, the pictogram is self-explanatory, but you may also see **Dames** (dahm) (*women*) or **Hommes** (ohhm) (*men*) written on the door.

Going to the Market

Outdoor markets are a delight. They're especially nice in small, country villages, where you can enjoy the local fare and delight in the noises, smells, and accents. But big cities have wonderful markets, too. Certain Paris districts have a market most days of the week in the morning, rain or shine.

Montréal is famous for its outdoor all-day markets during the summer months. The largest places and many small town squares also have **les halles** (ley ahl) (*an indoor market*). What better way to try out your French? After all, you can point to what you want and maybe learn the right word from a friendly vendor. Vendors in an outdoor market sell almost everything. In many of them, you can even find clothes, shoes, kitchen utensils, and, of course, flowers.

Making purchases with the verbs "acheter" and "vendre"

It is just too tempting to go to **le marché** (luh mahr-shey) (*outdoor market*) and not buy anything. These markets are great places to buy the freshest and most deliciously ripe fruit for your next snack, or some cheese and bread for your picnic. Whatever your purchases, you make them with the use of the verbs **acheter** (ahsh-tey) (*to buy*), and venders sell items with the verb **vendre** (vahN-druh) (*to sell*). **Vendre** is a regular **–re** verb (check out Chapter 2 for the conjugation of regular verbs) and **acheter** is a stem changing verb just like the verb **préférer** (prey-fey-rey) (*to prefer*), discussed in Chapter 6. Here are the conjugations of vendre and **acheter.**

Conjugation	Pronunciation
je vends	zhuh vahN
tu vends	tew vahN
il/elle/on vend	eel/ehl/ohN vahN
nous vendons	nooh vahN-dohN
vous vendez	vooh vahN-dey
ils/elles vendent	eel/ehl vahNd

Conjugation	Pronunciation
j'achète	zhah-sheht
tu achètes	tew ah-sheht
il/elle/on achète	eel/ehl/ohN ah-sheht
nous achetons	nooh-zah-shtohN
vous achetez	vooh-zah-shtey
ils/elles achètent	eel-/ehl-zah-sheht

Often, you use **acheter** in its infinitive form. For example, you may say **Je voudrais acheter des cerises** (zhuh vooh-dreh-zahsh-tey dey suh-reez) (*I would like to buy some cherries*). With so much variety at the fruit stands, you don't have to limit yourself. Here is a list of **fruits** (frwee) *(fruit)* you may find at **le marché** (for a list of meats, seafood, and vegetables available at these markets, refer to the lists in the earlier section "Perusing the menu"):

- **la pomme** (lah pohhm) (*apple*)
- **la banane** (lah bah-nahn) (*banana*)
- **la poire** (lah pwahr) (*pear*)
- **la pêche** (lah pehsh) (*peach*)
- **l'abricot** (m) (lah-bree-koh) (*apricot*)
- **la cerise** (lah suh-reez) (*cherry*)
- **la figue** (lah feeg) (*fig*)
- **le raisin** (luh reh-zaN) (*grape*)
- **l'ananas** (m) (lah-nah-nah) (*pineapple*)
- **la prune** (lah prewn) (*plum*)
- **la framboise** (lah frahN-bwahz) (*raspberry*)
- **l'orange** (f.) (lohr-ahNzh) (*orange*)
- **la fraise** (lah frehz) (*strawberry*)
- **la pastèque** (lah pahs-tehk) (*watermelon*)

Of course, you can't have only one grape or one raspberry, right? To make any of these fruit plural, just make the articles plural **(les)** (ley) (*the*) or ask for some by using the indefinite article **des** (dey) (*some*): for example, **Je voudrais des abricots** (zhuh vooh-dreh deyz-ah-bree-koh) (*I would like some apricots*). Also check out the following section on the metric system to buy a specific quantity.

Specifying how much you want

The metric system was adapted by the French in the 18th century and is used in the majority of countries around the world. If you travel to France or to any other country for that matter, being familiar with the metric system is very handy, especially when you want to buy something scrumptious at the market.

The basic metric unit of weight is the gram, and you usually buy fruit, vegetables, or meat in multiples of the basic gram. Table 8-1 lists the values for the gram.

Table 8-1	Measuring Amounts in Grams		
French	*Pronunciation*	*Translation*	*Conversion*
un gramme	uhN grahm	*1 gram (g)*	1 lb. = 453.60 (g)
un kilogramme/ un kilo	uhN kee-loh-grahm/uhN kee-loh	*1 kilogram (kg)*	1kg = 1000 g, about 2.2 lbs.
un demi-kilo/une livre	uhN duh-mee-kee-loh/ewn lee-vruh	*half a kilogram/a pound*	½ kg = 500 g, = about 1.1 lb.

If you want a pound of cherries, for example, make sure you ask for **une livre de cerises** (ewn lee-vruh duh suh-reez) (*a pound of cherries*) because if you ask for **un kilo de cerises** (uhN kee-loh duh suh-reez), you'll definitely get much more than you can eat!

Metric units are also important when you're traveling, especially when you have to determine distances (meters) or fill up your gas tank (liters). For information on the metric conversions for those units, head to Chapter 15.

Talkin' the Talk

Friday morning is **le jour du marché** (luh zhoohr dew mahr-shey) (*market day*). Madame Arnaud takes her nephew Thibaud along with her to go shopping at the local outdoor market.

Mme Arnaud:
Thibaud, qu'est-ce que tu aimes comme fruits?
tee-boh, kehs-kuh tew ehm kohhm frwee?
Thibaud, *what kind of fruit do you like?*

Thibaud:
Tous! Mais à cette saison, je préfère les pêches.
toohs! meh ah seht seh-zohN, zhuh prey-fehr ley pehsh.
All of them, but at this time of year, I prefer peaches.

Madame Arnaud and Thibaud wait in line at the fruit stand. When their turn comes, Madame Arnaud addresses **le vendeur** (luh vahN-duhr) (*the vendor*).

Mme Arnaud:	**Donnez-moi un kilo de pêches, s'il vous plaît.**
	dohh-ney-mwah uhN kee-loh duh pehsh, seel vooh pleh.
	Give me 1 kilogram (2.2 pounds) of peaches, please.

Le vendeur:	**Voilà madame, et avec ça?**
	vwah-lah mah-dahm, ey ah-vehk sah?
	Here you are, ma'am, anything else?

Mme Arnaud:	**Je voudrais aussi un demi-kilo d'abricots et un demi-kilo de raisins.**
	zhuh vooh-dreh oh-see uhN duh-mee kee-loh dah-bree-koh ey uhN duh-mee kee-loh duh reh-zaN.
	I would also like a pound of apricots and a pound of grapes.

Le vendeur:	**Très bien madame. C'est tout?**
	treh byaN mah-dahm. seh tooh?
	Very well, ma'am. Would that be all?

Mme Arnaud:	**C'est tout merci. Ça fait combien?**
	seh tooh mehr-see. sah feh kohN-byaN?
	That's all, thank you. How much is it?

Le vendeur:	**Huit euros.**
	weet-uh-roh.
	Eight euros.

Words to Know

tous	toohs	all of them
mais	meh	but
donnez-moi	dohh-ney-mwah	give me
Voilà	vwah-lah	There you go
Et avec ça?	ey ah-vehk sah	Anything else? And with that?
C'est tout	seh tooh	That's all
Ça fait combien?	sah feh kohN-byaN	How much is it?

Shopping at neighborhood food shops

When you don't have time to go to the outdoor market, or you can't find what you need at the little store, the supermarket comes in handy. France has some huge supermarkets that line the highways as you enter a city. Some of them are so large that they are called **hypermarchés** (ee-pehr-mahr-shey) (*hypermarkets*) instead of **supermarchés** (sew-pehr-mahr-shey) (*supermarkets*). Here, you can find absolutely everything: food, clothes, computers, large appliances, and sometimes even cars! They're certainly convenient, but if you visit France and have some time on your hands, go discover the little neighborhood food stores. You're sure to enjoy them.

Because supermarkets are often rather far from the inner city, the French do their daily shopping in the neighborhood stores. They can buy their bread, meat, and vegetables daily because the stores are so conveniently close to each other. Following are some of **les petits magasins** (ley puh-tee mah-gah-zaN) (*the little [food] stores*) that you would find in most neighborhoods throughout France:

- ✔ **la boulangerie** (lah booh-lahN-zhree) (*the bakery*). **La boulangerie** sells bread and bread products, like **des croissants** (dey krwah-sahN) (*croissants*), and **du pain aux raisins** (dew paN oh reh-zaN) (*raisin bread*).

- ✔ **la pâtisserie** (lah pah-tees-ree) (*the confectioner's shop*). These shops specialize in cakes and pastries, usually of a higher quality. They don't sell bread.

- ✔ **la boucherie** (lah booh-shree) (*the butcher shop*). Here you can find fresh cuts of all sorts of meats like beef, veal, lamb, goat, and chicken.

- ✔ **la charcuterie** (lah shahr-kew-tree) (*deli, butcher shop*). These shops specialize in pork and prepared foods.

- ✔ **la poissonnerie** (lah pwah-sohn-ree) (*the fish store*).

- ✔ **l'épicerie** (f) (ley-pees-ree) (*the grocery store*). **L'épicerie** is more like a general store.

- ✔ **la crèmerie** (lah krehm-ree) (*the dairy shop*). This is where you can buy dairy products and cheese.

- ✔ **le marchand de fruits et légumes** (luh mahr-shahN duh frwee ey ley-gewm) (*the produce vendor*). These stores have all kinds of fresh vegetables.

A fairly large number of people — mostly older — still go shopping for food every morning in France. They walk from store to store buying everything they need for the day's meals. It's also not unusual for the French, especially in big cities, to buy bread twice a day. French bread is made without preservatives and doesn't keep well, so buying in small quantities more often makes better sense. Plus, French bread tastes so good when it's freshly baked!

Fun & Games

Identify the items illustrated in each of the following pictures.

A. _____

B. _____

C. _____

D. _____

E. _____

F. _____

G. _____

H. _____

Chapter 9

Shopping Made Easy

• •

In This Chapter

▶ Browsing at the store and asking for help

▶ Using demonstrative adjectives and pronouns to point things out

▶ Recognizing sizes, colors, and materials

▶ Using comparatives and superlatives

• •

*L*e shopping (luh shoh-peeng) (*shopping*) — what a fun thing to do wherever you are. And when you're in a foreign country, you probably want to bring back that special souvenir, like a bottle of perfume, a lovely designer scarf or handbag, or a CD full of wonderful songs that remind you of your travels. Whether you're in Paris, Montreal, Geneva, or Brussels, you are in a shopper's paradise! Although what you buy in these places won't come cheap, you'll have your selection of the best of the best. And after all, **une fois n'est pas coutume** (ewn fwah neh pah kooh-tewm) (*once is not a habit, or once [in a while] does no harm*).

In this chapter, we explain everything you need to know to shop, including vocabulary for a variety of items, how to ask for assistance, what to say when you want to try something on, and more.

Going Shopping

Where you go shopping depends on what you want to buy. For some items, a discount store is the better choice; for others, only an upscale department store or boutique is the answer. Here are a few of your choices:

- ✔ **un hypermarché** (uhN-nee-pehr-mahr-shey) (*a hypermarket*). In these large discount stores, you can buy everything from food to electronic equipment.

- ✔ **un grand magasin** (uhN grahN mah-gah-zaN)(*a department store*).

- ✔ **un centre commercial** (uhN sahN-truh koh-mehr-syahl) (*a shopping mall*).

- ✔ **une boutique** (ewn booh-teek) (*a specialty shop/a boutique*).

   ✔ **une librairie** (ewn lee-brey-ree) (*a bookstore*)

   ✔ **une bijouterie** (ewn bee-zhooh-tree) (*a jewelry store*)

   ✔ **une dépanneuse** (ewn dey-pah-nuhz) (*a convenience store* [Québec])

Dépanner (dey-pah-ney) means *to help out,* and people in France and in Québec understand it that way but use it for different purposes. In Québec, **une dépanneuse** (ewn dey-pah-nuhz) is one of those convenience stores that are open all the time and where you can stop when you run out of bread or milk. In France, **une dépanneuse** is a tow-truck. They both help you out, don't they?

Pay attention to opening hours. Canada is pretty much the same as the United States. But in France, all department stores and malls are closed on Sundays. Many stores close at lunch time, especially outside of big cities, although this is less and less the case. Most stores are closed on Mondays, but department stores usually stay open. So before you go shopping, call ahead to find out about the store's hours. These questions can help:

   A quelle heure ouvrez-vous/fermez-vous? (ah keh-luhr ooh-vrey-vooh/fehr-mey-vooh?) (*At what time do you open/close?*)

   Etes-vous ouverts le dimanche? (eht-vooh-zooh-vehr luh dee-mahNsh?) (*Are you open on Sundays?*)

Shopping for clothes, item by item

You may be looking for clothes or shoes or something for yourself or for a loved one. Here's a list of **vêtements pour dames** (veht-mahN poohr dahm) (*women's clothes*) that may come in handy; some of these items can also be worn by men:

   ✔ **un chemisier** (uhN shuh-mee-zyey) (*a blouse*)

   ✔ **une chemise de nuit** (ewn shuh-meez duh nwee) (*a night gown*)

   ✔ **un costume de bain** (uhN kohs-tewm duh baN) (*a bathing suit* [Québec])

   ✔ **un foulard** (uhN fooh-lahr) (*a scarf*)

   ✔ **un imperméable** (uhN-naN-pehr-mey-ah-bluh) (*a raincoat*)

   ✔ **une jupe** (ewn zhewp) (*a skirt*)

   ✔ **un jean** (uhN jeen) (*jeans*)

   ✔ **un manteau** (uhN mahN-toh) (*a coat*)

   ✔ **un maillot de bain** (uhN mah-yoh duh baN) (*a bathing suit* [France])

   ✔ **un pantalon** (uhN pahN-tah-lohN) (*slacks*)

✔ **une robe** (ewn rohhb) (*a dress*)

✔ **une robe de chambre** (ewn rohhb duh shahN-bruh) (*a dressing gown/ a robe*)

✔ **des sous-vêtements** (m) (dey sooh-veht-mahN) (*underwear*)

✔ **un tailleur** (uhN tah-yuhr) (*a woman's suit*)

✔ **une veste** (ewn vehst) (*a jacket*)

And now for the **vêtements pour hommes** (veht-mahN pooh-rohhm) (*men's clothes*). Of course, some of these items can also be worn by women:

✔ **une ceinture** (ewn saN-tewr) (*a belt*)

✔ **un chapeau** (uhN shah-poh) (*a hat*)

✔ **des chaussettes** (dey shoh-seht) (*socks*)

✔ **une chemise** (ewn shuh-meez) (*a shirt*)

✔ **un complet** (uhN kohN-pleh) (*a man's suit* [France])

✔ **une cravate** (ewn krah-vaht) (*a tie*)

✔ **un habit** (uhN-nah-bee) (*a suit* [Québec])

✔ **un pardessus** (uhN pahr-duh-sew) (*an overcoat*)

✔ **un veston** (uhN vehs-tohN) (*a suit jacket*)

French has borrowed many English words for clothes; here are a few (keep in mind that some have a different meaning):

✔ **le jogging** (luh zhoh-geeng) (*warm-up suit*)

✔ **le pull** (luh pewl) (*sweater*)

✔ **le slip** (luh sleep) (*underpants*)

✔ **le sweat** (luh sweht) (*sweat shirt*)

✔ **le tee-shirt** (luh tee-shuhrt) (*T-shirt*)

When shopping for **une paire de chaussures** (ewn pehr duh shoh-sewr) (*a pair of shoes*), use these terms:

✔ **les baskets** (ley bahs-keht) (*sneakers*)

✔ **les bottes** (ley bohht) (*boots*)

✔ **les chaussons/les pantoufles** (ley shoh-sohN/ley pahN-tooh-fluh) (*slippers*)

✔ **les chaussures à talons** (ley shoh-sew-rah tah-lohN) (*high-heeled shoes*)

✔ **les sandales** (ley sahN-dahl) (*sandals*)

✔ **les tennis** (ley tey-nees) (*sneakers*)

Navigating your way around

Most stores have familiar layouts. Here are the terms you need to know to navigate your way around a store:

- ✔ **le rez-de-chaussée** (luh reyd-shoh-sey) (*the ground* [first] *floor*)
- ✔ **le premier étage** (luh pruh-myey-rey-tahzh) (*the first* [second] *floor*)
- ✔ **le deuxième étage** (luh duh-zee-ehm ey-tahzh) (*the second* [third] *floor*)
- ✔ **le troisième étage** (luh trwah-zee-ehm ey-tahzh) (*the third* [fourth] *floor*)
- ✔ **le sous-sol** (luh sooh-sohl) (*the basement*)
- ✔ **l'escalier roulant** (m) (lehs-kah-lyey rooh-lahN) (*the escalator*)
- ✔ **l'ascenseur** (m) (lah-sahN-suhr) (*the elevator*)
- ✔ **le rayon** (luh reh-yohN) (*department*)
- ✔ **les cabines d'essayage** (ley kah-been deh-sey-ahzh) (*fitting rooms*)
- ✔ **les toilettes** (ley twah-leht) (*restrooms*)

The French consider the first floor to be the ground floor and start counting *after* the ground floor.

Getting assistance

Although salesclerks won't bother you in discount and convenience stores, if you shop at department stores or boutiques, you'll probably hear a *saleslady,* **une vendeuse** (ewn vahN-duhz), asking you **Je peux vous aider?** (zhuh puh vooh-zey-dey) (*Can I help you?*). If you're just browsing and don't need help, you can say **Non, merci, je regarde seulement** (nohN, mehr-see, zhuh ruh-gahrd suhl-mahN) (*No thank you, I am just looking*). However, if you do need help, you may use any of the following phrases:

- ✔ **Pouvez-vous m'aider s'il vous plaît?** (pooh-vey-vooh mey-dey seel vooh pleh?) (*Can you help me, please?*)
- ✔ **Je voudrais un renseignement.** (zhuh vooh-dreh uhN rahN-seh-nyuh-mahN.) (*I would like some information.*)
- ✔ **Je cherche . . . .** (zhuh shehrsh. . . .) (*I am looking for . . . .*)

The French language does not make a distinction between the notions represented by *I can* and *I may*. Both use **je peux** (zhuh puh). The verb is the irregular **pouvoir** (pooh-vwahr). (Check out Chapter 8 for the conjugation of **pouvoir** in the conditional tense, which you use to make polite requests.) You conjugate the present tense as follows:

Conjugation	*Pronunciation*
je peux	zhuh puh
tu peux	tew puh
il/elle/on peut	eel/ehl/ohN puh
nous pouvons	nooh pooh-vohN
vous pouvez	vooh-pooh-vey
ils/elles peuvent	eel/ehl puhv

The verb **pouvoir** is always followed by an infinitive. Notice that when the sentence has an object pronoun, you place the object pronoun between the conjugated form of **pouvoir** and the infinitive (for more on indirect object pronouns, go to Chapter 13). Here are some examples:

> **Est-ce que vous pouvez me renseigner?** (ehs-kuh vooh pooh-vey muh rahN-sey-nyey?) (*Can you give me some information?*)

> **Est-ce que je peux l'essayer?** (ehs-kuh zhuh puh ley-sey-yey?) (*Can I try it on?*)

If no salesclerk is in sight, you can look for the *information counter,* **les renseignements** (ley rahN-seh-nyuh-mahN) or **le service clients** (luh sehr-vees klee-yahN). Most likely, someone there speaks English, but if not, don't worry. If you know the following phrases and responses, you can find your way around:

> **Pardon madame, où sont les parfums?** (pahr-dohN mah-dahm, ooh sohN ley pahr-faN?) (*Excuse me, ma'am, where are the perfumes?*)

> **Ici, au rez-de-chaussée.** (ee-see, oh reyd-shoh-sey.) (Here, on the ground floor.)

> **Les vêtements pour dames, s'il vous plaît.** (ley veht-mahN poohr dahm, seel vooh pleh.) (*Ladies' clothes, please.*)

> **C'est au troisième étage.** (seh-toh trwah-zee-ehm ey-tahzh.) (*It is on the third* [fourth] *floor.*)

Excusez-moi, je cherche les compacts disques. (eks-kew-zey-mwah, zhuh shehrsh ley kohN-pahkt deesk.) (*Excuse me, I am looking for the CDs.*)

Ils sont au sous-sol, à côté des livres. (eel sohN-toh sooh-sohl ah koh-tey dey lee-vruh.) (*They are in the basement, next to the books.*)

Finding the right fit

Clothes shopping involves finding the right size. In this section, we help you do just that.

In Canada, clothes sizes are the same as in the United States. In Europe, you may find different ways of measuring, depending on the country. Here are the rough equivalents for sizes of women's clothes:

Canadian and U.S. sizes	2	4	6	8	10	12	14	16	18	20
French sizes	32	34	36	38	40	42	44	46	48	50

For men's jacket and suit sizes, use the following approximate conversions:

Canadian and U.S. sizes	34	36	38	40	42	44	46	48	50
French sizes	44	46	48	50	52	54	56	58	60

Of course, if everything else fails, you can always ask for **petit** (puh-tee) (*small*), **moyen/médium** (mwah-yaN/mey-dyohhm) (*medium*), **large** (lahrzh) (*large*), or **extra-large** (ehks-trah lahrzh) (*extra-large*).

The French word for *size* is **la taille** (lah tahy). But often you don't even have to say the word, as these examples show:

Je fais du 36. (zhuh feh dew trahNt-sees.) (*I am a [size] 36.*)

Je voudrais essayer une robe en 40. (zhuh vooh-dreh ey-sey-yey ewn rohh-bahN kah-rahNt.) (*I would like to try a dress in [size] 40.*)

Est-que vous l'avez en plus petit? (ehs-kuh vooh lah-vey ahN plew puh-tee?) (*Do you have it in a small[er size]?*)

English has only one word for clothes and shoe sizes, but French has two words: **la taille** works for height and clothes, and **la pointure** (lah pwaN-tewr) is for shoes.

To describe how something fits, you use the phrase **Ça. . . va** (sah. . . vah) (_It fits. . ._). Between **Ça. . . va** you indicate who it fits. Here are some examples:

- ✔ **Ça me va.** (sah muh vah.) (_It fits me._)
- ✔ **Ça te va bien.** (sah tuh vah byaN.) (_It fits you well_ [informal]_._)
- ✔ **Ça vous va très bien.** (sah vooh vah treh byaN.) (_It fits you very well._ [formal])
- ✔ **Ça lui va mal.** (sah lwee vah mahl.) (_It fits him/her poorly._)

You can also use the following terms to more specifically describe the fit of an item of clothing:

- ✔ **ample** (ahN-pluh) (_loose_)
- ✔ **étroit/étroite/serré/serrée** (ey-trwah/ey-trwaht/seh-rey/seh-rey) (_tight_)
- ✔ **large** (lahrzh) (_wide_ [shoes])
- ✔ **trop court/courte** (troh koohr/koohrt) (_too short_)
- ✔ **trop grand/grande** (troh grahN/grahNd) (_too big_)
- ✔ **trop long/longue** (troh lohN/lohNg) (_too long_)
- ✔ **trop petit/petite** (troh puh-tee/puh-teet) (_too small_)

Here are some examples:

> **Cette jupe est trop courte.** (seht zhewp eh troh koohrt.) (_This skirt is too short._)

> **Ces chaussures sont étroites.** (sey shoh-sewr sohN-tey-trwaht.) (_These shoes are tight._)

Talkin' the Talk

 Cécile is shopping for a dress and has spotted one that she likes. The saleslady approaches her. (Track 9)

La vendeuse: **Je peux vous aider, madame?**
zhuh puh vooh-zey-dey, mah-dahm?
Can I help you, ma'am?

Cécile: **Oui, s'il vous plaît. Avez-vous cette robe en 36?**
wee, seel vooh pleh. ah-vey-vooh seht rohh-bahN trahNt-sees?
Yes, please. Do you have this dress in size 36?

La vendeuse: **Attendez un instant. Oui, nous l'avons. La voilà.**
ah-tahN-dey uhN-naN-stahN. wee, nooh lah-vohN. lah vwah-lah.
Wait a moment. Yes, we have it. There it is.

Cécile: **Est-ce que je peux l'essayer?**
ehs-kuh zhuh puh ley-sey-yey?
May I try it on?

La vendeuse: **Mais bien sûr, madame. Les cabines d'essayage sont au fond à gauche.**
meh byaN sewr, mah-dahm. ley kah-been dey-sey-yahzh sohN-toh-fohN ah gohsh.
But of course, ma'am. The fitting-rooms are in the back on the left.

A few minutes later, Cécile comes out of the fitting room with the dress on and asks the saleslady's opinion.

Cécile: **Qu'est-ce que vous en pensez?**
kehs-kuh vooh-zahN pahN-sey?
What do you think of it?

La vendeuse: **Je ne sais pas . . . elle est un peu trop grande, je crois.**
zhuhn seh pah . . . ehl eh-tuhN puh troh grahNd, zhuh krwah.
I don't know . . . it's a little too big, I think.

Cécile: **Moi, je trouve qu'elle ne me va pas du tout. Est-ce que vous l'avez en plus petit?**
mwah, zhuh troohv kehl nuh muh vah pah dew tooh. ehs-kuh vooh lah-vey ahN plew puh-tee?
I think it does not fit me at all. Do you have it in a smaller size?

La vendeuse: **Non, je suis désolée; c'est la plus petite taille.**
nohN, zhuh swee dey-zoh-ley; seh lah plew puh-teet tahy.
No, I am sorry; it is the smallest size.

Cécile: **Tant pis!**
tahN pee!
Too bad!

Words to know

attendez un instant	ah-tahN-dey uhN-naN-stahN	wait a moment
au fond	oh fohN	in the back
à gauche	ah gohsh	on the left
à droite	ah drwaht	on the right
je trouve/pense	zhuh troohv/pahNs	I think
un peu	uhN puh	a little
trop	troh	too much
pas du tout	pah dew tooh	not at all
tant pis	tahN pee	too bad

Pointing items out with "this," "that," "these," and "those"

Periodically, you want to draw attention to a particular item. If you don't know what the item is called (a fairly common situation when you're learning a language), you can always point to it, using these demonstrative adjectives:

- ✔ **ce** (suh) (*this, that*): Use **ce** in front of masculine singular nouns: **ce chemisier** (suh shuh-mee-zyey) (*this blouse, that blouse*), for example.

- ✔ **cet** (seht) (*this, that*): Use **cet** in front of masculine singular nouns that begin with a vowel or a mute h: **cet imperméable** (seh-taN-pehr-mey-ah-bluh) (*this raincoat, that raincoat*). (Go to Chapter 3 for more on the mute h.)

- ✔ **cette** (seht) (*this, that*): Use **cette** in front of feminine singular nouns: **cette veste** (seht vehst) (*this jacket, that jacket*), for example.

- ✔ **ces** (sey) (*these, those*): Use **ces** in front of masculine and feminine plural nouns: **ces chaussures** (sey shoh-sewr) (*these/those shoes*), for example.

Notice that the demonstrative adjectives mean both *this* and *that* in the singular, and *these* and *those* in the plural. If you need to distinguish between two items (this suit and that suit, for example, or these boots and those boots), then you add the suffixes **–ci** (–see) and **–là** (–lah) to the nouns:

- ✔ Adding the suffix **–ci** to a singular noun translates as *this*; adding **–ci** to a plural noun translates as *these*.

- ✔ Adding the suffix **–là** to a singular noun translates as *that*, adding **–là** to a plural noun translates as *those*.

Check out these examples:

> **Cette robe-ci est plus jolie que cette robe-là.** (seht rohhb-see eh plew zhoh-lee kuh seht rohhb-lah.) (*This dress is prettier than that dress.*)

> **Ces magasins-ci sont plus chers que ces magasins-là.** (sey-mah-gah-zahN-see sohN plew shehr kuh sey mah-gah-zahN lah.) (*These stores are more expensive than those stores.*)

Moving on to demonstrative pronouns

If you don't want to sound like a robot every time you speak, you can easily avoid being redundant by replacing the demonstrative adjective and the noun with a pronoun. Instead of saying *this dress is prettier than that dress,* for example, you can say *this one is prettier than that one* or *this dress is prettier than that one.* The French demonstrative pronouns need the suffix **–ci** and **–là** because they cannot stand alone. Table 9-1 lists the demonstrative pronouns.

Table 9-1	French Demonstrative Pronouns	
Demonstrative Pronouns	*Replaces*	*Example*
celui-ci, celui-là (suh-lwee-see, suh-lwee-lah) (*this one, that one*)	Masculine singular demonstrative adjective and noun	**ce chemisier-ci** (suh shuh-mee-zyey-see) (*this blouse*) becomes **celui-ci** (*this one*)
celle-ci, celle-là (sehl-see, sehl-lah) (*this one, that one*)	Feminine singular demonstrative adjective and noun	**cette chemise-là** (seht sheh-meez-lah) (*that shirt*) becomes **celle-là** (*that one*)
ceux-ci, ceux-là (suh-see, suh-lah) (*these ones, those ones*)	Masculine plural demonstrative adjective and noun	**ces vêtements-ci** (sey veht-mahN-see) (*these clothes*) becomes **ceux-ci** (suh-see) (*these ones*)
celles-ci, celles-là (sehl-see, sehl-lah) (*these ones, those ones*)	Feminine plural demonstrative adjective and noun	**ces bottes-là** (sey bohht-lah) (*those boots*) becomes **celles-là** (*those ones*)

Choosing the right fabric and color

When you're shopping for clothing, you may have a particular *fabric* — **le tissu** (luh tee-sew) — in mind. Being able to express your preference to the salesclerk gives her the information she needs to direct you to the right area. So here's a list of common fabrics:

✔ **la laine** (lah lehn) (*wool*)

✔ **la soie** (lah swah) (*silk*)

✔ **le coton** (luh koh-tohN) (*cotton*)

✔ **le velours côtelé** (luh vuh-loohr koht-ley) (*corduroy* [France]), or **le corduroy** (luh kohr-dew-rwah) (*corduroy* [Québec])

✔ **la flanelle** (lah flah-nehl) (*flannel*)

✔ **le lin** (luh laN) (*linen*)

✔ **le cuir** (luh kweer) (*leather*)

When talking about *fabrics*, you use **en** after the verb or **de** after the noun, as in these examples:

> **Cette veste est <u>en</u> laine.** (seht vehs-teh-tahN lehn) (*This jacket is [made] of wool.*)
>
> **C'est une veste <u>de</u> laine.** (seh-town vehst duh lehn.) (*It is a wool jacket.*)
>
> **Je voudrais un foulard <u>de</u> soie.** (zhuh vooh-dreh uhN fooh-lahr duh swah.) (*I would like a silk scarf.*)
>
> **Est-ce que ces chaussures sont <u>en</u> cuir?** (ehs-kuh sey shoh-sewr sohN-tahN kweer?) (*Are these shoes [made of] leather?*)

When you're picking out clothes, what's more important than the color? Remember that, when you're describing the color of an article of clothing, the color is an adjective. Like all adjectives, it must agree in gender and in number with the noun it modifies (refer to Chapter 2 for information on agreement). Following is a list of colors; those with an asterisk after them are *invariable,* meaning that they have only one form, even in the plural:

- **blanc/blanche** (blahN/blahNsh) (*white*)
- **bleu/bleue** (bluh) (*blue*)
- **jaune/jaune** (zhohn) (*yellow*)
- **marron*** (mah-rohN) (*brown*)
- **noir/noire** (nwahr) (*black*)
- **orange*** (oh-rahNzh) (*orange*)
- **rouge/rouge** (roohzh) (*red*)
- **vert/verte** (vehr/vehrt) (*green*)

The color adjective always follows the noun, as shown in these examples:

> **un pantalon noir** (uhN pahN-tah-lohN nwahr) (*black pants*)
>
> **des chaussures marron** (dey shoh-sewr mah-rohN) (*brown shoes*)
>
> **une jupe verte** (ewn zhewp vehrt) (*a green skirt*)

Talkin' the Talk

Vincent is looking for a sports jacket. He enters **une boutique de vêtements pour hommes** (ewn booh-teek duh veht-mahN pooh-rohhm) (*a men's clothing store*). At this time of year, many clothes are *on sale* (**en solde**) (ahN sohld). He is immediately greeted by **le vendeur** (luh vahN-duhr) (*the clerk*) and presents his request.

Vincent: **Je cherche une veste.**
zhuh shehr-shewn vehst.
I am looking for a jacket.

Le vendeur: **Quel genre de veste voulez-vous, monsieur, un blazer, un veston habillé?**
kehl zhahNr duh vehst vooh-ley-vooh, muh-syuh, uhN blah-zehr, uhN vehs-tohN ah-bee-yey?
What type of jacket do you want, sir, a blazer, a dressy suit jacket?

Vincent: **Non, plutôt une veste de sport.**
nohN, plew-toh ewn vehst duh spohr.
No, rather a sports jacket.

Le vendeur: **En quelle taille?**
ahN kehl tahy?
In what size?

Vincent: **En général, je porte du 50.**
ahN zhey-ney-rahl, zhuh pohrt dew saN-kahNt.
Usually, I wear a [size] 50.

Le vendeur: **Nous avons ce modèle, ou celui-ci en pure laine.**
nooh-zah-vohN suh moh-dehl, ooh suh-lwee-see ahN pewr lehn.
We have this style or this one in pure wool.

Vincent: **Je préfère une couleur plus foncée, bleu foncé, peut-être.**
zhuh prey-fehr ewn kooh-luhr plew fohN-sey, bluh fohN-sey, puh-teh-truh.
I prefer a darker color, dark blue, perhaps.

Vincent chooses a jacket and tries it on.

Le vendeur: **Oh, celle-ci vous va à merveille! Et elle est très à la mode.**
oh, sehl-see vooh vah ah mehr-vehy! ey ehl eh-treh-zah lah mohhd.
Oh, this one looks great on you! And it's very much in fashion.

Vincent: **Oui, vous avez raison et elle est en solde! Alors je la prends.**
wee, vooh-zah-vey rey-zohN ey ehl eh-tahN sohld! ah-lohr zhuh lah prahN.
Yes, you're right, and it's on sale! Then I'll take it.

Words to Know

foncé(e)	fohN-sey	dark
clair	klehr	light-colored
Ça vous va à merveille	sah vooh vah ah mehr-vehy	It looks great on you
à la mode	ah lah mohhd	in fashion, in style
les soldes	ley sohld	sales [France]

Making Comparisons: Good, Better, Best, and More

To make a comparison between two objects or two people, the French language uses the following constructions for all adjectives and adverbs:

- ✔ **plus . . . que** (plew . . . kuh) *(more . . . than)*
- ✔ **moins . . . que** (mwaN . . . que) *(less . . . than)*
- ✔ **aussi . . . que** (oh-see . . . kuh) *(as . . . as)*

Here are a few examples:

- ✔ **La librairie est plus grande que la bijouterie.** (lah lee-brey-ree eh plew grahNd kuh lah bee-zhooh-tree.) *(The bookstore is bigger than the jewelry store.)*

- ✔ **Les imperméables sont aussi chers que les manteaux.** (ley-zaN-pehr-mey-ah-bluh sohN-toh-see shehr kuh ley mahN-toh.) *(The raincoats are as expensive as the coats.)*

- ✔ **Ces chaussures-ci sont moins étroites que celles-là.** (sey shoh-sewr-see sohN mwaN-zey-trwaht kuh sehl-lah.) *(These shoes are less narrow than those.)*

When you want to say something is the best — or the most awful — you use a superlative in French as well as in English. Superlatives are constructed in two ways in French, depending on whether the adjective precedes or follows the noun. In both cases, the superlative construction always comes before the adjective; however, when the adjective follows the noun, the difference is that the definite articles **le, la,** or **les** precede both the noun and the superlative form.

> **C'est la moins jolie robe.** (seh lah mwaN zhoh-lee rohhb.) (*It is the least pretty dress.*) — adjective in front of the noun

> **Elle achète la robe la moins chère de la boutique.** (ehl ah-sheht lah rohhb lah mwaN shehr duh lah booh-teek.) (*She is buying the least expensive dress in the store.*) — adjective following the noun

You can't use the **plus . . . que** comparative construction for **bon** (bohN) (*good*). Just as the English word *good* has its own comparative (*better*) and superlative (*best*) forms, so does **bon:**

- ✔ **meilleur(s)/meilleure(s)** (meh-yuhr) (*better*). Here's an example:

  > **Les bottes de cuir sont meilleures que les bottes de caoutchouc.** (ley bohht duh kweer sohN meh-yuhr kuh ley bohht duh kah-ooh-tzhoohk.) (*Leather boots are better than rubber boots.*)

- ✔ **le/la/les meilleur(s)/meilleure(s)** (luh/lah/ley meh-yuhr) (*the best*). Here's an example:

  > **On trouve le meilleur chocolat en Suisse.** (ohN troohv luh meh-yuhr shoh-koh-lah ahN swees.) (*The best chocolate is found in Switzerland.*)

  > **Les meilleurs produits de cuir se trouvent en Italie.** (ley meh-yuhr proh-dwee duh kweer suh troohv ahN-nee-tah-lee.) (*The best leather products are found in Italy.*)

Talkin' the Talk

Nicole Verdier is shopping for shoes. After looking in the windows of several stores, Nicole sees a pair she really likes and so she goes in to inquire about them.

Nicole: **Bonjour, je voudrais voir les chaussures noires là dans la vitrine.**
bohN-zhoohr, zhuh vooh-dreh vwahr ley shoh-sewr nwahr lah dahN lah vee-treen.
Hello, I would like to see the black shoes there in the window.

La vendeuse: **Bien sûr, madame, en quelle pointure?**
byaN sewr, mah-dahm, ahN kehl pwaN-tewr?
Of course, ma'am, in what size?

Nicole: **Je fais du 38.**
zhuh feh dew trahNt-weet.
I am a 38.

La vendeuse: **Je regrette. En 38, nous les avons seulement en marron.**
zhuh ruh-greht. ahN trahNt-weet, nooh ley-zah-vohN suhl-mahN ahN mah-rohN.
I am sorry. In 38, we only have them in brown.

Nicole: **Bon, montrez-moi les marron.**
bohN, mohN-trey-mwah ley mah-rohN.
Okay, show me the brown ones.

Nicole puts the shoes on.

Nicole: **Elles sont trop étroites. Vous les avez en plus larges?**
ehl sohN troh-pey-trwaht. vooh ley-zah-vey ahN plew lahrzh?
They are too narrow. Do you have them in a wider size?

La vendeuse: **Ah non, madame. Voulez-vous voir un autre modèle?**
ah nohN, mah-dahm. vooh-ley-vooh vwah-ruhN-noh-truh moh-dehl?
No, ma'am. Do you want to see another style?

Nicole is not satisfied and moves on to another store, where she finds a pair she likes that fit her perfectly.

Nicole: **Combien coûtent celles-ci?**
kohN-byaN kooht sehl-see?
How much are these?

La vendeuse: **Cinquante euros.**
saN-kahNt uh-roh.
Fifty euros.

Nicole: **C'est un peu cher, mais elles sont très jolies et puis je dois absolument acheter des chaussures aujourd'hui. Allez, je les prends.**
seh-tuhN puh shehr, meh ehl sohN treh zhoh-lee ey pwee zhuh dwah ahb-soh-lew-mahN ahsh-tey dey shoh-sewr oh-zhoohr-dwee. ah-ley, zhuh ley prahN.
It is a little expensive, but they are very pretty, and I absolutely must buy shoes today. Okay, I'll take them.

La vendeuse: **C'est une très bonne décision, madame.**
seh-tewn treh bohhn dey-see-zyohN, mah-dahm.
It's a very good decision, ma'am.

Words to Know

voir	vwahr	to see
la vitrine	lah vee-treen	the (store) window
montrer	mohN-trey	to show
un autre	uhN-noh-truh	another
Combien coûte . . . ?	kohN-byaN kooht. . . ?	How much is . . . ?
aujourd'hui	oh-zhoohr-dwee	today
absolument	ahb-soh-lew-mahN	absolutely

The verb **devoir** (duh-vwahr) (*to have to*) is followed by an infinitive to express something that you have to do, ought to do, or must do. Here's the conjugation of **devoir** in the present tense:

Conjugation	*Pronunciation*
je dois	zhuh dwah
tu dois	tew dwah
il/elle/on doit	eel/ehl/ohN dwah
nous devons	nooh duh-vohN
vous devez	vooh duh-vey
ils/elles doivent	eel/ehl dwahv

Here are some examples using this verb: **Je dois acheter un manteau aujourd'hui** (zhuh dwah ahsh-tey uhN mahN-toh oh-zhoohr-dwee) (*I must buy, have to buy a coat today*). However **devoir** means *to owe* when followed by a noun: **Je dois cent euros à Catherine** (zhuh dwah sahN-tuh-roh ah kah-treen) (*I owe Catherine 100 euros*).

Fun & Games

identify all of the items of clothing that are labeled in the following drawing.

A. _____

B. _____

C. _____

D. _____

E. _____

F. _____

G. _____

H. _____

I. _____

J. _____

K. _____

Chapter 10

Going Out on the Town

*W*hen you visit a new city or town, you want to have fun trying out as much of the local entertainment as possible. In France, you can find something for everyone, from museums and theater to nightclubs and movies. This chapter has information you can use to discuss where you want to go, make plans with friends, and describe how much fun you had once you got there.

Going Out with the Verb "Sortir"

When you visit a new place, you don't want to just sit in your hotel room; you want to go out and explore the city and partake in everything it has to offer. You can visit the museums, take in a concert or play, or perhaps even go dancing at a nightclub. Whatever your activities, the verb **sortir** (sohr-teer) (*to go out*) will come in handy.

Sortir is an irregular verb, but it is not difficult to conjugate. Here is a little trick you can use to remember how to conjugate not only this verb but a few others like it, such as **partir** (pahr-teer) (*to leave*), **dormir** (dohr-meer) (*to sleep*), **servir** (sehr-veer) (*to serve*), and **mentir** (mahN-teer) (*to lie*):

✔ For the singular, you drop not only the **–ir** from the infinitive but also the consonant before the **–ir**, which leaves you with **sor–**, **par–**, **dor–**, **ser–**, and **men–**. Then you add **s, s, t**.

✔ For the plural, you drop the **–ir** from the infinitive and simply add **ons, ez, ent**.

Check out the conjugation of **sortir**:

Conjugation	*Pronunciation*
je sors	zhuh sohr
tu sors	tew sohr
il/elle/on sort	eel/ehl/ohN sohr
nous sortons	nooh sohr-tohN
vous sortez	vooh sorh-tey
ils/elles sortent	eel/ehl sohrt

Here are some sentences that use the verb **sortir**:

> **Nous sortons ce soir.** (nooh sohr-tohN suh swahr.) (*We are going out this evening.*)

> **Je sors avec mes amis.** (zhuh sohr ah-vehk mey-zah-mee.) (*I am going out with my friends.*)

Sortir is often used in its infinitive form after a verb of preference or wish. For example, you can say **Ils aiment sortir** (eel-zehm sohr-teer) (*They like going out*) or **Elle veut sortir ce soir** (ehl vuh sohr-teer suh swahr) (*She wants to go out this evening*).

Having Fun with the Verb "S'amuser"

What better way to express the fun you are having than with the verb **s'amuser** (sah-mew-zey) (*to have fun*). This verb is a *pronominal verb*, which means that it needs pronominal pronouns, also known as *reflexive pronouns,* which correspond to the subject of the verb.

There are three categories of pronominal verbs: reflexive, reciprocal, and idiomatic:

✔ A reflexive verb is one in which the subject does the action on itself: **Je me lave** (zhuh muh lahv) (*I wash myself*). See Chapter 5 for more on reflexive verbs.

✔ With a reciprocal verb, two or more people are doing the action on each other. For this reason, reciprocal verbs can only be plural: **Ils s'aiment** (eel sehm) (*They love each other*), for example, or **Nous nous écrivons** (nooh nooh-zey-kree-vohN) (*We write to each other*).

✔ An idiomatic verb is one whose meaning cannot be understood from a literal translation of the words. For example, the verb **ennuyer** (ahN-nwee-ey) means *to bother,* but when the same verb is pronominal, **s'ennuyer** (sahN- nwee-ey), it means *to be bored.*

Whatever the category, all pronominal verbs have an object pronoun that you place before the verb. These pronouns are **me** (muh) (*myself*), **te** (tuh) (*yourself*), **se** (suh) (*himself/herself*), **nous** (nooh) (*ourselves*), **vous** (vooh) (*yourself/yourselves*), and **se** (suh) (*themselves*). If the verb is a reflexive verb, these object pronouns are called *reflexive pronouns*. When the verb begins with a vowel or a mute h, you drop the **e** from **me**, **te**, and **se**.

Here is the conjugation of **s'amuser**:

Conjugation	*Pronunciation*
je m'amuse	zhuh mah-mewz
tu t'amuses	tew tah-mewz
il/elle/on s'amuse	eel/ehl/ohN sah-mewz
nous nous amusons	nooh nooh-zah-mew-zohN
vous vous amusez	vooh vooh-zah-mew-zey
ils/elles s'amusent	eel/ehl sah-mewz

These sentences show the verb **s'amuser** in action; notice the reflexive pronouns that appear before the verb:

> **Je m'amuse beaucoup.** (zhuh mah-mewz boh-kooh.) (*I'm having a lot of fun.*)
>
> **Nous nous amusons toujours.** (nooh nooh zah-mew-zohN tooh-zhoohr.) (*We always have fun.*)

When someone is going out, you would ordinarily say *Have fun,* which is the imperative form and therefore doesn't have a subject pronoun (the subject, *you,* is understood). For information on forming the imperative, go to Chapter 5. You form the imperative of pronominal verbs in the same way, except that you include the pronouns. Here are some examples:

> **Amuse-toi!** (ah-mewz-twah!) (*Have fun!* [singular *you*])
>
> **Amusons-nous!** (ah-mew-zohN-nooh!) (*Let's have fun!*)
>
> **Amusez-vous!** (ah-mew-zey-vooh!) (*Have fun!* [singular formal or plural *you*])

When the reflexive pronoun **te** comes after the verb, it becomes **toi** (twah). In the negative however, it goes back to being **te** and is placed before the verb: **Ne t'amuse pas!** (nuh tah-mewz pah!) (*Don't have fun!*) — now there's a sentence you never want to hear!

Oh, the Places You'll Go!

You've been dreaming about your ideal vacation and can't wait to get there. You may even have an itinerary planned of all the places you want to see and all the shows and entertainment you want to catch. You can have fun at almost any event, such as the following:

- **le ballet** (luh bah-leh) (*the ballet*)
- **l'opéra** (m) (loh-pey-rah) (*the opera*)
- **le concert** (luh kohN-sehr) (*the concert*)
- **le théâtre** (luh tey-ah-truh) (*the theater*)
- **le cinéma** (luh see-ney-mah) (*the movies*)
- **la soirée** (lah swah-rey) (*the party*)

Thanks to the Internet, the world is at your fingertips. You can find out what's playing where and at what time. Almost all museums and art galleries, theaters, and nightclubs have a website where you can get information at the click of your mouse. Or, if you prefer, pick up a local newspaper for entertainment listings. If you're in Paris, for example, and want to find local listings of cultural activities, grab one of the following publications: *Pariscope* (pah-ree-skohp), *L'Officiel des Spectacles* (loh-fee-syehl dey spehk-tah-kluh), or *Figaroscope* (fee-gah-roh-skohp), a supplement of the newspaper *Le Figaro* (luh fee-gah-roh). The Paris Tourist Office has a booklet you can pick up called *Paris Sélection* (pah-ree sey-lehk-syohN), or you can call the office's 24-hour English hotline at 01-49-52-53-56 to hear the entertainment listings .You can also watch for schedules of events posted around the city on the green, cylindrical kiosks.

Visiting museums and art galleries

You can visit many different museums in Paris. Perhaps the most famous is **Le Louvre** (luh looh-vruh). Originally built as a royal fortress, the Louvre is now home to artifacts dating from 5,000 B.C. to 1848, including some of the most famous sculptures and paintings in the world, such as the Winged Victory of Samothrace, the Venus de Milo, and Leonardo da Vinci's **La Joconde** (lah zhoh-kohNd) (*the Mona Lisa*). You can also see original 12th-century fortress foundations and drawbridge supports. Another famous museum, **le Musée D'Orsay** (luh mew-zey dohr-sey), is home to the world's finest collection of **van Gogh** (vahN guhg) paintings outside the van Gogh museum in Amsterdam, as well as to an impressive collection of impressionist art.

Museums in Paris are closed on different days. **Le Louvre** is closed on Tuesdays, for example, and **Le Musée D'Orsay** is closed on Mondays. Be sure to check out the hours before you go. (Check out the admission fees, too. Some museums have free admission on certain days. Admission to the Louvre, for instance, is free on the first Sunday of the month and on July 14, France's national holiday.)

If you're going to a museum, check into discounts (students, young children, and senior citizens often get a price break) and consider buying a museum pass, a **Carte Musées et Monuments** (kahrt mew-zey ey mohN-new-mahN). These passes, available at museum ticket offices, tourist offices, and subway stations, can add to your savings. For more information, contact the **Association InterMusées** (ah-soh-syah-syohN aN-tehr-mew-zhey) online at www.intermusees.fr.

You may also tour many of the **châteaux** (shah-toh) (castles) of France, such as **Versailles** (vehr-sahy), built as a hunting lodge in 1624 by Louis XIII and turned into the official residence of the French monarchy by Louis XIV in the second half of the 17th century. **Versailles** is quite impressive and is well worth a day trip.

Fontainebleau (fohN-tehn-bloh) is another famous **chateau** turned museum. Originally built as a hunting lodge during the Middle Ages, **Fontainebleau** was where Napoléon set up court in the early 19th century and signed his abdication papers in 1814. There are also many fairy tale castles along the **Loire** (lwahr) river valley, such as **Chambord** (shahN-bohr), **Blois** (blwah), **Chenonceau** (shuh-nohN-soh), **Azay-le-Rideau** (ah-zey luh ree-doh), and **Chinon** (shee-nohN).

As you tour these remarkable places, you may encounter signs such as the following:

- ✔ **Photos au flash interdites** (foh-toh oh flash aN-tehr-deet) (*No flash photography*)
- ✔ **Défense d'entrer** (dey-fahNs dahN-trey) (*No admittance*)

Spending an evening at the theater

French theater has been world famous for centuries and offers something for every taste and budget, from classical productions to the **avant-garde** (ah-vahN-gahrd) (*modern*). Paris alone has nearly 130 theaters; the most famous is one of the national theaters of France, **La Comédie Française** (lah kohh-mey-dee frahN-sehz), which was established in 1680 by Louis XIV and which stages performances of the classic plays of perhaps the greatest playwrights of the 17th century — **Pierre Corneille** (pyehr kohr-nehy), **Jean Racine** (zhahN rah-seen), and **Jean-Baptiste Poquelin** (zhahN-bah-pteest pohk-lahN), better known as **Molière** (moh-lyehr).

Reservations at one of the national theaters should be made in advance, unless you plan on trying to pick up some last minute "rush" tickets, which are usually on sale (and at a discount to students) 45 minutes before the show starts. Consider using one of the many known ticket services in Paris. These eliminate the need to go to the theater box office in advance. In addition, some offer discount tickets, especially for same-day performances, though there are restrictions. Check out these websites: **Kiosque-Théâtre** (kyohsk-tey-ah-truh) at www.kiosquetheatre.com, which is considered the best discount box office, selling discount tickets the day of the show, and **Alpha FNAC: Spectacles** (ahl-fah fnahk spehk-tah-kluhl) at www.fnacspectacles.com or www.fnac.com.

Going to the theater is an occasion: Men and women "dress" to go to the theater. Men wear dark suits, and women wear dresses. Opening nights call for more formal attire, such as tuxedos and evening gowns. Also, it is customary to tip the usher. Note that you're also expected to tip the attendant in the public restrooms, who is such a familiar character of the French scene that she has a name: **dame pipi** (dahm pee-pee).

If you're going to the theater, you'll need some key words to discuss your evening:

- **la pièce** (lah pyehs) (*the play*)

- **monter une pièce** (mohN-tey ewn pyehs) (*to put on a play*)

- **la représentation/le spectacle** (lah ruh-prey-zahN-tah-syohN/ luh spehk-tah-kluh) (*the performance*)

- **les costumes** (ley koh-stewm) (*the costumes*)

- **la comédie** (lah kohh-mey-dee) (*comedy*)

- **la tragédie** (lah trah-zhey-dee) (*tragedy*)

- **le rideau** (luh ree-doh) (*the curtain*)

- **le décor** (luh dey-kohr) (*the decor/scenery*)

- **la scène** (lah sehn) (*the stage*)

- **l'éclairage** (m) (ley-kleh-rahzh) (*the lighting*)

- **le billet** (luh bee-yeh) (*the ticket*)

- **le balcon** (luh bahl-kohN) (*the balcony*)

- **l'entracte** (m) (lahN-trahkt) (*the intermission*)

Here are some questions that you may want to ask or that someone may ask you:

Aimez-vous le théâtre? (ey-mey-vooh luh tey-ah-truh?) (*Do you like the theater?*)

Voulez-vous aller au théâtre? (vooh-ley-vooh-zah-ley oh tey-ah-truh?) (*Do you want to go to the theater?*)

Quelle pièce voulez-vous voir? (kehl pyehs vooh-ley-vooh vwahr?) (*What play do you want to see?*)

Qu'est-ce qu'on joue? (kehs-kohN zhooh?) (*What's playing?*)

Combien coûtent les billets? (kohN-byaN kooht ley bee-yeh?) (*How much do the tickets cost?*)

À quelle heure commence le spectacle? (ah kehl uhr kohh-mahNs luh spehk-tah-kluh?) (*What time does the show start?*)

Talkin' the Talk

Elise, a French student, and Steven, an American exchange student, are discussing going to the theater.

Elise: **Je voudrais aller au théâtre ce soir. Et toi?**
zhuh vooh-dreh-zah-ley oh tey-ah-truh suh swahr. ey twah?
I'd like to go to the theater tonight. And you?

Steven: **Oui, d'accord. Qu'est-ce qu'on joue?**
wee, dah-kohr. kehs kohN zhooh?
Okay. What's playing?

Elise: *Tartuffe,* **une comédie de Molière.**
tahr-tewf, ewn kohh-mey-dee duh moh-lyehr.
Tartuffe, a comedy by Molière.

Steven: **Je ne connais pas beaucoup le français. Ça va me plaire?**
zhuh nuh koh-ney pah boh-kooh luh frahN-seh. sah vah muh plehr?
I don't know a lot of French. Will I like it?

Elise: **Oui, bien sûr. C'est rigolo.**
wee, byaN syewr. seh ree-goh-loh.
Yes, of course. It's funny.

Later, Elise is buying tickets **au guichet** (oh gee-shey) (at the box office) from **le caissier** (luh key-syey), the ticket seller.

Elise: **Bonsoir. Je voudrais deux places à l'orchestre, s'il vous plaît.**
bohN-swahr. zhuh vooh-dreh duh plahs ah lohr-kehs-truh, seel vooh pleh.
Good evening. I'd like two orchestra seats, please.

Le caissier: **Tout est complet à l'orchestre.**
tooh-teh kohN-pleh ah lohr-kehs-truh.
The orchestra seats are sold out.

Elise: **Au balcon, s'il vous plaît.**
oh bahl-kohN, seel vooh pleh.
The balcony, please.

Le caissier: **Il y a deux places au premier rang au balcon.**
eel ee ah duh plahs oh pruh-myey rahN oh
bahl-kohN.
There are two seats in the front row of the balcony.

Elise: **C'est parfait! Combien coûtent les billets?**
seh pahr-feh! kohN-byaN kooht ley bee-yeh?
That's perfect! How much are the tickets?

Le caissier: **60 euros, s'il vous plaît.**
swah-sahNt uh-roh, seel vooh pleh.
Sixty euros, please.

Elise: **Le lever du rideau est à quelle heure?**
luh luh-vey dew ree-doh eh-tah kehl uhr?
What time does the curtain go up?

Le caissier: **Dans une demi-heure.**
dahN-zewn duh-mee uhr.
In half an hour.

Elise: **Merci, monsieur.**
mehr-see, muh-syuh.
Thank you, sir.

Words to Know

rigolo	ree-goh-loh	funny
la place	lah plahs	seat
à l'orchestre	ah lohr-kehs-truh	orchestra seats
Tout est complet	tooh-teh kohN-pleh	sold out
Le premier rang	luh pruh-myey rahN	front row
Le rideau se lève	luh ree-doh suh lehv	The curtain goes up

Heading to the movies

Are you **un cinéphile** (uhN see-ney-feel) (*a movie buff*)? Then we've got good news for you! When you're learning French — or any language for that matter — a great way to experience the language and practice your growing skills is to watch a film made in that language. Whether you plan to watch a film in a French-speaking country or see a foreign film at a cinema closer to home, the following terms may come in handy when you are speaking about the movie theater or films in general:

- **l'acteur/l'actrice** (lahk-tuhr/lahk-trees) (*actor/actress*)
- **le cinéaste** (luh see-ney-ahst) (*film maker*)
- **les effets spéciaux/les trucages** (ley-zeh-feh spey-syoh/ley trew-kahzh) (*special effects*)
- **le générique** (luh zhey-ney-reek) (*credits*)
- **le guichet** (luh gee-shey) (*ticket window*)
- **le long-métrage** (luh lohN mey-trahzh) (*feature film*)
- **le metteur-en-scène/le réalisateur** (luh meh-tuhr ahN sehn/luh rey-ah-lee-zah-tuhr) (*director*)
- **la séance** (lah sey-ahNs) (*a showing*)
- **la vedette** (lah veh-deht) (*[movie] star*)

Films marked **VO (version originale)** (vey oh [vehr-zyohN oh-ree-zhee-nahl]) are shown in their original language, with French subtitles. **VF (version française)** (vey ehf [vehr-zyohN frahN-sehz]) means that the film has been dubbed in French (dubbing is becoming more and more rare).

Most people have a favorite film genre. If someone asks you **Quels genres de films aimez-vous?** (kehl zhahN-ruh duh feelm ey-mey-vooh?) (*What kinds of films do you like?*), you can use the following list to indicate the one(s) you favor:

- **un film d'amour** (uhN feelm dah-moohr) (*a romance film*)
- **un film d'aventures** (uhN feelm dah-vahN-tewr) (*an adventure film*)
- **un film d'épouvante/d'horreur** (uhN feelm dey-pooh-vahNt/doh-ruhr) (*a horror film*)
- **un dessin animé** (uhN deh-sahN ah-nee-mey) (*a cartoon*)
- **un documentaire** (uhN doh-kew-mahN-tehr) (*a documentary*)
- **un film d'espionnage** (uhN feelm deh-spee-oh-nahzh) (*a spy film*)

✔ **un film policier** (uhN feelm poh-lee-syey) (*a detective film*)

✔ **un film de science-fiction** (uhN feelm duh syahNs fee-ksyohN)
(*a science-fiction film*)

✔ **un western** (uhN weh-stehrn) (*a western*)

The cinema, invented by Frenchmen, the brothers **Auguste** (oh-gewst) and
Louis (lwee) **Lumière** (lew-myehr), had its debut in Paris. The French film
industry has always seen itself as an artistic venue first and an industry
second. The French cinema is so popular that over 300 films are shown in
Paris per week, more than any other city in the world. **Le Festival de Cannes**
(luh feh-stee-vahl duh kahn) (*the Cannes Film Festival*) is an international film
festival that takes place every year in May in Cannes, in the south of France.
La Palme d'or (lah pahlm dohr) *(the Golden Palm)* is awarded each year to the
director of the best feature film in the competition. Each year, over 1,000 films
from around the globe are submitted to the festival in hopes of being selected.

Many theaters show a series of previews followed by commercials for as
long as a half hour before the show. Therefore, if you don't want to miss the
previews, it is best to go early. The showings, **les séances** (ley sey-ahNs), are
posted in the lobby of the movie theaters. You can also look them up online.

Talkin' the Talk

The following dialogue joins Madame and Monsieur Dumont and
their son Ben as they try to decide what to do today. (Track 10)

M. Dumont: **Qu'est-ce qu'on fait aujourd'hui? Je voudrais
visiter un musée.**
kehs-kohN feh oh-zhoohr-dwee? zhuh vooh-dreh
vee-zee-tey uhN mew-zey.
What shall we do today? I'd like to visit a museum.

Mme. Dumont: **Non, je voudrais visiter une cathédrale.**
nohN, zhuh vooh-dreh vee-zee-tey ewn
kah-tey-drahl.
No. I'd like to visit a cathedral.

Ben: **Ah non, pas de musées, pas de cathédrales!**
ah nohN, pah duh mew-zey, pah duh
kah-tey-drahl!
Oh no, no museums, no cathedrals!

M. Dumont: **D'accord. Voulez-vous aller au cinéma?**
dah-kohr. vooh-ley-vooh ah-ley oh see-ney-mah?
Okay. Do you want to go to the movies?

Ben:	**Super! Un film d'aventures!**
	sew-pehr! uhN feelm dah-vahN-tewr!
	Great! An adventure film!
Mme. Dumont:	**J'aime mieux les documentaires.**
	zhehm myuh ley doh-kew-mahN-tehr.
	I like documentaries better.
Ben:	**Non, un dessin animé!**
	nohN, uhN dey-saN ah-nee-mey!
	No, a cartoon!
M. Dumont:	**C'est moi qui décide. Je voudrais voir un film policier!**
	seh mwah kee dey-seed. zhuh vooh-dreh vwahr uhN feelm poh-lee-syey!
	I'll decide! I would like to see a detective film!

Words to Know

Je veux visiter. . . .	zhuh vuh vee-zee-tey	I want to visit. . . .
J'aime mieux	zhehm myuh	I prefer
C'est moi qui décide	seh mwah kee dey-seed	I'll decide
Je voudrais voir	zhuh vooh-dreh vwahr	I would like to see

Going to concerts

No matter what language you speak, music is international. If you're feeling overwhelmed by having to speak French all the time, try going to a concert. While there, you won't have to talk for a couple of hours, and you can relax and enjoy the music without worrying about making someone understand you. Check out these websites to find out what is playing where and much more: www.infoconcert.com or www.concerts.fr. Here are some general terms and different kinds of musical performances that may interest you:

✔ **une symphonie** (ewn saN-fohh-nee) (*a symphony*)

✔ **la musique classique** (lah mew-zeek klah-seek) (*classical music*)

✔ **la musique moderne** (lah mew-zeek moh-dehrn) (*modern music*)

✔ **la musique rock/le rock** (lah mew-zeek rohk/luh rohk) (*rock music/rock*)

✔ **la musique de jazz/le jazz** (lah mew-zeek duh zhahz/luh zhahz) (*jazz music/jazz*)

✔ **la musique techno/la techno** (lah mew-zeek tehk-noh/lah tehk-noh) (*techno music/techno*)

✔ **le rap** (luh rahp) (*rap music*)

✔ **un orchestre de chambre** (uhN-nohr-kehs-truh duh shahN-bruh) (*a chamber orchestra*)

Do not shout **Encore!** (ahN-kohr!) (Literally: *Again!*) at a French concert unless you want the performers to play the entire piece again. Instead, say **Bis!** (bees!), which means that you want them to play some more.

The verb **jouer** (zhooh-ey) is a regular **–er** verb meaning *to play*. It is used with either the preposition **de** (duh) or **à** (ah). (*Note*: These prepositions have no meaning — that is, they're not translated — when they're paired with the verb **jouer**.) When **jouer** is used with instruments, you use the preposition **de** + the definite articles **le** (luh), **la** (lah), and **les** (ley), depending on the gender and number of the instrument. The preposition **à** is used when referring to playing sports or games, or theatrical, cinematic, or musical performances. For more on sports, check out Chapter 12. Following are examples using **jouer**:

Je joue du piano. (zhuh zhooh dew pyah-noh.) (*I play the piano.*)

Tu joues de la guitare. (tew zhooh duh lah gee-tahr.) (*You play the guitar.*)

Il joue du violon. (eel zhooh dew vyoh-lohN.) (*He plays the violin.*)

Elles jouent au film de Truffaut. (ehl zhooh oh feelm duh trew-foh.) (*They are playing in Truffaut's film.*)

Enjoying the nightlife

If you're not exhausted after a full day of sightseeing, you may want to try visiting a more lively setting. Most large cities have plenty of nightclubs that offer everything from live music to dancing. What kind of **club** (kluhb) (*club*) do you want to go to? Here are a few options:

✔ **Une disco/discothèque** (ewn dees-koh/dees-koh-tehk) (*a disco*)

✔ **Une revue** (ewn ruh-vew) (*a review, show*)

✔ **Une boîte de nuit** (ewn bwaht duh nwee) (*a night club*)

Many Parisian clubs are officially private. This means they have the right to pick and choose their clientele. In general, word of mouth and weekly journals are the best guide to the current scene. Europeans also tend to dress up more for a night on the town than do their North American counterparts. To be admitted to one of the more exclusive clubs, you may need to accompany a regular customer. Here are some other things to know: The drinking age in France is 18. Women often receive discounts or are admitted free. The best advice is not to go alone, unless you're looking for a lot of attention. Weekday admission is much cheaper and not nearly as crowded.

Talkin' the Talk

Paul and Denise are finishing dinner and deciding what type of nightlife to pursue.

Paul:	**Veux-tu aller en boîte? Nous pouvons danser.** vuh-tew ah-ley ahN bwaht? nooh pooh-vohN dahN-sey. *Do you want to go to a night club? We could go dancing.*
Denise:	**Non, merci. Je suis trop fatiguée.** nohN, mehr-see. zhuh swee troh fah-tee-gey. *No, thanks. I'm too tired.*
Paul:	**Bon. Allons au club pour regarder une revue.** bohN. ahl-ohN-zoh kluhb poohr ruh-gahr-dey ewn ruh-vew. *Okay. Let's go to a club to watch a show.*
Denise:	**D'accord. Faut-il réserver?** dah-kohr. foh-teel rey-zehr-vey? *Okay. Is a reservation necessary?*
Paul:	**Nous allons devoir faire la queue.** nooh-zah-lohN duh-vwahr fehr lah kuh. *We'll have to stand in line.*
Denise:	**À quelle heure commence le spectacle?** ah kehl uhr kohh-mahNs luh spehk-tah-kluh? *What time does the show start?*
Paul:	**À 23h.** ah vaN-trwah-zuhr. *At 11:00 (p.m.).*

Denise: **Oh non! C'est trop tard!**
oh nohN! seh troh tahr!
Oh no! That's too late!

Words to Know

danser	dahN-sey	to dance
Je suis trop fatigué/ fatiguée	zhuh swee troh fah-tee-gey	I'm too tired.
Faut-il réserver?	foh-teel rey-zehr-vey	Is a reservation necessary?
faire la queue	fehr lah kuh	to wait in line
C'est trop tard	seh troh tahr	That's too late

Making Plans with Friends

Regardless of the activity, inviting a friend to come along always makes things much more fun. This section makes it easier to invite a friend as well as to accept or decline your friend's invitation.

Asking a friend to go out

When you ask a friend to go out, you use the **tu** (tew) (*you* [singular]) form. You may ask your friend what he is doing and whether he would like to go out and, if so, where. Here are a few questions that may come in handy when asking a friend out:

Qu'est-ce que tu fais (ce soir)? (kehs-kuh tew feh [suh swahr]?) (*What are you doing [this evening].?*)

Veux-tu sortir? (vuh-tew sohr-teer?) (*Do you want to go out?*)

Qu'est-ce que tu veux faire? (kehs-kuh tew vuh fehr?) (*What do you want to do?*)

Où veux-tu aller? (ooh vuh-tew ah-ley?) (*Where do you want to go?*)

Veux-tu aller au cinéma/au théâtre? (vuh-tew ah-ley oh see-ney-mah/ oh tey-ah-truh?) (*Do you want to go to the movies/to the theater?*)

Qu'est-ce que tu veux voir? (kehs-kuh tew vuh vwahr?) (*What do you want to see?*)

Accepting and declining invitations

When you have nothing to do or when you are bored, you'd gladly accept your friend's invitation . But when you're tired or don't feel like going out, you'll want to decline an invitation and perhaps even reschedule. With these phrases, you can do both:

Je veux bien. (zhuh vuh byaN.) (*I would like to.*)

J'aimerais vraiment aller au cinéma/au théâtre. (zhehm-reh vreh-mahN ah-ley oh see-ney-mah/oh tey-ah-truh.) (*I would really like to go to the movies/to the theatre.*)

J'aimerais/je voudrais voir le nouveau film de. . . . (zhehm-reh/zhuh vooh-dreh vwahr luh nooh-voh feelm duh. . . .) (*I would like to see the new film by. . . .*)

Je n'ai pas envie de sortir (ce soir). (zhuh ney pah-zahN-vee duh sohr-teer [suh swahr].) (*I don't feel like going out [this evening].*)

Peut-être demain/la semaine prochaine. (puh-teh-truh duh-maN/lah suh-mehn proh-shehn.) (*Perhaps tomorrow/next week.*)

FUN & GAMES

Identify the activity represented by each of these images.

A. _____

B. _____

C. _____

D. _____

E. _____

F. _____

Chapter 11

Taking Care of Business and Telecommunicating

. . . .

In This Chapter
▶ Conducting business via the phone and Internet
▶ Making an appointment
▶ Going to the post office
▶ Forming the past tense

. . . .

*N*ot all foreign travel is purely for pleasure's sake. In this time of international trade and global marketing, businesspeople may travel extensively or work with colleagues from all around the world. This chapter introduces you to the terms and phrases you would likely encounter while conducting business, working in an office, or communicating via phone, fax, or e-mail with a French-speaking colleague.

Getting Around — and Along — at the Office

If you're traveling to France or another French-speaking country for business — or just meeting with French colleagues via teleconferencing or online — be assured that everyone wants to make the encounter pleasant. Following are some of the professionals and staff members you may encounter:

✔ **le président-directeur général (PDG)** (luh prey-zee-dahN-dee-rehk-tuhr zhey-ney-rahl [pey dey zhey]) (*the head of the company who functions as CEO, chairman, and managing director*)

✔ **le gérant/la gérante** (luh zhey-rahN/lah zhey-rahNt) (*manager* [of a restaurant, hotel, shop])

✔ **le directeur/la directrice** (luh dee-rehk-tuhr/lah dee-rehk-trees) (*manager* [of a company, business])

✔ **le personnel** (luh pehr-sohh-nehl) (*staff, employees*)

✔ **le/la propriétaire** (luh/lah proh-pree-ey-tehr) (*owner*)

Although some French business practices may be different from your own, learning about and respecting these differences will not only impress your French-speaking counterparts but also bring you that much closer to achieving your goals. Here are a couple of things to know:

✔ During the 1980s, French businesses experienced an entrepreneurial explosion. The media and public utilities were privatized, and some of the newer and larger businesses were reorganized by American management consultants. These reorganized businesses tend to be more flexible and have a less centralized decision-making process than the older, family-owned businesses. Still, you may not find the same teamwork atmosphere that prevails in the United States and Canada. Expect **le président-directeur général** to make most decisions. Employees below the **PDG** follow a strict chain of command, with the junior staff handing problems over to superiors.

✔ You may also notice a rather elitist atmosphere in business. Being from the "right" families and going to the "right" schools often lead to positions in management.

✔ Women hold more senior positions than they used to, especially in the fields of advertising, retail, and media. The south of France still has a more traditional mind-set, however, and you may encounter some prejudice there against women in senior positions.

✔ Sexual harassment is more of an American concept. Don't be surprised if French men seem to treat businesswomen more flirtatiously. When entertaining on business in Belgium, American businesswomen should make payment arrangements in advance or indicate that their company is paying. Belgian businessmen usually don't allow a woman to pay under any other circumstances.

Taking notice of office supplies and equipment

No matter where you are, in your home office or abroad conducting business, your office includes things that are indispensable for working efficiently and accurately. Look around the office, and you'll see some very familiar **fournitures de bureau** (foohr-nee-tewr duh bew-roh) (*office supplies*), **matériel de bureau** (mah-tey-ree-ehl duh bew-roh) (*office equipment*), and **mobilier de bureau** (moh-bee-lyey duh bew-roh) (*office furniture*) that you can't do without:

✔ **l'agrafeuse** (f) (lah-grah-fuhz) (*stapler*)

✔ **les agrafes** (ley-zah-grahf) (*staples*)

✔ **le bureau** (luh bew-roh) (*desk*)

✔ **les ciseaux** (ley see-zoh) (*scissors*)

✔ **le classeur à tiroirs** (luh klah-suhr ah tee-rwahr) (*file cabinet*)

✔ **la corbeille à papiers** (lah kohr-behy ah pah-pyey) (*wastepaper basket*)

✔ **le crayon (**luh krey-ohN) (*pencil*)

✔ **les élastiques** (ley-zey-lah-steek) (*rubber bands*)

✔ **les enveloppes** (ley-zahN-vlohhp) (*envelopes*)

✔ **les fichiers** (ley fee-shyey) (*files*)

✔ **la gomme** (lah gohm) (*eraser*)

✔ **l'horloge** (f) (lohr-lohzh) (*clock*)

✔ **la lampe** (lah lahmp) (*lamp*)

✔ **la photocopieuse** (lah foh-toh-koh-pyuhz) (*copy machine*)

✔ **le ruban adhésif** (luh rew-bahN ahd-ey-zeef) (*tape*)

✔ **le siège/la chaise de bureau** (luh syehzh/lah shehz duh bew-roh)
(*office chair*)

✔ **le stylo** (luh stee-loh) (*pen*)

✔ **le tableau d'affichage** (luh tah-bloh dah-fee-shahzh) (*bulletin board*)

✔ **le télécopieur** (luh tey-ley-koh-pyuhr) (*fax machine*)

✔ **les trombones** (ley trohN-bohhn) (*paper clips*)

Using the computer and Internet

In French, the World Wide Web is sometimes called **la toile** (lah twahl), which literally means *the web.* More often, French speaking people call it **Le Web** (luh web). Here is a list of vocabulary pertaining to the computer and the Internet that will surely come in handy:

✔ **le clavier** (luh klah-vyey) (*keyboard*)

✔ **le curseur** (luh kewr-suhr) (*cursor*)

✔ **le fichier** (luh fee-shyey) (*file*)

✔ **l'icône** (f) (lee-kohn) (*icon*)

✔ **l'imprimante** (f) (laN-pree-mahNt) (*printer*)

✔ **le logiciel** (luh loh-zhee-syehl) (*software*)

✔ **le matériel** (luh mah-tey-ryehl) (*hardware*)

✔ **le moniteur** (luh moh-nee-tuhr) (*monitor*)

- ✔ **le mot de passe** (luh moh duh pahs) (*password*)
- ✔ **le navigateur** (luh nah-vee-gah-tuhr) (*web browser*)
- ✔ **l'ordinateur** (m) (lohr-dee-nah-tuhr) (*computer*)
- ✔ **la page d'accueil** (lah pahzh dah-kuhy) (*home page*)
- ✔ **le portable** (luh pohr-tah-bluh) (*laptop*)
- ✔ **le pseudo** (luh psuh-doh) (*user name*)
- ✔ **le réseau** (luh rey-zoh) (*network*)
- ✔ **le salon de chat** (luh sah-lohN duh chaht) (*chat room*)
- ✔ **la souris** (lah sooh-ree) (*mouse*)
- ✔ **surfer le Web** (sewr-fey luh wehb) (*to surf the Web*)
- ✔ **le système d'exploitation** (luh see-stehm dehks-plwah-tah-syohN) (*operating system*)
- ✔ **télécharger** (tey-ley-shahr-zhey) (*to download*)

Many French websites are bilingual, French and English. In addition, in Europe, each Internet address ends with letters identifying the country that hosts that address. In France, these two letters are `.fr`. For example, if you want to connect to the French Yahoo! site, you type `www.yahoo.fr`. Be forewarned! This site is entirely in French!

Sending an e-mail and a fax

With the Internet, the world has gotten smaller. Now you can stay in touch with your family and friends via **le courrier électronique/le mél** (luh kooh-ryey ey-lehk-troh-neek/luh meyl) (*e-mail*). Sending an e-mail is not only very easy but also very fast. Although specific instructions vary, in general, to send **une pièce jointe** (ewn pyehs zhwaNt) (*an attachment*), you do the following before clicking on **Envoyer** (ahN-vwah-yey) (*Send*): click on the icon **Insertion** (aN-sehr-syohN) (*Insert*), click on **Pièce jointe** (pyehs zhwaNt) (*Attachment*), choose the *file,* **fichier** (fee-shyey). Finally, click on the button **Joindre** (zhwaN-druh) (*Attach*).

You can also easily send **une télécopie/un fax** (ewn tey-ley-koh-pee/uhN fahks) (*a fax*) to someone in France. If you're dialing from the United States, enter the international access code (011) followed by the French country code (33) followed by the number. Then press Send.

Talkin' the Talk

Jean-Michel is showing his grandfather, André, how to send an e-mail.

André: **Quelle est la fonction d'un système d'exploitation?**
kehl eh lah fohN-ksyohN duhN see-stehm dehks-plwah-tah-syohN?
What is the function of an operating system?

Jean-Michel: **C'est de gérer les ressources de l'ordinateur comme le matériel, le logiciel, les fichiers.**
seh duh zhey-rey ley ruh-soohrs duh lohr-dee-nah-tuhr kohhm luh mah-tey-ryehl, luh loh-zhee-syehl, ley fee-shyey.
It's to manage the computer resources like the hardware, the software, the files.

André: **Que dois-je faire pour envoyer un courrier électronique?**
kuh dwah-zhuh fehr poohr ahN-vwah-yey uhN kooh-ryey ey-lehk-troh-neek?
What must I do to send an e-mail?

Jean-Michel: **D'abord, il faut avoir accès à ta messagerie et mettre ton pseudo et ton mot de passe.**
dah-bohr, eel foh-tah-vwahr ah-kseh ah tah meh-sah-zhree ey meh-truh tohN psuh-doh ey tohN moh duh pahs.
First, you have to access your e-mail account and put in your user name and password.

André: **Voilà, c'est fait. Et ensuite?**
vwah-lah, seh feh. ey ahN-sweet?
Okay, it's done. And then?

Jean-Michel: **Ensuite, choisis l'adresse électronique du destinataire, écris ton message et clique sur envoyer pour poster ton message.**
ahN-sweet, shwah-zee lah-drehs ey-lehk-troh-neek dew deh-stee-nah-tehr, ey-kree tohN meh-sahzh ey kleek sewr ahN-vwah-yey poohr pohs-tey tohN meh-sahzh.

Then choose the e-mail address of the addressee, write your message, and click on send to post your message.

André:	**C'est facile. Merci, Jean-Michel.**
	seh fah-seel. mehr-see, zhahN-mee-shehl.
	That's easy. Thank you, Jean-Michel.

Words to Know

gérer les ressources	zhey-rey ley ruh-soohrs	to manage the resources
d'abord	dah-bohr	first
il faut avoir accès	eel foh-tah-vwahr ah-kseh	you need access
ensuite	ahN-sweet	then/next
choisis	shwah-zee	choose
écris	ey-kree	write
c'est facile	seh fah-seel	it's easy

Sending mail the old-fashioned way

Although the Internet is a very fast way to keep in touch with family and friends as well as an effective way to conduct business, sometimes you want to make a little extra effort to send a postcard or a package through the regular postal mail. Just think of how excited you felt when **le facteur** (luh fahk-tuhr) (*the letter carrier*) brought you a card or a package from someone special. With the vocabulary and advice we share in this section, going to **la poste** (lah pohst) (*the post office*) will be a breeze.

Here is some general postal vocabulary, as well as some of the services provided by the post office in France:

- **l'expéditeur/l'expéditrice** (lehks-pey-dee-tuhr/lehks-pey-dee-trees) (*sender*)
- **le/la destinataire** (luh/lah deh-stee-nah-tehr)(*addressee*)
- **l'enveloppe** (f) (lahN-vlohhp) (*envelope*)
- **le timbre** (luh taN-bruh) (*stamp*)
- **le code postal** (luh kohhd poh-stahl) (*zip code*)
- **la lettre recommandée** (lah leh-truh ruh-kohh-mahN-dey) (*registered letter*)
- **la lettre exprès** (lah leh-truh ehks-prehs) (*express letter*)
- **l'envoi spécial** (m) (lahN-vwah spey-syahl) (*special delivery*)
- **le courrier** (luh kooh-ryey) (*mail*)
- **le paquet/le colis** (luh pah-keh/luh koh-lee) (*package*)
- **la boîte postale** (lah bwaht poh-stahl) (*post office box*)
- **l'affranchissement** (m) (lah-frahN-shees-mahN) (*postage*)
- **la balance** (lah bah-lahNs) (*scale*)
- **peser** (puh-zey) (*to weigh*)

In March of 2010, the post office in France became a publicly owned company. The post office is one of the largest employers in France. When you visit France, you cannot help but notice the bright yellow signs that indicate the post office as well as the bright yellow **boîtes aux lettres** (bwaht oh leh-truh) (*mailboxes*). Although the main post office in Paris is open 24 hours, typical postal hours are usually between 8 a.m. and 7 p.m. Monday through Friday, and between 8 a.m. and 12 noon on Saturday. Some post offices (especially in smaller towns) do close for a two-hour lunch break, usually between 12 noon and 2 p.m. The post office provides many services besides just mailing letters. You may purchase money orders, stamps, and phone cards, use a pay phone, send a fax, open a bank account, take out a loan, or invest money!

Making Appointments and Minding Business Hours

It is considered polite in European francophone countries to schedule appointments several weeks in advance. Be forewarned, however, that some may not confirm an appointment until the last minute.

Generally speaking, businesses are open from 8:00 (or 9:00) a.m. to noon, and from 2:00 to 5:00 (or 6:00) p.m. Monday through Friday. Many businesses open Mondays at 2:00 p.m. and are open Saturdays from 9:00 a.m. to noon or 1:00 p.m. Even though businesses may be open on Saturdays, don't try to schedule appointments then. Saturday is usually reserved for sales meetings and conferences. It may also be difficult to schedule appointments in Belgium on **Bourse** (boohrs) days, which are Mondays in Antwerp and Wednesdays in Brussels, because this is when businesspeople meet professional colleagues for lunch.

Europeans often take a longer lunch break than their North American counterparts. **Le déjeuner** (luh dey-zhuh-ney) (*lunch*) lasts anywhere from one-and-a-half to two hours, and business lunches are also more common than business dinners. Lengthy and lavish lunches are usually reserved for a first meeting or for celebrating the closing of a deal. However, don't be the first to initiate business conversation at a meal. Let your host decide whether to discuss business right away or to wait until the after-meal coffee has been served.

Don't plan on doing business during the two weeks before and after Christmas or Easter. Also avoid the months of July and August when stores, theaters, restaurants, and businesses often close for an annual vacation. (August is the vacation month for 80 percent of France.)

Talkin' the Talk

Dan Thompson, an American consultant, calls to set up an appointment with Monsieur Seiffert, the CEO of a chain of French **supermarchés** (sew-pehr-mahr-shey) (*supermarkets*). Monsieur Seiffert's secretary, **la secrétaire** (lah suh-krey-tehr), answers.

La secrétaire: **Compagnie France Supermarché, bonjour.**
kohN-pah-nyee frahNs sew-pehr-mahr-shey,
bohN-zhoohr.
Hello, France Supermarket Company.

Dan: **Bonjour. Dan Thompson à l'appareil. Passez-moi M. Seiffert, s'il vous plaît.**
bohN-zhoohr. Dan Thompson ah lah-pah-rehy.
pah-sey mwah muh-syuh see-fehr, seel vooh pleh.
Hello. This is Dan Thompson calling. Please transfer me to Mr. Seiffert.

La secrétaire:	**Un instant. Ne raccrochez pas. Il est dans son bureau. Je vous le passe.** uhN-naN-stahN. nuh rah-kroh-shey pah. eel eh dahN sohN bew-roh. zhuh vooh luh pahs. *One moment. Don't hang up. He's in his office. I'll transfer you to him.*
M. Seiffert:	**Allô, M. Thompson?** ah-loh, muh-syuh Thompson? *Hello, Mr. Thompson?*
Dan:	**Allô, M. Seiffert, bonjour. Je vais être à Nice le 14 juin. Je voudrais fixer un rendez-vous pour discuter votre stratégie de marketing.** ah-loh, muh-syuh see-fehr, bohN-zhoohr. zhuh veh-zeh-truh ah nees luh kah-tohrz zhwaN. zhuh vooh-dreh feek-sey uhN rahN-dey-vooh poohr dees-kew-tey vohh-truh strah-tey-zhee duh mahr-keh-teeng. *Hello Mr. Seiffert. I am going be in Nice on the 14th of June. I would like to arrange a meeting to discuss your marketing strategy.*
M. Seiffert:	**Ah, bon. Un instant. Je consulte mon calendrier. Ça va, je suis libre le 14 juin à 15h30.** ah, bohN. uhN-naN-stahN. zhuh kohN-sewlt mohN kah-lahN-dree-yey. sah vah, zhuh swee lee-bruh luh kah-tohrz zhwaN ah kaNz uhr trahNt. *Good. One moment. I'll consult my calendar. Okay, I'm free June 14th at 3:30 p.m.*
Dan:	**Très bien. Le 14 juin à 15h 30.** treh byaN. luh kah-tohrz zhwaN ah kaNz uhr trahNt. *Very well. June 14th at 3:30 p.m.*
M. Seifert:	**Au revoir.** ohr-vwahr. *Good bye.*

Words to Know

. . . à l'appareil	. . . ah lah-pah-rehy	This is . . . calling
Passez-moi. . .	pah-sey mwah. . .	Transfer me to. . .
un instant	uhN-naN-stahN	one minute
Ne raccrochez pas/ ne quittez pas	nuh rah-kroh-shey pah/nuh kee-tey pah	Don't hang up
Il est/n'est pas dans son bureau	eel eh/neh pah dahN sohN bew-roh	He's in/out of his office
Je vous le/la passe	zhuh vooh luh/lah pahs	I'll transfer you to him/her
Je consulte mon calendrier	zhuh kohN-sewlt mohN kah-lahN-dree-yey	I'll check my calendar
Je suis libre . . .	zhuh swee lee-bruh. . .	I'm free . . .
un rendez-vous	uhN rahN-dey-vooh	an appointment

Making a Phone Call

Whether you're visiting France, Canada, or any other francophone country, making phone calls is much easier than it used to be. Most people now have **un mobile/un portable** (uhN moh-beel/uhN pohr-tah-bluh) (*a cell phone*). Just in case, there are some public pay phones in France that take **une télé-carte** (ewn tey-ley-kahrt) (*a calling card*). Because of cell phones, however, the number of public phones has decreased dramatically.

In France, most families have one phone line and only one or two phones. The phone is usually in the living room, with an extension either in the den or master bedroom. Very rarely do you find a phone in the kitchen. When calling someone's residence, keep in mind that calling before 8:00 a.m. and after 8:00 p.m. is usually for emergencies, unless the person is expecting your call. Avoid calling during lunch and dinner hours because doing so is considered impolite.

French has two words for *hello.* You use **allô** (ah-loh) when answering the telephone and **bonjour** (bohN-zhoohr) when greeting people elsewhere. Also, in French, a telephone says **dring, dring** (dreen, dreen), not *ring, ring.*

Talkin' the Talk

Pierre is calling to tell Monique what time the movie starts. Monique's mother, Mme. La Grange, answers the phone. (Track 11)

Mme. La Grange: **Allô?**
ah-loh?
Hello?

Pierre: **Bonjour madame. C'est Pierre.**
bohN-zhoohr mah-dahm. seh pyehr.
Hello Ma'am. It's Pierre.

Mme. La Grange: **Oui, Pierre. Ça va?**
wee, pyehr. sah vah?
Yes, Pierre. How are you?

Pierre: **Ça va bien. Est-ce que Monique est là?**
sah vah byaN. ehs-kuh moh-neek eh lah?
I'm fine. Is Monique there?

Mme. La Grange: **Oui, un moment, s'il te plaît. Ne raccroche pas.**
wee, uhN moh-mahN, seel tuh pleh. nuh rah-krohsh pah.
Yes, just a minute. Don't hang up.

Monique: **Allô, Pierre?**
ah-loh, pyehr?
Hello, Pierre?

Pierre: **Monique, le film commence à 18h (heures).**
moh-neek, luh feelm kohh-mahNs ah deez-weet-uhr.
Monique, the movie starts at 6:00 p.m.

Monique:	**C'est super! À bientôt.**
	seh sew-pehr! ah byaN-toh.
	Super! I'll see you later.
Pierre:	**Au revoir. À bientôt.**
	ohr-vwahr. ah byaN-toh.
	Good-bye. See you later.

Words to Know

Est-ce que . . . est là?	ehs-kuh. . . eh lah?	Is. . . there?
un moment, s'il te plaît	uhN moh-mahN seel tuh pleh	one minute please
ne raccroche pas/ne quitte pas	nuh rah-krohsh pah/ nuh keet pah	don't hang up
à bientôt	ah byaN-toh	see you later

Did you notice the informal tone of the preceding conversation? That's because it was between people who are well acquainted with each other. Had Pierre and Monique been strangers, the conversation would have been more formal. Go to Chapter 2 for more about informal versus formal forms of address.

Many times, the person you're trying to reach is not available. In that case, you can leave a message on **un répondeur** (uhN rey-pohN-duhr) (*an answering machine*) or in person.

Livin' in the Past: Using the Past Tense

In French, you form the past tense, **le passé composé** (luh pah-sey kohN-poh-zey), by conjugating the helping verb, called an *auxiliary verb,* in the present tense and adding a past participle. The two auxiliary verbs are **avoir** (ahv-wahr) (*to have*) and **être** (eh-truh) (*to be*). Most verbs use **avoir;** a small percentage use **être.**

Creating the past tense with "avoir"

Here's the conjugation of **avoir** (*to have*) in the present tense:

Conjugation	*Pronunciation*
j'ai	zhey
tu as	tew ah
il/elle/on a	eel/ehl/ohN ah
nous avons	nooh-zah-vohN
vous avez	vooh-zah-vey
ils/elles ont	eel-/ehl-zohN

You make regular past participles from the infinitive of the verbs:

- The past participle for **–er** verbs ends in **é**; just drop the **r** of the infinitive and add **un accent aigu** (uhN-nahk-sahN-tey-gew) (*an acute accent*) to the **e**.

    - **téléphoner** (tey-ley-fohh-ney) (*to telephone or call*): **J'ai téléphoné à Monique.** (zhey tey-ley-fohh-ney ah moh-neek.) (*I called Monique.*)

    - **laisser** (leh-sey) (*to leave*): **Nous avons laissé un message.** (nooh-zah-vohN leh-sey uhN meh-sahzh.) (*We left a message.*)

- The past participle for **-ir** verbs ends in **i**; just drop the **r** from the infinitive.

    - **choisir** (shwah-zeer) (*to choose*): **Il a choisi un mot de passe.** (eel ah shwah-zee uhN moh duh pahs.) (*He chose a password.*)

    - **finir** (fee-neer) (*to finish*): **Elles ont fini leur conversation.** (ehl-zohN fee-nee luhr kohN-vehr-sah-syohN.) (*They finished their conversation.*)

- The past participle for **-re** verbs ends in **u**; drop the **re** from the infinitive and add a **u**.

    - **attendre** (ah-tahN-druh) (*to wait, to wait for*): **Tu as attendu le bus.** (tew ah ah-tahN-dew luh bewhs.) (*You waited for the bus.*)

    - **répondre** (rey-pohN-druh) (*to answer*): **Vous avez répondu à la question.** (vooh-zah-vey rey-pohN-dew ah lah kehs-tyohN.) (*You answered the question.*)

French also has several irregular past participles. The irregular verbs don't have a set pattern like the regular verbs do, so you just have to memorize them. Table 11-1 lists the most common irregular past participles.

Table 11-1	Common Irregular Past Participles	
Infinitive	*Past Participle*	*Example*
être (eh-truh) (*to be*)	**été** (ey-tey)	**Nous avons été en retard.** (nooh-zah-vohN-zey-tey ahN reh-tahr.) (*We were late.*)
avoir (ahv-wahr) (*to have*)	**eu** (ew)	**Il a eu un message.** (eel ah ew uhN mey-sahzh.) (*He had a message.*)
faire (fehr) (*to do, to make*)	**fait** (feh)	**Qu'est-ce que tu as fait?** (kehs-kuh tew ah feh?) (*What did you do?*)
voir (vwahr) (*to see*)	**vu** (vew)	**J'ai vu le directeur** (zhey vew luh dee-rehk-tuhr.) (*I saw the director, manager.*)
pouvoir (pooh-vwahr) (*to be able to*)	**pu** (pew)	**Vous avez pu téléphoner à votre bureau.** (vooh-zah-vey pew tey-ley-fohh-ney ah vohh-truh bew-roh.) (*You were able to call your office.*)
vouloir (vooh-lwahr) (*to wish, to want*)	**voulu** (vooh-lew)	**J'ai voulu un rendez-vous** (zhey vooh-lew uhN rahN-dey-vooh.) (*I wanted an appointment.*)
prendre (prahN-druh) (*to take*)	**pris** (pree)	**Ils ont pris l'avion.** (eel-zohN pree lah-vyohN.) (*They took the plane.*)

Using the past tense with être

A few verbs are conjugated with the auxiliary verb **être** instead of **avoir**. Most of these are verbs of motion, such as

- **aller** (ah-ley) (*to go*)
- **arriver** (ah-ree-vey) (*to arrive*)
- **descendre** (dey-sahN-druh) (*to go down, to get off*)
- **devenir** (duh-vuh-neer) (*to become*)
- **entrer** (ahN-trey) (*to enter*)
- **monter** (mohN-tey) (*to go up, to climb, to get on*)
- **mourir** (mooh-reer) (*to die*)
- **naître** (neh-truh) (*to be born*)
- **partir** (pahr-teer) (*to leave*)
- **passer** (pah-sey) (*to pass [by]*)
- **rentrer** (rahN-trey) (*to return, to go home*)

✔ **rester** (rehs-tey) (*to stay*)

✔ **retourner** (ruh-toohr-ney) (*to return, to go back*)

✔ **revenir** (ruh-vuh-neer) (*to come back*)

✔ **sortir** (sohr-teer) (*to go out*)

✔ **tomber** (tohN-bey) (*to fall*)

✔ **venir** (vuh-neer) (*to come*)

The main difference between forming past tense with the verb **avoir** and the verb **être** is that, when you use **être,** the past participle must agree in number and gender with the subject. The rules for making past participles agree with the number and gender of the subject are as follows:

✔ If the subject is masculine singular, the past participle doesn't change.

✔ The past participle changes spelling only in the following cases:

  • If the subject is feminine singular, add an **–e** to the past participle.

  • If the subject is masculine plural, add an **-s** to the past participle.

  • If the subject is feminine plural, add and **–es** to the past participle.

Here are examples of the past tense using the most common **être** (eh-truh) verbs:

Nous sommes restés ici. (nooh sohm rehs-tey ee-see.) (*We stayed here.*)

Il est tombé. (eel eh tohN-bey.) (*He fell.*)

Ils sont descendus. (eel sohN dey-sahN-dew.) (*They went downstairs.*)

Elle est entrée au bureau. (ehl eh-tahN-trey oh bew-roh.) (*She entered the office.*)

Vous êtes sortis. (vooh-zeht sohr-tee.) (*You* [masculine plural] *went out.*)

Even though the past participle must agree in number and gender with the subject, the pronunciation doesn't change if the past participle ends in a vowel. Consider these examples, which use **être** and the past participle of **aller**; notice how, in each pair, the pronunciation of the past participle stays the same, even though its spelling changes between the masculine and feminine, the singular and the plural:

✔ Feminine singular: **Je suis allée à la poste.** (zhuh swee-zah-ley ah lah pohst.) (*I went to the post office.*)

Masculine singular: **Je suis allé à la poste.** (zhuh swee-zah-ley ah lah pohst.) (*I went to the post office.*)

✔ Feminine singular: **Tu es allée à la poste.** (tew eh-zah-ley ah lah pohst.) (*You went to the post office.*)

Masculine plural: **Nous sommes allés à la poste.** (nooh sohm-zah-ley ah lah pohst.) (*We went to the post office.*)

✔ Feminine plural: **Elles sont allées à la poste.** (ehl sohN-tah-ley ah lah pohst.) (*They went to the post office.*)

However, if the past participle ends in a consonant, you do hear the difference between the masculine and feminine endings. Here are some examples:

Il est mort en 1863. (eel eh mohr ahN deez-wee sahN swah-sahNt-trwah.) (*He died in 1863.*)

Elle est morte en 1863. (ehl eh mohr-tahN deez-wee sahN swah-sahNt-trwah.) (*She died in 1863.*)

Fun & Games

Activity 1: In the blanks provided, identify each item in the office.

A. _____

B. _____

C. _____

D. _____

E. _____

F. _____

G. _____

H. _____

I. _____

J. _____

Activity 2: Fill in the blanks with the correct form of the past participle.

A. Je suis _____en avance. (arriver) (*I arrived early.*)

B. Elles ont _____ au téléphone. (parler) (*They talked on the phone.*)

C. Il a _____un nouveau bureau. (vouloir) (*He wanted a new office, desk.*)

D. Nous sommes_____ tard. (rentrer) (*We came home late.*)

E. Qu'est-ce que vous avez _____? (faire) (*What did you do?*)

F. Il a _____le personnel. (choisir) (*He chose the staff.*)

G. J'ai _____ un ordinateur. (avoir) (*I had a computer.*)

Chapter 12

Recreation and the Outdoors

. . . .

In This Chapter

▶ Playing team and individual sports with the verbs **jouer** and **faire**

▶ Focusing on a few popular pastimes

▶ Enjoying a good book with the verb **lire**

. . . .

All work and no play makes **Jacques un garçon ennuyeux** (zhahk uhN gahr-sohN ahN-nwee-yuh) (*Jack a dull boy*). Whether you're playing or watching sports, going to the beach, camping, or pursuing quieter hobbies, you're sure to have a good time if you know some of the language. In this chapter, we give you ample sports and activity-related vocabulary terms so that you can converse with others about the kinds of things you like to do. We also explain when to use the verb **faire de** (fehr duh) versus when to use **jouer à** (zhooh-ey ah), both of which mean *to play*.

Playing Sports and Games

It seems that every nation has a national pastime. In the U.S. **le base-ball** (luh behz-bohl) (*baseball*), **le basket (ball)** (luh bahs-keht [bohl]) (*basketball*), and **le football américain** (luh fooht-bohl ah-mey-ree-kaN) (*American football*) are popular, as is **le hockey** (luh oh-keh) (*hockey*) in Canada. Some of these sports — **le football américain** and **le base-ball**, for example — remain uncommon in Europe. Here are some pastimes that are important in a few French-speaking countries and regions:

   ▶ **Le cyclisme** (luh see-kleez-muh) (*cycling*) is very popular in France and Belgium.

   ▶ **Le foot(ball)** (luh fooht[bohl]) (*soccer*) is a favorite sport in Canada, France, Belgium, and in many African francophone countries. ***Note:*** In Canada, soccer is called **le soccer** (luh soh-kuhr).

   ▶ **Le rugby** (luh rewg-bee) (*rugby*) is popular in Southern France.

✔ **Le ski** (luh skee) (*skiing*) is popular in Switzerland.

✔ **Le hockey (sur glace)** (luh hoh-keh [sewr glahs]) ([*ice*] *hockey*) is popular in Canada.

Among the most popular **sports-spectacles** (spohr-spehk-tah-kluh) (*spectator sports*) are **le foot(ball)**, **les courses de chevaux** (ley koohrs duh shuh-voh) (*horse racing*), and **les courses automobiles** (ley koohrs oh-toh-moh-beel) (*automobile racing*). The best known horse race is **le Grand Prix de Longchamp** (luh grahN pree duh lohNg-shahN) in Paris. As for **les courses automobiles,** there are two extremely famous ones: **les 24 heures du Mans** (ley vaNt kah-truhr dew mahN) (*24 Hours of Le Mans*) and **le Rallye de Monte-Carlo** (luh rah-lee duh mohN-tey-kahr-loh) (*Monte Carlo Rally*).

First held in 1903, **Le Tour de France** (luh toohr duh frahNs) is the largest **course du cycliste** (koohrs dew see-kleest) (*cycling race*) in the world. Every summer, cyclists from all over the world bike over 2,000 miles (3,200 kilometers). The race begins in a different city each year but always ends in Paris, along the **Champs-Elysées** (shahN-zeh-lee-zey). The course is very demanding, traveling through the Alps and Pyrenees mountain regions and under difficult weather conditions. **Le maillot jaune** (luh mah-yoh zhohn) (*the yellow jersey*) is awarded to the winner.

The French use two different verbs when talking about playing sports: **faire de** (fehr duh) is mostly used for individual sports and **jouer à** (zhooh-ey ah) for team sports or games. Both verbs essentially mean *to play*, although the specific translation varies by activity. They can also be used interchangeably. The following sections have the details.

Using "faire" for individual sports

Individual sports such as **la natation** (lah nah-tah-syohN) (*swimming*), **le tennis** (luh tey-nees) (*tennis*), **la randonnée** (lah rahN-doh-ney) (*hiking*), **le cyclisme** (luh see-kleez-muh) (*cycling*), **la voile** (lah vwahl) (*sailing*), and **la planche à voile** (lah plahNsh ah vwahl) (*windsurfing*) are also popular.

When you talk about individual sports, you use the verb **faire**. **Faire** is an irregular verb, and it uses the preposition **de** (duh) and a definite article *the* — **le** (luh) or **la** (lah), depending on the gender of the sport. (Keep in mind that **de + le** contracts to form **du**, whereas **de + la** remains **de la**.) With sports, the verb **faire** can be translated in a number of ways, such as *to play* or *to do,* and sometimes, it's not translated at all. In such cases, the sport serves as the verb, such as *to hike* or *to ski.*

Table 12-1 shows sentences using **faire** so that you can easily see how the form changes with the gender of the sport. (To see the general conjugation of **faire,** refer to Chapter 2.)

Table 12-1	The Verb "faire" When Used with Sports	
French	*Pronunciation*	*Translation*
Je fais du tennis.	zhuh feh dew tey-nees.	*I play tennis.*
Tu fais du vélo.	tew feh dew vey-loh.	*You bike, You go biking.*
Il/Elle/On fait du ski.	eel/ehl/ohN feh dew skee.	*He/She/One skis, He/She/One goes skiing.*
Nous faisons de la natation.	nooh fuh-zohN duh lah nah-tah-syohN.	*We swim, We go swimming.*
Vous faites une randonnée.	vooh feh-tewn rahN-doh-ney.	*You hike, You go hiking.*
Ils/Elles font du cheval.	eel/ehl fohN dew shvahl.	*They go horseback riding.*

Here is a list of some individual sports or activities that you may enjoy — and that use the verb **faire:**

- ✔ **faire une promenade** (fehr ewn prohm-nahd) (*to take a walk, to stroll*)

- ✔ **faire du surf** (fehr dew sewrf) (*to surf, to go surfing*)

- ✔ **faire du vélo** (fehr dew vey-loh) (*to bike, to go biking*)

- ✔ **faire du jogging** (fehr dew zhoh-geeng) (*to jog, to go jogging*)

- ✔ **faire de l'exercice** (fehr duh lehk-sehr-sees) (*to exercise*)

- ✔ **faire du patin à roulettes/à glace** (fehr dew pah-taN ah rooh-leht/ah glahs) (*to roller skate, to ice skate*)

- ✔ **faire du roller** (fehr dew roh-luhr) (*to rollerblade*)

- ✔ **faire du cheval/de l'équitation** (fehr dew shvahl/duh ley-kee-tah-syohN) (*to go horseback riding*)

For more winter and summer sports, head to the sections "Going Downhill — or Cross-country — Skiing" and "Going to the Beach."

Using "jouer" for team sports

Today, the French are much more sports minded than in the past. Young people regularly join teams and compete in sports such as **le basket**, **le foot(ball)**, and **le rugby**. When talking about team sports, you usually use the verb **jouer**.

Jouer is a regular **–er** verb. It uses the preposition **à** (ah) (*to, at, in*) and the definite articles **le, la,** or **les,** depending on the gender and number of the sport or game. (You also use **jouer** when you talk about playing musical instruments, but you use it with the preposition **de;** check out Chapter 10 for more on that.) Table 12-2 shows sentences using **jouer** so that you can see how the form changes with the gender of the sport. (For information on conjugating regular verbs, refer to Chapter 2.)

Table 12-2	The Verb "jouer" When Used with Sports	
French	*Pronunciation*	*Translation*
Je joue au basket.	zhuh zhooh oh bahs-keht.	*I play basketball.*
Tu joues au golf.	tew zhooh oh gohlf.	*You play golf.*
Il/Elle/On joue au volley-ball.	eel/ehl /ohN zhooh oh voh-leh-bohl.	*He/She/One plays volleyball.*
Nous jouons au foot(ball).	nooh zhooh-ohN oh fooht(bohl).	*We play soccer.*
Vous jouez au hockey.	vooh zhooh-ey oh oh-keh.	*You play hockey.*
Ils/Elles jouent au football américain.	eel/ehl zhooh oh fooht-bohl ah-mey-ree-kaN.	*They play football.*

The following is a list of group or team sports with the verb **jouer**:

- ✔ **jouer au tennis** (zhooh-ey oh tey-nees) (*to play tennis*)

- ✔ **jouer au foot(ball)** (zhooh-ey oh fooht[bohl]) (*to play soccer*)

- ✔ **jouer au football américain** (zhooh-ey oh fooht-bohl ah-mey-ree-kaN) (*to play football*)

- ✔ **jouer au basket(ball)** (zhooh-ey oh bahs-keht[bohl]) (*to play basketball*)

- ✔ **jouer au golf** (zhooh-ey oh gohlf) (*to play golf*)

- ✔ **jouer au volley-ball** (zhooh-ey oh voh-leh-bohl) (*to play volleyball*)

- ✔ **jouer au base-ball** (zhooh-ey oh behz-bohl) (*to play baseball*)

- ✔ **jouer au hockey** (zhooh-ey oh oh-keh) (*to play hockey*)

- ✔ **jouer au hockey sur gazon** (zhooh-ey oh oh-keh sewr gah-zohN) (*to play field hockey*)

- ✔ **jouer au rugby** (zhooh-ey oh rewg-bee) (*to play rugby*)

- ✔ **jouer au lacrosse** (zhooh-ey oh lah-krohs) (*to play lacrosse*)

Because French schools and universities are built solely around academics, there are no official sport teams. Many students join sports clubs, which is a good way to meet new people and make new friends. These clubs are also open to foreign students. Each sport has a **Fédération** (fey-dey-rah-syohN) that supplies all information regarding affiliated clubs and associations. The **Fédération** also sponsors regional and national public events.

Talkin' the Talk

Paul is at a soccer game, and Marc sits down beside him. (Track 12)

Marc: **Zut! J'ai manqué le coup d'envoi!**
zewt! zhey mahN-key luh kooh dahN-vwah!
Darn! I missed the kick-off!

Paul: **Tu n'as pas manqué beaucoup. Ils sont à égalité.**
tew nah pah mahN-key boh-kooh. eel sohN-tah ey-gah-lee-tey.
You didn't miss much. The score's tied.

Marc: **Oh, excellent. Joues-tu au foot?**
oh, ehk-seh-lahN. zhooh tew oh fooht?
Oh, excellent. Do you play soccer?

Paul: **Non, je joue au basket.**
nohN, zhuh zhooh oh bahs-keht.
No, I play basketball.

Marc: **Je joue au basket aussi. Je cherche une équipe.**
zhuh zhooh oh bahs-keht oh-see. zhuh shehrsh ewn ey-keep.
I play basketball, too. I'm looking for a team.

Paul: **Nous jouons au club local.**
nooh zhooh-ohN oh kluhb loh-kahl.
We play at the local club.

Marc: **Eh, regarde! Il a marqué un but!**
ey, ruh-gahrd! eel ah mahr-key uhN bewt!
Hey, look! He scored a goal!

Paul: **Super! Nous avons gagné!**
sew-pehr! nooh-zah-vohN gah-nyey!
Super! We won!

Words to Know

manquer	mahN-key	to miss
le coup d'envoi	luh kooh dahN-vwah	kick-off
un club de sport/ local	uhN kluhb duh spohr/ loh-kahl	a sports/local club
être à égalité	eh-truh ah ey-gah-lee-tey	tied score
une équipe	ewn ey-keep	a team
gagner	gah-nyey	to win
marquer un point/but	mahr-key uhN pwaN/ bewt	to score a point/ goal

Going Downhill — or Cross-country — Skiing

Whether you're in Switzerland, France, or Canada, you can find plenty of opportunities for **le ski alpin** (luh skee ahl-paN) (*downhill skiing*), **le ski de fond** (luh skee duh fohN) (*cross-country skiing*), and **la planche à neige** (lah plahNsh ah nehzh) (*snowboarding*). In France, the Alps are the best for downhill skiing and the Pyrenees for cross-country. Resorts in France tend to be modern and efficient; in Switzerland the emphasis is on tradition and character. Switzerland has nearly 200 villages and small towns equipped for downhill skiing. And Montreal skiing conditions are billed as the "best in the East." You can even cross-country ski through the **Parc du Mont-Royal** (pahrk dew mohN-rwah-yahl) in Montreal proper.

You use the verb **faire du** with **ski alpin** and **ski de fond,** and the verb **faire de la** with **planche à neige:**

✔ **faire du ski (alpin)** (fehr dew skee [ahl-paN]) (*to [downhill] ski, to go downhill skiing*)

✔ **faire du ski de fond** (fehr dew skee duh fohN) (*to cross-country ski, to go cross-country skiing*)

✔ **faire de la planche à neige** (fehr duh lah plahNsh ah nehzh) (*to snowboard, to go snowboarding*)

The following vocabulary will come in handy when you're heading out for an afternoon of wintery fun:

✔ **le forfait** (luh fohr-feh) (*lift pass*)

✔ **les conditions** (ley kohN-dee-syohN) (*[ski] conditions*)

✔ **la neige** (lah nehzh) (*snow*)

✔ **poudreuse** (pooh-druhz) (*powdery [snow]*)

✔ **l'équipement** (ley-keep-mahN) (*equipment*)

✔ **les leçons de ski** (ley luh-sohN duh skee) (*skiing lessons*)

✔ **les skis** (ley skee) (*skis*)

Talkin' the Talk

Antoine and his girlfriend, Françoise, have come to the mountains to ski.

Françoise:	**Il fait très froid aujourd'hui.** eel feh treh frwah oh-zhoohr dwee. *It's really cold today.*
Antoine:	**Oui! Et il y a beaucoup de neige.** wee! ey eel ee ah boh-kooh duh nehzh. *Yes! And there's a lot of snow.*
Françoise:	**Mais, bien sûr. Il a neigé hier soir.** meh, byaN sewr. eel ah neh-zhey yehr swahr. *But of course. It snowed last night.*
Antoine:	**La neige est poudreuse, aussi.** lah nehzh eh pooh-druhz, oh-see. *The snow is powdery, too.*
Françoise:	**Oui, les conditions sont excellentes.** wee, ley kohN-dee-syohN sohN-teh-kseh-lahNt. *Yes, the conditions are excellent.*
Antoine:	**Reste ici. J'achète les forfaits.** rehst ee-see. zhah-sheht ley fohr-feh. *Stay here. I'll buy the lift passes.*

At the ski resort, Antoine buys lift tickets from Anne.

Antoine: **Je voudrais deux forfaits pour une journée, s'il vous plaît.**
zhuh vooh-dreh duh fohr-feh poohr ewn zhoohr-ney, seel vooh pleh.
I would like two one-day passes, please.

Anne: **Voulez-vous louer de l'équipement, monsieur?**
vooh-ley-vooh looh-ey duh ley-keep-mahN, muh-syuh?
Do you want to rent some equipment, sir?

Antoine: **Oui, je voudrais louer des skis, s'il vous plaît.**
wee, zhuh vooh-dreh looh-ey dey ski, seel vooh pleh.
Yes, I'd like to rent some skis, please.

Anne: **Voulez-vous des leçons de ski?**
vooh-ley vooh dey luh-sohN duh ski?
Do you want (ski) lessons?

Antoine: **Non, merci.**
nohN, mehr-see.
No, thank you.

Anne: **Ça coûte 125 euros, s'il vous plaît.**
sah kooht sahN vaN-saNk uh-roh, seel vooh pleh.
That will be 125 euros, please.

Words to Know

Il fait très froid	eel feh treh frwah	It's very cold
rester	rehs-tey	to stay
acheter	ahsh-tey	to buy
Je voudrais . . .	zhuh vooh-dreh . . .	I'd like . . .
louer	looh-ey	to rent

Going to the Beach

Allons à la plage! (ah-lohN-zah lah plahzh!) (*Let's go to the beach!*) Nothing is more relaxing than a day spent lounging on the sand or playing in the water. **La Côte d'Azur** (lah koht dah-zewr) (*the Azure Coast*), also known as the French Riviera, is situated on the southern coast of France, along the Mediterranean. Its numerous beaches are quite crowded during the months of July and August. Swimming is quite safe because most beaches are supervised by **les surveillants de plage/de baignade** (ley sewr-vehy-ahN duh plahzh/duh beh-nyahd) (*lifeguards*).

When you go to the beach, here are some activities you may find amusing:

- ✔ **le ski nautique** (luh skee noh-teek) (*water skiing*)
- ✔ **la plongée sous-marine** (lah plohN-zhey sooh-mah-reen) (*scuba diving*)
- ✔ **la plongée libre** (lah plohN-zhey lee-bruh) (*snorkeling*)
- ✔ **la voile** (lah vwahl) (*sailing*)
- ✔ **la planche à voile** (lah plahN-shah vwahl) (*windsurfing*)
- ✔ **la natation** (lah nah-tah-syohN) (*swimming*)

For each of the preceding activities, you use the verb **faire** (fehr) plus the preposition **de** (duh) and the appropriate definite article — **le** (luh) or **la** (lah). Refer to the earlier section "Using the verb 'faire' when talking about individual sports" for details.

Topless sunbathing is accepted on most French beaches, and there are also nudist beaches, primarily around **Saint-Tropez** (sahN troh-pey) and **l'île du Levant** (leel dew luhv-ahN). Before disrobing completely, look around to see what is acceptable! As they say, "When in Rome . . ."!

With a couple of towels, some suntan lotion, a refreshing drink, and these vocabulary words, you're all set to spend a day at the beach:

- ✔ **la mer** (lah mehr) (*the sea*)
- ✔ **le bord de la mer/au bord de la mer** (luh bohr duh lah mehr/oh bohr duh lah mehr) (*the seashore/by the seashore*)
- ✔ **la plage** (lah plahzh) (*the beach*)
- ✔ **le sable** (luh sah-bluh) (*sand*)
- ✔ **le banc de sable** (luh bahN duh sah-bluh) (*sand bank*)
- ✔ **la dune de sable** (lah dewn duh sah-bluh) (*sand dune*)
- ✔ **le château de sable** (luh shah-toh duh sah-bluh) (*sand castle*)

- ✔ **la vague** (lah vahg) (*wave*)

- ✔ **les coquillages** (ley kohh-kee-yahzh) (*seashells*)

- ✔ **l'algue** (lahlg) (*seaweed*)

- ✔ **la serviette** (lah sehr-vyeht) (*towel*)

- ✔ **les lunettes de soleil** (ley lew-neht duh soh-lehy) (*sunglasses*)

- ✔ **la lotion/la crème solaire** (lah loh-syohN/lah krehm soh-lehr) (*suntan lotion/sunscreen*)

- ✔ **le bronzage** (luh brohN-zahzh) (*suntan*)

- ✔ **bronzer** (brohN-zey) (*to tan*)

- ✔ **se faire bronzer** (suh fehr brohN-zey) (*to get a tan*)

- ✔ **le coup de soleil** (luh kooh duh soh-lehy) (*sunburn*)

- ✔ **la visière** (lah vee-zyehr) (*[sun] visor*)

If you see a sign posted that reads **Baignade interdite** (beh-nyahd aN-tehr-deet), beware. That means *No swimming!*

Talkin' the Talk

Mme. Lafarge and her two sons Gaston and Henri are spending the day at the beach.

Gaston et Henri: **Maman! Nous allons nager.**
mah-mahN! nooh-zah-lohN nah-zhey.
Mom! We're going swimming.

Mme. Lafarge: **Attendez! Vous oubliez la crème solaire.**
ah-tahN-dey! Vooh-zooh-blee-yey lah krehm soh-lehr.
Wait! You're forgetting your suncreen.

Gaston: **Oh, maman! Dépêche-toi!**
oh mah-mahN! dey-pehsh-twah!
Oh, Mom! Hurry up!

Henri: **Gaston, regarde les très grandes vagues!**
gah-stohN, ruh-gahrd ley treh grahNd vahg!
Gaston, look at those really big waves!

Gaston:
> **C'est super! Maman, as-tu mon tuba et mes palmes? Nous allons faire de la plongée libre.**
> seh sew-pehr! mah-mahN, ah-tew mohN tew-bah ey mey pahlm? nooh-zah-lohN fehr duh lah plohN-zhey lee-bruh.
> *It's great! Mom, do you have my snorkel and flippers? We are going snorkeling.*

Mme. Lafarge:
> **Oui, ils sont dans le sac. Je vais bronzer. Amusez-vous bien!**
> wee, eel sohN dahN luh sahk. zhuh veh brohN-zey. ah-mew-zey-vooh byaN.
> *Yes, they are in the bag. I'm going to tan. Have fun!*

Words to Know

nager	nah-zhey	to swim
oublier	ooh-blee-yey	to forget
se dépêcher	suh dey-peh-shey	to hurry
le tuba	luh tew-bah	snorkel
les palmes	ley pahlm	flippers
s'amuser	sah-mew-zey	to have fun
Amusez-vous!	ah-mew-zey-vooh!	Have fun!

Setting Up Camp

Camping is a great way to get away from it all. Traditionally in France, the months of July and August are when the French, especially the Parisians, head to the hills, so to speak. Highways are jammed with cars and campers escaping from the city. Along the French Riviera, traffic has been known to be stalled for hours as cars wind their way to the coast.

Camping along the coast is very well organized. Most campgrounds have showers and restaurants, as well as separate sites for bicycles and tent campers. Many are situated along the beaches. If you plan to go, making reservations well in advance is a good idea, especially during the months of July and August. Off-road camping is illegal.

The following vocabulary words and phrases pertain to camping and fishing that will be useful in case you want to pursue this fun-filled — and perhaps a little rugged — activity.

- **la tente** (lah tahNt) (*tent*)
- **monter la tente** (mohN-tey lah tahNt) (*to pitch the tent*)
- **les allumettes** (ley-zah-lew-meht) (*matches*)
- **faire un feu de camp** (fehr uhN fuh duh kahN) (*start a campfire*)
- **le sac de couchage** (luh sahk duh kooh-shahzh) (*sleeping bag*)
- **les douches** (ley doohsh) (*showers*)
- **les toilettes** (ley twah-leht) (*the toilets*)
- **les services** (ley sehr-vees) (*the facilities*)
- **pêcher** (peh-shey) (*to fish, to go fishing*)
- **attrapper** (ah trah-pey) (*to catch*)
- **le poisson** (luh pwah-sohN) (*fish*)
- **la canne à pêche** (lah kahn ah pehsh) (*fishing pole*)

You can find many **terrains de camping** (tehr-ehn duh kahN-peeng) (*campgrounds*) in France. To find out where to camp in France and for other important details about booking your ideal spot, check out these websites:

- www.campingfrance.com
- about-france.com/tourism/camping.htm
- gofrance.about.com/od/lodging/a/camping.htm

The Laurentian Mountains are about an hour's drive north of Montreal. This area, inhabited by the Algonquin Indians, is full of natural beauty. The long, narrow glacial lakes are fed by freezing cold streams coursing down wooded slopes of yellow birch, beech, pine, and maple trees. Camping along these river banks is one of the best ways to appreciate the rugged splendor of the mountains. Advance reservations are usually not required at park campgrounds operated by the Québec government.

For camping information in the Québec region, check out these websites:

- www.camping-canada.com
- www.campcanada.com

Talkin' the Talk

 Etienne and Christine are going camping. Christine has been napping in the car. (Track 13)

Etienne: **Lève-toi! Nous sommes arrivés.**
            lehv-twah! nooh sohm-zah-ree-vey.
            Get up! We're here.

Christine: **Oh! C'est très joli, n'est-ce pas?**
            oh! seh treh zhoh-lee, nehs-pah?
            Oh! It's very pretty, isn't it?

Etienne: **Oui. Montons la tente.**
            wee. mohN-tohN lah tahNt.
            Yes. Let's pitch the tent.

Christine: **D'accord. Quels services y-a-t-il?**
            dah-kohr. kehl sehr-vees ee-ah-teel?
            Okay. What facilities are there?

Etienne: **Il y a des toilettes et des douches.**
            eel ee ah dey twah-leht ey dey doohsh.
            There are toilets and showers.

Christine: **Voilà les sacs de couchage.**
            vwah-lah ley sahk duh kooh-shahzh.
            Here are the sleeping bags.

Etienne: **Merci. Peux-tu trouver les allumettes?**
            mehr-see. puh-tew trooh-vey ley-zah-lew-meht?
            Thanks. Can you find the matches?

Christine: **Oui, les voilà.**
            wee, ley vwah-lah.
            Yes, here they are.

Etienne: **Bon. Je vais faire un feu de camp.**
            bohN. zhuh veh fehr uhN fuh duh kahN.
            Good. I'll start a campfire.

After their campsite is set up for the evening, the friends talk about how to spend their afternoon.

Etienne: **Christine, je vais pêcher.**
            krees-teen, zhuh veh peh-shey.
            Christine, I'm going fishing.

Christine:	**Je n'aime pas pêcher. Je vais lire mon livre.** zhuh nehm pah peh-shey. zhuh veh leer mohN lee-vruh. *I don't like fishing. I'm going to read my book.*
Etienne:	**J'espère attraper des poissons pour le dîner.** zhehs-pehr ah-trah-pey dey pwah-sohN poohr luh dee-ney. *I hope to catch some fish for dinner.*
Christine:	**Tu as ta canne à pêche?** tew ah tah kahn ah pehsh? *Do you have your fishing pole?*
Etienne:	**Oui et des vers aussi.** wee ey dey vehr oh-see. *Yes, and some worms, too.*
Christine:	**Dégoûtant! Va-t-en!** dey-gooh-tahN! vah-tahN! *Disgusting! Go away!*

Words to Know

se lever	suh luh-vey	to get up
lève-toi!	lehv-twah!	get up!
Nous sommes arrivés.	nooh sohm-zah-ree-vey	We're here, We've arrived.
je n'aime pas...	zhuh nehm pah...	I don't like...
lire	leer	to read
les vers	ley vehr	worms
dégoûtant	dey-gooh-tahN	disgusting

Enjoying Quieter Pursuits

Sometimes you don't feel like venturing out but want to stay at home. You can do many things at home to entertain or occupy yourself. Of course, you can watch your favorite television program, read a good book, or tend to your garden. You can also play a board game or cards with your family.

Having fun with board games

Few things are more fun on rainy days than staying indoors and playing a game or two with your loved ones. There are a number of **jeux de société/ jeux de plateau** (zhuh duh soh-see-ey-tey/zhuh duh plah-toh) (*board games*), most of which are those that you're probably already familiar with, like Monopoly, Scrabble, Cranium, and so on. Other options include **jeux de voyage** (zhuh duh voh-yahzh) (*travel games*) and **puzzles** (puhzl), more appropriately called **jeux de patience** (zhuh duh pah-syahNs) (*games of patience*). Other games that you can play at home include **le jeu d'échecs** (luh zhuh dey-shehk) (*chess*), **le jeu de dames** (luh zhuh duh dahm) (*checkers*), and **les jeux de cartes** (ley zhuh duh kahrt) (*card games*).

You use the verb **jouer à** (zhooh-ey ah) (*to play*) plus the definite articles **le/ la/les** (luh/lah/ley) (*the*) to say that you are playing cards or card games. Here are some examples: **jouer aux échecs** (zhooh-ey oh-zey-shehk) (*to play chess*), **jouer aux dames** (zhooh-ey oh dahm) (*to play checkers*), **jouer aux cartes** (zhooh-ey oh kahrt) (*to play cards*), **jouer au poker** (zhooh-ey oh poh-kehr) (*to play poker*), and so on.

Reading with the verb "lire"

Another favorite quiet activity is reading, which is a wonderful way to let your imagination soar as you travel in time and space to the farthest corners of the earth and the universe. You can read with the verb **lire** (leer) (*to read*) which is an irregular verb. Here is the conjugation of **lire**:

Conjugation	*Pronunciation*
je lis	zhuh lee
tu lis	tew lee
il/elle/on lit	eel/ehl/ohN lee
nous lisons	nooh lee-zohN
vous lisez	vooh lee-zey
ils/elles lisent	eel/ehl leez

Here is a list of the types of reading material you may be interested in:

- ✔ **un journal** (uhN zhoohr-nahl) (*a newspaper*)

- ✔ **un magazine** (uhN mah-gah-zeen) (*a magazine*)

- ✔ **une bande dessinée** (ewn bahNd dey-see-ney) (*a comic strip*)

- ✔ **un conte/une nouvelle** (uhN kohNt/ewn nooh-vehl) (*a short story*)

- ✔ **un roman** (uhN roh-mahN) (*a novel*)

- ✔ **un roman d'amour/de science-fiction/d'aventures/policier** (uhN roh-mahN dah-moohr/duh syahNs-fee-ksyohN/dah-vahN-tewr/poh-lee-syey) (*a love story/a science-fiction story/an adventure story/a detective story*)

- ✔ **un recueil de poèmes** (uhN ruh-kuhy duh poh-ehm) (*a collection of poems*)

Tending to the garden

Not only is gardening very relaxing for many people, but it is also very rewarding. Whether you are planting an herb, vegetable, or flower garden, in time, you get to enjoy the "fruits" of your labor. Here is some general gardening vocabulary:

- ✔ **faire du jardinage** (fehr dew zhahr-dee-nahzh) (*to garden*)

- ✔ **planter** (plahN-tey) (*to plant*)

- ✔ **arroser** (ah-roh-zey) (*to water*)

- ✔ **arracher les mauvaises herbes** (ah-rah-shey ley moh-veh-zehrb) (*to pull out the weeds*)

- ✔ **tondre la pelouse/le gazon** (tohN-druh lah puh-loohz/luh gah-zohN) (*to mow the lawn*)

- ✔ **une tondeuse à gazon** (ewn tohN-duhz ah gah-zohN) (*a lawn mower*)

- ✔ **le sol** (luh sohl) (*the soil*)

- ✔ **labourer la terre** (lah-booh-rey lah tehr) (*to dig, to till the soil*)

- ✔ **le tuyau d'arrosage** (luh tewy-oh dah-roh-zahzh) (*garden hose*)

- ✔ **les outils de jardinage** (ley-zooh-tee duh zhahr-dee-nahzh) (*garden tools*)

- ✔ **la plante** (lah plahNt) (*plant*)

- ✔ **les graines** (ley grehn) (*seeds*)

- ✔ **les gants de jardinage** (ley gahN duh zhahr-dee-nahzh) (*gardening gloves*)

- ✔ **le transplantoir** (luh trahNs-plahN-twahr) (*trowel*)

Les jardins d'herbes (aromatiques) (ley zhahr-daN dehrb [ah-roh-mah-teek]) (*herb gardens*) are generally easy to grow and allow you to bring fresh flavors to your kitchen all year round. Here are a few herbs you may want to include:

- ✔ **l'aneth** (lah-neht) (*dill*)
- ✔ **le basilic** (luh bah-zee-leek) (*basil*)
- ✔ **le cerfeuil** (luh sehr-fuhy) (*chervil*)
- ✔ **l'estragon** (lehs-trah-gohN) (*tarragon*)
- ✔ **la menthe** (lah mahNt) (*mint*)
- ✔ **le persil** (luh pehr-see) (*parsley*)
- ✔ **le romarin** (luh roh-mah-raN) (*rosemary*)
- ✔ **la sauge** lah sohzh) (*sage*)
- ✔ **le thym** (luh taN) (*thyme*)

Want to plant **un jardin d'agrément** (uhN zhahr-daN dah-grey-mahN) (*a flower garden*)? Here are some lovely plants to include in **la plate-bande** (lah plaht-bahNd) (*the flower bed*):

- ✔ **les bégonias** (ley bey-goh-nyah) (*begonias*)
- ✔ **les hortensias** (ley-zohr-tahN-syah) (*hydrangeas*)
- ✔ **les jonquilles** (ley zhohN-keey) (*daffodils*)
- ✔ **les oeillets** (ley-zuh-yeh) (*carnations*)
- ✔ **les marguerites** (ley mahr-gah-reet) (*daisies*)
- ✔ **les roses** (ley rohz) (*roses*)
- ✔ **les tulipes** (ley tew-leep) (*tulips*)
- ✔ **les violettes** (ley vyoh-leht) (*violets*)

If you're interested in **un potager** (uhN poh-tah-zhey) (*a vegetable garden*), head to Chapter 8 for a long list of vegetables you may want your garden to contain!

Fun & Games

Identify, in French, the activity shown in each of the following pictures.

A. _____

B. _____

C. _____

D. _____

E. _____

F. _____

G. _____

H. _____

I. _____

J. _____

Part III
French on the Go

In this part . . .

At some point, you may very well find yourself traveling to a country in which French is spoken, and that's what this part is all about. We cover all aspects of travel, from planning a trip and going through customs, to handling emergencies and seeking medical assistance. Furthermore, this part covers exchanging money, using public transportation, and reserving a hotel room.

Chapter 13

Planning a Trip

- -

- -

Traveling is a way to get away, relax, and perhaps seek a new adventure. Planning your travels in advance is the first step to a rewarding, fulfilling time. Whatever you're looking for— adventure, history, natural wonders, or cultural enlightenment — France and other French-speaking countries have it all. In this chapter, we help you decide where you want to go, show you how to make the appropriate travel plans, and get you ready to take that trip you always dreamed of.

Where Do You Want to Go?

When planning a trip to France — or any French-speaking country — one of the first things to do is to decide where you want to go and what you'd like to see. A trip to France, for example, offers these delights: the ocean and beaches, olive trees and vineyards, rolling green meadows bounded by straggling hedgerows, dazzling expanses of naked rock and arid ruddy soil, former homes or playgrounds of kings, counts, and feudal lords, Romanesque village churches and spectacular Gothic cathedrals, and ruins of Roman architecture and medieval monasteries. Here's a sampling of the wonderful places you can go:

- ✔ **Les Alpes** (ley-zahlp) (*the Alps*), in the southeast

- ✔ **Les Pyrénées** (ley pee-rey-ney) (*the Pyrenees*) in the southwest

- ✔ **La Côte d'Azur** (lah koht dah-zewhr) (*the Riviera*), along the Mediterranean coast, **la Méditerranée** (lah mey-dee-teh-rah-ney)

- ✔ **Le Jura** (luh zhew-rah) mountains in the east

- ✔ **Les Vosges** (ley vohzh) mountains in the east

✔ **Le Massif Central** (luh mah-seef sahN-trahl), the rugged, dry mountains in central France.

✔ **La Bretagne** (lah bruh-tah-nyuh) (*Brittany*), in the northwest

You can even tour the country by water, by way of France's four major rivers — **la Seine** (lah sehn) (the Seine also runs through Paris), **la Loire** (lah lwahr), **la Garonne** (lah gah-rohn), **le Rhône** (luh rohn) — and many others that crisscross the entire country.

If you want your trip to be more exotic, you can choose to visit an *overseas department of France,* **Départements et Régions d'outre-mer (DROM)** (dey-pahrt-mahN ey rey-zhyohN dooh-truh-mehr [drohm]), such as **la Martinique** (lah mahr-tee-neek) in the French West Indies, or an *overseas collectivity,* **Collectivité d'outre-mer (COM)** (koh-leh-ktee-vee-tey dooh-truh-mehr [kohm]), such as **Tahiti** (tah-ee-tee) in French Polynesia.

If you prefer to visit a French-speaking region closer to home, **Québec** (key-behk) and **Montréal** (mohN-rey-ahl) are all you can ask for. You can wander around the old city, visit the botanical gardens and the Basilica of Notre Dame. What about catching a hockey game at the Olympic stadium or attending the biggest winter festival in the world? If summer concerts are more your style, Québec is the place to be in July.

Using geographical prepositions

Wherever you're going, you have to use the verb **aller** (ah-ley) (*to go*) — see Chapter 2 for the conjugation of this verb — followed by a preposition. Which preposition you use depends on whether the place is a city, province, state, or country.

To indicate that you're from a certain place, you use the verb **être** (eh-truh) (*to be*) or the verb **venir** (vuh-neer) (*to come*), followed by a preposition that means *from.* Here's the present tense conjugation of the verb **venir** (head to Chapter 2 for the conjugation of **être**).

Conjugation	Pronunciation
je viens	zhuh vyaN
tu viens	tew vyaN
il/elle/on vient	eel/ehl/ohN vyaN
nous venons	nooh vuh-nohN
vous venez	vooh vuh-ney
ils/elles viennent	eel/ehl vyehn

Saying what city you're from

In French, as in English, you can say *I come from* as well as *I am from.* Use **être** when you want to simply say that you *are from* some place; use the verb **venir** when you want to say that you *come from* some place. Consider these examples:

> **Je suis de New York.** (zhuh swee duh New York.) (*I am from New York.*)
>
> **Nous sommes de Paris.** (nooh sohm duh pah-ree.) (*We are from Paris.*)
>
> **Je viens de Montréal.** (zhuh vyaN duh mohN-rey-ahl.) (*I come from Montreal.*)
>
> **Il vient de Boston.** (eel vyaN duh Boston.) (*He comes from Boston.*)

In French, the question *Where are you from?* is actually *From where are you?* In an interrogative sentence that has a preposition, the preposition is always placed at the beginning of the question. To say *from* in French, you use the preposition **de** (duh). Check out the following examples (notice that **de** becomes **d'** in front of a vowel):

> **D'où êtes-vous?/D'où es-tu?** (dooh eht-vooh?/dooh eh-tew?) (*Where are you from?* [formal/informal])
>
> **D'où venez-vous?/D'où viens-tu?** (dooh vuh-ney-vooh?/dooh vyaN-tew?) (*Where do you come from?* [formal/informal])

Sounds easy, doesn't it? But notice that the places mentioned in the preceding examples (New York, Paris, Montreal, and Boston) are cities. It gets a little more complicated when you start talking about the state, province, country, or continent you come from, as the next section explains.

Saying what state, province, country, or continent you're from

In French, states, provinces, countries, and continents can be masculine or feminine: **la France** (lah frahNs) and **le Canada** (luh kah-nah-dah), for example. (The state, province, country, and continent names that end in **e** are usually feminine.) Table 13-1 presents a sample list of countries with their genders.

Table 13-1	Genders of Countries
Feminine	*Masculine*
L'Algérie (lahl-zhey-ree) (*Algeria*)	**Le Canada** (luh kah-nah-dah) (*Canada*)
L'Allemagne (lahl-mah-nyuh) (*Germany*)	**Les États-Unis*** (ley-zey-tah-zew-nee) (*the United States*)
L'Angleterre (lahN-gluh-tehr) (*England*)	**Le Portugal** (luh pohr-tew-gahl) (*Portugal*)

(continued)

Table 13-1 (continued)

Feminine	Masculine
La Belgique (lah behl-zheek) (*Belgium*)	**Le Japon** (luh zhah-pohN) (*Japan*)
L'Espagne (lehs-pah-nyuh) (*Spain*)	**Le Sénégal** (luh sey-ney-gahl) (*Senegal*)
La France (lah frahNs) (*France*)	**Le Maroc** (luh mah-rohk) (*Morocco*)
La Grèce (lah grehs) (*Greece*)	**Le Danemark** (luh dahn-mahrk) (*Denmark*)
L'Inde (laNd) (*India*)	**Les Pays-Bas*** (ley pey-ee-bah) (the Netherlands)
L'Italie (lee-tah-lee) (*Italy*)	**Le Liban** (luh lee-bahN) (*Lebanon*)
La Suisse (lah swees) (*Switzerland*)	**Le Mexique** (luh mehk-seek) (*Mexico*)

** Both **Les États-Unis** and **Les Pays-Bas** are masculine, plural.*

Notice that all feminine countries end with the letter **e**. One exception is **le Mexique** (luh mehk-seek) (Mexico), which is masculine, even though it ends in **e**.

The following list shows you how to indicate going to or coming from different types of places. Keep in mind that these are general rules; some exceptions do exist.

Table 13-2   Geographical Prepositions

City or Island	
Preposition	**Example**
à (ah) (*to go to or be in*)	**Je vais à Rennes.** (zhuh veh-zah rehn.) (*I am going to Rennes.*)
	Il va à Tahiti. (eel vah ah tah-ee-tee.) (*He is going to Tahiti.*)
de (d') (duh) (*to be from or come from*)	**Je viens de Rennes.** (zhuh vyaN duh rehn.) (*I come from Rennes.*)
	Il vient de Tahiti. (eel vyaN duh tah-ee-tee.) (*He comes from Tahiti.*)
Feminine states, provinces, countries (or masculine beginning with a vowel)	
Preposition	**Example**
en (ahN) (*to go to or be in*)	**Nous allons en Californie/en Normandie/en Espagne/en Iran.** (nooh-zah-lohN ahN kah-lee-fohr-nee/ahN nohr-mahN-dee/ahN-neh-spah-nyuh/ahN ee-rahN.) (*We are going to California/to Normandy/to Spain/to Iran.*)
de (d') (duh) (*to be from or come from*)	**Nous sommes de Californie/de Normandie/d'Espagne/d'Iran.** (nooh sohm duh kah-lee-fohr-nee/duh nohr-mahN-dee/deh-spah-nyuh/dee-rahN.) (*We are from California/Normandy/Spain/Iran.*)

Masculine states, provinces, countries	
Preposition	**Example**
au (oh) (*to go to or be in*)	**Ils vont au Canada/au Portugal/au Maroc.** (eel vohN-toh kah-nah-dah/oh pohr-tew-gahl/oh mah-rohk.) (*They are going to Canada/to Portugal/to Morocco.*)
du (dew) (*to be from or come from*)	**Ils viennent du Canada/du Portugal/du Maroc.** (eel vyehn dew kah-nah-dah/dew pohr-tew-gahl/dew mah-rohk.) (*They come from Canada/from Portugal/from Morocco.*)

Masculine plural countries	
Preposition	**Example**
aux (oh) (*to go to or be in*)	**Elle va aux Etats-Unis/aux Pays-Bas.** (ehl vah oh-zey-tah-zew-nee/oh pey-ee-bah.) (*She is going to the United States/to the Netherlands.*)
des (dey) (*to be from or come from*)	**Elle est des Etats-Unis/des Pays-Bas.** (ehl eh deh-zey-tah-zew-nee/dey pey-ee-bah.) (*She is from the United States/from the Netherlands.*)

Because the verb **être** means *to be,* you can use it to mean being *in* a city or country, as well as being *from* a city or country.

Talkin' the Talk

Lynne is on the phone with her friend Anne in Paris. Anne and her husband Michel want Lynne and her husband David to join them during the holidays.

Anne: **Écoute, Lynne. J'ai une proposition. Que faites-vous pendant les fêtes?**
ey-kooht, leen. zhey ewn proh-poh-zee-syohN. kuh feht-vooh pahN-dahN ley feht?
Listen, Lynne. I have a proposition. What are you doing during the holidays?

Lynne: **Nous? Pas grand-chose. Nous allons beaucoup dormir et nous détendre.**
nooh? pah grahN-shohz. nooh-zah-lohN boh-kooh dohr-meer ey nooh dey-tahN-druh.
Us? Not much. We are going to sleep a lot and relax.

Anne: **Nous aussi. Mais voilà ma proposition: Venez à Nice avec nous!**
          nooh-zoh-see. meh vwah-lah mah proh-poh-zee-syohN: vuh-ney ah nees ah-vehk nooh!
          Us too. But here is my proposition: Come to Nice with us!

Lynne: **À Nice? Comment ça?**
          ah nees? koh-mahN sah?
          To Nice? How come?

Anne: **Nous allons louer une petite maison. Pour vous et pour nous.**
          nooh-zah-lohN looh-ey ewn puh-teet meh-zohN. poohr vooh ey poohr nooh.
          We are going to rent a little house. For you and for us.

Lynne: **Oh là là, Anne. C'est fantastique! Je vais l'annoncer à David. Nice! Mon rêve! Je vais te rappeler.**
          oh lah lah, ahn. seh fahN-tah steek! zhuh veh lah-nohN-sey ah dah-veed. Nees! mohN rehv! zhuh veh tuh rah-pley.
          Oh wow, Anne! That's fantastic! I'm going to announce it to David. Nice! My dream! I am going to call you back.

Words to Know

les fêtes [f]	ley feht	holidays
pas grand-chose	pah grahN-shohz	not much
dormir	dohr-meer	to sleep
se détendre	suh dey-tahN-druh	to relax (reflexive)
nous allons louer	nooh-zah-lohN looh-ey	we are going to rent

Making plans with the future tense

When you plan a trip, you are looking ahead to the future. French has two main future tenses: the immediate or near future and the simple future. As Chapter 2 explains, you form the immediate future by conjugating the verb **aller** in the present followed by an infinitive. The immediate future means *to be going to do something.* The other form of the future tense in French is the simple future. In English, the simple future uses the word *will* plus the verb, as in *I will travel this summer.* In French, you use only the verb but conjugate it in the future tense, which implies *will.*

To form the simple future with **–er, –ir, –re** verbs, take the infinitive (drop the **e** of **–re** verbs because the future stem ends in an **r**) and add the following endings: **–ai, –as, –a, –ons, –ez,** and **–ont.** These endings come from the verb **avoir** (ah-vwahr) (*to have*), except that you drop the **av–** in front of the **nous** (nooh) (*we*) and **vous** (vooh) (*you*) verb forms. To see what we mean, take a look at the conjugation of three verbs — **arriver** (ah-ree-vey) (*to arrive*), **finir** (fee-neer) (*to finish*), and **attendre** (ah-tahN-druh) (*to wait [for]*) — which represent the three main verb categories: **–er, –ir, –re.**

Conjugation	*Pronunciation*
j'arriverai	zhah-reev-rey
tu arriveras	tew ah-reev-rah
il/elle/on arrivera	eel/ehl/ohN ah-reev-rah
nous arriverons	nooh-zah-reev-rohN
vous arriverez	vooh-zah-reev-rey
ils/elles arriveront	eel-/ehl-zah-reev-rohN

Conjugation	*Pronunciation*
je finirai	zhuh fee-nee-rah
tu finiras	tew fee-nee-rah
il/elle/on finira	eel/ehl/ohN fee-nee-rah
nous finirons	nooh fee-nee-rohN
vous finirez	vooh fee-nee-rey
ils/elles finiront	eel/ehl fee-nee-rohN

Conjugation	Pronunciation
j'attendrai	zhah-tahN-drey
tu attendras	tew ah-tahN-drah
il/elle/on attendra	eel/ehl/ohN ah-tahN-drah
nous attendrons	nooh-zah-tahN-drohN
vous attendrez	vooh-zah-tahN-drey
ils/elles attendront	eel-/ehl-zah-tahN-drohN

There are also many verbs that have irregular stems but regular endings. To conjugate these verbs in the future tense, you follow the same pattern noted earlier but change the stem as appropriate for the particular verb being conjugated. **Aller** is one of these verbs. The stem of **aller** in the future is **ir**. Here's the conjugation of **aller** in the simple future tense:

Conjugation	Pronunciation
j'irai	zhee-rey
tu iras	tew ee-rah
il/elle/on ira	eel/ehl/ohN ee-rah
nous irons	nooh-zee-rohN
vous irez	vooh-zee-rey
ils/elles iront	eel-/ehl-zee-rohN

Table 13-3 shows these types of verbs and their stems.

Table 13-3   Verbs with Irregular Stems but Regular Endings

Verb	Stem
aller (ah-ley) (*to go*)	**ir** (eer)
avoir (ah-vwahr) (*to have*)	**aur** (ohr)
courir (kooh-reer) (*to run*)	**courr** (koohr)
devoir (duh-vwahr) (*to owe, to have to*)	**devr** (duh-vruh)
envoyer (ahN-vwah-yey) (*to send*)	**enverr** (ahN-vehr)
être (eh-truh) (*to be*)	**ser** (suhr)
faire (fehr) (*to do, to make*)	**fer** (fuhr)
mourir (mooh-reer) (*to die*)	**mourr** (moohr)
pouvoir (pooh-vwahr) (*to be able to*)	**pourr** (poohr)

Verb	Stem
recevoir (ruh-suh-vwahr) (*to receive*)	**recevr** (ruh-suh-vruh)
savoir (sah-vwahr) (*to know*)	**saur** (sohr)
venir (vuh-neer) (*to come*)	**viendr** (vyehn-druh)
voir (vwahr) (*to see*)	**verr** (vehr)
vouloir (vooh-lwahr) (*to want*)	**voudr** (vooh-druh)

Here are some sentences that use the future tense with these irregular verbs:

> **Je serai prêt/prête.** (zhuh suh-rey preh/preht.) (*I will be ready.*)

> **Nous recevrons les passeports.** (nooh ruh-suh-vrohN ley pahs-pohr.) (*We will receive the passports.*)

Getting Ready for Your Trip

When you plan your trip, you're likely to hear the questions **Où voulez-vous aller?** (ooh vooh-ley-vooh-zah-ley?) (*Where do you want to go?*). To answer this question, you simply say **Je voudrais aller à. . . .** (zhuh vooh-dreh-zah-ley ah. . . .) (*I would like to go to. . . .*). If you're working with a travel agent, you may also hear **Quand voulez-vous partir?** (kahN vooh-ley-vooh pahr-teer?) (*When do you want to leave?*) and **Quand voulez-vous revenir?** (kahN vooh-ley-vooh ruh-vuh-neer?) (*When do you want to come back?*) Refer to Chapter 4 for information on making date references. If you're reserving seats, you will be asked **Pour combien de personnes?** (poohr kohN-byaN duh pehr-sohhn?) (*For how many people?*) To answer, simply say **Pour. . . personnes** (poohr. . . pehr-sohhn) (*For. . . people*).

Talkin' the Talk

While her friends are in New York making their own travel arrangements, Anne is at a Paris travel agency booking her and her husband's flight to Nice. (Track 14)

Anne: **Bonjour, monsieur.**
               bohN-zhoohr, muh-syuh.
               Good morning, sir.

Agent: **Bonjour, madame. Vous désirez?**
               bohN-zhoohr, mah-dahm. vooh dey-zee-rey?
               Good morning, ma'am. Can I help you?

Anne: **Nous voudrions prendre l'avion pour Nice en décembre.**
noo vooh-dree-ohN prahN-druh lah-vyoN poohr nees ahN dey-sahN-bruh.
We would like to take a plane to Nice in December.

Agent: **C'est pour combien de personnes?**
seh poohr kohN-byaN duh pehr-sohhn?
For how many people?

Anne: **Pour deux personnes, monsieur.**
poohr duh pehr-sohhn, muh-syuh.
For two people, sir.

Agent: **Et pour quelle date? Vous voulez rester pour combien de jours?**
ey poohr kehl daht? vooh vooh-ley reh-stey poohr kohN-byaN duh zhoohr?
And for which date? How many days do you want to stay?

Anne: **Dix jours: du 22 décembre au 2 janvier.**
dee zhoohr: dew vahNt-duh dey-sahN-bruh oh duh zhahN-vyey.
Ten days: from the 22nd of December to the 2nd of January.

Agent: **Vous avez de la chance. J'ai encore deux places. Votre nom?**
vooh-zah-vey duh lah shahNs. zhey ahN-kohr duh plahs. vohh-truh nohN?
You're lucky. I still have two seats. Your name?

Anne: **Anne et Michel Brasse: B-R-A-S-S-E.**
ahn ey mee-shehl brahs: bey ehr ah dooh-bluh ehs uh.
Anne and Michel Brasse: B-R-A-S-S-E.

Agent: **C'est le vol Air France 6002 qui part à 10 heures de Charles de Gaulle. Ça vous convient?**
seh luh vohl ehr frahNs see meel duh kee pahr ah deez-uhr duh shahrl duh gohl. sah vooh kohN-vyaN?
It's the Air France flight #6002 which leaves at 10 a.m. from Charles de Gaulle. Does that suit you?

Anne: **Oui, c'est parfait. À quelle heure est-ce qu'il arrive?**
wee, seh pahr-feh. ah kehl uhr ehs-keel ah-reev?
Yes, that's perfect. At what time does it arrive?

Agent: **Il arrive à Nice à 11h30.**
eel ah-reev ah nees ah ohNz uhr trahNt.
It arrives in Nice at 11:30 a.m.

Anne: **Bon. Pouvez-vous réserver deux sièges pour nous?**
bohN. pooh-vey-vooh rey-sehr-vey duh syehzh poohr nooh?
Good. Can you reserve two seats for us?

Agent: **Mais oui, bien sûr.**
meh wee, byaN sewr.
Yes, of course.

Words to Know

je reviens	zhuh ruh-vyaN	I am coming back
voyager	voh-yah-zhey	to travel
le vol	luh vohl	the flight
le siège	luh syehzh	the seat
le lendemain	luh lahN-duh-mahN	the next day

Introducing the indirect object pronouns

The preceding dialogue uses the phrase **Ça vous convient?** (sah vooh kohN-vyaN?), which translates as *Does that suit you?* or *Is that convenient for or suitable to you?* The **vous** in this sentence is the indirect object pronoun. The indirect object pronoun replaces the indirect object (the noun) that follows the preposition **à** in the sentence). For example, in the sentence **Je parle à Pierre** (zhuh pahrl ah pyehr) (*I am speaking to Pierre*), **Pierre** is the indirect object. You can replace **à Pierre** with the indirect object pronoun **lui** (lwee) (*to him*) to form the sentence **Je lui parle** (zhuh lwee pahrl) (*I am speaking to him*). Table 13-4 shows the French indirect object pronouns.

Note that sometimes in English, the indirect object pronoun is translated as *(for)* instead of *(to)* as in the earlier example **Ça vous convient?**

Table 13-4	French Indirect Object Pronouns
Pronoun	*Example*
me (muh) (*to me*)	**Ça me convient.** (sah muh kohN-vyaN.) (*That suits me.*)
te (tuh) (*to you*)	**Ça te convient.** (sah tuh kohN-vyaN.) (*That suits you.*)
lui (lwee) (*to him, to her*)	**Ça lui convient.** (sah lwee kohN-vyaN.) (*That suits him/her.*)
nous (nooh) (*to us*)	**Ça nous convient.** (sah nooh kohN-vyaN.) (*That suits us.*)
vous (vooh) (*to you*)	**Ça vous convient.** (sah vooh kohN-vyaN.) (*That suits you.*)
leur (luhr) (*to them*)	**Ça leur convient.** (sah luhr kohN-vyaN.) (*That suits them.*)

By the way, only **lui** and **leur** differ from the direct object pronouns, which are **le**, **la, les**; the others coincide. (See Chapter 16 for more information on direct object pronouns.)

In the following sentence, you can see how an indirect object pronoun replaces an indirect object noun with **à: Ça convient à M. (**or **à Mme) Paulet** (sah kohN-vyaN ah muh-syuh [*or* ah mah-dahm] poh-leh) (*It suits Mr.* [*or Mrs.*] *Paulet*) becomes **Ça lui convient** (sah lwee kohN-vyaN)(*It suits him* [or *her*]).

Securing passports and visas

The requirements to enter different countries can vary. If you're a U.S. citizen, you need a valid **passeport** (pahs-pohr) (*passport*), and depending on how long you stay, you may also need a visa. (If you plan to stay in Europe for less than three months, no visa is required, for example). To find out more about entry requirements anywhere in the world (Tahiti? Martinique? Madagascar?), you can browse on the Internet at travel.state.gov. Here are some terms and phrases that can get you the information you need:

- ✔ **le consulat français** (luh kohN-sew-lah frahN-seh) (*the French consulate*)

- ✔ **voyager** (voh-yah-zhey) (*to travel*)

- ✔ **un passeport valide** (uhN pahs-pohr vah-leed) (*a valid passport*)

- ✔ **Est-ce qu'il faut un visa pour aller en/au/aux. . . ?** (ehs-keel foh-tuhN vee-zah pooh-rah-ley ahN/oh/oh. . . ?) (*Do you need a visa to go to. . .?*)

- ✔ **Je veux rester. . . jours/semaines en/au/aux. . . .** (zhuh vuh rehs-tey. . . zhoohr/suh-mehn ahN/oh/oh. . . .) (*I want to stay. . . days/weeks in . . . .*)

Be sure to check the expiration date on your passport early because getting it renewed can take weeks. Don't even dream that you can get it renewed overnight! If you need a brand new passport because you've never had one, make sure you start procedures at least six weeks before you want to leave. If you're traveling to Europe, once you're there, you can hop from country to country to your heart's desire. In most cases, you won't even be asked to show your passport.

Packing your suitcases with your belongings: Using possessive adjectives

Regardless of when you're going or what you plan to do, when you pack for your trip, you want to bring along some of your most comfortable clothes (Chapter 9 has a list) and shoes. You may also want to bring your sunglasses, your hat, your suntan lotion, and so on — all of which you can do with possessive adjectives.

Possessive adjectives in English are *my, your, his, her, our,* and *their.* In French, because every noun has a gender, the possessive adjectives must agree in gender and in number with the object that is possessed, not with the person possessing the object. That is the reason that, in French, there is no difference, for example, between *his* sunglasses or *her* sunglasses. Table 13-5 lists the possessive adjectives.

Table 13-5	French Possessive Adjectives	
Masculine Singular	*Feminine Singular*	*Masculine/FemininePlural*
mon (mohN) (*my*)	**ma** (mah) (*my*)	**mes** (mey) (*my*)
ton (tohN) (*your*)	**ta** (tah) (*your*)	**tes** (tey) (*your*)
son (sohN) (*his, her*)	**sa** (sah) (*his, her*)	**ses** (sey) (*his, her*)
notre (nohh-truh) (*our*)	**notre** (nohh-truh) (*our*)	**nos** (noh) (*our*)
votre (vohh-truh) (*your*)	**votre** (vohh-truh) (*your*)	**vos** (voh) (*your*)
leur (luhr) (*their*)	**leur** (luhr) (*their*)	**leurs** (luhr) (*their*)

Here are some examples of the possessive adjectives:

> **Elle a un sac. C'est son sac.** (ehl ah uhN sahk. seh sohN sahk.) (*She has a bag. It's her bag.*) — In this example, notice that the possessive adjective **son** does not agree with the feminine subject, **elle**, but with the masculine, singular noun **sac**.

> **Il porte une chemise. C'est sa chemise.** (eel pohrt ewn shuh-meez. seh sah shuh-meez.) (*He is wearing a shirt. It's his shirt.*) — Here, the possessive adjective **sa** agrees with **chemise**, which is feminine singular, not with the masculine subject **il**.

Keep in mind the local expectations regarding appropriate attire. When you visit historical monuments in France, such as cathedrals and churches, for example, you don't see locals wearing clothing that is too revealing (very short shorts or skirts, for example, or very low-cut tank tops), and you shouldn't either.

Talkin' the Talk

Lynne and her husband, David, have never been to the south of France, so she calls up her friend Anne, who lives in France, to ask about what type of clothing to take.

Lynne: **Anne, je fais nos valises. Qu'est-ce que tu me conseilles comme vêtements?**
ahn, zhuh feh noh vah-leez. kehs-kuh tew muh kohN-sehy kohm veht-mahN?
Anne, I am packing our suitcases. What do you advise me about clothes?

Anne: **C'est facile. Des choses légères mais un pull pour le soir.**
seh fah-seel. dey shohz ley-zhehr meh uhN pewl poohr luh swahr.
That's easy. Light things, but a sweater for the evening.

Lynne: **Okay. Alors, je vais prendre mes shorts et mes t-shirts pour la plage.**
Oh-keh. ah-lohr, zhuh veh prahN-druh mey shohrt ey mey tee-shuhrt poohr lah plahzh.
Okay. So, I am going to take my shorts and my t-shirts for the beach.

Anne: **Et peut-être ta robe rouge et ta jupe noire pour sortir. Pour David, apporte son costume et sa cravate.**
ey puh-teh-truh tah rohhb roohzh ey tah zhewp nwahr poohr sohr-teer. poohr dah-veed, ah-pohrt sohN koh-stewm ey sah krah-vaht.
And maybe your red dress and your black skirt for going out. For David, bring his suit and his tie.

Lynne: **Ah oui, et ses chaussures.**
ah wee, ey sey shoh-sewr.
Oh yes, and his shoes.

Anne: **Voilà. Mais ne prenez pas trop de choses.**
vwah-lah. meh nuh pruh-ney pah trohd shohz.
That's it. But don't take too many things.

Lynne: **Et nos sandales et nos baskets, ça suffit?**
ey noh sahN-dahl ey noh bahs-keht, sah sew-fee?
And our sandals and our sneakers, is that enough?

Anne: **Oui. N'oubliez pas vos lunettes de soleil!**
wee. nooh-blee-yey pah voh lew-neht duh soh-lehy!
Yes. Don't forget your sunglasses!

Fun & Games

In the blanks provided, write the French term for each of the identified countries.

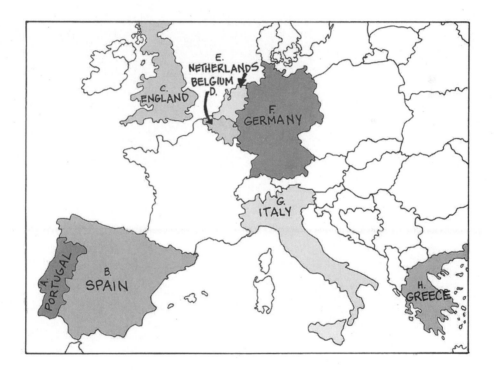

A._____ B._____

C._____ D._____

E._____ F._____

G._____ H._____

Chapter 14

Dealing with Money in a Foreign Land

. . . .

In This Chapter
▶ Understanding French currency
▶ Changing money and cashing checks
▶ Using an ATM and credit cards

. . . .

Money, **l'argent** (lahr-zhahN), makes the world go 'round, they say, and you need money to go 'round the world. If you have the opportunity — and pleasure — of traveling to a French-speaking country, you need to know what the currency is and how to complete numerous monetary transactions, like exchanging currency, cashing traveler's checks, using bank machines, and more. In this chapter, we give you the information and phrases you need to express your needs clearly through several kinds of money transactions.

Getting Current with Currency

Unified Europe — the block of countries that are part of the European Union — has made it easier to cross the borders within the EU without the hassle of going through border check points. Furthermore, many countries within the EU have a common currency, the euro (€), which has been legal currency since January 1, 1999. As of January 1, 2011, 17 out of 27 European Union countries, including France, use the euro. Here is a list of French-speaking regions and countries around the world that use the euro:

  ✔ **In Europe**: France, Monaco, Belgium, Luxemburg, Corsica

  ✔ **In the Americas:** French Guiana, St. Pierre, and Miquelon

  ✔ **In the Caribbean:** Martinique, Guadeloupe, St. Barthélemy, and St. Martin

  ✔ **In the Indian Ocean:** Mayotte and La Réunion

Of course, not all French-speaking countries are part of the European Union, nor do they all use euros. If you travel to any of these countries, you'll want to know the currency used there. The following sections tell you what you need to know.

Getting familiar with euros and cents

The euro, like all other monetary units, comes in the form of coins and bills in several denominations. There are seven different denominations of euro notes, or bills, and each has a distinct color and size. These notes are the same for all countries in the Euro zone, that is, the 17 countries that have adopted the euro. The coins, however, have a common front side, but the designs on the back of the coins are specific to each country. The following sections have the details. For more information, go to `http://en.wikipedia.org/wiki/euro`.

Getting the bills straight

There are seven different denominations of the euro: €5, €10, €20, €50, €100, €200, €500. Unlike U.S. dollar bills, which all have the same size and color, the euro bills increase in size with the denomination and are very colorful. The notes, which are the same for all countries in the Euro zone, denote European symbols such as European architecture, a map of Europe, the name "Euro" in Greek and Latin, the 12 stars of the European flag, and so on. The front features windows and gateways, and the back depicts European bridges. Figure 14-1 shows the front and back of a euro bill.

Figure 14-1: All euros are the same from country to country. (Not actual size.)

Looking at the coins

Euro coins come in denominations ranging from 1 **centime** (sahN-teem) (*cent*) to 50 **centimes** (sahN-teem) (*cents*): There are also €1 and €2 coins. There are eight coins in all: € 0.01, € 0.02, € 0.05, € 0.10, € 0.20, € 0.50, €1, and € 2.

The coins have a common front side, but the backside of the coins differs by country, and they can be used interchangeably throughout the various countries that use the euro. The French coins include these three symbols (see Figure 14-2):

✔ **La Marianne** (lah mah-ree-ahn), representing the French Republic of **Liberté, Egalité, Fraternité** (lee-behr-tey, ey-gah-lee-tey, frah-tehr-nee-tey) (*Liberty, Equality, Fraternity*), is on €0.01, €0.02, and €0.05 cent coins.

✔ **La Semeuse** (lah seh-muhz) (*the Sower*), a theme carried over from the French Franc, is on €0.10, €0.20, and €0.50 cent coins.

✔ **L'Arbre** (lahr-bruh) (*the Tree*) surrounded by a hexagon is on €1 and €2 coins. The tree symbolizes life, continuity, and growth, and the hexagon symbolizes France, which is also called **l'Hexagone** (leh-ksah-gohn) (*the Hexagon*) because of its six-sided shape.

Figure 14-2: From left: **La Marianne**, **la Semeuse**, and **l'Arbre**.

La Marianne   The Sower   Tree

The coins vary in size, but, just like U.S. coins, they don't necessarily grow in proportion to the denomination.

When you do your banking or shopping, keep in mind that the French separate euros and **centimes** with a comma, not with a period. For example, 100,00 in French euros is written in English as 100.00.

Beyond Europe and the euro: Currency in other French-speaking countries

As mentioned previously, not all French-speaking countries use the euro. Table 14-1 lists the currencies of several countries where French is either the official language or one of the official languages. (French is also spoken in many more places, such as many regions of Africa, although it is not the official language; this list doesn't include those countries):

Table 14-1   Currency in Other Countries Where French Is Spoken

Country/Region	Currency (in English)	Currency (in French)
Switzerland	Swiss franc (CHF)	**le franc suisse** (luh frahN swees)
Québec, Canada	Canadian dollar (CAD)	**le dollar canadien** (luh doh-lahr kah-nah-dyaN)
Haiti	Haitian gourdes (HTG)	**la gourde haïtienne** (lah goohrd ah-ee-syehn)
Madagascar	Malagasy ariary (MGA)	**L'ariary malgache** (lah-ree-ah-ree mahl-gahsh)
Tahiti	CFP* franc (XPF)	**Le franc pacifique** (luh frahN pah-see-feek)
New Caledonia	CFP* franc (XPF)	**Le franc pacifique** (luh frahN pah-see-feek)
Vanuatu	Vanuatu vatu (VUV)	**Le Vanuatu vatu** (luh vah-new-ah-tew vah-tew)
Wallis-et-Futuna	CFP* franc (XPF)	**Le franc pacifique** (luh frahN pah-see-feek)

* CFP stands for Cour de Franc Pacifique, translated as the Pacific Franc.

Going to the Bank

When you travel to another country, one of the first places you probably need to go is to **la banque** (lah bahNk) (*the bank*), where you can exchange currency, cash a traveler's check, or change large bills into smaller denominations. The following vocabulary terms can help you navigate your way to the right people and areas of a bank and request what you need:

- **la caisse** (lah kehs) (*cash register*)
- **le caissier/la caissière** (luh key-syey/lah key-syehr) (*teller*)
- **le client/la cliente** (luh klee-yahN/lah klee-yahNt) (*customer*)
- **le guichet de change** (luh gee-sheh duh shahNzh) (*cashier's window*)
- **en argent liquide** (ahN nahr-zahN lee-keed) (*in cash*)
- **le reçu** (luh ruh-sew) (*receipt*)
- **la signature** (lah see-nyah-tewr) (*signature*)

Banking hours, **heures d'ouverture et de fermeture** (uhr dooh-vehr-tewr ey duh fehr-muh-tewr), can range between **8h** (wee-tuhr) (*8:00 a.m.*) and **10h** (dee-zuhr) (*10:00 a.m.*), and **14h** (kah-tohrz uhr) (*2:00 p.m.*) and **17h** (dee-seht uhr) (*5:00 p.m.*); refer to Chapter 4 for telling time in French. Some banks close during lunch break, which can last up to two hours.

Getting — and requesting — assistance

When you enter a bank, someone there may ask you how he or she can help you. You may hear one of these phrases, both of which mean *Can I help you?*

- ✔ **Vous désirez?** (vooh dey-zee-rey?)
- ✔ **Je peux vous aider?** (zhuh puh vooh-zey-dey?)

Instead of waiting to be offered help, you can also just walk up to an employee and state what you want. Start your request with **Je voudrais . . .** (zhuh vooh-dreh. . .) (*I would like . . .*) and then add the specifics, for example, **changer des dollars en euros** (shahN-zhey dey doh-lahr ahN uh-roh) (*to change dollars into euros*) or **encaisser un chèque** (ahN-key-sey uhN shehk) (*to cash a check*).

To say *I need something* in French, you express it as *I have need of something*. You pick the appropriate form of the verb **avoir** (ah-vwahr) (*to have*) — head to Chapter 2 for the conjugation of **avoir** — add **besoin de** (buh-zwaN duh) (*need of*), and then follow it with whatever you need. All together, it looks like this: **J'ai besoin de. . . .** (zhey buh-zwaN duh. . . .) (*I need. . . .*) + a noun or a verb in the infinitive form. Here are some examples:

> **J'ai besoin d'une pièce d'identité.** (zhey buh-zwaN dewn pyehs dee-dahN-tee-tey.) (*I need identification.*)

> **Christine a besoin d'argent.** (krees-teen ah buh-zwaN dahr-zhahN.) (*Christine needs money.*)

> **Avez-vous besoin de changer des dollars?** (ah-vey-vooh buh-zwaN duh shahN-zhey dey doh-lahr?) (*Do you need to change dollars?*)

Exchanging money

Because the majority member states of the European Union use the euro as the shared currency, you have only one exchange rate to deal with for most European countries. Wonderful, right? And perfect for travelers. When you have **une devise (étrangère)** (ewn duh-veez [ey-trahN-zhehr]) (*foreign* *currency*), you can go to any of the following three convenient places to exchange money at a reasonable rate:

- ✔ **les banques** (ley bahNk) (*banks*). Especially in smaller towns, banks are often the most convenient place to exchange currency because small towns are less likely to have a specific currency exchange office. Banks charge an additional fee (which may vary from bank to bank) to exchange currency.

- ✔ **un bureau de change** (uhN bew-roh duh shahNzh) (*a currency exchange office*). These businesses are everywhere in big cities. However, check the rates and commissions first because they can vary greatly. A bank is often a good alternative when no currency exchange office is available.

- ✔ **la poste** (lah pohst) (*the post office*). In France, you can change money in many post offices. They open at 8:00 a.m. (**8h**) and close at around 7:00 p.m. (**19h**). If you happen to walk into a post office that doesn't offer currency exchange, the postal clerks can direct you to the nearest place that does offer this service.

Other places, such as hotel lobbies, may exchange currency, but their rates are usually less favorable. Likewise, although you may have to change a few dollars at the money exchange counter of the airport upon your arrival, you can usually get a better deal if you wait until you are in town to change money at a bank.

As a general guide, the U.S. dollar is worth less than the euro and slightly more than the Canadian dollar. To find more precise, current exchange rates go to www.finance.yahoo.com. Alternatively, you can simply ask for the current exchange rate with this question: **Quel est votre taux de change?** (kehl eh vohh-truh toh duh shahNzh?) (*What is your exchange rate?*). Here are some other phrases that may come in handy:

Est-ce qu'on peut changer de l'argent ici? (ehs-kohN puh shahN-zhey duh lahr-zhahN ee-see?) (*Can one exchange money here?*)

Je voudrais changer des dollars américains pour. . . . (zhuh vooh-dreh shahN-zhey dey doh-lahr ah-mey-ree-kaN poohr. . . .) (*I would like to change U.S. dollars for. . . .*)

Quels sont vos frais de change? (kehl sohN voh freh duh shahNzh?) (*How much do you charge to change money?*)

Talkin' the Talk

 Martin, a Canadian tourist, walks into a money exchange office in Nice to exchange his Canadian dollars into euros. (Track 15)

L'employée: **Bonjour, monsieur, vous désirez?**
bohN-zhoohr, muh-syuh, vooh dey-zee-rey?
Hello, sir, what can I do for you?

Martin: **Bonjour, madame. Je voudrais changer cent dollars canadiens.**
bohN-zhoohr, mah-dahm. zhuh vooh-dreh shahN-zhey sahN doh-lahr cah-nah-dyaN.
Hello, ma'am. I would like to change one hundred Canadian dollars.

L'employée: **Très bien, monsieur. Un moment, s'il vous plaît. . . . Bon, ça fait 75 euros. . . . Voilà, et votre reçu.**
treh byaN, muh-syuh. uhN moh-mahN, seel vooh pleh. . . . bohN, sah feh swah-sahN kaNz uh-roh. . . . vwah-lah, ey vohh-truh ruh-sew.
Very well, sir. One moment, please. . . . Well, it's 75 euros. . . . Here you are, and your receipt.

Martin: **Merci, et au revoir.**
mehr-see, ey ohr-vwahr.
Thank you, and good-bye.

L'employée: **Au revoir, monsieur.**
ohr-vwahr, muh-syuh.
Good-bye, sir.

Cashing checks and checking your cash

Cashing **un chèque de voyage** (uhN shehk duh voh-yahzh) (a *traveler's check*) is another task you can take care of in **la banque**. When you go to cash your checks, you can say **Je voudrais encaisser. . . .** (zhuh vooh-dreh ahN-key-sey. . . .) (*I would like to cash. . . .*). You'll be asked to provide **une pièce d'identité** (ewn pyehs dee-dahN-tee-tey) (*an I.D.*) and **votre signature** (vohh-truh see-nyah-tewr) (*your signature*).

You can save yourself a lot of trouble by getting these checks in your destination's local currency. Cashing local checks is **gratuit** (grah-twee) (*free of charge*). If it isn't, go to another bank. If your traveler's checks aren't in the local currency, you have to pay a fee to get them exchanged into local money. Another benefit is that many stores accept local checks just as they would cash.

As convenient as it may be to have your traveler's checks made in the local currency, traveler's checks in U.S. dollars may be useful as a back-up source in the event that your plans change, you decide to stretch your visit to another country, or if U.S. dollars just make you feel better in a security blanket sort of way.

Making change

Large bills can be inconvenient. Pulling out a very large bill to pay for a very inexpensive item can make you feel conspicuous. In addition, some businesses may not accept bills over a certain amount, and you may be asked **Avez-vous de la (petite) monnaie?** (ah-vey-vooh duh lah [puh-teet] moh-neh?) (*Do you have [small] change?*). The same question in Quebec is **Avez-vous du p'tit change?** (ah-vey-vooh dew ptee shahNzh?). Plus, having a variety of small bills makes it a little easier to keep track of how much you're spending and how much change you should get back, which is particularly helpful when you're still learning to count out a new and unfamiliar currency. So when you want to get some change, you can use these phrases:

> **J'ai besoin de monnaie.** (zhey buh-zwaN duh moh-neh.) (*I need change [coins]*.)

> **Je voudrais faire du change.** (zhuh vooh-dreh fehr dew shahNzh.) (*I would like to get some change.*) — Quebec

> **Je voudrais faire de la monnaie.** (zhuh vooh-dreh fehr duh lah moh-neh.) (*I would like to get some change.*) — France

Be careful not to accidentally translate the English word *money* to **monnaie**. Although *money* and **monnaie** look and sound so much alike, the word French word for *money* is actually **argent** (ahr-zhahN*)*.

Talkin' the Talk

Susan is in a bank, wanting to cash her traveler's checks. She speaks to **la caissière** (lah key-syehr) (*the teller*).

Susan: **Bonjour, mademoiselle. Je voudrais encaisser mes chèques de voyage.**
                bohN-zhoohr, mahd-mwah-zehl. zhuh vooh-dreh ahN-key-sey mey shehk duh voh-yahzh.
                Hello, miss. I would like to cash my traveler's checks.

La caissière: **Ils sont en euros?**
                eel sohN-tahN uh-roh?
                Are they in euros?

Susan: **Oui, en euros.**
                wee, ahN uh-roh.
                Yes, in euros.

La caissière: **Bon. J'ai besoin d'une pièce d'identité.**
                bohN. zhey buh-zwaN dewn pyehs dee-dahN-tee-tey.
                Very well. I need identification.

Susan: **J'ai mon passeport et une carte de crédit, c'est bon?**
                zhey mohN pahs-pohr ey ewn kahrt duh krey-dee, seh bohN?
                I've got my passport and a credit card. Will that do?

La caissière: **Le passeport, c'est parfait . . . merci. Et votre sigature, s'il vous plaît.**
                luh pahs-pohr, seh pahr-feh . . . mehr-see. ey vohh-truh see-nyah-tewr, seel vooh pleh.
                The passport, that's perfect . . . thank you. And your signature, please.

Susan: **Ah oui, bien sûr . . . voilà.**
                ah wee, byaN sewr . . . vwah-lah.
                Oh yes, certainly . . . here you go.

Using Credit Cards and ATMs

Sometimes a store may not accept your local traveler's check — a situation that happens more frequently in Europe than in the United States. In that event, you'll want to have some extra cash when you go shopping. Another option is to use **une carte de crédit** (ewn kahrt duh krey-dee) (*a credit card*) or **un distributeur (de billets)** (uhN dees-tree-bew-tuhr [duh bee-yeh]) (*an automated teller machine, ATM*).

You can find ATMs in big and small towns, usually at a bank, in a shopping area, at train stations, at post offices, and all sorts of other places. You can access them all day and night. . . unless, of course, they are temporarily out of order. But nothing is perfect, right?

Credit cards are widely accepted in French-speaking countries, but some stores have a minimum purchase requirement. For example, they may not accept credit cards if you spend under 20 euros.

If you use your ATM card to exchange money, the exchange rate you get is definitely the most favorable because you're making a direct bank exchange between the ATM's bank and your bank. The fee is slightly more if you use your credit card to access cash at an ATM because most credit cards charge a fee for cash advances.

Machines basically work the same way elsewhere as they do in the U.S. Usually you can choose your prompts to be in English, but just in case the machine doesn't give you a language choice, here are the French phrases and instructions you need to know to use an ATM:

- **Insérez votre carte svp.** (aN-sey-rey vohh-truh kahrt seel vooh pleh.) (*Insert your card, please.*)

- **Tapez votre code svp.** (tah-pey vohh-truh kohhd seel vooh pleh.) (*Type your PIN, please.*)

- **Retrait d'espèces.** (ruh-treh deh-spehs.) (*Cash withdrawal.*)

- **Voulez-vous un reçu?** (vooh-ley-vooh uhN ruh-sew?) (*Would you like a receipt?*)

- **Carte en cours de vérification.** (kahrt ahN koohr duh vey-ree-fee-kah-syohN.) (*Checking your balance.*)

- **Patientez svp.** (pah-syaN-tey seel vooh pleh.) (*Wait, please.*)

- **Reprenez votre carte svp.** (ruh-pruh-ney vohh-truh kahrt, seel vooh pleh.) (*Take your card, please.*)

- **Prenez votre argent svp.** (pruh-ney vohh-truh ahr-zhahN seel vooh pleh.) (*Take your money, please.*)

✓ **N'oubliez pas votre reçu.** (nooh-blee-yey pah vohh-truh ruh-sew.)
(*Don't forget your receipt.*)

Saying that you can, want, or have to do something

Verbs such as **pouvoir** (pooh-vwahr) (*to be able to*), **vouloir** (vooh-lwahr) (*to want*), or **devoir** (duh-vwahr) (*to have to, to must*) require a verb after them in the infinitive form to express what you can, want, and must do or have to do. Here are some examples:

✓ **Tu peux aller au distributeur.** (tew puh ah-ley oh dees-tree-bew-tuhr.)
(*You can go to the ATM.*)

✓ **Vous pouvez insérer votre carte.** (vooh pooh-vey aN-sey-rey vohh-truh kahrt.) (*You can insert your card.*)

✓ **Pouvez-vous signer ici?** (pooh-vey vooh see-nyey ee-see?) (*Can you sign here?*)

✓ **Je veux changer de l'argent.** (zhuh vuh shahN-zhey duh lahr-zhahN.)
(*I want to change money.*)

✓ **Il doit aller à la banque.** (eel dwah-tah-ley ah lah bahNk.) (*He has to go to the bank.*)

✓ **Vous devez taper votre code.** (vooh duh-vey tah-pey vohh-truh kohhd.)
(*You have to type in your PIN.*)

For the conditional form and usage of the verbs **pouvoir** and **vouloir,** refer to Chapter 8. You can find the present tense conjugations of **pouvoir** and **devoir** in Chapter 9.

Using disjunctive pronouns

After prepositions such as **pour** (poohr) (*for*), **avec** (ah-vehk) (*with*), **sans** (sahN) (*without*), and so on, the French use *disjunctive,* or *stress,* pronouns to refer to people. Table 14-2 lists the disjunctive pronouns.

Table 14-2	French Disjunctive Pronouns
Pronoun	*Example*
moi (mwah) (*me*)	**pour moi** (poohr mwah) (*for me*)
toi (twah) (*you* [singular])	**avec toi** (ah-vehk twah) (*with you*)

(continued)

Table 14-2 (continued)

Pronoun	Example
lui/elle (lwee/ehl) (*him/her*)	**sans lui** (sahN lwee) (*without him*); **pour elle** (poohr ehl) (*for her*)
nous (nooh) (*us*)	**avec nous** (ah-vehk nooh) (*with us*)
vous (vooh) (*you* [singular formal or plural])	**sans vous** (sahN vooh) (*without you*)
eux/elles (uh/ehl) (*them* [masc. plural/ fem. plural])	**pour eux** (poohr uh) (*for them*); **avec elles** (ah-vehk ehl) (*with them*)

Here are some sentences using these disjunctive pronouns:

> **Pouvez-vous traduire pour moi?** (pooh-vey-vooh trah-dweer poohr mwah?) (*Can you translate for me?*)

> **Avez-vous votre carte de crédit avec vous?** (ah-vey-vooh vohh-truh kahrt duh krey-dee ah-vehk vooh?) (*Do you have your credit card with you?*)

> **Il a une pièce d'identité avec lui.** (eel ah ewn pyehs dee-dahN-tee-tey ah-vehk lwee.) (*He has an ID with him.*)

When you are conducting any type of transaction, instead of always using **je** (zhuh) (*I*) or **nous** (nooh) (*we*), you can use the impersonal **on** (ohN) (*one*) in French. For example, you can ask **On peut payer ici?** (ohN puh pey-yey ee-see?) (*Can we can pay here?* [Literally, *Can one pay here?*]) **On peut** sounds a lot better to French ears than the good old **je peux** (zhuh puh) (*I can*) or **nous pouvons** (nooh pooh-vohN) (*we can*) form. **On** (ohN) (*one*, in the impersonal meaning) is what you usually hear. Sometimes **on** also replaces the *they* form, maybe just to be more casual: **Ah, ils ouvrent!** (ah, eel-zooh-vruh!) becomes **Ah, on ouvre!** (ah, ohN-nooh-vruh!), both of which mean *Ah, they are opening!* For more on **on**, check out Chapter 2.

Talkin' the Talk

Julie bought a couple of travel guides and tells **le vendeur** (luh vahN-duhr) (*the salesperson*) that she wants to pay with her credit card. Unfortunately, the store does not accept credit cards. (Track 16)

Julie: **Bonjour, monsieur, vous acceptez les cartes de crédit?**
bohN-zhoohr, muh-syuh, vooh-zah-kseh-ptey ley kahrt duh krey-dee?
Hello, sir, do you accept credit cards?

Le vendeur: **Ah, non, désolé.**
ah, nohN, dey-zoh-ley.
Oh, no, sorry.

Julie: **Zut! Alors, où est-ce qu'il y a un distributeur près d'ici?**
zewt! ah-lohr, ooh ehs-keel ee ah uhN dees-tree-bew-tuhr preh dee-see?
Darn! Then, where is there an ATM close to here?

Le vendeur: **Il y en a un en face.**
eel ee ahN-nah uhN ahN fahs.
There is one across the street.

Julie: **Je reviens tout de suite. Pouvez-vous garder mes guides?**
zhuh ruh-vyaN tooht sweet. pooh-vey-vooh gahr-dey mey geed?
I'll be back right away. Can you hold my guides?

Le vendeur: **Avec plaisir. Ne vous inquiétez pas.**
ah-vehk pleh-zeer. nuh vooh-zaN-kee-ey-tey pah.
Gladly. Don't worry.

Julie: **Merci, à tout de suite.**
mehr-see, ah tooht sweet.
Thank you, I'll be right back.

Words to Know

vous acceptez	vooh-zah-kseh-ptey	you accept
alors	ah-lohr	then, so then
en face	ahN fahs	across the street
je reviens	zhuh ruh-vyaN	I'll come back
à tout de suite	ah tooht sweet	I'll be right back
ne vous inquiétez pas	nuh vooh-zaN-kee-ey-tey pah	don't worry

Fun & Games

Identify each of the following French coins and indicate what symbol appears on the back.

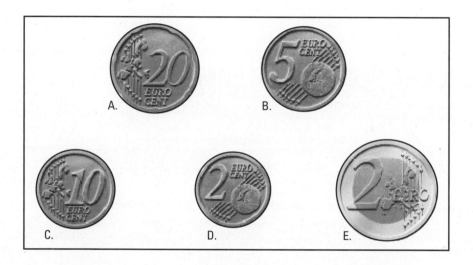

	Coin	Symbol
A.	_____	_____
B.	_____	_____
C.	_____	_____
D.	_____	_____
E.	_____	_____

Chapter 15

Getting Around: Planes, Trains, Taxis, and More

In This Chapter

▶ Getting through the airport

▶ Navigating public transportation

▶ Taking a taxi

▶ Renting a car and getting gas

---

*W*hen you travel, your first concern may be getting to your destination country, but as soon as you are there, you want to get around. After all, that's why you came in the first place, right? This chapter can help you navigate your way through the airport, train station, or subway system, as well as rent a car or flag down a taxi to get where you're going.

Getting through the Airport

On the day of your departure, try to arrive at **l'aéroport** (lah-ey-roh-pohr) (*the airport*) early, usually two to two-and-a-half hours before your departure. Remember that, if you are in the front of the line when you check in, you get to choose where you sit on **l'avion** (lah-vyohN) (*the plane*). Have **votre passeport** (vohh-truh pahs-pohr) (*your passport*) and other important documents handy, and in no time, you'll be all set to proceed to the boarding gate.

Before the day of your flight, make sure to check your airline carrier to see how many pieces of luggage you're entitled to bring with you and the maximum allotted weight of each. By adhering to the airline's regulations, you can avoid unpleasant surprises like being charged extra for your luggage.

Finding your way around the airport

Because of their size and the number of people who go through them every day, airports can be overwhelming places, especially when you're unfamiliar with the layout and the language. This section helps you identity some important areas in the airport, such as

- **départs** (dey-pahr) (*departures*)
- **arrivées** (ah-ree-vey) (*arrivals*)
- **enregistrement des bagages** (ahN-reh-zhee-struh-mahN dey bah-gahzh) (*baggage check*)

Your first task when you go to the airport is to find **l'aérogare** (lah-ey-roh-gahr) (*the terminal*) for **la ligne aérienne** (lah lee-nyuh ah-ey-ree-ehn) (*the airline*) you are flying. Then look for **le numéro du vol** (luh new-mey-roh dew vohl) (*the flight number*). After you arrive at **le comptoir** (luh kohN-twahr) (*the airline ticket counter*), you **enregistrer les bagages/les valises** (ahN-reh-zhee-strey ley bah-gahzh/ley vah-leez) (*check your bags/suitcases*). At that time, you'll be given **une carte d'embarquement** (ewn kahrt dahN-bahr-kuh-mahN) (*a boarding pass*). Then you can go to **la porte** (lah pohrt) (*the gate*) and wait until called to board your plane.

Up, up, and away — On the plane

If you're flying to France from New York, your trip should take about seven-and-a-half hours. Before landing, you'll be asked to fill out a custom's form which pertains to the purpose and the length of your stay. You'll also be asked if you have anything to declare. If you are traveling with your family, only one form is necessary for all of you.

Once on the plane, sit back and relax. **Un steward/une hôtesse de l'air** (uhN stee-wahr/ewn oh-tehs duh lehr) (*flight attendant*) will be around to see to your comfort, offering reading material, pillows, beverages, and so on.

At different points during the flight, you may hear the following:

- **Attachez votre ceinture** (ah-tah-shey vohh-truh saN-tewr) (*Fasten your seatbelt*)
- **Restez assis** (reh-stey ah-see) (*Remain seated*)
- **Ne fumez pas/Interdiction de fumer** (nuh few-mey pah/aN-tehr-dee-ksyohN duh few-mey) (*Don't smoke/No smoking*)
- **Éteignez tout appareil électronique** (ey-taN-nyey tooh-tah-pah-rehy ey-leh-ktroh-neek) (*Turn off all electronic devises*)

The pilot will also share information with you when the plane is going **décoller** (dey-koh-ley) (*to take off*), **atterrir** (ah-teh-reer) (*to land*), or **faire une escale** (fehr ewn eh-skahl) (*to stop over*).

Going through customs

When you arrive in any French-speaking country, you're instantly surrounded by a flood of French language: The porter, the taxi driver, and the customs people all address you in French. Your first hurdle is making it through customs.

Look for signs directing you to **la douane** (lah dooh-ahn) (*customs*). Have your passport(s) and custom form handy, as well as any other documents that may apply, like student or work permits or an extended visa. (A visa is not needed for most of the European countries if you are planning to stay for less than 3 months.) One at a time, you (or your family if you're traveling together) will be called for questioning. Common questions include

- ✓ **Quelle est la raison de votre voyage?** (kehl eh lah reh-zohN duh vohh-truh voh-yahzh?) (*What is the reason for your trip?*)
- ✓ **Combien de temps restez-vous à/en/au/aux. . . ?** (kohN-byaN duh tahN reh-stey-vooh ah/ahN/oh/oh. . .?) (*How much time are you staying in. . . . ?*) (For more on the geographical prepositions, refer to Chapter 13.)

Most likely, you will only need to show your passport and custom form to the custom's officer; occasionally, you may be picked out for further questioning. In this case, you may hear the following questions:

- ✓ **Avez-vous quelque chose à déclarer?** (ah-vey-vooh kehl-kuh shoh-zah dey-klah-rey?) (*Do you have something to declare?*)
- ✓ **Pouvez-vous ouvrir votre sac?** (pooh-vey-vooh-zooh-vreer vohh-truh sahk?) (*Can you open your bag?*)

After you answer the questions, **le douanier/la douanière** (luh dooh-ah-nyey/lah dooh-ah-nyehr) (*the custom officer*) will then stamp your passport, and you'll be on your way.

It's best not to joke around with an immigration or customs officer. He also has to control his sense of humor. He's there for serious business.

Talkin' the Talk

Le douanier, the custom's officer, is the first person Nicola encounters in the French airport. She hands him her passport and her customs slip, and he starts **le contrôle des passeports** (luh kohN-trohl dey pahs-pohr) (*the passport check*).

Le douanier: **Bonjour. Bienvenue en France. Allez-vous rester en France pendant tout votre séjour?**
bohN-zhoohr. byaN-vuh-new ahN frahNs. ah-ley-vooh reh-stey ahN frahNs pahN-dahN tooh vohh-truh sey-zhoohr?
Hello. Welcome to France. Are you going to stay in France during your entire stay?

Nicola: **Non, je vais aussi à Bruxelles et en Suisse.**
nohN, zhuh veh-zoh-see ah brewk-sehl ey ahN swees.
No, I am also going to Brussels and to Switzerland.

Le douanier: **Et la raison de votre voyage?**
ey lah reh-zohN duh vohh-truh vwah-yahzh?
And the reason for your trip?

Nicola: **C'est pour les affaires et le plaisir.**
seh poohr ley-zah-fehr ey luh pleh-zeer.
It's for business and pleasure.

Le douanier: **Combien de temps restez-vous en tout?**
kohN-byaN duh tahN reh-stey-vooh-zahN tooh?
How much time are you staying altogether?

Nicola: **Deux semaines.**
duh suh-mehn.
Two weeks.

Le douanier: **Avez-vous quelque chose à déclarer?**
ah-vey-vooh kehl-kuh shoh-zah dey-klah-rey?
Do you have something to declare?

Nicola: **Non, je n'ai rien à déclarer.**
nohN, zhuh ney ryaN ah dey-klah-rey.
No, I have nothing to declare.

Le douanier: **Pouvez-vous ouvrir votre sac?**
pooh-vey-vooh ooh-vreer vohh-truh sahk?
Can you open your bag?

Nicola: **Oui, monsieur . . . voilà.**
wee, muh-syuh. . . vwah-lah.
Yes, sir . . . here you go.

Le douanier: **Je vous souhaite un bon séjour!**
zhuh vooh sweht uhN bohN sey-zhoohr!
I wish you a nice stay!

Nicola: **Merci, monsieur. Au revoir.**
mehr-see, muh-syuh. ohr-vwahr.
Thank you, sir. Good-bye.

Words to Know

pendant	pahN-dahN	during
séjour	sey-zhoohr	stay
pour les affaires	poohr ley-zah-fehr	for business
combien de temps	kohN-byaN duh tahN	how much time
en tout	ahN tooh	in all
une/la semaine	ewn/lah suh-mehn	a/the week
je vous souhaite	zhuh vooh sweht	I wish you
rien à declarer	ryaN ah dey-klah-rey	nothing to declare

When you are talking about staying in a city, you use **à** (ah) to express the English *in,* such as **à Paris** (ah pah-ree) (*in Paris*) or **à Bruxelles** (ah brewk-sehl) (*in Brussels*). For countries, you usually use **en** (ahN) for the country names ending in **e** or beginning with a vowel: **la France** (lah frahNs), **la Suisse** (lah swees), **l'Italie** (lee-tah-lee), and so on. If this is not the case, then for countries such as **le Canada** (luh kah-nah-dah), **le Portugal** (luh pohr-tew-gahl), **les États-Unis** (ley-zey-tah-zew-nee), and so on, you use **au(x)** (oh). For more details on geographical prepositions, see Chapter 13.

Navigating Buses, Trains, and Subways

The public transportation system in most major cities of Europe and Canada is excellent. This section gives general information so you can research some fun and economical ways of getting to your favorite destinations. Check out the following list for ideas on the range of choices available for getting around in various cities:

- ✔ **Montreal:** Bus, subway, STCUM (urban train system), Amtrak, and VIA Rail (national train system)
- ✔ **Brussels:** Subway, bus, tramway, and SNCB (national train system)
- ✔ **Geneva:** Tramway, bus, trolleybus, and CFF (national train system)
- ✔ **Paris:** Subway and RER (express trains between Paris and its suburbs), bus, SNCF (national train system), and tourist boats

When you get on the bus, or before you get on the train or subway, be sure to validate your ticket in a machine installed for that purpose. It gets awfully expensive when **le contrôleur** (luh kohN-troh-luhr) (*the conductor, the ticket inspector*) gets on and checks everybody. And they do!

Boarding the bus

If you have time, **le bus** (luh bews) (*the bus*) is probably the most wonderful way to get not only an impression of the different **quartiers** (kahr-tyey) (neighborhoods) of a city but also to experience that city's people a bit. Busses are clean and pleasant and usually run on 15 to 30 minute intervals. The majority of bus stops in major cities are equipped with an electronic device, which shows when the next bus is expected. Also displayed in the bus stops are **les lignes de bus** (ley lee-nyuh duh bews) (*bus routes*) and neighborhood maps. Major cities have **des excursions en bus** (dey-zehk-skewr-zyohN ahN bews) (*bus tours*), which are a great and inexpensive way to see the city.

You can usually buy **un billet** (uhN bee-yeh) (*a ticket*) from **le conducteur de bus** (luh kohN-dew-ktuhr duh bews) (*the bus driver*), but remember that large bills are not welcome; it's best to have the correct change (Chapter 14 covers money). Generally, buying tickets in a book of ten, **un carnet** (uhN kahr-neh), is cheaper. You can purchase these at metro stations or at any **distributeur automatique** (dees-tree-bew-tuhr oh-toh-mah-teek) (*automated ticket vending machine*). You may also purchase tickets at **le guichet** (luh gee-shey) (*the ticket window*). In many cities, the subway system is connected with the bus system, so you can use the same tickets.

Talkin' The Talk

Mr. and Mrs. Meyer are at a bus stop. They are reading the bus schedule, but they're not sure whether they've read it correctly. Bus number 82 is arriving. Mr. Meyer turns to **la jeune femme** (lah zhuhn fahm) (*the young woman*) next to him for help. (Track 17)

Mr. Meyer:	**Excusez-moi, mademoiselle. C'est bien le bus pour l'hôtel de ville?** ehk-skew-zey mwah, mahd-mwah-zehl. seh byaN luh bews poohr loh-tehl duh veel? *Excuse me, Miss. Is that the correct bus to City Hall?*
La jeune femme:	**Non, il faut prendre le bus numéro 67.** nohN, eel foh prahN-druh luh bews new-mey-roh swah-sahN seht. *No, you have to take bus number 67.*
Mr. Meyer:	**À quelle heure est-ce qu'il arrive?** ah kehl uhr ehs-keel ah-reev? *What time does it come?*
La jeune femme::	**Il passe tous les quarts d'heure, mais il est souvent en retard.** eel pahs tooh ley kahr duhr, meh eel eh sooh-vahN ahN ruh-tahr. *It comes every 15 minutes, but it is often late.*
Mr. Meyer:	**Et c'est à combien d'arrêts d'ici?** ey seh ah kohN-byaN dah-reh dee-see? *And how many stops is it from here?*
La jeune femme:	**Ce n'est pas très loin, c'est le prochain arrêt. Ah, le voilà! Il est à l'heure!** suh neh pah treh lwaN, seh luh proh-sheh-nah-reh. ah, luh vwah-lah! eel eh-tah luhr! *It's not very far. It's the next stop. Ah, there it is! It's on time!*
Mr. Meyer:	**Merci beaucoup. Au revoir.** mehr-see boh-kooh. ohr-vwahr. *Thank you very much. Good-bye.*

Words to Know

l'hôtel de ville	loh-tehl duh veel	city hall
il faut prendre	eel foh prahN-druh	you need to take
il passe	eel pahs	it comes
tous les quarts d'heure	tooh ley kahr duhr	every fifteen minutes
souvent	sooh-vahN	often
combien d'arrêts	kohN-byaN dah-reh	how many stops
d'ici	dee-see	from here
le prochain arrêt	luh proh-sheh-nah-reh	the next stop

The adjective or pronoun **tout** (tooh) *(all, every)* has four forms (**tout, toute, tous, toutes**) because it agrees in gender and number with the noun it modifies or, as a pronoun, with the noun it replaces. **Tous** or **toutes** mean *every* when they are connected with a time definition in the plural, as in these examples:

tous les quarts d'heure (tooh ley kahr duhr) *(every quarter of an hour)*

tous les jours (tooh ley zhoohr) *(every day)*

toutes les vingt minutes (tooht ley vaN mee-newt) *(every 20 minutes)*

When **tout** is connected with time definitions in the singular, however, it takes on a different meaning — *all* or *something in its entirety*, as these examples show:

toute la matinée (tooht lah mah-tee-ney) *(all morning long, the whole morning, the entire morning)*

toute la journée (tooht lah zhoohr-ney) *(all day long, the whole day, the entire day)*

toute la vie (tooht lah vee) *(the entire life, the whole life)*

Using the subway

The **métro** (mey-troh) (*subway*) is an economical and fast way to get around the city. Paris, Brussels, Lille, and Lyon, as well as Montreal, all have very efficient subway systems. Big maps in each station make the systems easy to use, and the hours of operation (usually from 5:30 a.m. to 1:00 a.m.) make it very convenient. In these cities, the fare is standard, no matter how far you travel. Here are some words that may come in handy when you're at the métro:

- **la correspondance** (lah koh-reh-spohN-dahNs) (*transfer point, connection*)
- **le guichet** (luh gee-sheh) (*ticket window*)
- **la ligne** (lah lee-nyuh) ([*métro*] *line*)
- **la place/le siège** (lah plahs/luh syehzh) (*seat*)
- **le plan** (luh plahN) (*map*)
- **le quai** (luh key) (*platform*)
- **la sortie** (lah sohr-tee) (*the exit*)
- **la station de métro** (lah stah-syohN duh mey-troh) (*métro station*)
- **la voiture** (lah vwah-tewr) (*métro, car, train car*)

Looking for ticket packages

A number of packages are available for tourists, which can include day or multiple-day passes, as well as weekly passes (you can read about these options in an upcoming list). If you are visiting Paris, for example, you should explore one of the several options available:

- The **Paris Visite** (pah-ree vee-zeet) (*a Paris visit pass*), which you can use for unlimited trips on the métro, the bus, and the **RER (Réseau Express Régional)** (ehr uh ehr [rey-zoh ehk-sprehs rey-zhee-oh-nahl]), or the **Montmartre Funiculaire** (mohN-mahr-truh few-nee-kew-lehr), which saves you from climbing all those stairs when visiting **Montmartre** in the 18th district. This pass lets you choose the zones in which you'd like to travel, as well as the number of days. For more information, go to www.parispass.com.

- The **Navigo Découverte** (nah-vee-goh dey-kooh-vehrt) (*Navigo discover pass*), which is valid from Monday through Sunday, can be purchased to include unlimited use of the métro, RER, busses, transportation to the two airports, **Charles de Gaulle** (shahrl duh gohl) and **Orly** (ohr-lee), as well as **le Château de Versailles** (luh shah-toh duh vehr-sahy) (*the palace of Versailles*) and Disney Park. For more information on the

Navigo Découverte, check out www.transilien.com or http://
parisbytrain.com/paris-train-metro-week-pass-navigo-
decouverte.

✔ **Un carnet** (uhN kahr-neh) (*a book of 10 tickets*), which you can share
with others traveling with you.

You can purchase any of these passes at ticket windows or ticket vending
machines at métro, RER, or train stations. Some passes are also available at
the Paris tourist office.

Buying your ticket

Most employees in the métro speak enough English to sell tickets and answer
your questions. But just in case, here are some helpful phrases:

Un billet, s'il vous plaît. (uhN bee-yeh, seel vooh pleh.) (*One ticket, please.*)

Un carnet, s'il vous plaît. (uhN kahr-neh, seel vooh pleh.) (*A book of
[ten]) tickets, please.*)

Comment aller à. . . ? (koh-mahN-tah-ley ah. . . ?) (*How do I get to. . . ?*)

Quelle est la ligne pour. . . ? (kehl eh lah lee-nyuh poohr. . . ?) (*Which
line is it for. . .?*)

Est-ce le bon sens pour aller à. . . ? (ehs luh bohN sahNs poohr ah-ley
ah. . . ?) (*Is this the right direction to go to. . . ?*)

Est-ce qu'il faut prendre une correspondance? (ehs-keel foh prahN-
drewn koh-reh-spohN-dahNs?) (*Do I need to transfer?*)

Où est la sortie, s'il vous plaît? (ooh eh lah sohr-tee, seel vooh pleh?)
(*Where is the exit, please?*)

Talkin' the Talk

Mr. Meyer and Mrs. Meyer split up for the morning to see different
museums. Now it's time to meet for lunch. Mr. Meyer wants to try
out the subway, but he thinks he needs a map and stops at a kiosk.

Mr. Meyer:	**Bonjour. Est-ce que vous avez un plan de métro?** bohN-zhoohr. ehs-kuh vooh-zah-vey uhN plahN duh mey-troh? *Hello. Do you have a metro map?*
L'employée	**Le voici. . . . Est-ce que je peux vous aider?** luh vwah-see. . . . ehs-kuh zhuh puh vooh-zey-dey? *Here it is. . . . Can I help you?*

Mr. Meyer:	**Oui, pour la Grande Place, c'est quelle ligne?**
	wee, poohr lah grahNd plahs, seh kehl lee-nyuh?
	Yes, to Grande Place, which line is it?

L'employée:	**C'est direct avec la ligne 3.**
	seh dee-rehkt ah-vehk lah lee-nyuh trwah.
	You can go directly with line 3.

Mr. Meyer:	**Combien de temps est-ce qu'il faut?**
	kohN-byaN duh tahN ehs-keel foh?
	How long does it take?

L'employée:	**Disons . . . 20 minutes.**
	dee-zohN. . .vaN mee-newt.
	Let's say . . . 20 minutes.

Mr. Meyer:	**Merci beaucoup, madame.**
	mehr-see boh-kooh, mah-dahm.
	Thank you very much, ma'am.

L'employée:	**Je vous en prie.**
	zhuh vooh-zahN pree.
	You're welcome.

Je vous en prie (zhuh vooh-zahN pree) is a more formal way of saying *You are welcome.* The more casual expression is **Pas de quoi** (paht kwah) a phrase you can make more formal by not abbreviating it: **Il n'y a pas de quoi** (eel nyah paht kwah). You can also say **De rien** (duh ryaN) (*It's nothing*).

Getting around by train

If you'd like to travel through Europe, there is no better way than by rail. Trains in Europe are modern, clean, fast, and efficient. For long distance travel through Europe, trains are equipped with restaurants or café cars, as well as **des couchettes** (dey kooh-sheht) (*berths*) if you choose this option. A number of rail passes allow you to travel to the countries of your choice, but remember to purchase them ahead of time. Student and age discounts are also available, so don't forget to ask for those. For more information on these rail passes, go to www.raileurope.com.

In addition, for long-distance traveling between France, Belgium, and the Netherlands, you may want to try the **Train à Grande Vitesse (TGV)** (traN ah grahNd vee-tehs [tey zhey vey]), an extra-high-speed train that you can use only with reservations. It is very fast and efficient, can take you across France in no time, and is truly worth the experience. The **TGV Thalys** (tey-zhey-vey tah-lee) runs Paris to Brussels to Amsterdam and back.

Also convenient, **l'Eurostar/Le Shuttle** (luh-roh stahr/luh shuh-tuhl) is a passenger Channel Tunnel link from London's Waterloo train station to Paris and Brussels with no reservations necessary. The **SNCF (Société Nationale des Chemins de Fer Français)** (ehs ehn sey ehf [soh-see-ey-tey nah-syoh-nahl dey shuh-maN duh fehr frahN-seh]) is the French National Railroad System. There are six major **gares** (gahr) (*train stations*) in Paris alone.

Here are some useful words and phrases that can come in handy when you're traveling by train:

- ✔ **le guichet** (luh gee-sheh) (*ticket window*)
- ✔ **le quai** (luh key) (*platform*)
- ✔ **les renseignements** (ley rahN-seh-nyuh-mahN) (*the information desk*)
- ✔ **la consigne** (lah kohN-see-nyuh) (*baggage room*)
- ✔ **la salle d'attente** (lah sahl dah-tahNt) (*waiting room*)
- ✔ **le bureau des objets trouvés** (leh bew-roh dey-zohb-zheh trooh-vey) (*lost-and-found*)
- ✔ **un [billet] aller-simple** (uhN bee-yeh ah-ley-saN-pluh) (*a one way [ticket]*)
- ✔ **un [billet] aller-retour** (uhN bee-yeh ah-ley-ruh-toohr) (*a round trip [ticket]*)
- ✔ **le compartiment** (luh kohN-pahr-tee-mahN) (*compartment*)
- ✔ **composter** (kohN-poh-stey) (*to validate [a ticket]*)
- ✔ **la gare** (lah gahr) (*train station*)
- ✔ **les heures de pointe** (ley-zuhr duh pwaNt) (*rush hour, peak*)
- ✔ **la période creuse** (lah pey-ree-ohd kruhz) (*off peak*)
- ✔ **l'horaire** (loh-rehr) (*the schedule*)
- ✔ **l'indicateur (automatique)** (laN-dee-kah-tuhr [oh-toh-mah-teek]) (*automated train schedule*)
- ✔ **un tarif réduit** (uhN tah-reef rey-dwee) (*reduced fare*)
- ✔ **la voie** (lah vwah) (*track*)
- ✔ **à bord** (ah bohr) (*on board*)
- ✔ **à destination de** (ah deh-stee-nah-syohN duh) (*bound for*)
- ✔ **direct(e)** (dee-rehkt) (*direct, non-stop*)

Getting help at the train station

Train stations around the world are always busy, noisy, and confusing, but you can usually find helpful people around, such as the police and station employees, that you can turn to for direction.

You can use these questions to find what you're looking for:

- **Pardon, où sont. . . ?** (pahr-dohN, ooh sohN. . . ?) (*Pardon, where are . . .?*)

- **Excusez-moi, où est. . . ?** (ehk-skew-zey-mwah, ooh eh. . . ?) (*Excuse me, where is . . . ?*)

Consider these examples:

> **Pardon, où sont les guichets?** (pahr-dohN, ooh sohN ley gee-sheh?) (*Pardon, where are the ticket windows?*)

> **Excusez-moi, où est la salle d'attente?** (ehk-skew-zey-mwah, ooh eh lah sahl dah-tahNt?) (*Excuse me, where is the waiting room?*)

When asking questions involving the words *which* or *what,* you use **quel(s)/quelle(s)** (kehl), depending on whether the noun referred to is masculine or feminine and singular or plural. **Quel** and its other forms are adjectives and must be either followed by a noun with which they agree or separated from the noun by the verb **être** (eh-truh) (*to be*). Here are some examples:

- **Il arrive par quel train?** (eel ah-reev pahr kehl traN?) (*Which train is he arriving on?*)

- **De quelle ville es-tu?** (duh kehl veel eh-tew?) (*Which city are you from?*)

- **Quelles places avez-vous?** (kehl plahs ah-vey-vooh?) (*Which seats do you have?*)

- **Quel est le nom de la gare?** (kehl eh luh nohN duh lah gahr?) (*What is the name of the train station?*)

- **Quelles sont les heures de pointe?** (kehl sohN ley-zuhr duh pwaNt?) (*What are the peak hours?*)

Buying tickets and checking the schedule

When you are traveling, you undoubtedly need to ask questions about plane and train schedules. Here are a few questions and answers that may come in handy.

- **Quand voulez-vous partir?** (kahN vooh-ley-vooh pahr-teer?) (*When do you want to leave?*)

- ✔ **Où voulez-vous aller?** (ooh vooh-ley-vooh-zah-ley?) (*Where do you want to go?*)

- ✔ **Voulez-vous un aller-retour ou un aller-simple?** (vooh-ley-vooh-zuhN ah-ley-ruh-toohr ooh uhN ah-ley-saN-pluh?) (*Do you want a round trip or a one way?*)

- ✔ **Pour combien de personnes?** (poohr kohN-byaN duh pehr-sohhn?) (*For how many people?*)

Similarly, you may have some questions of your own:

- ✔ **A quelle heure y a-t-il un train pour. . . ?** (ah kehl uhr ee ah-teel uhN traN poohr. . .?) (*What time is there a train for. . . ?*)

- ✔ **Est-ce que le train est à l'heure?** (ehs-kuh luh traN eh-tah luhr?) (*Is the train on schedule/time?*)

To this last question, you may get any of the following answers:

- ✔ **Le train est à l'heure.** (luh traN eh-tah luhr.) (*The train is on time.*)

- ✔ **Le train est en avance.** (luh traN eh-tahN-nah-vahNs.) (*The train is early.*)

- ✔ **Le train est en retard.** (luh traN eh-tahN ruh-tahr.) (*The train is late.*)

Talkin' the Talk

Susan wants to meet her old friend Julie in Versailles. So she takes a day off from her group and is trying her luck on her own. (Track 18)

L'employé:	**Bonjour, madame. Vous désirez?**
	bohN-zhoohr, mah-dahm. vooh dey-zee-rey?
	Good morning, ma'am. Can I help you?

Susan:	**Je voudrais un billet pour Versailles, s'il vous plaît.**
	zhuh vooh-dreh uhN bee-yeh poohr vehr-sahy, seel vooh pleh.
	I would like a ticket to Versailles, please.

L'employé:	**Aller-simple ou aller-retour?**
	ah-ley-saN-pluh ooh ah-ley-ruh-toohr?
	One way or round trip?

Susan:	**Aller-retour, s'il vous plaît. Deuxième classe.**
	ah-ley-ruh-toohr, seel vooh pleh. duh-zee-ehm klahs.
	Round trip, please. Second class.

L'employé:	**C'est pour combien de personnes?**
	seh poohr kohN-byaN duh pehr-sohhn?
	For how many people?

Susan:	**Pour une personne, monsieur.**
	poohr ewn pehr-sohhn, muh-syuh.
	For one person, sir.

L'employé:	**Vous avez de la chance. J'ai encore une place. Ça fait douze euros.**
	vooh-zah-vey duh lah shahNs. zhey ahN-kohr ewn plahs. sah feh doohz uh-roh.
	You're lucky. I still have one seat. That'll be 12 euros.

Susan:	**Est-ce que je dois changer de train?**
	ehs-kuh zhuh dwah shahN-zhey duh traN?
	Do I have to change trains?

L'employé:	**Oui, vous avez une correspondance à Issy.**
	wee, vooh-zah-vey ewn koh-reh-spohN-dahN-sah ee-see.
	Yes, you have a connecting train in Issy.

Susan:	**Et de quel quai part le train?**
	ey duh kehl key pahr luh traN?
	And from which platform does the train leave?

L'employé:	**Quai 12A.**
	key doohz ah.
	Platform 12A.

Susan:	**Merci. Au revoir.**
	mehr-see. ohr-vwahr.
	Thank you. Good-bye.

Getting Around by Car

If convenience and fast service are more important to you than paying the fare, then taking a taxi is a good way to get around. Or, if you're more adventurous and like driving, you may want to rent a car. This way, you can stop wherever you want, visit local towns, meander through the **marchés** (mahr-shey) (*outdoor markets*), and change plans according to the weather or your mood. The following sections tell you what you need to know.

Hailing a taxi

Taxis are readily available at all airports and train stations, as well as all over major cities. Although taxis come in all colors, depending on the country you are visiting, they are easily recognizable because of the international word on them: Taxi. (Keep in mind though, that taxis have a passenger as well as a luggage limit.)

Although many taxi drivers in large international cities have a basic knowledge of English, have your destination address printed out to avoid any misunderstandings. Be prepared to pay in cash because some taxis do not take credit or debit cards.

The following terms and phrases are ones you'll use when you take a taxi:

- **le chauffeur de taxi** (luh shoh-fuhr duh tah-ksee) (*cab driver*)
- **le tarif** (luh tah-reef) (*fare*)
- **la station de taxi** (lah stah-syohN duh tah-ksee) (*taxi stand*)
- **Où voulez-vous aller?** (ooh vooh-ley-vooh-zah-ley?) (*Where do you want to go?*)
- **Je voudrais aller à. . . .** (zhuh vooh-dreh-zah-ley ah….) (*I would like to go to. . . .*)

Tipping is optional in Belgium, although it is customary to round up to the nearest euro, but in other European countries, expect to leave about a 10 percent tip.

Talkin' the Talk

Karen and Derek want to take a taxi from the airport to their hotel. They were lucky enough to get the attention of a taxi driver right away.

Le chauffeur de taxi:	**Où voulez-vous aller?** ooh vooh-ley-vooh-zah-ley? *Where do you want to go?*
Karen:	**Bruxelles, Hôtel Gillon, s'il vous plaît.** brewk-sehl, oh-tehl zhee-lohN, seel vooh pleh. *Brussels, Hotel Gillon, please.*
Le chauffeur de taxi:	**Avec plaisir. C'est dans quelle rue?** ah-vehk pleh-zeer. seh dahN kehl rew? *With pleasure. Which street is that on?*

Derek:	**Voyons . . . c'est 22 rue Albert. C'est combien?**
	vwah-yohN. . . seh vaNt-duh rew ahl-behr. seh kohN-byaN?
	Let's see . . . it's 22 Albert Street. How much is it?
Le chauffeur de taxi:	**35 euros. C'est le tarif normal. Est-ce que je mets les valises dans le coffre?**
	trahN-saNk uh-roh. seh luh tah-reef nohr-mahl. ehs-kuh zhuh meh ley vah-leez dahN luh koh-fruh.
	35 euros. That's the normal fare. Do I put the suitcases in the trunk?
Karen:	**Très bien, mais je garde mon sac à dos avec moi.**
	treh byaN, meh zhuh gahrd mohN sahk ah doh ah-vehk mwah.
	Very well, but I am keeping my backpack with me.

Words to Know

la rue	lah rew	the street
C'est combien?	seh kohN-byaN?	How much is it?
je mets	zhuh meh	I put
le coffre	luh koh-fruh	the trunk (of a vehicle)
garder	gahr-dey	to keep
le sac à dos	luh sahk ah doh	backpack

Driving in a foreign land

Louer une voiture (looh-ey ewn vwah-tewr) (*renting a car*) in Europe may be a little more expensive than renting one in the U.S. However, if you share the car with two or three others, this option may be less expensive than purchasing individual rail passes. If you decide to rent a car and drive yourself, it is always best to do your research and to talk to your rental agency about your travel plans. Keep these points in mind:

✔ The minimum driving age for car rentals in Europe is between 21 and 25, and the maximum age is usually 70. If you are a younger or older driver, you may be asked to pay additional insurance against collision damage. Purchasing additional insurance anyway just for your peace of mind may be a good idea, but that is totally up to you. Check with your credit card company to see whether they cover the insurance on rental cars.

✔ When you are renting a car, make sure you tell the agency about your travel plans because some agencies may have border restrictions or limits and you may need to pay extra insurance fees for this. Also if you are renting a car in one country and would like to drop it off in another, you may be required to pay drop-off fees.

✔ In most countries all you need is your normal, valid driver's license. In others, they may ask you for your International Drivers' Permit, or IDP, which is basically a translation of your license in many different languages. It is a good idea to get an IDP anyway, especially if you are not certain where your car travels may take you or if you are stopped by the police. You can purchase an IDP for about $15.00 at any automobile association which is authorized by the Department of State to issue IDPs, such as AAA or CAA. You need two passport photos as well as your valid driver's license to get an IDP.

✔ Many French **autoroutes** (oh-toh-rooht) (*highways*) require **des péages** (dey pey-ahzh) (*tolls*), and they are not cheap. Always have coins handy, although most of the time you pick up a ticket at the point of entry and pay at the exit. In France, tollbooths usually accept credit cards: Just insert your ticket into a machine at the tollbooth, then your credit card, wait, get your receipt, and make sure you pull your card out again.

Here are some words and phrases related to driving and **la circulation** (lah seer-kew-lah-syohN) (*traffic*):

✔ **le rond-point** (luh rohN-pwaN) (*roundabout*)

✔ **le stationnement/le stationnement interdit** (luh stah-syohNn-mahN/ luh stah-syohNn-mahN aN-tehr-dee) (*parking/no parking*)

✔ **le piéton/la piétonne** (luh pyey-tohN/lah pyey-tohhn) (*pedestrian*)

✔ **le trottoir** (luh troh-twahr) (*sidewalk*)

✔ **la sortie** (lah sohr-tee) (*exit*)

✔ **le carrefour** (luh kahr-foohr) (*intersection*)

✔ **l'embouteillage** (lahN-booh-teh-yahzh) (*traffic jam*)

✔ **le sens unique** (luh sahNs ew-neek) (*one way*)

✔ **le pont** (luh pohN) (*bridge*)

✔ **ralentir** (rah-lahN-teer) (*to slow down*)

✔ **rouler vite** (rooh-ley veet) (*to drive fast*)

✔ **demi-tour** (duh-mee-toohr) (*U turn*)

Filling up at the gas station

As you probably are aware, **faire le plein** (fehr luh plaN) (*to fill the gas tank*) in Europe, or in France specifically, costs more than it does here at home. Don't get too excited when you see postings at the **station-service** (stah-syohN-sehr-vees) (*gas station*) for 1.55; that's in euros and per liter, not per gallon. A gallon of **essence** (eh-sahNs) (*gas*) is 3.78 liters. Although gas prices fluctuate, gas is usually cheaper at supermarkets and hypermarkets than it is on major highways.

Just like in North America, in France you have a choice of **sans-plomb** (sahN-plohN) (*unleaded*), **ordinaire** (ohr-dee-nehr) (*regular unleaded*), **super** (sew-pehr) (*super unleaded*), and **gazole/diesel** (gah-zohl/dyey-zehl) (*diesel*).

If you travel to Europe, make sure you're familiar with the metric system and its three most common units: the meter, the gram, and the liter. One kilometer equals 0.621 of a mile. For example, from the center of Paris to Versailles is about 21 kilometers, or approximately 13 miles. For more information on weights, check out Chapter 8.

Gas stations on the major highways do have **des pompistes** (dey pohN-peest) (*gas station attendants*), but others may not. Generally, you pump your gas first and then pay. Although you can pay a cashier with a credit card, a credit card may not work in the automated machines. Some European countries, including France, have adapted "chip-and-pin cards," which are the only ones accepted at self-serve pay at the pump stations.

The following little phrases can help you out when you are looking to fill up the tank:

> **Où est-ce qu'il y a une station-service?** (ooh ehs-keel ee ah ewn stah-syohN-sehr-vees?) (*Where is there a gas station?*)

> **Est-ce qu'il y a une station-service près d'ici?** (ehs-keel ee ah ewn stah-syohN sehr-vees preh dee-see?) (*Is there a gas station near here?*)

> **Le plein, s'il vous plaît.** (luh plaN, seel vooh pleh.) (*Fill it up, please.*)

When talking about unspecified quantities, French uses an article called the **partitif** (pahr-tee-teef) (*partitive*) because it describes a "part" of a quantity. You construct it by combining the preposition **de** (*of*) and the definite article **le, la, les:**

- **de + le = du** (dew)
- **de + la = de la** (duh lah)
- **de + les = des** (dey)
- **de + l' = de l'** (duhl)

You can translate these constructions as *some*, as in this example: **Je voudrais du carburant** (zhuh vooh-dreh dew kahr-bew-rahN) (*I would like some fuel.*) Check out Chapter 2 for more on the partitive.

Here's a little advice: Fill up during the day at a manned station and keep some cash on hand in case the automated machines don't accept your credit card. Also be aware that gas stations in town may be closed on Sundays. This is not the case on the highways.

Getting help when you have car trouble

Hopefully, your journey will be smooth and trouble-free, but in the event you have car trouble or see **un avertisseur lumineux** (uhN ah-vehr-tee-suhr lew-mee-nuh) (a *warning light*), you may need to talk to **un mécanicien** (uhN mey-kah-nee-syaN) (*a mechanic*). Here are some words and phrases that can help you identify what the trouble is:

- ✔ **la batterie** (lah bah-tree) (*battery*)
- ✔ **le capot** (luh kah-poh) (*the hood*)
- ✔ **l'essuie-glace** (ley-swee-glahs) (*windshield wiper*)
- ✔ **les freins** (ley fraN) (*the brakes*)
- ✔ **le pare-brise** (luh pahr-breez) (*windshield*)
- ✔ **les phares** (ley fahr) (*headlights*)
- ✔ **le pneu/le pneu crevé** (luh pnuh/luh pnuh kruh-vey) (*tire/flat tire*)
- ✔ **tomber (être) en panne** (tohN-bey [eh-truh] ahN pahn) (*to break down [car]*)
- ✔ **vérifier (les niveaux)** (vey-ree-fyey [ley nee-voh]) (*check [the levels]*)
- ✔ **la vidange** (lah vee-dahNzh) (*oil change*)

Deciphering road signs

You can't travel safely on your own without being able to understand **les panneaux routiers** (ley pah-noh rooh-tyey) (*road signs*). Although many signs are easily recognizable — like the stop and yield signs — others have less obvious meanings. You must review these before you get behind the wheel. The following information is a good start.

To avoid **une contravention** (ewn kohN-trah-vahN-syohN) (*a ticket*), keep in mind that **les limitations de vitesse** (ley lee-mee-tah-syohN duh vee-tehs) (*speed limits*) in France (indicated by a round sign with a red border) are approximately 80 mph or 130 km/h on the highways, 55 mph or 90 km/h on open roads, and 30 mph or 50 km/h in the city. Speed limits are strictly enforced, and you pay a fine on the spot. Also the traffic arriving on the right always has **la priorité à droite** (lah pree-oh-ree-tey ah dwaht) (*the right of way*; Literally: *priority to the right*).

Here are some important signs that you have to be aware of:

- ✔ **arrêt** (ah-reh) (*stop*)
- ✔ **cédez le passage** (sey-dey luh pah-sahzh) (*yield*)
- ✔ **chaussée rétrécie** (shoh-sey rey-trey-see) (*road narrows*)
- ✔ **chaussée glissante** (shoh-sey glee-sahNt) (*slippery road*)
- ✔ **interdiction de faire demi-tour** (aN-tehr-dee-ksyohN duh fehr duh-mee-toohr) (*no U Turn*)
- ✔ **passage interdit** (pah-sahzh aN-tehr-dee) (*no entry*)
- ✔ **passage piéton** (pah-sahzh pyey-tohN) (*pedestrian crossing*)
- ✔ **risque de chutes de pierre** (reesk duh shewt duh pyehr) (*falling rocks*)
- ✔ **sens unique** (sahNs ew-neek) (*one way*)
- ✔ **travaux** (trah-voh) (*road work*)
- ✔ **virage à droite/virage à gauche** (vee-rahzh ah dwaht/vee-rahzh ah gohsh) (*bend to the right/bend to the left*)

Road signs are distinguishable by shape, color, and by graphics. Here are a few you should become familiar with:

- ✔ Triangles with a red border indicate a warning or a danger. Example: **Chaussée glissante**.
- ✔ Round signs with a thick red border indicate restrictions. Example: **Interdiction de faire demi-tour.**
- ✔ Round signs with blue background indicate what you are required to do. Example: **obligation de tourner à gauche.**
- ✔ Square and rectangular signs guide you. Example: **Autoroute** (oh-toh-rooht) (*highway*), which always begins with a capital **A** (for **Autoroute)** followed by the highway number.

Fun & Games

One part of driving safely is understanding and obeying road signs. To see how well you'd do on a French road, match each French road sign to its English translation.

PASSAGE A PIÉTON

AUTOROUTE

OBLIGATION DE TOURNER À DROITE

TRAVAUX

RISQUE DE CHUTES DE PIERRES

INTERDICTION DE FAIRE DEMI-TOUR

CEDEZ LE PASSAGE

CHAUSSÉE GLISSANTE

1._____Road Work

2._____Pedestrian crossing

3._____Slippery road

4._____Right turn only

5._____Highway

6._____Yield

7. _____No U turn

8. _____Falling rocks

A. Obligation de tourner à droite

B. Autoroute

C. Interdiction de faire demi-tour

D. Chaussée glissante

E. Cédez le passage

F. Passage piéton

G. Risque de chutes de pierres

H. Travaux

Chapter 16

Finding a Place to Stay

• •

• •

*N*ot everybody is so lucky as to have good friends abroad with whom they can stay when they're traveling. Most likely, you'll need to book a hotel room as part of your trip planning, right along with composing an itinerary of the sights you want to see. Even if you're traveling on business and your choice of hotel is limited to those selected by your company, you may still have questions about the accommodations.

In this chapter, you get the information you need to find accommodations, make reservations, and check in and check out of your hotel.

Finding Accommodations

Hotels are your home away from home — even if you just consider it a place to lay your head after a day on the go — so it's good to know how to secure the kind of lodging you prefer. When thinking about what you want in a hotel, price is a consideration, but price alone does not determine whether a place is a wonderful one to stay in. Each type of accommodation — whether you want **un hôtel une étoile** (uhN-noh-tehl ewn ey-twahl) (*a one-star hotel*) or **un hôtel cinq étoiles** (uhN-noh-tehl saNk ey-twahl) (*a five-star hotel*) — offers advantages that may be just what you're looking for.

Les hôtels (ley-zoh-tehl) (*hotels*) range from basic one-star accommodations to luxury five-star establishments. Room prices vary according to amenities, size, rating, and location. Most hotels offer breakfast (usually a continental breakfast, which includes either a croissant or a roll with butter and jam, and coffee or tea), but not all have a restaurant. The names for different types of hotels may vary a little throughout the French-speaking countries.

Hôtel garni (oh-tehl gahr-nee) means *bed and breakfast,* and **maison de logement** (meh-zohN duh lohzh-mahN) in French-speaking Canada refers to a smaller hotel or tourist home, which in other countries is sometimes also called **une pension (de famille)** (ewn pahN-syohN [duh fah-meey]) (*a boarding house*) or **une auberge** (ewn oh-behrzh) (*inn*).

And then, in France, there are also those exquisite **châteaux** (shah-toh) (*castles*), which have been refurbished into hotels. Sure, they tend to be on the more expensive side, but the ambiance and the high-quality service are hard to surpass if you're looking for something special.

In recent years, alternatives to traditional hotels have become increasingly popular, such as **les gîtes ruraux** (ley zheet rew-roh) in France, which are furnished holiday cottages or flats, farmhouse arrangements in Belgium, chalets in Switzerland, or even former monasteries.

Finally, for the young and young at heart, France alone has about 200 **auberges de jeunesse** (oh-behrzh duh zhuh-nehs) (*youth hostels*), well scattered throughout the country, with varying facilities. Your national youth hostel association can give you details, or you can go online. For information about Canadian youth hostels, for example, go to www.hostellingmontreal.com and for hostels in other parts of the world, check out www.hostels.com.

Of course, when planning a trip to Europe, you can always get more information by browsing the Internet. The following sites, many of which provide virtual tours so that you can "visit" before you go, may help you:

- ✔ www.hotels.com can help you find a hotel in any part of the world.
- ✔ www.hotels.fr is entirely in French and can help you find hotels throughout France.
- ✔ www.hotels.be can help you find hotels in some parts of Europe like Belgium and the Netherlands.
- ✔ www.relaischateaux.fr gives you information about luxury hotels around the world.

The closer your hotel is to the center of the city, the more expensive it is likely to be. Also remember to figure in the city tax of about one euro per day per person, which is typically not included in the hotel rate.

Choosing your amenities

After you do your research and know exactly what kind of hotel you want to stay in, you should think about the kinds of amenities that you may be looking for. Here is a list of expressions that will tell you more about your accommodations:

✔ **la climatisation** (lah klee-mah-tee-zah-syohN) (*air conditioning*)

✔ **la piscine** (lah pee-seen) (*swimming pool*)

✔ **la salle de gym** (lah sahl duh zheem) (*fitness room*)

✔ **le site historique** (luh seet ee-stoh-reek) (*historic site*)

✔ **la blanchisserie** (lah blahN-shee-sree) (*laundry service*)

✔ **la navette d'aéroport** (lah nah-veht dah-ey-roh-pohr) (*airport shuttle*)

✔ **une connexion Wi-Fi** (ewn kohN-neh-ksyohN wee-fee) (a *Wi-Fi connection*)

In many countries, **un lavabo** (uhN lah-vah-boh) (*a bathroom sink*) and **une baignoire** (ewn beh-nywahr) (*a bathtub*) and/or **une douche** (ewn doohsh) (*a shower*) are separate from the toilet and the bidet, an arrangement which is wonderful, of course. However, some showers are hand-held in the bathtub with no curtain around it, and that method takes a bit getting used to, but works fine, too.

Many hotels and other types of lodgings have Internet access, which is pretty affordable and reliable. Often you find computers in the hotel lobby, which you may be able to use free of charge or for a small fee. If your hotel doesn't provide this service, don't worry: Numerous Internet cafés and **cybercafés** (see-behr kah-fey) (*cybercafés)* are located throughout major cities. Most hotels also provide Internet jacks into which you can plug your Ethernet cable.

The voltage in Europe is 220 volts as opposed to 110 volts used in the U.S. and Canada. If you're bringing any type of electronic equipment (hair dryer, electric shaver, laptop, and so on), you'll want to buy an adapter to bring with you. You can purchase these at any electronics store. In case you forget your adapter, you may buy one in an electronics store or any hypermarket in the country you are visiting.

Making reservations

You usually book a room online or through a travel agent, but just in case you call in person, you need to know what to say. This section includes some questions and phrases that can get you started.

When you call a hotel, you will probably first be connected to **le/la standardiste** (luh/lah stahN-dahr-deest) (*the switchboard operator*). You need to tell that person why you're calling. You can say something like the following:

> **Je voudrais retenir/réserver une chambre, s'il vous plaît.** (zhuh vooh-dreh ruh-tuh-neer/rey-zehr-vey ewn shahN-bruh, seel vooh pleh.) (*I would like to reserve a room please.*)

> **Avez-vous une chambre libre?** (ah-vey-vooh ewn shahN-bruh lee-bruh?) (*Do you have a room available?*)

You also need to say how long you'll be staying. To tell the operator or hotel clerk that you are staying from a certain date to a certain date, you use **du** (dew) (*from*) and **au** (oh) (*to*). For example, if you are staying *from June 4 to June 9,* you say **du quatre juin au neuf juin** (dew kah-truh zhwaN oh nuhf zhwaN). Alternatively, you can say **du 4 au 9 juin** (dew kaht-ruh oh nuhf zhwaN), which means the same thing. If you are staying from the first of the month or to the first of the month, then say **du premier** (dew pruh-myey) (*from the first*) and **au premier** (oh pruh-myey) (*to the first*). For example, **du premier au sept juillet** (dew pruh-myey oh seht zhwee-yeh) (*from the first to the seventh of July* [or *from July 1 to July 7*]). Chapter 4 has more on setting specific dates.

Specifying the kind of room you want

When you call to reserve a room, you have to tell them what type of room you're interested in. For example, do you want a single or a double room? Do you want one bed or two beds? Do you want the room to be facing the garden, the beach, or the court yard? To state the type of room you want, place any of these terms after the phrase **une chambre**… (ewn shahN-bruh…).

- **simple** (sahN-pluh) (*single*)
- **double** (dooh-bluh) (*double*)
- **pour deux/trois/quatre personnes** (poohr duh/trwah/kaht-ruh pehr-sohhn) (*for two/three/four people*)
- **à un lit/à deux lits** (ah uhN lee/ah duh lee) (*with one bed/with two beds*)
- **à deux lits jumeaux** (ah duh lee zhew-moh) (*with two twin beds*)

Do you want a room that faces or looks onto somewhere beautiful or romantic? Then you use the expression **donner sur** (dohh-ney sewr) (*facing, overlooking*). The verb **donner** (dohh-ney), whose literal meaning is *to give,* is a regular **–er** verb, which you conjugate the same way you conjugate the verb **parler** (pahr-ley) (*to speak*). (For the conjugation of regular verbs, refer to Chapter 2.) You would say **Je voudrais une chambre qui donne sur. . . .** (zhuh vooh-dreh ewn shahN-bruh kee dohhn sewr. . . .) (*I would like a room that faces. . . .*) and then specify any of the following:

- **le jardin** (luh zhahr-daN) (*the garden*)
- **la piscine** (lah pee-seen) (*the swimming pool*)
- **la montagne** (lah mohN-tah-nyuh) (*the mountain*)
- **la cour** (lah koohr) (*the court yard*)
- **la plage** (lah plahzh) (*the beach*)
- **la mer** (lah mehr) (*the sea*)
- **le lac** (luh lahk) (*the lake*)

Asking about the price

An important consideration before booking a room is the price. When you ask about room prices, also consider asking about whether a deposit is needed and whether the establishment accepts credit cards. The following sequence of questions and answers may help you:

Quel est le prix de la chambre? (kehl eh luh pree duh lah shahN-bruh?) (*What is the price of the room?*)

Le prix est 250 euros par jour. (luh pree eh duh-sahN saN-kahNt uh-roh par jour.) (*The price is 250 euros per day.*)

Est-ce qu'il faut un acompte/des arrhes? (ehs-keel foh uhN-nah-kohNt/ dey-zahr?) (*Do you need a deposit?*)

Il faut un acompte/des arrhes de 20 pour cent. (eel foh uhN-nah-kohNt/ dey-zahr duh vaN poohr sahN.) (*You need a 20 percent deposit.*)

Acceptez-vous des cartes de crédit? (ah-kseh-ptey-vooh dey kahrt duh krey-dee?) (*Do you accept credit cards?*)

Oui, bien sûr. (wee, byahN sewr.) (*Yes, of course.*)

Talkin' the Talk

Mr. and Mrs. Dalton are tired from driving and decide to call it a day in Annecy, a beautiful, small, French town close to the Swiss border. They stop at a pretty country inn. (Track 19)

Mr. Dalton: **Bonjour! Nous voudrions une chambre avec des lits jumeaux.**
bohN-zhoohr! nooh vooh-dree-ohN ewn shahN-bruh ah-vehk dey lee zhew-moh.
Hello! We would like a room with twin beds.

Le concierge: **Côté cour ou côté rue?**
koh-tey koohr ooh koh-tey rew?
Looking out on the court yard or the street?

Mrs. Dalton: **Côté cour. Et avec salle de bains et une baignoire, s'il vous plaît. Quel est le prix?**
koh-tey koohr. ey ah-vehk sahl duh baN ey ewn beh-nywahr, seel vooh pleh. kehl eh luh pree?
On the court yard. And with a bathroom and a bathtub, please. What is the price?

Le concierge: **Je vérifie . . . au rez-de-chaussée ça coûte 150 euros.**
zhuh vey-ree-fee . . . oh reyd-shoh-sey sah kooht sahN saN-kahNt uh-roh.
I am checking . . . on the ground floor, that'll cost 150 euros.

Mrs. Dalton: **Et au premier étage?**
ey oh pruh-myey-rey-tahzh?
And on the second floor?

Le concierge: **Je regrette. Le premier étage est complet.**
zhuh ruh-greht. luh pruh-myey-rey-tahzh eh kohN-pleh.
I'm sorry. The second floor is booked.

Mr. Dalton: **Pas de problème. Le rez-de-chaussée nous convient bien.**
pahd proh-blehm. luh reyd-shoh-sey nooh kohN-vyaN byaN.
No problem. The ground floor suits us fine.

Words to Know

côté cour	koh-tey koohr	facing the court yard
côté rue	koh-tey rew	facing the street
je vérifie	zhuh vey-ree-fee	I am checking
le rez-de-chaussée	luh reyd-shoh-sey	ground floor
ça coûte	sah kooht	that costs
au premier étage	oh pruh-myey-rey-tahzh	on the second floor
il nous convient	eel nooh kohN-vyaN	it suits us

Checking In to a Hotel

After a long trip, arriving at a hotel is probably your first highlight . . . and perhaps your first interaction with French. You may wonder how to address the hotel staff, especially when you arrive to inquire about a room. The titles **Monsieur** (muh-syuh) (*Sir, Mister [Mr.]*), **Madame** (mah-dahm) (*Ma'am, Misses [Mrs.]*), and **Mademoiselle** (mahd-mwah-zehl) (*Miss*) are used in French much more than in English and do not sound as formal. In fact, it is polite to add them after **bonjour** (bohN-zhoohr) (*hello, good morning*), especially when addressing someone you don't know.

Using direct object pronouns

In a conversation, you wouldn't sound very natural if you kept repeating the same words: "I would like a room. Can I see the room? Let's go and see the room." Instead, you'd say, "I would like a room. Can I see it? Let's go and see it," which sounds a lot better. So drop the direct object and replace it with one of the following direct object pronouns:

- ✔ **me** (muh) (*me*)
- ✔ **te** (tuh) (*you* [singular informal])
- ✔ **le** (luh) (*him, it*)
- ✔ **la** (lah) (*her, it*)
- ✔ **nous** (nooh) (*us*)
- ✔ **vous** (vooh) (*you* [singular formal or plural])
- ✔ **les** (ley) (*them*)

Just remember that the pronoun you choose depends on whether the noun it replaces is feminine or masculine, singular or plural. The placement of the pronoun is also important. You must put the direct object pronoun in front of the conjugated verb.

The object pronouns **me**, **te**, **nous**, and **vous** are easy to remember because each has only one form for both masculine and feminine. For example,

Est-ce que tu me vois? (ehs-kuh tew muh vwah?) (*Do you see me?*)

Oui, je te vois. (wee, zhuh tuh vwah.) (*Yes, I see you.*)

Est-ce qu'il nous appelle? (ehs-keel nooh-zah-pehl?) (*Is he calling us?*)

Oui, il vous appelle. (wee, eel vooh-zah-pehl.) (*Yes, he is calling you.*)

Things are a little trickier with the direct object pronouns in the third person, **le**, **la**, and **les**. The French forms of these pronouns change based on the gender and number of the noun they replace. Follow these rules:

- ✔ Use **le** when the noun being replaced is masculine singular. For example, the sentence **Il voit l'hôtel** (eel vwah loh -tehl) (*He sees the hotel*) changes to **Il le voit** (eel luh vwah) (*He sees it*).

- ✔ Use **la** when the noun being replaced is feminine singular. For example, the sentence **Nous suivons la réceptionniste** (nooh swee-vohN lah rey-sehp-syohN-neest) (*We are following the receptionist*) becomes **Nous la suivons** (nooh lah swee-vohN) (*We are following her*).

- ✔ In the third person plural, there is only one pronoun that replaces both a masculine and a feminine plural noun: **les**. For example, the sentence **Elle vérifie les dates** (ehl vey-ree-fee ley daht) (*She is checking the dates*) becomes **Elle les vérifie** (ehl ley vey-ree-fee) (*She's checking them*).

Naturally, there is an exception to the rule that the direct object pronoun must appear in front of the conjugated verb: When you have a helping verb plus an infinitive in your sentence, you need to put the object pronoun in front of the infinitive form, as in the following examples:

Il veut voir la chambre. (eel vuh vwahr lah shahN-bruh.) (*He wants to see the room.*) — direct object

Il veut la voir. (eel vuh lah vwahr.) (*He wants to see it.*) — direct object pronoun

Je dois vérifier les prix. (zhuh dwah vey-ree-fyey ley pree.) (*I must check out the prices.*) — direct object

Je dois les vérifier. (zhuh dwah ley vey-ree-fyey.) (*I must check them out.*) — direct object pronoun

Filling out a registration form

When you arrive at a hotel, chances are, you have to fill out **une fiche** (ewn feesh) (*a registration form*). This form may ask you for these items:

- ✔ **nom/prénom** (nohN/prey-nohN) ([*last*] *name/first name*)

- ✔ **lieu de résidence/adresse** (lyuh duh rey-zee-dahNs/ahd-rehs) (*address*)

- ✔ **rue/numéro** (rew/new-mey-roh) (*street/number*)

- ✔ **ville/code postal** (veel/kohhd poh-stahl) (*city/zip code*)

- ✔ **état/pays** (ey-tah/pey-ee) (*state/country*)

- ✔ **numéro de téléphone** (new-mey-roh duh tey-ley-fohhn) (*telephone number*)

- **nationalité** (nah-syoh-nah-lee-tey) (*nationality*)

- **date/lieu de naissance** (daht/lyuh duh neh-sahNs) (*date/place of birth*)

- **numéro de passeport** (new-mey-roh duh pahs-pohr) (*passport number*)

- **signature** (see-nyah-tewr) (*signature*)

- **numéro d'immatriculation de la voiture** (new-mey-roh dee-mah-tree-kew-lah-syohN duh lah vwah-tewr) (*license plate number*)

- **date de l'arrivée** (daht duh lah-ree-vey) (*date of arrival*)

- **date du départ** (daht dew dey-pahr) (*date of departure*)

Should you tip hotel staff such as bellboys and maids? A service charge is generally included in hotel and restaurant bills. However, if the service has been particularly good, you may want to leave an extra tip.

Talkin' the Talk

Carol is checking in at the reception desk while Max brings in the luggage with the doorman's help.

Carol:	**Nous prenons la belle chambre au troisième étage.** nooh pruh-nohN lah behl shahN-bruh oh trwah-zee-ehm ey-tahzh. *We'll take the beautiful room on the fourth floor.*
Le réceptionniste:	**Bon. Veuillez remplir cette fiche, s'il vous plaît, et j'ai besoin de vos passeports.** bohN. vuh-yey rahN-pleer seht feesh, seel vooh pleh, ey zhey buh-zwaN duh voh pahs-pohr. *Good. Would you please fill out this form, and I need your passports.*
Carol:	**Les voilà . . . et la fiche . . . . C'est fait.** ley vwah-lah . . . ey lah feesh . . . . seh feh. *Here they are . . . and the (registration) form.... It's done.*
Le réceptionniste:	**Merci, madame. L'ascenseur est à gauche. Je vous souhaite une bonne soirée.** mehr-see, mah-dahm. lah-sahN-suhr eh-tah gohsh. zhuh vooh sweht ewn bohhn swah-rey. *Thank you, ma'am. The elevator is on the left. I wish you a nice evening.*

Carol:	**Merci. À quelle heure fermez-vous la porte principale?**
	mehr-see. ah kehl uhr fehr-mey-vooh lah pohrt praN-see-pahl?
	Thank you. What time do you close the main door?

Le réceptionniste:	**À minuit, mais vous pouvez toujours sonner.**
	ah mee-nwee, meh vooh pooh-vey tooh-zhoohr sohh-ney.
	At midnight, but you can always ring.

Words to Know

veuillez remplir	vuh-yey rahN-pleer	would you please fill out
j'ai besoin de	zhey buh-zwaN duh	I need
l' ascenseur	lah-sahN-suhr	the elevator
je vous souhaite	zhuh vooh sweht	I wish you
vous fermez	vooh fehr-mey	you close
la porte principale	lah pohrt praN-see-pahl	main door
vous pouvez sonner	vooh pooh-vey sohh-ney	you can ring

Asking for towels and other essentials

Okay, you're settling in to your hotel room, but you discover you need more towels, blankets, and pillows. Or maybe you discover that the light bulb is out, or there's no more toilet paper. If you need any of these items, you would call down to the desk and say **Il nous faut. . . .** (eel nooh foh. . . .) (*We need. . . .*) and add the articles from the following list, as appropriate:

- ✔ **une/des couverture(s)** (ewn/dey kooh-vehr-tewr) (a *blanket/blankets*)

- ✔ **un/des oreiller(s)** (uhN/dey-zoh-reh-yey) (a *pillow/pillows*)

- ✔ **une/des serviette(s)** (ewn/dey sehr-vee-eht) (a *towel/towels*)

- ✔ **des cintres** (dey sahN-truh) (*hangers*)

- ✔ **une/des ampoule(s)** (ewn/dey-zahN-poohl) (a *light bulb/light bulbs*)

- ✔ **du savon** (dew sah-vohN) (*soap*)

- ✔ **du papier hygiénique/de toilette** (dew pah-pyey ee-zhee-ey-neek/duh twah-leht) (*toilet paper*)

In Chapter 7, we discuss the impersonal expression **il faut** (eel foh) (*it is necessary*) followed by the infinitive. However, you can personalize this construction by adding an indirect object pronoun of your choice in front of the verb: **me** (muh) (*to me*), **te** (tuh) (*to you*), **lui** (lwee) (*to him/to her*), **nous** (nooh) (*to us*), **vous** (vooh) (*to you*), and **leur** (luhr) (*to them*). (Check out the indirect object pronouns in Chapter 13.) Look at the following examples but note that you cannot translate these examples literally:

> **Il me faut des serviettes.** (eel muh foh dey sehr-vee-eht.) (*I need towels.*)

> **Il nous faut du savon.** (eel nooh foh dew sah-vohN.) (*We need soap.*)

Checking Out of a Hotel

For whatever reason, the checkout time is hardly ever convenient, but you probably realize that rooms have to be cleaned before the next guest arrives. Of course, before leaving, you have to pay your bill or at least verify it to see whether you have accrued any additional charges during your stay. The following phrases can come in handy when it's time to check out:

- ✔ **À quelle heure faut-il libérer la chambre?** (ah kehl uhr foh-teel lee-bey-rey lah shahN-bruh?) (*At what time do I/we have to check out?*)

- ✔ **Ces frais supplémentaires sont corrects/incorrects.** (sey freh sew-pley-mahN-tehr sohN koh-rehkt/aN-koh-rehkt.) (*These additional charges are correct/incorrect.*)

- ✔ **J'ai une question en ce qui concerne la note.** (zhey ewn kehs-tyohN ahN skee kohN-sehrn lah nohht.) (*I have a question regarding the bill.*)

- ✔ **Je voudrais un reçu.** (zhuh vooh-dreh uhN ruh-sew.) (*I'd like a receipt.*)

You may have to remove your belongings from your room before you're ready to depart from your location. Fortunately, many hotels allow you to leave your luggage in the lobby or some other place until you leave. To find out whether your hotel offers this service, ask **Je peux laisser mes bagages ici jusqu'à . . . .?** (zhuh puh ley-sey mey bah-gahzh ee-see zhews-kah. . .?) (*Can I leave my luggage here until. . . ?*)

Talkin' the Talk

Judy Cole's plane is leaving in the evening. So she wants to spend her last day in town and get the luggage later. (Track 20)

Judy:	**À quelle heure faut-il libérer la chambre?** ah kehl uhr foh-teel lee-bey-rey lah shahN-bruh? *At what time do we have to vacate the room (check out)?*
La réceptionniste:	**Avant midi, madame.** ah-vahN mee-dee, mah-dahm. *Before noon, ma'am.*
Judy:	**Je peux laisser mes bagages ici jusqu'à seize heures?** zhuh puh ley-sey mey bah-gahzh ee-see zhews-kah sehz uhr? *Can I leave my luggage here until 4:00 p.m.?*
La réceptionniste:	**Oui, vous pouvez les laisser ici. Voulez-vous la note maintenant?** wee, vooh pooh-vey ley ley-sey ee-see. vooh-ley-vooh lah nohht maN-tuh-nahN? *Yes, you can leave them here. Would you like the bill now?*
Judy:	**Oui, s'il vous plaît. Voyons, les coups de téléphone . . . le minibar . . . Très bien. Vous acceptez les cartes de crédit, n'est-ce pas?** wee, seel vooh pleh. vwah-yohN, ley kooh duh tey-ley-fohhn. . . luh mee-nee-bar. . . treh byaN. vooh-zah-kseh-ptey ley kahrt duh krey-dee, nehs-pahs? *Yes, please. Let's see, the phone calls . . . the minibar . . . Very well. You accept credit cards, don't you?*

La réceptionniste:	**Oui, Visa ou Mastercard . . . merci . . . et voici votre reçu.**
	wee, vee-zah ooh mah-stehr-kahrd . . . mehr-see . . . ey vwah-see vohh-truh ruh-sew.
	Yes, Visa or Mastercard . . . thank you . . . and here is your receipt.

Judy:	**Merci. Pouvez-vous m'appeler un taxi, s'il vous plaît?**
	mehr-see. pooh-vey-vooh mah-pley uhN tah-ksee, seel vooh pleh?
	Thank you. Can you call a taxi for me, please?

La réceptionniste:	**Bien sûr.**
	byaN sewr.
	Of course.

Words to Know

je peux laisser	zhuh puh ley-sey	I can leave (behind)
ici	ee-see	here
jusqu'à	zhews-kah	until
la note	lah nohht	bill
un coup de téléphone	uhN kooh duh tey-ley-fohhn	telephone call
le reçu	luh ruh-sew	receipt

Fun and Games

There seems to be a mistake on your hotel bill, so you are going over the details with the desk clerk. You had a room for two with twin beds and a bathtub, on the second floor, facing the street, for two nights. Correct him as needed by circling the correct response and clarifying any answers as needed.

L'employé: Je vérifie. Une chambre double?

A. You: Oui/Non. _____

L'employé: Avec douche?

B. You: Oui/Non. _____

L'employé: Au rez-de-chaussée?

C. You: Oui/Non. _____

L'employé: Côté rue?

D. You: Oui/Non. _____

L'employé: Pour trois nuits?

E. You: Oui/Non. _____

Chapter 17

Handling Emergencies

. . . .

In This Chapter
▶ Getting medical help
▶ Asking for help from the police

. . . .

*I*t goes without saying that emergencies are no fun. They're bad enough when you're on home turf, but they're even worse when you're in a foreign environment. Hopefully, the only help you'll ever need to ask for when you're traveling is where the nearest bus terminal is or what local cuisine your hosts would recommend. But if you do find yourself in an emergency situation, you can use the information and vocabulary in this chapter to get the help you need.

We've divided this chapter into two main sections: The first half deals with health problems, and the second half deals with legal matters.

Getting Help Fast

If you're ever in an accident or have an emergency, the following key French phrases will alert those nearby and get you help right away:

▸ **À l'aide! Vite!** (ah lehd! veet!) (*Help! Fast!*)

▸ **Au secours!** (oh skoohr!) (*Help!*)

▸ **Au feu!** (oh fuh!) (*Fire!*)

▸ **Arrêtez-le/la!** (ah-reh-tey-luh/lah!) (*Stop him/her!*)

▸ **Au voleur!** (oh voh-luhr!) (*Catch the thief!*)

▸ **Police!** (poh-lees!) (*Police!*)

The emergency number for the entire European Union is 112. When you call this number, it connects you to the local first responders. Be sure you give them your location, the type of emergency, and your telephone number.

You may also find it helpful to have on hand specific emergency numbers for the country you're visiting. In France, the numbers are as follows (in the provinces, all the emergency numbers are on one page of the telephone book):

- **La police** (lah poh-lees) (*police*): 17
- **L'ambulance** (lahN-bew-lahNs) (*ambulance*): 15
- **Le feu** (luh fuh) (*fire*): 18

The French are required by law to provide assistance in an emergeny. At the very least, they will stop, ask you what the problem is (if it's not evident), and call or tell you which number to call for the particular type of emergency.

Chances are that one of the first responders will speak enough English to communicate with you directly or will call someone who does. Just in case, you can always ask for someone who speaks English by saying **Est-ce qu'il y a quelqu'un qui parle anglais?** (ehs-keel ee ah kehl-kuhN kee pahrl ahN-gleh?) (*Is there someone who speaks English?*)

Getting Medical Help

If you have a medical concern — you have **une maladie** (ewn mah-lah-dee) (*an illness*), for example — you may simply need to go **chez le médecin** (shey luh meyd-saN) (*to the doctor's office*) or **au cabinet médical** (oh kah-bee-neh mey-dee-kahl) (*to the medical office*). To do this, you'll want to **prendre rendez-vous** (prahN-druh rahN-dey-vooh) (*make an appointment*). Although doctors usually have consultation hours for patients who don't have appointments, you may have to wait a long time. (If you are too ill to go to the doctor, don't worry. They can come to your hotel room or wherever you're staying.)

Your hotel can provide the addresses and phone numbers of local doctors or specialists. You can also get this information from a pharmacist. On Sundays, holidays, or after-hours, the local **gendarmerie** (zhahN-dahr-muh-ree) (*police station*) can also provide the number of **le médecin de garde** (luh meyd-saN duh gahrd) (*the doctor on duty*) or **la pharmacie de garde** (lah fahr-mah-see duh gahrd) (*the 24-hour pharmacy*).

If you have been involved in an accident, you may need to go to **un hôpital** (uhN-noh-pee-tahl) (*a hospital*) or **les urgences** (f) (ley-zewr-zhahNs) (*the emergency room*). In such an emergency, you can use either of the following phrases:

> ✔ **Il me faut un docteur.** (eel muh foh tuhN dohk-tuhr.) (*I need a doctor.*)
>
> ✔ **Il lui faut une ambulance.** (eel lwee foh-tewn ahN-bew-lahNs.) (*He/She needs an ambulance.*)

Before leaving home, check with your insurance provider to see whether your policy covers emergencies or doctor visits abroad. If emergencies or medical treatments abroad aren't covered, you may need to purchase coverage for the dates you're traveling. If you need any sort of medical services while abroad, simply show your providers proof of your insurance in the United States. Also be sure to call your insurance company back home to explain what's happening. Usually you'll have to pay your bill (with your credit card) when you receive medical care, but your insurance company will reimburse you when you present the detailed bill back home. Remember to keep all your receipts and any **feuilles de soins** (fuhy duh swaN) (*medical claim forms*) that you sign.

Talking with doctors when you're ill or injured

France has one of the best healthcare systems in the world. Rest assured that, whether you're simply not feeling well and want to discuss your symptoms with **un médecin/un docteur** (uhN meyd-saN/uhN dohk-tuhr) (*a doctor*) or have been hurt in an accident, you'll receive world-class care.

Describing what body part hurts

To describe what's bothering you, you need to be able to convey to the doctor what body part hurts or feels uncomfortable:

> ✔ **la bouche** (lah boohsh) (*mouth*)
>
> ✔ **le bras** (luh brah) (*arm*)
>
> ✔ **la cheville** (lah shuh-veey) (*ankle*)
>
> ✔ **les côtes** (f.) (ley koht) (*ribs*)
>
> ✔ **le cou** (luh kooh) (*neck*)
>
> ✔ **le doigt** (luh dwah) (*finger*)
>
> ✔ **le dos** (luh doh) (*back*)

- **l'épaule** (ley-pohl) (*shoulder*)

- **l'estomac/le ventre** (leh-stoh-mah/luh vahN-truh) (*stomach*)

- **la figure** (lah fee-gewr) (*face*)

- **le genou** (luh zhuh-nooh) (*knee*)

- **la gorge** (lah gohrzh) (*throat*)

- **la jambe** (lah zhahNb) (*leg*)

- **la main** (lah maN) (*hand*)

- **le nez** (luh ney) (*nose*)

- **le pied** (luh pyey) (*foot*)

- **la poitrine** (lah pwah-treen) (*chest*)

- **l'oeil/les yeux** (luhy/ley-zyuh) (*eye/eyes*)

- **l'oreille** (loh-rehy) (*ear*)

- **l'orteil** (lohr-tehy) (*toe*)

- **la tête** (lah teht) (*head*)

To tell the doctor that something hurts, simply use the expression **J'ai mal à (à la/au/aux). . . .** (zhey mahl ah (ah lah/oh/oh. . . .) (*My . . . hurts*) and follow this with the body part. This construction uses the verb **avoir** (ah-vwahr) (*to have*) conjugated in the present (refer to Chapter 2 for the conjugation of this verb) plus the preposition **à** (ah). Whether you use **à la/au/aux** before the body part depends on the gender and number of the body part: If the body part is masculine singular, use **au;** if it is feminine singular, use **à la,** and if it's masculine or feminine plural, use **aux**. Here are some examples:

> **J'ai mal au bras.** (zhey mahl oh brah.) (*My arm hurts.*)
>
> **J'ai mal à la poitrine.** (zhey mahl ah lah pwah-treen.) (*My chest hurts.*)
>
> **J'ai mal aux pieds.** (zhey mahl oh pyeh.) (*My feet hurt.*)

You can also indicate what hurts on someone else by changing the subject pronoun at the beginning and conjugating the verb **avoir** appropriately, as shown in these examples:

> **Il a mal au dos**. (eel ah mahl oh doh.) (*His back hurts.*)
>
> **Nous avons mal à la tete.** (nooh-zah-vohN mahl ah lah teht.) (*Our head hurts, We have a headache.*)

Describing other symptoms

If you don't feel well — you have a fever or feel nauseous or faint, for example — you'll want to explain those symptoms to the doctor. In this case, you want to be able to tell the doctor *I have a fever* or *I am nauseous*. To create many of these expressions, you use the verb **avoir**, as explained in the preceding sections, but without the preposition **à**. You say, for example, **j'ai** (zhey) (*I have*) and follow it with the appropriate symptom. Following are some symptoms:

- **de la fièvre** (duh lah fyeh-vruh) (*a fever*)

- **de la température** (duh lah tahN-pey-rah-tuhr) (*a temperature*)

- **des problèmes à respirer** (dey proh-blehm ah reh-spee-rey) (*problems breathing*)

- **de l'asthme** (duh lah-smuh) (*asthma*)

- **une migraine** (ewn mee-grehn) (*a migraine*)

- **un (gros) rhume** (uhN [groh] rewm) (*an [awful] cold*)

- **la grippe** (lah greep) (*the flu*)

- **le nez bouché** (luh ney booh-shey) (*a stuffy nose*)

- **une toux** (ewn tooh) (*a cough*)

- **une eruption/des taches rouges** (ewn ey-rewp-syohN/dey tahsh roohzh) (*a rash/red spots*)

- **la diarrhée** (lah dyah-rey) (*diarrhea*)

- **une coupure** (ewn kooh-pewr) (*a cut*)

Keep in mind that the English translation may not actually include the verb *to have,* as these examples show:

J'ai de la nausée/J'ai mal au coeur. (zhey duh lah noh-zey/zhey mahl oh kuhr.) (*I am nauseous.*)

J'ai des vertiges. (zhey dey vehr-teezh.) (*I am dizzy.*)

Talkin' the Talk

Julia has not been feeling well, so she calls her doctor's office in order to make an appointment. She explains her symptoms to the receptionist. (Track 21)

Julia: **Bonjour. C'est Julia Mills au téléphone. Est-ce que je pourrais prendre rendez-vous le plus tôt possible?**
bohN-zhoohr. seh zhew-lyah meels oh tey-ley-fohhn. ehs-kuh zhuh pooh-reh prahN-druh rahN-dey-vooh luh plew toh poh-see-bluh?
Hello. This is Julia Mills speaking. Could I have an appointment as soon as possible?

La réceptionniste:	**De quoi souffrez-vous?** duh kwah sooh-frey-vooh? *What are you suffering from?*
Julia:	**Je suis tombée et maintenant j'ai très mal à la tête.** zhuh swee tohN-bey ey maN-tuh-nahN zhey treh mahl ah lah teht. *I fell and now I have a bad headache.*
La réceptionniste:	**Avez-vous mal au coeur?** ah-vey-vooh mahl oh kuhr? *Do you feel nauseous?*
Julia:	**Oui, je ne me sens pas très bien.** wee, zhuh nuh muh sahN pah treh byahN. *Yes, I don't feel very well.*
La réceptionniste:	**Pouvez-vous venir tout de suite?** pooh-vey-vooh vuh-neer tooht sweet? *Can you come in right away?*
Julia:	**Oui, merci. À tout à l'heure.** wee, mehr-see. ah tooh-tah luhr. *Yes, thank you. See you shortly.*

Saying that you broke, sprained, twisted, or cut something

In French, to express that you have broken your arm, sprained or twisted your ankle, or cut a part of your body, you use reflexive verbs. (Check out the explanation and conjugation of such verbs in the present in Chapter 5. For more on the past tense, refer to Chapter 11.) To form the past tense of reflexive verbs, take the present tense conjugation of the auxiliary **être** (eh-truh) (*to be*) and follow it with a past participle. Here is an example of the verb **se casser** (suh kah-sey) (*to break*) in the **passé composé** (pah-sey kohN-poh-zey) (*the past tense* [*compound past*]):

Je me suis cassé la jambe. (zhuh muh swee kah-sey lah zhahNb.) (*I broke my leg.*)

Tu t'es cassé la cheville. (tew teh kah-sey lah shuh-veey.) (*You broke your ankle.*)

Il/Elle s'est cassé la bras. (eel/ehl seh kah-sey lah brah.) (*He/She broke his/her arm.*)

Nous nous sommes cassé les orteils. (nooh nooh sohm kah-sey ley-zohr-tehy.) (*We broke our toes.*)

Vous vous êtes cassé les doigts. (vooh vooh-zeht kah-sey ley dwah.) (*You broke your fingers.*)

Ils/Elles se sont cassé les côtes. (eel/ehl suh sohN kah-sey ley koht.) (*They broke their ribs.*)

Follow this pattern with other verbs and then add the part of the body that is affected. Here are examples using other verbs:

- **Je me suis foulé. . . .** (zhuh muh swee fooh-ley. . . .) (*I sprained. . . .*)
- **Je me suis tordu. . . .** (zhuh muh swee tohr-dew. . . .) (*I twisted. . . .*)
- **Je me suis coupé. . . .** (zhuh muh swee kooh-pey. . . .) (*I cut. . . .*)

English uses the possessive adjectives with the parts of the body, but French uses the definite articles. For example, in English, you say *I broke my foot.* In French, **je me suis cassé le pied** (zhuh muh swee kah-sey luh pyey), which means *I broke my foot* but translates literally as *I broke the foot to me.*

Undergoing a medical examination

When you go to the doctor, he or she will undoubtedly ask you a few questions, such as **Où avez-vous mal?** (ooh ah-vey-vooh mahl?) (*Where does it hurt?*) or **Quels sont vos symptômes?** (kehl sohN voh saN-ptohm?) (*What are your symptoms?*). To answer these questions, use the terms and phrases provided in the preceding sections. Unless the problem is very obvious and easy-to-treat, other questions and procedures may be required, as the following sections explain.

If you've been involved in an accident and hurt yourself, a frequently used idiomatic expression is the question **Qu'est-ce qui s'est passé?** (kehs-kee seh pah-sey?) (*What happened?*) Another common expression is **Ça fait mal!** (sah feh mahl!) (*That hurts!*) You'll want to memorize both of these.

Sharing information about existing conditions

The doctor may ask you questions, such as the following, to determine whether you have other conditions he or she needs to know about:

Êtes-vous cardiaque? (eht-vooh kahr-dyahk?) (*Do you have a heart condition?*)

Êtes-vous diabétique? (eht-vooh dee-ah-bey-teek?) (*Are you a diabetic?*)

Avez-vous de l'hypertension? (ah-vey-vooh duh lee-pehr-tahN- syohN?) (*Do you have high-blood pressure?*)

Êtes-vous allergique à. . .? (eht-vooh-zah-lehr-zheek ah . . .?) (*Are you allergic to. . .?*)

Prenez-vous des médicaments? (pruh-ney-vooh dey mey-dee-kah-mahN?) (*Are you taking any medications?*)

Of course, you can also offer this information before you're asked, by using these phrases:

- ✔ **Je suis cardiaque.** (zhuh swee kahr-dyahk.) (*I have a heart condition.*)

- ✔ **J'ai de l'hypertension.** (zhey duh lee-pehr-tahN-syohN.) (*I have high blood pressure.*)

- ✔ **Je suis diabétique/allergique à . . . .** (zhuh swee dee-ah-bey-teek/ ah-lehr-zheek ah. . . .) (*I am diabetic/allergic to . . . .*)

Talking about tests

After you tell the doctor what your concern is, he or she will examine you and may want to **prendre votre pouls** (prahN-druh vohh-truh poohl) (*take your pulse*) and **ausculter votre coeur** (oh-skewl-tey vohh-truh kuhr) (*listen to your heart*) or even do the following, as warranted:

- ✔ **prendre votre tension artérielle** (prahN-druh vohh-truh tahN-syohN ahr-tey-ree-ehl) (*to take your blood pressure*)

- ✔ **faire une prise de sang** (fehr ewn preez duh sahN) (*to take, draw blood*)

- ✔ **faire une radiographie** (fehr ewn rah-dyoh-grah-fee) (*to do an x-ray*)

When the exam is complete, the doctor will tell you what you need to do. The doctor may **prescrire des médicaments** (preh-skreer dey mey-dee-kah-mahN) (*prescribe medication*), which you can get at a pharmacy.

Talkin' the Talk

Julia arrives at the doctor's office and is given an examination.

Le médecin: **Depuis quand vous sentez-vous comme ça?**
duh-pwee kahN vooh sahN-tey-vooh kohm sah?
How long have you been feeling like this?

Julia: **Depuis hier, quand je suis tombée.**
duh-pwee yehr, kahN zhuh swee tohN-bey.
Since yesterday, when I fell.

Le médecin: **Avez-vous perdu l'appétit?**
ah-vey-vooh pehr-dew lah-pey-tee?
Have you lost your appetite?

Julia: **Oui, et j'ai mal au coeur.**
wee, ey zhey mahl oh kuhr.
Yes, and I feel nauseous.

Le médecin: **Vous avez une légère commotion cérébrale. Reposez-vous bien pendant quelques jours. Est-ce que vous prenez des médicaments?**
vooh-zah-vey ewn ley-zhehr koh-moh-syohN sey-rey-brahl. ruh-poh-zey-vooh byaN pahN-dahN kehl-kuh zhoohr. ehs-kuh vooh pruh-ney dey mey-dee-kah-mahN?
You have a light concussion. Take it very easy for a few days. Do you take any medication?

Julia: **Non. Mais je suis allergique à l'aspirine.**
nohN. meh zhuh swee-zah-lehr-zheek ah lah-spee-reen.
No. But I am allergic to aspirin.

Le médecin: **Bon. Voilà une ordonnance . . . en cas de douleur. Prenez un comprimé toutes les quatre heures et revenez dans trois jours.**
bohN. vwah-lah ewn ohr-doh-nahNs . . . ahN kah duh dooh-luhr. pruh-ney uhN kohN-pree-mey tooht ley kah-truhr ey ruh-vuh-ney dahN trwah zhoohr.
Good. Here is a prescription . . . in case of pain. Take one pill every four hours and come back in three days.

Julia: **Merci, docteur. Au revoir.**
mehr-see, dohk-tuhr. ohr-vwahr.
Thank you, doctor. Good-bye.

Words to Know

je suis tombé(e)	zhuh swee tohN-bey	I fell
se sentir	suh sahN-teer	to feel
depuis quand/ depuis hier	duh-pwee kahN/duh-pwee yehr	since when/since yesterday
perdre	pehr-druh	to lose
une commotion cérébrale	ewn koh-moh-syohN sey-rey-brahl	a concussion
pendant quelques jours	pahN-dahN kehl-kuh zhoohr	for a few days
revenir	ruh-vuh-neer	to come back

To form the past tense in French, you need the auxiliary verbs **avoir** or **être** plus the past participle, as in **j'ai eu** (zhey ew) (*I had*). Chapter 11 covers the past tense.

Going to a pharmacy for minor ailments and medications

The French pharmacists' duties far surpass those of the pharmacists in the U.S., so the pharmacy is often the first place you go in France for minor medical concerns. In addition to filling **des ordonnances** (dey-zohr-doh-nahNs) (*prescriptions*), the highly trained **pharmacien/pharmacienne** (fahr-mah-syaN/fahr-mah-syehn) (*pharmacist*) can dress wounds; give advice on how to remedy a bad cold, migraines, sunburn, and so on; and give nutritional advice as well. French pharmacies are easily recognizable by the big green cross on them.

When you go to a pharmacist for medical care, you can ask **Pourriez-vous me donner un conseil?** (pooh-ree-ey-vooh muh dohh-ney uhN kohN-sehy) (*Could you give me some advice?*). If the problem is more serious and requires further medical attention, the pharmacist will refer you to the doctors in the area.

In addition, unlike in the U.S., **les médicaments** (ley mey-dee-kah-mahN) (*medication*) in France is sold only in pharmacies, not in supermarkets or anywhere else. The following vocabulary can help you request the medication you need:

- ✔ **les antibiotiques** (ley-zahN-tee-bee-oh-teek) (*antibiotics*)
- ✔ **l'aspirine** (lah-spee-reen) (*aspirin*)
- ✔ **les pastilles** (ley pah-steey) (*lozenges*)
- ✔ **le sirop (pour la toux)** (luh see-roh [poohr lah tooh]) (*syrup [cough syrup]*)
- ✔ **les vitamines** (ley vee-tah-meen) (*vitamins*)

If you need medication, provide the generic name of the medication to the pharmacist because the name brand may not exist in the country where you are traveling. For example, you can say **acétaminophène** (ah-sey-tah-mee-noh-fehn) (*acetaminophen*) or **ibuprofène** (ee-bew-proh-fehn) (*ibuprophen*).

Even though you probably won't need a fully stocked **trousse de secours** (troohs duh skoohr) (*first-aid kit*), you can also get some basic items like **de l'alcool** (duh lahl-kohhl) (*[rubbing] alcohol*) and **des pensements** (dey pahN-suh-mahN) (*bandages*) at pharmacies, too.

Pharmacy hours are usually Monday to Saturday 9:00 a.m. to 7:00 p.m. and closed on Sundays. For night and Sunday hours, there is always **une pharmacie de garde** (ewn fahr-mah-see duh gahrd) (*a 24-hour pharmacy* [Literally: *a pharmacy on duty*]) nearby.

Braving the dentist

Anything can happen while traveling. You may get **une rage de dents** (ewn razh duh dahN) (*a violent toothache*) or lose a filling. If this happens, you can ask for the name of a local **dentiste** (dahN-teest) (*dentist*) at your hotel or inquire at the nearest pharmacy. Here's some vocabulary pertaining to common ailments involving your teeth:

- ✔ **un abcès** (uhN-nahp-seh) (*an abscess*)
- ✔ **une couronne cassée** (ewn kooh-rohn kah-sey) (*a broken crown*)
- ✔ **la dent (sensible)** (lah dahN [sahN-see-bluh]) ([*sensitive*] *tooth*)
- ✔ **les gencives saignantes** (ley zhahN-seev seh-nyahNt) (*bleeding gums*)
- ✔ **le plombage est tombé** (luh plohN-bahzh eh tohN-bey) (*the filling fell out*)

Handling Legal Matters

Most vacations and trips take place without any sort of issues that would require you to talk to the police or need help from your consulate. But occasionally, you may find yourself in a situation where such conversations are necessary. Perhaps your wallet or purse has been stolen, you've been involved in or have witnessed an accident, or you've lost your passport. This section provides you with the information you need to deal with such incidents if they should occur.

Talking to the police

You should report any accident, emergency, theft, and so on to **le commissariat de police** (luh koh-mee-sah-ree-aht duh poh-lees) (*the police station*) in major cities or to **la gendarmerie** (lah zhahN-dahr-muh-ree) in smaller towns. (See the earlier section "Getting Help Fast" for emergency numbers.) To find the nearest police station, you can say **Où est le commissariat de police le plus proche?** (ooh eh luh koh-mee-sah-ree-aht duh poh-lees luh plew prohsh?) (*Where is the closest police station?*). Once there, you can explain your purpose by saying **Je veux signaler . . .** (zhuh vuh see-nyah-ley) (*I want to report . . .*) and filling in with the following phrases:

✔ **un accident** (uhN-nah-ksee-dahN) (*an accident*)

✔ **une agression** (ew-nah-greh-syohN) (*a mugging*)

✔ **un cambriolage** (uhN kahN-bree-oh-lahzh) (*a burglary*)

✔ **un vol** (uhN vohl) (*a theft*)

At this point, the conversation is likely to go beyond the French you know. In that case, you can say **Est-ce qu'il y a quelqu'un qui parle anglais?** (ehs-keel ee ah kehl-kuhN kee pahrl ahN-gleh?) (*Is there anyone who speaks English?*)

Reporting an accident

In the event of an accident, report the accident to **un agent de police** (uhN-nah-zhahN duh poh-lees) (*a police officer*) to make a report of major accidents in towns, or to **un gendarme** (uhN zhahN-dahrm) (*a police officer*) for accidents on country roads. You can say **Il y a eu un accident. . . .** (eel ee ah ew uhN-nah-ksee-dahN. . . .) (*There has been an accident. . . .*) and then follow this with these phrases:

✔ **sur l'autoroute** (sewr loh-toh-rooht) (*on the highway*)

✔ **sur la route** (sewr lah rooht) (*on the road*)

✔ **près de....** (preh duh...) (*near. . . .*)

When the police arrive, they usually ask a great many questions, such as the following:

✔ **Est-ce que je peux voir votre . . . ?** (ehs-kuh zhuh puh vwahr vohh-truh) (*Can I see your . . . ?*)

> **permis de conduire** (pehr-mee duh kohN-dweer) (*driver's license*)

> **carte d'assurance** (kahrt dah-sew-rahNs) (*insurance card*)

> **carte grise** (kahrt greez) (*vehicle registration document*)

✔ **Quel est votre nom et adresse?** (kehl eh vohh-truh nohN ey ah-drehs?) (*What is your name and address?*)

✔ **À quelle heure est-ce que ça s'est passé?** (ah kehl uhr ehs-kuh sah seh pah-sey?) (*At what time did this happen?*)

✔ **Est-ce qu'il y a des témoins?** (ehs-keel ee ah dey tey-mwaN?) (*Are there any witnesses?*)

They may also say **Vous devez venir au commissariat pour faire une déposition** (vooh duh-vey vuh-neer oh koh-mee-sah-ree-ah poohr fehr ewn dey-poh-zee-syohN) (*You have to come to the station to make a statement*) or **Vous devez payer une amende** (vooh duh-vey pey-yey ewn ah-mahNd) (*You have to pay a fine*).

The following phrases may help you explain what happened:

Il m'est rentré dedans. (eel meh rahN-trey duh-dahN.) (*He ran into me.*)

Elle a conduit trop vite/près. (ehl ah kohN-dwee troh veet/preh.)
(*She drove too fast/close.*)

Je faisais . . . kilomètres à l'heure. (zhuh fuh-zeh . . . kee-loh-meh-truh
ah luhr) (*I was doing . . . kilometers per hour.*)

At any time, feel free to say **Je voudrais un interprète/un avocat.** (zhuh
vooh-dreh–zuhN-naN-tehr-preht/uhN-nah-voh-kah.) (*I would like an
interpreter/a lawyer.*)

Talkin' the Talk

As André drives across an intersection, a driver runs through a red
light and hits him from behind. A police officer is called to the scene.

Le gendarme:	**Qu'est-ce qui s'est passé?** kehs-kee seh pah-sey? *What happened?*
André:	**Je traversais le carrefour quand cette voiture a brûlé un feu rouge et m'est rentré dedans.** zhuh trah-vehr-seh luh kahr-foohr kahN seht vwah-tewr ah brew-ley uhN fuh roozh ey meh rahN-trey duh-dahN. *I was crossing the intersection when this car ran a red light and hit me from behind.*
Le gendarme:	**Etes-vous blessé?** eht-vooh bley-sey? *Are you hurt?*
André:	**Non, monsieur, mais le pare-chocs est bosselé.** nohN, muh-syuh, meh luh pahr-shohk eh bohhs-ley. *No, sir, but the bumper is dented.*
Le gendarme:	**Donnez-moi votre permis de conduire et votre carte grise.** dohh-ney-mwah vohh-truh pehr-mee duh kohN-dweer ey vohh-truh kahrt greez. *Give me your license and your vehicle registration.*

André:	**Les voici.**
	ley vwah-see.
	Here they are.

Words to Know

traverser	trah-vehr-sey	to cross
le carrefour	luh kahr-foohr	the intersection
brûler un feu rouge	brew-ley uhN fuh roohzh	to go through a red light
blessé(e)	bley-sey	hurt, wounded
le pare-chocs	luh pahr-shohk	the bumper
bosselé(e)	bohhs-ley	dented
les voici	ley vwah-see	here they are

Describing what was stolen

If things have been stolen from you, a police officer will ask **Qu'est-ce qui vous manque?** (kehs-kee vooh mahNk?) (*What is missing?*). You can say **On m'a volé . . . .** (ohN mah voh-ley. . . .) (*They stole. . . .*) and add the item stolen. Here are some items that are commonly stolen:

- **mon appareil-photo** (mohN-nah-pah-rehy foh-toh) (*my camera*)
- **mes cartes de crédit** (mey kahrt duh krey-dee) (*my credit cards*)
- **mon sac** (mohN sahk) (*my bag*)
- **mon argent** (mohN-nahr-zhahN) (*my money*)
- **mon passeport** (mohN pahs-pohr) (*my passport*)
- **mon porte-monnaie** (mohN pohrt-moh-neh) (*my wallet*)

The officer may also ask **Pouvez-vous décrire la personne?** (pooh-vey-vooh dey-kreer lah pehr-sohhn?) (*Can you describe the person?*). If you happened to see the culprit, you can say **C'était quelqu'un . . . .** (sey-teh kehl-kuhN. . . .) (*It was someone . . . .*) and then fill in the following descriptors:

- **aux cheveux blonds/bruns/roux/gris** (oh shuh-vuh blohN/bruhN/ rooh/gree) (*with blond/brown/red/gray hair*)

- **un peu chauve** (uhN puh shohv) (*balding*)

- **grand/petit/mince/gros** (grahN/puh-tee/maNs/groh) (*tall/short/ skinny/fat*)

- **d' environ . . . ans** (dahN-vee-rohN . . . ahN) (*of about . . . years [of age]*)

You may also be able to describe what that person was wearing. Go to Chapter 9 for clothing-related vocabulary.

Getting legal help

As a foreigner, you may feel overwhelmed and welcome some help. You can ask to do one of the following things:

J'ai besoin d'un avocat qui parle anglais. (zhey buh-zwaN duhN- nah-voh-kah kee pahrl ahN-gleh.) (*I need a lawyer who speaks English.*)

Je voudrais téléphoner à un/e ami/e en ville. (zhuh vooh-dreh tey-ley-fohh-ney ah uhN/ewn ah-mee ahN veel.) (*I would like to call a friend in town.*)

Je dois contacter le consulat. (zhuh dwah kohN-tah-ktey luh kohN- sew-lah.) (*I have to contact the consulate.*)

While you're in a foreign country, the laws of that country override the laws of your own. In an emergency, your consul is the most appropriate person to help you. He or she is on your side, more so than any local lawyer or police. To find out before your trip where the American or Canadian consulates are located, go to http://france.usembassy.gov. Other French-speaking countries may have similar websites for locating your country's consulate.

Fun & Games

Your friend is learning to surf, and as fate would have it, you're the first person to find him after he fell off his board over some reefs. He seems okay, but just to make sure, you ask him about each body part. Write the French words for the body parts on the corresponding lines.

1. chest _____

2. shoulder_____

3. eye_____

4. head_____

5. nose_____

6. mouth_____

7. neck_____

8. arm_____

9. hand_____

10. stomach_____

11. leg_____

12. foot_____

13. ankle_____

14. knee_____

Part IV
The Part of Tens

The 5th Wave
By Rich Tennant

Obviously you're pronouncing the phrase "Throw us a...," correctly in French, but the word for "lifesaver" just isn't coming out right.

Amis de la Mer

In this part . . .

Every *For Dummies* book includes top-ten lists, and this book has some good ones. In addition to offering tips on how to learn French quickly, we provide you with French phrases to avoid, French expressions you shouldn't hesitate to use, and French phrases that will make you sound French.

Chapter 18

Ten Ways to Pick Up French Quickly

● ●

*W*hether you took French in high school or college and neglected it since then, or you came to love this wonderful language "later in life" and are anxious to speak it, there are several ways you can broaden your exposure to French in order to learn it more quickly. This chapter offers a few fun suggestions that can help you memorize French words, get used to the cadence of the French language, and get into the swing of speaking French.

Label the Things in Your House

If you are interested in picking up a lot of everyday words fast, cut up a bunch of paper into little pieces (or use sticky pads), get out your English-French dictionary, and do the following: Look up the French word for everything you can touch in your house, such as **le mur** (luh mewr) (*the wall*), **la porte** (lah pohrt) (*the door*), **le sofa** (luh soh-fah) (*the couch*), **le réfrigérateur** (luh rey-free-zhey-rah-tuhr) (*the refrigerator*), **une tasse** (ewn tahs) (*a cup*), **le robinet** (luh roh-bee-neh) (*the faucet*), and so on. Then write each word on one of those pieces of paper and tape it, stick it, or pin it to whatever it describes. Then every time you pass by that object, say the word aloud. By employing this strategy, you can't help but memorize these words quickly!

Write Your Shopping Lists in French

When you make out your grocery list, do it in French. Write the English equivalents after the French, though, so that you don't get annoyed in the store when you can't remember that **de l'ail** (duh lahy) means *garlic* or **des pommes** (dey pohm) means *apples*.

Listen to French Music

You can buy French CDs — preferably with the text printed in a companion booklet, which gives you an idea of what the musicians are singing about — or download French songs. Also consider searching for the lyrics of your favorite songs on the Internet. Listening to the French and trying to imitate the sounds can help you not only learn the vocabulary but also improve your pronunciation.

Watch French Movies

A fun way to pick up expressions, accent, cultural habits, and the like is by watching French films, preferably as they were originally released. (If you get a movie with subtitles, try your best to ignore them; otherwise, you'll end up enjoying the movie but not learning any French!) You can get French movies online or through a film service such as Netflix.

If you can, watch the same film a few times and try to imitate the intonation and sounds of phrases and sentences that you hear.

Tune in to TV5

TV5 is a 24-hours-a-day, 7-days-a-week French language channel that you can access if you have cable or satellite. This station airs programs from France, Switzerland, Belgium, Canada, and French-speaking Africa. The programs include news broadcasts, films, cultural and entertainment programs, documentaries, sports, and so on. To see what providers in your area offer TV5, go to www.tv5. org/cms/USA and enter your zip code in the available box. Remember that the more you listen to French, the more your comprehension improves.

Read French Publications

Reading French newspapers and magazines is a great way to keep up with current events and fashion trends and, at the same time, pick up some catchy phrases from headlines and ads. Reading the ads is a guaranteed eye-opener! In addition, you can read children's books. The photographs and artwork in these publications can help you follow along, even when the words are unfamiliar. If you are a little more adventurous, you can try out short stories in French.

Take a Class

Many local community colleges and adult education programs offer language classes. The advantage of being in a classroom is that you're in an interactive environment and have a live person who can answer any specific questions you may have. You will also have the benefit of being able to hear and practice speaking the French language with your instructor and other students.

Join a French Association

You can find French associations throughout the United States and Canada. One of the most famous is the Alliance Française, which is a non-profit association whose mission is to promote the French language and the French and Francophone cultures. The Alliance Française offers classes, film series, lectures, and much more. Find out what and where the nearest French association is in your area and join. You'll meet interesting people and perhaps even find someone with whom you can converse and practice your French. To find out more about this organization and locate chapters near you, go to www.afusa.org

Surf the 'Net for Topics That Interest You — in French

The Internet has many opportunities for you to learn French, from basic vocabulary to in-depth articles. Get on your favorite search engine and type in **.fr**, instead of **.com,** and you'll have the francophone world at your finger tips. Select whatever interests you: culture, hobbies, economy, food and cooking, media, business, or any other area. Browse around in English or in French and pick out words you know.

Join an Online Chat or Pen Pal Forum

Go to a French chat room just to listen, if you'd like. You may be surprised how much you can pick up by listening to informal conversations. You can also join a pen pal forum. Just search the Internet and find one you feel comfortable with, such as www.french.about.com or www.french-chat.com. You can have your questions answered and share your language successes and concerns with others. ***Note:*** As with any interactive site on the Internet, be extra cautious and don't provide any personal information.

Chapter 19

Ten Things Never to Say in French

∙ ∙

Have you ever had foreign visitors say something that made you just want to crack up laughing or hold your breath and hope no one else heard? Well, even the best of us linguists make mistakes like this, but people new to a language are particularly susceptible to these errors. This chapter offers some pointers to help you avoid the worst pitfalls!

Using "Tu" When You Mean "Vous"

When speaking to anyone other than children, be sure to never use the familiar form of address: **tu** (tew) (*you*) or **ton/ta/tes** (tohN/tah/tey) (*your*). For example, when you meet someone and want to say *How are you?* you say **Comment allez-vous?** (koh-mahN-tah-ley-vooh?), not **Comment vas-tu?** (koh-mahN vah-tew?). If you use the familiar form in the wrong situations, you'll be perceived as uneducated; in the worst cases, your listeners may even take it as an insult!

Wait until the other party offers the familiar form — **Mais on peut se tutoyer!** (meh ohN puh suh tew-twah-yey!) (*But we can use the familiar form with each other!*). This is the green light, of course, that lets you know that using the familiar form is fine. In fact, turning the offer down would be considered pretty insulting!

Using "Bonne nuit!" for Good-Bye

When you say good-bye to someone at night, you don't want to say **Bonne nuit!** (bohn nwee) (*Good night!*) unless you mean to make a point of the fact that you are going straight to bed. Stick to **Au revoir!** (ohr-vwahr) (*Good-bye!*) or **Bonsoir!** (bohN-swahr) (*Good evening!*).

Using "Garçon" or "Porteur" to Address Service Staff

When you want to get the waiter's attention in a restaurant, don't call out **Garçon!** (gahr-sohN!) (*Boy!*). And in airports and train stations, you want to avoid the term **porteur** (pohr-tuhr) (*porter*). The attendants absolutely hate being referred to by these terms, which are considered condescending. Say **monsieur** (muh-syuh) (*sir*) instead.

Saying "Je suis excité(e)" to Indicate Excitement

If you are excited about something, don't say **Je suis excité/excitée** (zhuh swee-zehk-see-tey) (*I am excited*) because the phrase has a sexual connotation. Even though French has no direct equivalent for the phrase *I'm excited*, you can convey the same sentiment by saying **J'ai hâte de. . . .** (zhey aht duh. . . .) (*I look forward to. . . .*) or **Je suis très heureux/heureuse. . . .** (zhuh swee treh-zuh-ruh/uh-ruhz. . . .) (*I am very happy. . . .*).

Saying "Je suis chaud(e)/froid(e)" to Say You're Hot or Cold

When you are hot or cold, be sure not to say **Je suis chaud/chaude** (zhuh swee shoh/shohd) (*I am hot*) or **Je suis froid/froide** (zhuh swee frwah/frwahd) (*I am cold*) because these phrases actually mean that you're in heat or frigid, which is probably not your intent! Instead, say **J'ai chaud/chaude** (zhey shoh/shohd) or **J'ai froid/ froide** (zhey frwah/frwahd), both of which use the verb **avoir** (ah-vwahr) (*to have*).

Saying *"Je suis plein/e"* to Mean You're Full

If someone asks whether you'd like another helping at dinner and you're full, you certainly don't want to translate the word *full* into French. Saying **Je suis plein/pleine** (zhuh swee plahN/plehn) means *I am pregnant*. Instead, you can say **J'ai fini** (zhey fee-nee) (*I'm finished*) or **J'ai assez/trop mangé** (zhey ah-sey/troh mahN-zhey) (*I ate enough/too much*).

Using *"de la glace"* to Request Ice

When you're in a restaurant and you want ice cubes in your drink, you usually have to say so. The trouble is, if you ask for **de la glace** (duh lah glahs), the waiter may ask you **Quel parfum?** (kehl pahr-faN?) (*What flavor?*). The reason? In this context, **la glace** refers to *ice cream*. Instead, you want to request **des glaçons** (dey glah-sohN) (*ice cubes*).

Using *"Je suis . . . ans"* to Tell Your Age

If someone asks you your age, don't translate literally from the English and say **Je suis 30 ans** (zhuh swee trahN-tahN) (*I am 30 years old.*) Use instead the verb **avoir** (ah-vwahr) (*to have*) because the French say **J'ai 30 ans** (zhey trahN-tahN) which literally means *I have 30 years*.

Asking for Change with *"J'ai besoin de change"*

When you want change for your large bills, don't say **J'ai besoin de change** (zhey buh-zwaN duh shahNzh) because the listener may think you need a fresh set of clothes. You want to say instead **J'ai besoin de monnaie** (zhey buh-zwaN duh moh-neh) (*I need change*).

Using the Verb "Visiter" in Reference to People

One way to guarantee a good laugh when you're telling someone that you're going to visit friends is to say something like **Je vais visiter mon ami Paul** (zhuh veh vee-zee-tey mohN-nah-mee pohl). Why so funny? Because the verb **visiter** (vee-zee-tey) (*to visit*) is used for places and monuments — for sightseeing — not for people. You probably don't plan to walk around your friend or your aunt in the same way that you walk around a monument, right? Instead, say **Je vais voir Paul** (zhuh veh vwahr pohl) (*I am going to see Paul*) or use the expression that is used to visit people, **rendre visite à** (rahN-druh vee-zeet ah) (*to pay a visit to, to visit [a person]*) as in **Je vais rendre visite à Paul** (zhuh veh rahN-druh vee-zeet ah pohl) (*I'm going to visit Paul*).

Chapter 20

Ten Favorite French Expressions

After you get tuned into French a little, you may suddenly hear people use very French expressions that seem to just sort of slip out at any given occasion. You may even have heard some of these already; now it's time to casually use them yourself.

"À mon avis"

If you want to express your opinion in French, you use this handy phrase. **À mon avis** (ah mohN-nah-vee) means *in my opinion.* You can use the expression before or after you state your opinion.

"C'est pas vrai"

If you hear something that is hard to believe, you say **C'est pas vrai** (seh pah vreh) (*No way!, You don't say!*) This expression's literal meaning is *It is not true.* Note that, grammatically, this expression should be **Ce n'est pas vrai** (suh neh pah vreh); however, in oral French, the **ne** is often omitted, and you only hear the **pas.**

"Avec plaisir"

Avec plaisir (ah-vehk pleh-zeer) means *with pleasure,* and it's a great way to accept an invitation to lunch or to see a film, for example. You can also use this expression to show that you are willing and happy to do a favor for someone.

"Bon appétit!"

Bon appétit! (bohN-nah-pey-tee!) literally means *Good appetite!* However, it certainly is not commenting on anyone's good or bad appetite. You use this phrase when you begin to eat or when you see someone eating and want to express your desire that that person enjoy the meal. **Bon appétit!** is much like the English *Enjoy!* except that the French say **Bon appétit!** much more freely.

"C'est génial"

Use **C'est génial** (seh zhey-nyahl) to convey excitement about something. It means *It's fantastic!* or *It's great!* It can also suggest that something is really clever or, as the British say, *It's brilliant.*

"À votre santé"

When the French raise their glasses, they say **À votre santé** (ah vohh-truh sahN-tey) in the singular formal or plural, or **À ta santé** (ah tah sahN-tey) in the familiar form. These phrases literally mean *to your health,* but their general meaning is the same as their English counterpart: *Cheers!*

"À vos souhaits"

When someone sneezes, in English you say *Bless you.* In French, you say **À vos souhaits** (ah voh sweh) (*to your wishes*), which is more formal, or **À tes souhaits** (ah tey sweh), which is more familiar or informal. Both expressions mean that you hope the sneezer's wishes come true.

"Quelle horreur!"

Quelle horreur! (kehl oh-ruhr!) means *What a horror!* You use it not only for real horrors but also to express any kind of disgust, as in these expressions: *What a terrible thought! How nasty!* and *I can't believe it!* You also use this expression when something looks, sounds, or smells terrible.

"À bientôt"

The literal translation of **À bientôt** (ah byaN-toh) is *Until soon*. You use this expression when you expect to see the departing person within a reasonable time frame.

"Pas mal"

Use **pas mal** (pah mahl) (*not bad*) when you want to express that something isn't great, but it's not terrible either; instead it's in-between. Generally, you use this phrase in response to someone asking you how you are feeling or how things are going.

Chapter 21

Ten Phrases That Make You Sound French

• •

Chapter 20 provides you with some typically French expressions that almost everyone who speaks a little French knows and uses. The phrases in this chapter go a few steps beyond those common ones: These expressions are so very French that you may even pass for a native French speaker when you use them!

"Passez-moi un coup de fil!"

Passez-moi un coup de fil! (pah-sey mwah uhN kooht feel!) means *Give me a call!* You could say, of course, **Appelez-moi!** (ah-pley-mwah) or **Téléphonez-moi!** (tey-ley-fohh-ney-mwah!) (*Call me!*), both of which mean the same thing, but those phrases don't sound as sophisticated! You can also use the **tu** (tew) (*you* [singular]) form with these expressions: **Passe-moi un coup de fil** (pahs-mwah uhN kooht feel!), **appelle-moi** (ah-pehl-mwah), and **téléphone-moi** (tey-ley-fohhn-mwah).

"On y va!" or "Allons-y!"

On y va! (oh-nee vah!) or **Allons-y!** (ah-lohN-zee!) both mean *Let's go* [*there*]! You can also send someone off somewhere with the imperative **Allez-y!** (ah-ley-zee!) (*Go ahead!*) — or **Vas-y!** (vah-zee!) for the familiar form — if you want to get a little insistent about it.

"Je n'en sais rien"

To indicate you're in the dark about something, say **Je n'en sais rien** (zhuh nahN seh ryaN) (*I don't know anything about it*). In casual speech, you can also say (and this is what you hear most of the time) **J'en sais rien** (zhahN seh ryaN) to indicate the same thing. Technically, **J'en sais rien** is grammatically incorrect because it is missing the **ne** (nuh) before the pronoun, but in spoken French, the **ne** is often dropped.

"Je n'en reviens pas"

If you hear something surprising or unbelievable, you can say **Je n'en reviens pas** (zhuh nahN ruh-vyaN pah) or you can omit the **n'** and say **J'en reviens pas** (zhahN ruh-vyaN pah). Both mean *I can't get over it* or *I'm amazed*. If you were to translate this expression literally, it wouldn't make sense: *I am not coming back from it*.

"Ça vaut la peine"

To express that something is worth the trouble, you can say **Ça vaut la peine** (sah voh lah pehn) or even **Ça vaut le coup** (sah voh luh kooh), which both mean *It's worth it*. The literal translations of theses expressions are *It's worth the pain* and *It's worth the effort*. You can also use these expressions in the negative: **Ça ne vaut pas la peine** (sah nuh voh pah lah pehn) or even **Ça ne vaut pas le coup** (sah nuh voh pas luh kooh), which mean *It's not worth it*. As with the expressions in the preceding sections, the **ne** is often dropped in spoken French, and you may hear **Ça vaut pas la peine** (sah voh pah lah pehn) or even **Ça vaut pas le coup** (sah voh pah luh kooh).

"C'est pas grave"

Literally, **C'est pas grave** (seh pah grahv) means *It isn't serious (grave)*, but the colloquial translation is *It's no big deal*. The full expression is **Ce n'est pas grave** (suh neh pah grahv), but the **ne** is eliminated when speaking, and the emphasis is on **pas**.

"Ça m'est égal"

If you don't mind one way or another about something, then use the expression **Ça m'est égal** (sah meh-tey-gahl), which means *I don't mind* or *I don't care.* The literal translation is *It's equal to me.*

"N'importe"

N'importe (naN-pohrt) is a very common and versatile expression because it can be followed by so many interrogative adverbs, pronouns, or adjectives. By itself, the phrase means *no matter*, and when you tack on an interrogative expression, such as **qui** (kee) (*who*), **où** (ooh) (*where*), **quand** (kahN) (*when*), **comment** (koh-mahN) (*how*), **quoi** (kwah) (*what*), and so on, it means *No matter who, where, when, how,* or *what,* respectively.

"Tu cherches midi à 14h"

Tu cherches midi à 14h (tew shehrsh mee-dee ah kah-tohrz uhr) has to be the best one of all. Try to translate this literally and what you come up with is *You are looking for noon at 2 p.m.* Not sure what that means? Well, the meaning is fairly complex, but this phrase is so neat and so heavily used that you're very likely to hear it, and if you want to sound French, you'll want to say it, too. So here goes: **Tu cherches midi à 14h** means that so-and-so is making things more difficult than necessary, that he or she is sort of off the mark, has lost perspective, and is complicating the issue. You can also practice saying **Il ne faut pas chercher midi à 14h!** (eel nuh foh pah shehr-shey mee-dee ah kah-tohrz uhr!) (*You shouldn't get so obsessive about it!*)

Use **Tu cherches midi à 14h** when you're talking to the person who is making things unnecessarily difficult; use **Il/Elle cherche midi à 14h** (eel/ehl shehrsh mee-dee ah kah-tohrz uhr) when you're describing someone else.

"Prenons un pot!"

Use **Prenons un pot** (pruh-nohN-zuhN poh) when you want to say. . . *Let's take a pot*? No, that can't be it, or can it? Well, if you stretch your imagination a bit, you can see that the phrase actually means *Let's have a drink!* (Not a whole potful maybe, but . . . .) You can also use the expression **Prenons un verre** (pruh-nohN-zuhN vehr), which means *Let's have a drink* (it's literal translation is *Let's have a glass*).

Part V
Appendixes

The 5th Wave   By Rich Tennant

In this part . . .

Last but not least, we give you the appendixes, which you will no doubt find quite useful. In addition to a pretty comprehensive mini-dictionary, we also provide verb tables that show you how to conjugate regular and irregular verbs, answers to the Fun & Game sections throughout the book, and a guide to the audio CD that's attached to the back of the book.

French-English Mini-Dictionary

A

à bientôt (ah byaN-toh): see you soon

à côté de (ah koh-tey duh): next to

à demain (ah duh-mahN): see you tomorrow

à droite (ah drwaht): on the right

à gauche (ah gohsh): on the left

à l'heure (ah luhr): on time

abricot (ah-bree-koh) m: apricot

absolument (ahb-soh-lew-mahN): absolutely

accepter (ah-kseh-pley): to accept

acheter (ahsh-tey): to buy

addition (ah-dee-syohN) f: check

adorer (ah-doh-rey): to love, to adore

adresse (ah-drehs) f: address

adresse électronique (ah-dreh-sey-lehk-troh-neek) f: e-mail address

aérogare (ah-ey-roh-gahr) f: airport terminal

affaires (ah-fehr) fpl: business

affranchissement (ah-frahN-shee-smahN) m: postage

agneau (ah-nyoh) m: lamb

agrafe (ah-grahf) f: staple

agrafeuse (ah-grah-fuhz) f: stapler

agréable (ah-grey-ah-bluh): pleasant

aider (ey-dey): to help

aimer (eh-mey): to like, to love

aller (ah-ley): to go

aller-retour (ah-ley-ruh-toohr) m: round trip

aller-simple (ah-ley-saN-pluh) m: one-way (ticket)

allumette (ah-lew-meht) f: match

ami/amie (ah-mee) m/f: friend

ananas (ah-nah-nah) m: pineapple

aneth (ah-neht) m: dill

antibiotique (ahN-tee-bee-oh-teek) m: antibiotic

août (ooht) m: August

appareil-photo (ah-pah-rehy foh-toh) m: camera

appeler/s'appeler (ah-pley/sah-pley): to call/to call oneself, to be named

architecte (ahr-shee-tehkt) m/f: architect

argent (ahr-zhahN) m: money

armoire (ahr-mwahr) f: armoire

arrêt (ah-reh) m: stop

arrivée (ah-ree-vey) f: arrival

arriver (ah-ree-vey): to arrive

arroser (ah-roh-zey): to water

ascenseur (ah-sahN-suhr) m: elevator

asperge (ah-spehrzh) f: asparagus

assiette (ah-syeht) f: plate

attendre (ah-tahN-druh): to wait

attrapper (ah-trah-pey): to catch

au fond (oh fohN): in the back

au revoir (ohr-vwahr): good-bye

aubaine (oh-behn) f: sales [Quebec]

aujourd'hui (oh-zhoohr-dwee): today

aussi (oh-see): also

auteur (oh-tuhr) m: author

automne (oh-tohn) m: fall

avion (ah-vyohN) m: plane

avocat/avocate (ah-voh-kah/ah-voh-kaht) m/f: lawyer

avoir (ah-vwahr): to have

avoir faim (ah-vwahr faN): to be hungry

avoir soif (ah-vwahr swahf): to be thirsty

avril (ah-vreel) m: April

B

baignoire (beh-nywahr) f: bathtub

balance (bah-lahNs) f: scale

banane (bah-nahn) f: banana

bande dessinée (bahNd deh-see-ney) f: comic strip

banque (bahNk) f: bank

basilic (bah-zee-leek) m: basil

basket (bahs-keht) m: basketball

baskets (bahs-keht) fpl: sneakers

beau/belle (boh/behl) m/f: nice, beautiful, handsome

beurre (buhr) m: butter

bicyclette (bee-see-kleht) f: bicycle

bien sûr (byaN sewr): of course

bière (byehr) f: beer

bifteck (beef-tehk) m: steak

bijouterie (bee-zhooh-tree) f: jewelry store

billet (bee-yeh) m: ticket

bizarre (beez-ahr): weird, bizarre

blanc/blanche (blahN/blahNsh) m/f: white

blazer (blah-zehr) m: blazer

bleu/bleue (bluh) m/f: blue

boeuf (buhf) m: beef

boire (bwahr): to drink

boîte aux lettres (bwaht oh leh-truh) f: mailbox

bon/bonne (bohN/bohhn) m/f: good

bonheur (boh-nuhr) m: happiness

bonjour (bohN-zhoohr): hello, good day

bonne nuit (bohhn nwee) f: good night (when going to bed)

bonsoir (bohN-swahr) m: good evening, good night

bottes (bohht) fpl: boots

bouche (boohsh) f: mouth

boucherie (booh-shree) f: butcher shop

boulangerie (booh-lahN-zhree) f: bakery

bras (brah) m: arm

bronzer (brohN-zey): to tan

brosse (brohs) f: brush

bruyant/bruyante (brwee-ahN/brwee-ahNt) m/f: noisy

bureau (bew-roh) m: office, desk

bureau de change (bew-roh duh shahNzh) m: currency exchange office

C

ça va (sah vah): okay

cabine d'essayage (kah-been dey-sey-ahzh) f: fitting room

café (kah-fey) m: coffee, café

caisse (kehs) f: cash register

caissier/caissière (key-syey/key-syehr) m/f: cashier

calendrier (kah-lahN-dree-yey) m: calendar

cambriolage (kahN-bree-oh-lahzh) m: burglary

campagne (kahN-pah-nyuh) f: countryside

canapé (kah-nah-pey) m: sofa

canard (kah-nahr) m: duck

canne à pêche (kahn ah pehsh) f: fishing pole

capot (kah-poh) m: hood (of a car)

carotte (kah-roht) f: carrot

carrefour (kahr-foohr) m: intersection

carte d'embarquement (kahrt dahN-bahr-kuh-mahN) f: boarding pass

carte de crédit (kahrt duh krey-dee) f: credit card

casse-croûte (kahs-krooht) m: snack

ceinture (saN-tewr) f: belt

celui-ci/celle-ci (suh-lwee-see/sehl-see) m/f: this one

celui-là/celle-là (suh-lwee-lah/sehl-lah) m/f: that one

centre commercial (sahN-truh koh-mehr-syahl) m: mall

cerfeuil (sehr-fuhy) m: chervil

cerise (suh-reez) f: cherry

champignon (shahN-pee-nyohN) m: mushroom

chanter (shahN-tey): to sing

chapeau (shah-poh) m: hat

charmant/charmante (shahr-mahN/shahr-mahNt) m/f: charming

château (shah-toh) m: castle

chaud/chaude (shoh/shohd) m/f: warm, hot

chaussettes (shoh-seht) fpl: socks

chaussons (shoh-sohN) mpl: slippers

chaussures (shoh-sewr) f pl: shoes

chemise (shuh-meez) f: shirt

chemisier (shuh-mee-zyey) m: blouse

cher/chère (shehr) m/f: expensive, dear

cheville (shuh-veey) f: ankle

choisir (shwah-zeer): to choose

chou (shooh) m: cabbage

chou-fleur (shooh-fluhr) m: cauliflower

choux de Bruxelles (shooh duh brewk-sehl) mpl: Brussels sprouts

cinéaste (see-ney-ahst) m/f: filmmaker

cinéma (see-ney-mah) m: movies

cinq (saNk): five

ciseaux (see-zoh) mpl: scissors

clair/claire (klehr) m/f: light-colored

classeur à tiroirs (klah-suhr ah tee-rwahr) m: file cabinet

clavier (klah-vyey) m: keyboard

climatisation (klee-mah-tee-zah-syohN) f: air conditioning

code postal (kohhd poh-stahl) m: zip code

coffre (koh-fruh) m: trunk

colis (koh-lee) m: package

collègue (koh-lehg) m/f: colleague, coworker

combien (kohN-byaN): how much

comment (koh-mahN): how

commode (koh-mohhd) f: dresser

compagnie (kohN-pah-nyee) f: company

complet (kohN-pleh) m: suit [France]

composter (kohN-poh-stey): to validate a ticket

comptoir (kohN-twahr) m: counter

conduire (kohN-dweer): to drive

confiture (kohN-fee-tewr) f: jam

consigne (kohN-see-nyuh) f: baggage room

conte de fée (kohNt duh fey) m: fairy tale

contravention (kohN-trah-vahN-syohN) f: traffic ticket

coquilles Saint-Jacques (koh-keey saN zhahk) fpl: scallops

corbeille à papiers (kohr-behy ah pah-pyey) m: wastepaper basket

coriandre (koh-ree-ahN-druh) m: coriander

costume de bains (kohs-tewm duh baN) m: bathing suit [Québec]

côtes (koht) f: coast

côtes (koht) fpl: ribs

cou (kooh) m: neck

couleur (kooh-luhr) f: color

cour (koohr) f: courtyard

courir (kooh-reer): to run

couteau (kooh-toh) m: knife

couverts (kooh-vehr) mpl: silverware

couverture (kooh-vehr-tewr) f: blanket

cravate (krah-vaht) f: tie

crayon (krey-ohN) m: pencil

crème (krehm) f: cream

crémerie (kreym-ree) f: dairy product and cheese store

crevettes (kruh-veht) fpl: shrimp

crudités (krew-dee-tey) fpl: mixed greens, raw vegetables

cuillère (kwee-yehr) f: spoon, teaspoon

cuir (kweer) m: leather

cuisinière (kwee-zee-nyehr) f: stove

D

d'accord (dah-kohr): all right, okay

dans (dahN): in, inside

danser (dahN-sey): to dance

décembre (dey-sahN-bruh) m: December

dehors (duh-ohr): outside

déjeuner (dey-zhuh-ney) m: lunch (as a verb: to have lunch)

demi-tour (duh-mee-toohr) m: U turn

dent (dahN) f: tooth

dentifrice (dahN-tee-frees) m: toothpaste

dentiste (dahN-teest) m/f: dentist

départ (dey-pahr) m: departure

derrière (deh-ryehr): behind

descendre (dey-sahN-druh): to go down, to get off

désolé/désolée (dey-zoh-ley) m/f: sorry

dessert (deh-sehr) m: dessert

dessin animé (deh-sahN ah-nee-mey) m: cartoon

détester (dey-teh-stey): to hate

deux (duh): two

devant (duh-vahN): in front of

devenir (duh-vuh-neer): to become

devoir (duh-vwahr): to have to

dinde (daNd) f: turkey

directeur/directrice (dee-rehk-tuhr/dee-rehk-trees) m/f: manager (of a company, business)

distributeur (de billets) (dees-tree-bew-tuhr [duh bee-yey]) m: ATM

dix (dees): ten

dix-huit (deez-weet): eighteen

dix-neuf (deez-nuhf): nineteen

dix-sept (dee-seht): seventeen

docteur (dohk-tuhr) m: doctor

documentaire (doh-kew-mahN-tehr) m: documentary

doigt (dwah) m: finger

donner (dohh-ney): to give

donner sur (dohh-ney sewr): facing, overlooking

dormir (dohr-meer): to sleep

dos (doh) m: back

doux/douce (dooh/doohs) m/f: mild, sweet

douze (doohz): twelve

draps (drah) mpl: sheets

E

échecs (ey-shehk) mpl: chess

éclairage (ey-kleh-rahzh) m: lighting

eau (oh) f: water

effets spéciaux (ey-feh spey-syoh) mpl: special effects

égalité (ey-gah-lee-tey) f: equality

élastique (ey-lah-steek) m: rubber band

elle (ehl) f: she

elles (ehl) fpl: they

embouteillage (ahN-booh-teh-yahzh) m: traffic jam

employé/employée (ahN-plwah-yey) m/f: employee

en face de (ahN fahs duh): across from, in front of

en retard (ahN ruh-tahr): late

enchanté/enchantée (ahN-shahN-tey) m/f: delighted

enfant (ahN-fahN) m/f: child

ennuyeux/ennuyeuse (ahN-nwee-uh/ahN-nwee-uhz): m/f: boring

entre (ahN-truh): between

entrée (ahN-trey) f: appetizer, entrance

entrer (ahN-trey): to enter

enveloppe (ahN-vlohhp) f: envelope

envoyer (ahN-vwah-yey): to send

épaule (ey-pohl) f: shoulder

épicerie (ey-pees-ree) f: grocery store, general store

épinards (ey-pee-nahr) mpl: spinach

époux/épouse (ey-pooh/ey-poohz) m/f: spouse

escalier roulant (ehs-kah-lyey rooh-lahN) m: escalator

essence (ey-sahNs) f: gas

essuie-glace (ey-swee-glahs) m: windshield wiper

est (ehst): east

estragon (ehs-trah-gohN) m: tarragon

été (ey-tey) m: summer

être (eh-truh): to be

étroit/étroite (ey-trwah/ey-trwaht) m/f: narrow

évier (ey-vyey) m: kitchen sink

F

facile (fah-seel): easy

faire (fehr): to do, to make

faire du jardinage (fehr dew zhahr-dee-nahzh): to garden

faire le plein (fehr luh plaN): to fill the gas tank

fatigué/fatiguée (fah-tee-gey) m/f: tired

femme (fahm) f: woman, wife

fenêtre (fuh-neh-truh) f: window

fêtes (feht) fpl: holidays

février (fey-vryey) m: February

fichier (fee-shyey) m: file

fier/fière (fyehr) m/f: proud

figue (feeg) f: fig

figure (fee-gewr) f: face

fille (feey) f: daughter or girl

film d'amour (feelm dah-moohr) m: romance film

film d'aventures (feelm dah-vahN-tewr) m: adventure film

film d'épouvante/d'horreur (feelm dey-pooh-vahNt/doh-ruhr) m: horror film

film d'espionnage (feelm deh-spee-oh-nahzh) m: spy film

film de science-fiction (feelm duh syahNs fee-ksyohN) m: science-fiction film

film policier (feelm poh-lee-syey) m: a detective film

fils (fees) m: son

fin (fahN) f: end

finir (fee-neer): to finish

flanelle (flah-nehl) f: flannel

fleur (fluhr) f: flower

foncé/foncée (fohN-sey) m/f: dark

football/soccer (fooht-bohl/soh-kehr) m: soccer

football américain (fooht-bohl ah-mey-ree-kaN) m: (American) football

foulard (fooh-lahr) m: scarf

four à micro-ondes (foohr ah mee-kroh-ohNd) m: microwave

fourchette (foohr-sheht) f: fork

fraise (frehz) f: strawberry

framboise (frahN-bwahz) f: raspberry

freins (fraN) mpl: brakes (of a car)

frère (frehr) m: brother

froid (frwah): cold

fromage (froh-mahzh) m: cheese

fruits (frwee) mpl: fruit

G

gagner (gah-nyey): to win

garçon (gahr-sohN) m: boy

gare (gahr) f: train station

gâteau (gah-toh) m: cake

générique (zhey-ney-reek) m: credits

genou (zhuh-nooh) m: knee

gérant/gérante (zhey-rahN/zhey-rahNt) m/f: manager (restaurant, hotel, shop)

gigot d'agneau (zhee-goh dah-nyoh) m: leg of lamb

glace (glahs) f: ice cream

gomme (gohm) f: eraser

goûter (gooh-tey) m: snack (as a verb: to taste)

graine (grehn) f: seed

grand/grande (grahN/grahNd) m/f: big, tall, large

grand magasin (grahN mah-gah-zaN) m: department store

grippe (greep) f: flu

gros/grosse (groh/grohs) m/f: large, fat, thick

guichet (gee-shey) m: ticket window

guitare (gee-tahr) f: guitar

H

habit (ah-bee) m: suit [Québec]

habiter (ah-bee-tey): to live

haricots verts (ah-ree-koh vehr) mpl: green beans

heure de pointe (uhr duh pwaNt) f: rush hour, peak

heureux/heureuse (uh-ruh/uh-ruhz) m/f: happy

hiver (ee-vehr) m: winter

homard (oh-mahr) m: lobster

horaire (oh-rehr) m: schedule

horloge (ohr-lohzh) f: clock

hortensia (ohr-tahN-syah) m: hydrangea

hôtel (oh-tehl) m: hotel

hôtesse de l'air (oh-tehs duh lehr) f: flight attendant

huit (weet): eight

huitres (wee-truh) fpl: oysters

I

icône (ee-kohn) f: icon

idée (ee-dey) f: idea

il (eel) m: he

il y a (eel ee ah): there is, there are

ils (eel) mpl: they

imperméable (aN-pehr-mey-ah-bluh) m: raincoat (n); rainproof (adj)

imprimante (aN-pree-mahnt) f: printer

infirmier/infirmière (aN-feer-myey/aN-feer-myehr) m/f: nurse

informaticien/informaticienne (aN-fohr-mah-tee-syaN/aN-fohr-mah-tee-syehn) m/f: computer scientist

ingénieur (aN-zhey-nyuhr) m: engineer

J

jambe (zhahNb) f: leg

jambon (zhahN-bohN) m: ham

janvier (zhahN-vyey) m: January

jardin (zhahr-daN) m: yard, garden

jardin d'agrément (zhahr-daN dah-grey-mahN) m: flower garden

jaune (zhohn): yellow

je (zhuh): I

jean (jeen) m: jeans

joindre (zhwaN-druh): to attach

joli/jolie (zhoh-lee) m/f: pretty

jonquille (zhohN-keey) f: daffodil

jouer (zhooh-ey): to play

jour (zhoohr) m: day

journal (zhoohr-nahl) m: newspaper

juillet (zhwee-yeh) m: July

juin (zhwaN) m: June

jupe (zhewp) f: skirt

jusqu'à (zhews-kah): until

L

là-bas (lah-bah): over there

lac (lahk) m: lake

laine (lehn) f: wool

lait (leh) m: milk

laitue (ley-tew) f: lettuce

lancer (lahN-sey): to launch, to throw

large (lahrzh): large, wide

lavabo (lah-vah-boh) m: bathroom sink

lave-vaisselle (lahv veh-sehl) m: dishwasher

lecteur de CD/de DVD (lehk-tuhr duh sey dey/duh dey vey dey) m: CD, DVD player

légumes (ley-gewm) mpl: vegetables

lendemain (lahN-duh-mahN) m: next day

liberté (lee-behr-tey) f: freedom

librairie (lee-brey-ree) f: bookstore

limonade (lee-moh-nahd) f: lemonade

lin (laN) m: linen

lire (leer): to read

lit (lee) m: bed

livre (lee-vruh) f: pound = 500 g, about 1.1lb.; m: book

logiciel (loh-zhee-syehl) m: software

long-métrage (lohN mey-trahzh) m: feature film

lui (lwee) m: him

lunettes de soleil (lew-neht duh soh-lehy) fpl: sunglasses

M

madame (mah-dahm) f: ma'am, missus

mademoiselle (mahd-mwah-zehl) f: miss

magasin (mah-gah-zaN) m: store

mai (meh) m: May

maillot de bains (mah-yoh duh baN) m: bathing suit

main (maN) f: hand

maintenant (maN-tuh-nahN): now

mais (meh): but

maison (meh-zohN) f: house

maladie (mah-lah-dee) f: illness

manger (mahN-zhey): to eat

manquer (mahN-key): to miss

manteau (mahN-toh) m: coat

marchand/marchande (mahr-shahN/mahr-shahNd) m/f: vendor

margarine (mahr-gah-reen) f: margarine

marguerite (mahr-gah-reet) f: daisy

mari (mah-ree) m: husband

marron (mah-rohN): brown

mars (mahrs) m: March

matériel (mah-tey-ryehl) m: equipment, material

mauvais/mauvaise (moh-veh/moh-vehz) m/f: bad

médecin (meyd-saN) m: physician

mél (mehl) m: e-mail

même (mehm): even, same

mémoire (mey-mwahr) f: memory

menthe (mahNt) f: mint

mentir (mahN-teer): to lie

mer (mehr) f: ocean

merci (mehr-see): thank you

mère (mehr) f: mother

messagerie (mey-sah-zhree) f: e-mail account

metteur-en-scène (meh-tuhr-ahN-sehn) m: film director

mettre (meh-truh): to put, to place

mille (meel) m: thousand

miroir (mee-rwahr) m: mirror

mobile (moh-beel) m: cell phone

moderne (moh-dehrn) m/f: modern

moi (mwah): me

moniteur (moh-nee-tuhr) m: monitor

monsieur (muh-syuh) m: mister

montagne (mohN-tah-nyuh) f: mountain

monter (mohN-tey): to go up, to climb, to get on

montre (mohN-truh) f: watch

montrer (mohN-trey): to show

moquette (moh-keht) f: carpet

mot de passe (moh duh pahs) m: password

mourir (mooh-reer): to die

moyen/moyenne (mwah-yaN/mwah-yehn) m/f: average

N

naissance (neh-sahNs) f: birth

naître (neh-truh): to be born

natation (nah-tah-syohN) f: swimming

navigateur (nah-vee-gah-tuhr) m: web browser

neige (nehzh) f: snow

nettoyer (neh-twah-yey): to clean

neuf (nuhf): nine

neuf/neuve (nuhf/nuhv) m/f: brand new

nez (ney) m: nose

noir/noire (nwahr) m/f: black

nom (nohN) m: last name

nord (nohr) m: north

nous (nooh): we

nouveau/nouvelle (nooh-voh/nooh-vehl) m/f: new

novembre (noh-vahN-bruh) m: November

nuage (new-ahzh) m: cloud

numéro de téléphone (new-mey-roh duh tey-ley-fohhn) m: phone number

O

octobre (ohk-toh-bruh) m: October

oeil/yeux (uhy/yuh) m: eye/eyes

oeillet (uh-yeh) m: carnation

oignon (ohh-nyohN) m: onion

oiseau (wah-zoh) m: bird

oncle (ohN-kluh) m: uncle

onze (ohNz) eleven

orange (oh-rahNzh) f: orange

ordinateur (ohr-dee-nah-tuhr) m: computer

oreille (oh-rehy) f: ear

oreiller (oh-rehy-ey) m: pillow

orteil (ohr-tehy) m: toe

oseille (oh-zehy) f: sorrel

où (ooh): where

ou (ooh): or

ouest (ooh-wehst) m: west

P

page d'accueil (pahzh dah-kuhy) f: home page

pain (paN) m: bread

pantalon (pahN-tah-lohN) m: pants, slacks

pantoufles (pahN-tooh-fluh) fpl: slippers

pardessus (pahr-duh-sew) m: overcoat

pare-brise (pahr-breez) m: windshield

parfait/parfaite (pahr-feh/pahr-feht) m/f: perfect

parler (pahr-ley): to speak, to talk

partir (pahr-teer): to leave

pas du tout (pah dew tooh): not at all

passeport (pahs-pohr) m: passport

passer (pah-sey): to pass [by]

pastèque (pahs-tehk) f: watermelon

pastille (pah-steey) f: lozenge

pâtes (paht) fpl: pasta

pâtisserie (pah-tees-ree) f: pastry shop

pays (pey-ee) m: country

PDG (pey dey zhey): CEO

pêche (pehsh) f: peach

pêcher (pehsh-ey): to go fishing

peigne (peh-nyuh) m: comb

pensée (pahN-sey) f: thought

pensement (pahN-suh-mahN) m: bandage

penser (pahN-sey): to think

père (pehr) m: father

période creuse (pey-ree-ohd kruhz) f: off peak

permis de conduire (pehr-mee duh kohN-dweer) m: driver's license

persil (pehr-see) m: parsley

personnes (pehr-sohhn) fpl: people

peser (puh-zey): to weigh

petit/petite (puh-tee/puh-teet) m/f: small, short

petit déjeuner (puh-tee dey-zhuh-ney) m: breakfast

petite-fille (puh-teet feey) f: granddaughter

petit-fils (puh-tee fees) m: grandson

petits pois (puh-tee pwah) mpl: peas

petits-enfants (puh-tee-zahN-fahN) mpl: grandchildren

photo (foh-toh) f: picture

photocopieuse (foh-toh-koh-pyuhz) f: copy machine

piano (pyah-noh) m: piano

pièce (pyehs) f: room, theatrical play

pièce jointe (pyehs zhwaNt) f: attachment

pied (pyey) m: foot

piéton/piétonne (pyey-tohN/pyey-tohhn) m/f: pedestrian

piscine (pee-seen) f: swimming pool

place (plahs) f: seat, city or town square

plage (plahzh) f: beach

plan (plahN) m: map

planche à voile (plahNsh ah vwahl) f: windsurfing

plate-bande (plaht-bahNd) f: flowerbed

pneu (pnuh) m: tire

pointure (pwaN-tewr) f: shoe size

poire (pwahr) f: pear

poireau (pwah-roh) m: leak

poisson (pwah-sohN) m: fish

poissonnerie (pwah-sohn-ree) f: fish store

poitrine (pwah-treen) f: chest

poivre (pwah-vruh) m: pepper

police (poh-lees) f: police

pomme (pohhm) f: apple

pommes de terre (pohhm duh tehr) fpl: potatoes

pont (pohN) m: bridge

porc (pohr) m: pork

portable (pohr-tah-bluh) m: laptop

porte (pohrt) f: door

portefeuille (pohrt-fuhy) m: wallet

porter (pohr-tey): to wear, to carry

poste (pohst) f: post office

potager (poh-tah-zhey) m: vegatable garden, vegetable

poulet (pooh-leh) m: chicken

pourboire (poohr-bwahr) m: tip

pourquoi (poohr-kwah): why

pouvoir (pooh-vwahr): to be able to

préférer (prey-fey-rey): to prefer

prendre (prahN-druh): to take

prénom (prey-nohN) m: first name

présenter (prey-zahN-tey): to introduce

printemps (praN-tahN) m: spring

professeur (proh-feh-suhr) m: high school teacher, college professor

promenade (prohm-nahd) f: walk

propriétaire (proh-pree-ey-tehr) m/f: owner

prune (prewn) f: plum

pseudo (psooh-doh) m: username

publicité (pew-blee-see-tey) f: advertisement

puis (pwee): then

pull (pewl) m: sweater

Q

quai (key) m: platform

quand (kahN): when

quatorze (kah-tohrz): fourteen

quatre (kah-truh): four

quel/quelle (kehl) m/f: which

quelque chose (kehl-kuh shohz): something

qu'est-ce que/quoi (kehs-kuh/kwah): what

qui (kee): who

quinze (kaNz): fifteen

R

raisin (reh-zaN) m: grape

ralentir (rah-lahN-teer): to slow down

randonnée (rahN-doh-ney) f: hike

rasoir (rah-zwahr) m: razor

réalisateur/réalisatrice (rey-ah-lee-zah-tuhr/rey-ah-lee-zah-trees) m/f: director

recevoir (ruh-suh-vwahr): to receive

reçu (ruh-sew) m: receipt

réfrigérateur (rey-free-zhey-rah-tuhr) m: refrigerator

regarder (ruh-gahr-dey): to watch

rendez-vous (rahN-dey-vooh) m: appointment

rendre (rahN-druh): to return (something)

rendre visite à (rahN-druh vee-zeet ah): to visit a person

renseignement (rahN-seh-nyuh-mahN) m: information

rentrer (rahN-trey): to return, to go home

repas (ruh-pah) m: meal

répondre (rey-pohN-druh): to answer

représentation (ruh-prey-zahN-tah-syohN) f: performance

réseau (rey-zoh) m: network

rester (rehs-tey): to stay

retraité/retraitée (ruh-treh-tey) m/f: retiree

réveil (rey-vehy) m: alarm clock

rez-de-chaussée (reyd shoh-sey) m: ground [first] floor

rhume (rewm) m: a cold

rideau (ree-doh) m: curtain

riz (ree) m: rice

robe (rohhb) f: dress

roman (roh-mahN) m: novel

romarin (roh-mah-raN) m: rosemary

rouge (roohzh): red

ruban adhésif (rew-bahN ahd-ey-zeef) m: tape

rue (rew) f: street

S

s'abonner (sah-boh-ney): to subscribe

s'amuser (sah-mew-zey): to have fun

s'en aller (sahN-nah-ley): to leave

s'habiller (sah-bee-yey): to get dressed

sable (sah-bluh) m: sand

sac (sahk) m: bag

sac de couchage (sahk duh kooh-shahzh) m: sleeping bag

saison (seh-zohN) f: season

salade verte (sah-lahd vehrt) f: green salad, salad with lettuce only

salle d'attente (sahl dah-tahNt) f: waiting room

salon de chat (sah-lohN duh chaht) m: chat room

salut (sah-lew): hi

sandales (sahN-dahl) fpl: sandals

sauge (sohzh) f: sage

saumon (soh-mohN) m: salmon

savoir (sah-vwahr): to know

savon (sah-vohN) m: soap

se doucher (suh dooh-shey): to shower

se laver (suh lah-vey): to wash

se lever (suh-luh-vey): to get up

se réveiller (suh rey-vey-yey): to wake up

séance (sey-ahNs) f: (a movie) showing

secrétaire (suh-krey-tehr) m/f: secretary

seize (sehz): sixteen

séjour (sey-zhoohr) m: stay

sel (sehl) m: salt

semaine (suh-mehn) f: week

sens unique (sahNs ew-neek) m: one way

sept (seht): seven

septembre (sehp-tahN-bruh) m: September

serveur/serveuse (sehr-vuhr/sehr-vuhz) m/f: waiter/waitress

serviette (sehr-vyeht) f: napkin, towel

seulement (suhl-mahN): only

siège (syehzh) m: seat

siffler (see-fley): to whistle

six (sees): six

slip (sleep) m: underpants, briefs

soeur (suhr) f: sister

soie (swah) f: silk

soirée (swah-rey) f: evening, party

sol (sohl) m: soil

soldes (sohld) mpl: sales [France]

soleil (soh-lehy) m: sun

sortie (sohr-tee) f: exit

sortir (sohr-teer): to exit, to go out

soucoupe (sooh-koohp) f: saucer

souris (sooh-ree) f: mouse

sous (sooh): under, underneath

sous-vêtements (sooh-veht-mahN) m: underwear

souvent (sooh-vahN): often

sportif/sportive (spohr-teef/spohr-teev) m/f: athletic

stationnement (stah-syohn-mahN) m: parking

station-service (stah-syohN-sehr-vees) f: gas station

steward/hôtesse de l'air (stee-wahr/oh-tehs duh lehr) m/f: flight attendant

stylo (stee-loh) m: pen

sucre (sew-kruh) m: sugar

sud (sewd) m: south

supermarché (sew-pehr-mahr-shey) m: supermarket

sur (sewr): on, on top of

surveillant/surveillante de plage, de baignade (sewr-vehy-ahN/sewr-vehy-ahNt duh plahzh, duh beh-nyahd) m/f: lifeguard

sweat (sweht) m: sweatshirt

T

tableau d'affichage (tah-bloh dah-fee-shahzh) m: bulletin board

tailleur (tahy-uhr) m: women's suit

tant pis (tahN pee): too bad

tante (tahNt) f: aunt

tapis (tah-pee) m: rug

tarif réduit (tah-reef rey-dwee) m: reduced fare

tarte aux pommes (tahr-toh-pohhm) f: apple tart

tasse (tahs) f: cup

taux de change (toh duh shahNzh) m: exchange rate

télécharger (tey-ley-shahr-zhey): to download

télécopie (tey-ley-koh-pee) f: fax

télécopieur (tey-ley-koh-pyuhr) m: fax machine

téléphoner (tey-ley-fohh-ney): to telephone or call

tennis (tey-nees) m: tennis

tête (teht) f: head

thé (tey) m: tea

thon (tohN) m: tuna

thym (taN) m: thyme

timbre (taN-bruh) m: stamp

toi (twah): you

tomate (toh-maht) f: tomato

tomber (tohN-bey): to fall

tondeuse à gazon (tohN-duhz ah gah-zohN) f: lawn mower

tondre la pelouse/le gazon (tohN-druh lah puh-loohz/luh gah-zohN): to mow the lawn

toujours (tooh-zhoohr): always

tous (toohs): all

tout le monde (tooh luh mohNd): everyone, everybody

toux (tooh) f: a cough

train (traN) m: train

travailler (trah-vah-yey): to work

travailleur/travailleuse (trah-vah-yuhr/ trah-vah-yuhz) m/f: hardworking

treize (trehz): thirteen

trois (twah): three

trop (troh): too much

trottoir (troh-twahr) m: sidewalk

trucages (trew-kahzh) mpl: special effects

truite (trweet) f: trout

tu (tew): you, informal, singular

tuyau d'arrosage (tewy-oh dah-roh-zahzh) m: garden hose

U

un/une (uhN/ewn) m/f: one

V

vague (vahg) f: wave

valise (vah-leez) f: suitcase

veau (voh) m: veal, calf

vedette (veh-deht) f: [movie] star

vendre (vahN-druh): to sell

venir (vuh-neer): to come

verre (vehr) m: glass

vert/verte (vehr/vehrt) m/f: green

veste (vehst) f: jacket (for men and women)

veston (vehs-tohN) m: man's suit jacket

viande (vyahNd) f: meat

victoire (veek-twahr) f: victory

vidange (vee-dahNzh) f: oil change

vieux/vieille (vyuh/vyehy) m/f: old

ville (veel) f: city/town

vin (vaN) m: wine

vingt (vaN): twenty

violon (vyoh-lohN) m: violin

visiter (vee-zee-tey): to visit (a place)

vitrine (vee-treen) f: store window

voie (vwah) f: track

voile (vwahl) f: sailing

voir (vwahr): to see

voiture (vwah-tewr) f: car

vol (vohl) m: flight, theft

vouloir (vooh-lwahr): to want

vous (vooh): you, singular formal or plural

voyage d'affaires (voh-yahzh dah-fehr) m: business trip

voyager (voh-yah-zhey): to travel

English-French Mini-Dictionary

A

absolutely: **absolument** (ahb-soh-lew-mahN)

(to) accept: **accepter** (ah-kseh-ptey)

across from, in front of: **en face de** (ahN fahs-duh)

address: **adresse** (ah-drehs) f

adventure film: **film d'aventures** (feelm dah-vahN-tewr) m

advertisement: **publicité** (pew-blee-see-tey) f

air conditioning: **climatisation** (klee-mah-tee-zah-syohN) f

airport terminal: **aérogare** (ah-ey-roh-gahr) f

alarm clock: **réveil** (rey-vehy) m

all right, okay: **d'accord** (dah-kohr)

all: **tous** (toohs)

also: **aussi** (oh-see)

always: **toujours** (tooh-zhoohr)

American football: **foot(ball) américain** (fooht[bohl] ah-mey-ree-kaN) m

ankle: **cheville** (shuh-veey) f

(to) answer: **répondre** (rey-pohN-druh)

antibiotic: **antibiotique** (ahN-tee-bee-oh-teek) m

appetizer, entrance: **entrée** (ahN-trey) f

apple tart: **tarte aux pommes** (tahr-toh-pohhm) fpl

apple: **pomme** (pohhm) f

appointment: **rendez-vous** (rahN-dey-vooh) m

apricot: **abricot** (ah-bree-koh) m

April: **avril** (ah-vreel) m

architect: **architecte** (ahr-shee-tehkt) m/f

arm: **bras** (brah) m

armoire: **armoire** (ahr-mwahr) f

arrival: **arrivée** (ah-ree-vey) f

(to) arrive: **arriver** (ah-ree-vey)

asparagus: **asperge** (ah-spehrzh) f

athletic: **sportif/sportive** (spohr-teef/spohr-teev) m/f

ATM: **distributeur (de billets)** (dees-tree-bew-tuhr [duh bee-yey]) m

attach: **joindre** (zhwaN-druh)

attachment: **pièce jointe** (pyehs zhwaNt) f

August: **août** (ooht) m

aunt: **tante** (tahNt) f

author: **auteur** (oh-tuhr) m

average: **moyen/moyenne** (mwah-yaN/mwah-yehn) m/f

B

back: **dos** (doh) m

bad: **mauvais/mauvaise** (moh-veh/moh-vehz) m/f

bag: **sac** (sahk) m

baggage room: **consigne** (kohN-see-nyuh) f

bakery: **boulangerie** (booh-lahN-zhree) f

banana: **banane** (bah-nahn) f

bandage: **pensement** (pahN-suh-mahN) m

bank: **banque** (bahNk) f

basil: **basilic** (bah-zee-leek) m

basketball: **basket** (bahs-keht) m

bathing suit: **maillot de bain/costume de bains** (Québec) (mah-yoh duh baN/kohs-tewm duh baN) m

bathroom sink: **lavabo** (lah-vah-boh) m

bathtub: **baignoire** (beh-nywahr) f

(to) be: **être** (eh-truh)

beach: **plage** (plahzh) f

(to) be able to: **pouvoir** (pooh-vwahr)

(to) be born: **naître** (neh-truh)

(to) become: **devenir** (duh-vuh-neer)

bed: **lit** (lee) m

beef: **boeuf** (buhf) m

beer: **bière** (byehr) f

behind: **derrière** (deh-ryehr)

belt: **ceinture** (saN-tewr) f

between: **entre** (ahN-truh)

bicycle: **bicyclette** (bee-see-kleht) f

big, tall, large: **grand/grande** (grahN/ grahNd) m/f

bird: **oiseau** (wah-zoh) m

birth: **naissance** (neh-sahNs) f

black: **noir/noire** (nwahr) m/f

blanket: **couverture** (kooh-vehr-tewr) f

blazer: **blazer** (blah-zehr) m

blouse: **chemisier** (shuh-mee-zyey) m

blue: **bleu/bleue** (bluh) m/f

boarding pass: **carte d'embarquement** (kahrt dahN-bahr-kuh-mahN) f

bookstore: **librairie** (lee-brey-ree) f

boots: **bottes** (bohht) fpl

boring: **ennuyeux/ennuyeuse** (ahN-nwee-uh/ahN-nwee-euhz) m/f

boy: **garçon** (gahr-sohN) m

brakes (of a car): **freins** (fraN) mpl:

bread: **pain** (paN) m

breakfast: **petit déjeuner** (puh-tee dey-zhuh-ney) m

bridge: **pont** (pohN) m

brother: **frère** (frehr) m

brown: **marron** (mah-rohN)

brush: **brosse** (brohs) f

Brussels sprouts: **choux de Bruxelles** (shooh duh brewk-sehl) mpl

bulletin board: **tableau d'affichage** (tah-bloh dah-fee-shahzh) m

burglary: **cambriolage** (kahN-bree-oh-lahzh) m

business trip: **voyage d'affaires** (voh-yahzh dah-fehr) m

business: **affaires** (ah-fehr) f pl

but: **mais** (meh)

butcher shop: **boucherie** (booh-shree) f

butter: **beurre** (buhr) m

(to) buy: **acheter** (ahsh-tey)

C

cabbage: **chou** (shooh) m

cake: **gâteau** (gah-toh) m

calendar: **calendrier** (kah-lahN-dree-yey) m

(to) call/to call oneself, to be named: **appeler/s'appeler** (ah-pley/sah-pley)

camera: **appareil-photo** (ah-pah-rehy foh-toh) m

car: **voiture** (vwah-tewr) f

carnation: **oeillet** (uh-yeh) m

carpet: **moquette** (moh-keht) f

carrot: **carotte** (kah-roht) f

cartoon: **dessin animé** (deh-sahN ah-nee-mey) m

cashier: **caissier/caissière** (key-syeh/ key-syehr) m/f

cash register: **caisse** (kehs) f

castle: **château** (shah-toh) m

(to) catch: **attraper** (ah-trah-pey)

cauliflower: **chou-fleur** (shooh-fluhr) m

CD, DVD player: **lecteur de CD/de DVD** (lehk-tuhr duh sey dey/duh dey vey dey) m

cell phone: **mobile** (moh-beel) m

CEO: **PDG** (pey dey zhey)

charming: **charmant/charmante** (shahr-mahN/shahr-mahNt) m/f

chat room: **salon de chat** (sah-lohN duh chaht) m

check: **addition** (ah-dee-syohN) f

cheese: **fromage** (froh-mahzh) m

cherry: **cerise** (suh-reez) f

chervil: **cerfeuil** (sehr-fuhy) m

chess: **échecs** (ey-shehk) mpl

chest: **poitrine** (pwah-treen) f

chicken: **poulet** (pooh-leh) m

child: **enfant** (ahN-fahN) m/f

(to) choose: **choisir** (shwah-zeer)

city/town: **ville** (veel) f

(to) clean: **nettoyer** (neh-twah-yey)

clock: **horloge** (ohr-lohzh) f

cloud: **nuage** (new-ahzh) m

coast: **côtes** (koht) f

coat: **manteau** (mahN-toh) m

coffee, café: **café** (kah-fey) m

cold (noun): **rhume** (rewm) m

cold: **froid/froide** (frwah/frwahd) m/f

colleague, coworker: **collègue** (koh-lehg) m/f

color: **couleur** (kooh-luhr) f

comb: **peigne** (peh-nyuh) m

(to) come: **venir** (vuh-neer)

comic strip: **bande dessinée** (bahNd deh-see-ney) f

company: **compagnie** (kohN-pah-nyee) f

computer scientist: **informaticien/informaticienne** (aN-fohr-mah-tee-syaN/aN-fohr-mah-tee-syehn) m/f

computer: **ordinateur** (ohr-dee-nah-tuhr) m

copy machine: **photocopieuse** (foh-toh-koh-pyuhz) f

coriander: **coriandre** (koh-ree-ahN-druh) m

cough (noun): **toux** (tooh) f

counter: **comptoir** (kohN-twahr) m

country: **pays** (pey-ee) m

countryside: **campagne** (kahN-pah-nyuh) f

courtyard: **cour** (koohr) f

cream: **crème** (krehm) f

credit card: **carte de crédit** (kahrt duh krey-dee) f

credits: **générique** (zhey-ney-reek) m

cup: **tasse** (tahs) f

currency exchange office: **bureau de change** (bew-roh duh shahNzh) m

curtain: **rideau** (ree-doh) m

D

daffodil: **jonquille** (zhohN-keey) f

dairy product and cheese store: **crémerie** (kreym-ree) f

daisy: **marguerite** (mahr-gah-reet) f

(to) dance: **danser** (dahN-sey)

dark: **foncé/foncée** (fohN-sey) m/f

daughter, girl: **fille** (feey) f

day: **jour** (zhoohr) m

dear, expensive: **cher/chère** (shehr) m/f

December: **décembre** (dey-sahN-bruh) m

delighted: **enchanté/enchantée** (ahN-shahN-tey) m/f

dentist: **dentiste** (dahN-teest) m/f

department store: **grand magasin** (grahN mah-gah-zaN) m

departure: **départ** (dey-pahr) m

dessert: **dessert** (deh-sehr) m

detective film: **film policier** (feelm poh-lee-syey) m

(to) die: **mourir** (mooh-reer)

dill: **aneth** (ah-neht) m

director (film): **metteur-en-scène/réalisateur/réalisatrice** (meh-tuhr-ahN-sehn/rey-ah-lee-zah-tuhr/rey-ah-lee-zah-trees) m/f

director/manager (of a company or business): **directeur/directrice** (dee-rehk-tuhr/dee-rehk-trees) m/f

dishwasher: **lave-vaisselle** (lahv veh-sehl) m

(to) do, to make: **faire** (fehr)

doctor: **docteur** (dohk-tuhr) m

documentary: **documentaire** (doh-kew-mahN-tehr) m

door: **porte** (pohrt) f

(to) download: **télécharger** (tey-ley-shahr-zhey)

dress: **robe** (rohhb) f

dresser: **commode** (koh-mohhd) f

(to) drink: **boire** (bwahr)

(to) drive: **conduire** (kohN-dweer)

driver's license: **permis de conduire** (pehr-mee duh kohN-dweer) m

duck: **canard** (kah-nahr) m

E

ear: **oreille** (oh-rehy) f

easy: **facile** (fah-seel)

(to) eat: **manger** (mahN-zhey)

eight: **huit** (weet)

eighteen: **dix-huit** (deez-weet)

elevator: **ascenseur** (ah-sahN-suhr) m

eleven: **onze** (ohNz)

e-mail account: **messagerie** (mey-sah-zhree) f

e-mail address: **adresse électronique** (ah-dreh-sey-lehk-troh-neek) f

e-mail: **mél** (mehl) m

employee: **employé/employée** (ahN-plwah-yey) m/f

end: **fin** (fahN) f

engineer: **ingénieur** (aN-zhey-nyuhr) m

(to) enter: **entrer** (ahN-trey)

envelope: **enveloppe** (ahN-vlohhp) f

equality: **égalité** (ey-gah-lee-tey) f

equipment, material: **matériel** (mah-tey-ryehl) m

eraser: **gomme** (gohm) f

escalator: **escalier roulant** (ehs-kah-lyey rooh-lahN) m

even, same: **même** (mehm)

evening party: **soirée** (swah-rey) f

everyone, everybody: **tout le monde** (tooh luh mohNd)

exchange rate: **taux de change** (toh duh shahNzh) m

exit: **sortie** (sohr-tee) f

(to) exit, to go out: **sortir** (sohr-teer)

expensive: **cher/chère** (shehr) m/f

eye/eyes: **oeil /yeux** (uhy/yuh) m

F

face: **figure** (fee-gewr) f

facing, overlooking: **donner sur** (dohh-ney sewr)

fairy tale: **conte de fée** (kohNt duh fey) m

fall: **automne** (oh-tohn) m

(to) fall: **tomber** (tohN-bey)

fat, large: **gros/grosse** (groh/grohs) m/f

father: **père** (pehr) m

fax machine: **télécopieur** (tey-ley-koh-pyuhr) m

fax: **télécopie** (tey-ley-koh-pee) f

feature film: **long-métrage** (lohN mey-trahzh) m

February: **février** (fey-vryey) m

fifteen: **quinze** (kaNz)

fig: **figue** (feeg) f

file cabinet: **classeur à tiroirs** (klah-suhr ah tee-rwahr) m

file: **fichier** (fee-shyey) m

(to) fill the gas tank: **faire le plein** (fehr luh plaN)

filmmaker: **cinéaste** (see-ney-ahst) m/f

finger: **doigt** (dwah) m

(to) finish: **finir** (fee-neer)

first name: **prénom** (prey-nohN) m

fish store: **poissonnerie** (pwah-sohn-ree) f

fish: **poisson** (pwah-sohN) m

fishing pole: **canne à pêche** (kahn ah pehsh) f

fitting room: **cabine d'essayage** (kah-been dey-sey-ahzh) f

five: **cinq** (saNk)

flannel: **flanelle** (flah-nehl) f

flight attendant: **steward/hôtesse de l'air** (stee-wahr/oh-tehs duh lehr) m/f

flight: **vol** (vohl) m

flower garden: **jardin d'agrément** (zhahr-daN dah-grey-mahN) m

flower: **fleur** (fluhr) f

flowerbed: **plate-bande** (plaht-bahNd) f

flu: **grippe** (greep) f

foot: **pied** (pyey) m

fork: **fourchette** (foohr-sheht) f

four: **quatre** (kah-truh)

fourteen: **quatorze** (kah-tohrz)

freedom: **liberté** (lee-behr-tey) f

friend: **ami/amie** (ah-mee) m/f

fruit: **fruits** (frwee) mpl

G

(to) garden: **faire du jardinage** (fehr dew zhahr-dee-nahzh) garden hose: **tuyau d'arrosage** (tewy-oh dah-roh-zahzh) m

gas station: **station-service** (stah-syohN-sehr-vees) f

gas: **essence** (ey-sahNs) f

glass: **verre** (vehr) m

(to) get dressed: **s'habiller** (sah-bee-yey)

(to) get up: **se lever** (suh-luh-vey)

(to) give: **donner** (dohh-ney)

(to) go: **aller** (ah-ley)

(to) go down, to get off: **descendre** (dey-sahN-druh)

(to) go fishing: **pêcher** (pehsh-ey)

(to) go up, to climb, to get on: **monter** (mohN-tey)

good: **bon/bonne** (bohN/bohhn) m/f

good-bye: **au revoir** (ohr-vwahr)

good day, hello: **bonjour** (bohN-zhoohr)

good evening, good night: **bonsoir** (bohN-swahr) m

good night (when going to bed): **bonne nuit** (bohhn nwee) f

grandchildren: **petits-enfants** (puh-tee-zahN-fahN) mpl

granddaughter: **petite-fille** (puh-teet feey) f

grandson: **petit-fils** (puh-tee fees) m

grape: **raisin** (reh-zaN) m

green beans: **haricots verts** (ah-ree-koh vehr) mpl

green salad, salad with lettuce only: **salade verte** (sah-lahd vehrt) f

green: **vert/verte** (vehr/vehrt) m/f

grocery store, general store: **épicerie** (ey-pees-ree) f

ground [first] floor: **rez-de-chaussée** (reyd shoh-sey) m

guitar: **guitare** (gee-tahr) f

H

ham: **jambon** (zhahN-bohN) m

hand: **main** (maN) f

happiness: **bonheur** (boh-nuhr) m

happy: **heureux/heureuse** (uh-ruh/uh-ruhz) m/f

hardworking: **travailleur/travailleuse** (trah-vah-yuhr/trah-vah-yuhz) m/f

hardware: **matériel** (mah-tey-ree-ehl) m

hat: **chapeau** (shah-poh) m

(to) hate: **détester** (dey-teh-stey)

(to) have: **avoir** (ah-vwahr)

(to) have fun: **s'amuser** (sah-mew-zey)

(to) have to: **devoir** (duh-vwahr)

he: **il** (eel) m

head: **tête** (teht) f

(to) help: **aider** (ey-dey)

hi: **salut** (sah-lew)

high school teacher, college professor: **professeur** (proh-feh-suhr) m

hike: **randonnée** (rahN-doh-ney) f

him: **lui** (lwee) m

holidays: **fêtes** (feht) fpl

home page: **page d'accueil** (pahzh dah-kuhy) f

hood (of a car): **capot** (kah-poh) m

horror film: **film d'épouvante/d'horreur** (feelm dey-pooh-vahnt/doh-ruhr) m

hotel: **hôtel** (oh-tehl) m

house: **maison** (meh-zohN) f

how much: **combien** (kohN-byaN)

how: **comment** (koh-mahN)

(to be) hungry: **avoir faim** (ah-vwahr faN)

husband: **mari** (mah-ree) m

hydrangea: **hortensia** (ohr-tahN-syah) m

I

I: **je** (zhuh)

ice cream: **glace** (glahs) f

icon: **icône** (ee-kohn) f

idea: **idée** (ee-dey) f

illness: **maladie** (mah-lah-dee) f

in front of: **devant** (duh-vahN)

in the back: **au fond** (oh fohN)

in, inside: **dans** (dahN)

information: **renseignement** (rahN-sehn-yuh-mahN) m

intersection: **carrefour** (kahr-foohr) m

(to) introduce: **présenter** (prey-zahN-tey)

J

jacket (for men and women): **veste** (vehst) f

jam: **confiture** (kohN-fee-tewr) f

January: **janvier** (zhahN-vyey) m

jeans: **jean** (jeen) m

jewelry store: **bijouterie** (bee-zhooh-tree) f

July: **juillet** (zhwee-yeh) m

June: **juin** (zhwaN) m

K

keyboard: **clavier** (klah-vyey) m

kitchen sink: **évier** (ey-vyey) m

knee: **genou** (zhuh-nooh) m

knife: **couteau** (kooh-toh) m

(to) know: **savoir** (sah-vwahr)

L

lake: **lac** (lahk) m

lamb: **agneau** (ah-nyoh) m

laptop: **portable** (pohr-tah-bluh) m

large, wide: **large** (lahrzh) m/f

last name: **nom** (nohN) m

late: **en retard** (ahN ruh-tahr)

(to) launch, to throw: **lancer** (lahN-sey)

lawn mower: **tondeuse à gazon** (tohN-duhz ah gah-zohN) f

lawyer: **avocat/avocate** (ah-voh-kah/ ah-voh-kaht) m/f

leak: **poireau** (pwah-roh) m

leather: **cuir** (kweer) m

(to) leave: **partir/s'en aller** (pahr-teer/ sahN-nah-ley)

leg of lamb: **gigot d'agneau** (zhee-goh dah-nyoh) m

leg: **jambe** (zhahNb) f

lemonade: **limonade** (lee-moh-nahd) f

lettuce: **laitue** (ley-tew) f

(to) lie: **mentir** (mahN-teer)

lifeguard: **surveillant/surveillante de plage, de baignade** (sewr-vehy-ahN/sewr-vehy-ahNt duh plahzh, duh beh-nyahd) m/f

light-colored: **clair/claire** (klehr) m/f

lighting: **éclairage** (ey-kleh-rahzh) m

(to) like, to love: **aimer** (eh-mey)

linen: **lin** (laN) m

(to) live: **habiter** (ah-bee-tey)

lobster: **homard** (oh-mahr) m

(to) love, to adore: **adorer** (ah-doh-rey)

lozenge: **pastille** (pah-steey) f

lunch (as a verb: to have lunch): **déjeuner** (dey-zhuh-ney) m

M

ma'am, missus: **madame** (mah-dahm) f

mailbox: **boîte aux lettres** (bwaht oh leh-truh) f

(to) make, to do: **faire** (fehr)

mall: **centre commercial** (sahN-truh koh-mehr-syahl) m

man's suit jacket: **veston** (vehs-tohN) m

manager (of a company, business): **directeur/directrice** (dee-rehk-tuhr/ dee-rehk-trees) m/f

manager (restaurant, hotel, shop): **gérant/ gérante** (zhey-rahN/zhey-rahNt) m/f

map: **plan** (plahN) m

March: **mars** (mahrs) m

margarine: **margarine** (mahr-gah-reen) f

match: **allumette** (ah-lew-meht) f

May: **mai** (meh) m

me: **moi** (mwah)

meal: **repas** (ruh-pah) m

meat: **viande** (vyahNd) f

memory: **mémoire** (mey-mwahr) f

microwave: **four à micro-ondes** (foohr ah mee-kroh-ohNd) m

mild, sweet: **doux/douce** (dooh/doohs) m/f

milk: **lait** (leh) m

mint: **menthe** (mahNt) f

mirror: **miroir** (mee-rwahr) m

miss (title): **mademoiselle** (mahd-mwah-zehl) f

(to) miss: **manquer** (mahN-key)

mister: **monsieur** (muh-syuh) m

mixed greens, raw vegetables: **crudités** (krew-dee-tey) fpl

modern: **moderne** (moh-dehrn) m/f

money: **argent** (ahr-zhahN) m

monitor: **moniteur** (moh-nee-tuhr) m

mother: **mère** (mehr) f

mountain: **montagne** (mohN-tah-nyuh) f

mouse: **souris** (sooh-ree) f

mouth: **bouche** (boohsh) f

movie star: **vedette** (veh-deht) f

movies: **cinéma** (see-ney-mah) m

(to) mow the lawn: **tondre la pelouse/le gazon** (tohN-druh lah puh-loohz/luh gah-zohN)

mushroom: **champignon** (shahN-pee-nyohN) m

N

napkin, towel: **serviette** (sehr-vyeht) f

narrow: **étroit/étroite** (ey-trwah/ey-trwaht) m/f

neck: **cou** (kooh) m

network: **réseau** (rey-zoh) m

new, brand new: **neuf/neuve** (nuhf/nuhv) m/f

new: **nouveau/nouvelle** (nooh-voh/nooh-vehl) m/f

newspaper: **journal** (zhoohr-nahl) m

next day: **lendemain** (lahN-duh-mahN) m

next to: **à côté de** (ah koh-tey duh)

nice, beautiful, handsome: **beau/belle** (boh/behl) m/f

nine: **neuf** (nuhf)

nineteen: **dix-neuf** (deez-nuhf)

noisy: **bruyant/bruyante** (brwee-ahN/brwee-ahNt) m/f

north: **nord** (nohr) m

nose: **nez** (ney) m

not at all: **pas du tout** (pah dew tooh)

novel: **roman** (roh-mahN) m

November: **novembre** (noh-vahN-bruh) m

now: **maintenant** (maN-tuh-nahN)

nurse: **infirmier/infirmière** (aN-feer-myey/aN-feer-myehr) m/f

O

ocean: **mer** (mehr) f

October: **octobre** (ohk-toh-bruh) m

of course: **bien sûr** (byaN sewr)

off peak: **période creuse** (pey-ree-ohd kruhz) f

office, desk: **bureau** (bew-roh) m

often: **souvent** (sooh-vahN)

oil change: **vidange** (vee-dahNzh) f

okay: **ça va** (sah vah)

old: **vieux/vieille** (vyuh/vyehy) m/f

on the left: **à gauche** (ah gohsh)

on the right: **à droite** (ah drwaht)

on time: **à l'heure** (ah luhr)

on, on top of: **sur** (sewr)

one way: **sens unique** (sahNs ew-neek) m

one: **un/une** (uhN/ewn) m/f

one-way ticket: **aller-simple** (ah-ley saN-pluh) m

onion: **oignon** (ohh-nyohN) m

only: **seulement** (suhl-mahN)

or: **ou** (ooh)

orange: **orange** (oh-rahNzh) f

outside: **dehors** (duh-ohr)

over there: **là-bas** (lah-bah)

overcoat: **pardessus** (pahr-duh-sew) m

owner: **propriétaire** (proh-pree-ey-tehr) m/f

oysters: **huitres** (wee-truh) fpl

P

package: **colis** (koh-lee) m

parking: **stationnement** (stah-syohn-mahN) m

parsley: **persil** (pehr-see) m

(to) pass (by): **passer** (pah-sey)

passport: **passeport** (pahs-pohr) m

password: **mot de passe** (moh duh pahs) m

pasta: **pâtes** (paht) fpl

pastry shop: **pâtisserie** (pah-tees-ree) f

peach: **pêche** (pehsh) f

pear: **poire** (pwahr) f

peas: **petits pois** (puh-tee pwah) mpl

pedestrian: **piéton/piétonne** (pyey-tohN/ pyey-tohhn) m/f

pen: **stylo** (stee-loh) m

pencil: **crayon** (krey-ohN) m

people: **personnes** (pehr-sohhn) fpl

pepper: **poivre** (pwah-vruh) m

perfect: **parfait/parfaite** (pahr-feh/ pahr-feht) m/f

performance: **représentation** (ruh-prey-zahN-tah-syohN) f

phone number: **numéro de téléphone** (new-mey-roh duh tey-ley-fohhn) m

physician: **médecin** (meyd-saN) m

piano: **piano** (pyah-noh) m

picture: **photo** (foh-toh) f

pillow: **oreiller** (oh-rehy-ey) m

pineapple: **ananas** (ah-nah-nah) m

plane: **avion** (ah-vyohN) m

plate: **assiette** (ah-syeht) f

platform: **quai** (key) m

(to) play: **jouer** (zhooh-ey)

pleasant: **agréable** (ah-grey-ah-bluh)

plum: **prune** (prewn) f

police: **police** (poh-lees) f

pork: **porc** (pohr) m

post office: **poste** (pohst) f

postage: **affranchissement** (ah-frahN-shee-smahN) m

potatoes: **pommes de terre** (pohhm duh tehr) fpl

pound (f) (500 g, about 1.1 lb), book(m): **livre** (lee-vruh)

(to) prefer: **préférer** (prey-fey-rey)

pretty: **joli/jolie** (zhoh-lee) m/f

printer: **imprimante** (aN-pree-mahnt) f

proud: **fier/fière** (fyehr) m/f

(to) put, to place: **mettre** (meh-truh)

R

raincoat (n), rainproof (adj): **imperméable** (aN-pehr-mey-ah-bluh) m

raspberry: **framboise** (frahN-bwahz) f

razor: **rasoir** (rah-zwahr) m

(to) read: **lire** (leer)

receipt: **reçu** (ruh-sew) m

(to) receive: **recevoir** (ruh-suh-vwahr)

red: **rouge** (roohzh)

reduced fare: **tarif réduit** (tah-reef rey-dwee) m

refrigerator: **réfrigérateur** (rey-free-zhey-rah-tuhr) m

retiree: **retraité/retraitée** (ruh-treh-tey) m/f

(to) return (something): **rendre** (rahN-druh)

(to) return, to go home: **rentrer** (rahN-trey)

ribs: **côtes** (koht) fpl

rice: **riz** (ree) m

romance film: **film d'amour** (feelm dah-moohr) m

room, theatrical play: **pièce** (pyehs) f

rosemary: **romarin** (roh-mah-raN) m

round trip: **aller-retour** (ah-ley ruh-toohr) m

rubber band: **élastique** (ey-lah-steek) m

rug: **tapis** (tah-pee) m

(to) run: **courir** (kooh-reer)

rush hour, peak: **heure de pointe** (uhr duh pwaNt) f

S

sage: **sauge** (sohzh) f

sailing: **voile** (vwahl) f

sales [France]: **soldes** (sohld) mpl

sales [Quebec]: **aubaine** (oh-behn) f

salmon: **saumon** (soh-mohN) m

salt: **sel** (sehl) m

sand: **sable** (sah-bluh) m

sandals: **sandales** (sahN-dahl) fpl

saucer: **soucoupe** (sooh-koohp) f

scale: **balance** (bah-lahNs) f

scallops: **coquilles Saint-Jacques** (koh-keey saN zhahk) fpl

scarf: **foulard** (fooh-lahr) m

schedule: **horaire** (oh-rehr) m

science-fiction film: **film de science-fiction** (feelm duh syahNs fee-ksyohN) m

scissors: **ciseaux** (see-zoh) mpl

season: **saison** (seh-zohN) f

seat, city or town square: **place** (plahs) f

seat: **siège** (syehzh) m

secretary: **secrétaire** (suh-krey-tehr) m/f

(to) see: **voir** (vwahr)

see you soon: **à bientôt** (ah byaN-toh)

see you tomorrow: **à demain** (ah duh-mahN)

seed: **graine** (grehn) f

(to) sell: **vendre** (vahN-druh)

September: **septembre** (sehp-tahN-bruh) m

(to) send: **envoyer** (ahN-vwah-yey)

seven: **sept** (seht)

seventeen: **dix-sept** (dee-seht)

she: **elle** (ehl) f

sheets: **draps** (drah) mpl

shirt: **chemise** (shuh-meez) f

shoe size: **pointure** (pwaN-tewr) f

shoes: **chaussures** (shoh-sewr) f pl:

shoulder: **épaule** (ey-pohl) f

(to) show: **montrer** (mohN-trey)

(to) shower: **se doucher** (suh dooh-shey)

showing (a movie): **séance** (sey-ahNs) f

shrimp: **crevettes** (kruh-veht) fpl

sidewalk: **trottoir** (troh-twahr) m

silk: **soie** (swah) f

silverware: **couverts** (kooh-vehr) mpl:

sister: **soeur** (suhr) f

six: **six** (sees)

sixteen: **seize** (sehz)

skirt: **jupe** (zhewp) f

slacks, pants: **pantalon** (pahN-tah-lohN) m

(to) sleep: **dormir** (dohr-meer)

sleeping bag: **sac de couchage** (sahk duh kooh-shahzh) m

(to) sing: **chanter** (shahN-tey)

slippers: **chaussons/pantoufles** (shoh-sohN/ pahN-tooh-fluh) mpl/fpl

(to) slow down: **ralentir** (rah-lahN-teer)

small, short: **petit/petite** (puh-tee/puh-teet) m/f

snack (as a verb: to taste): **goûter** (gooh-tey) m

snack: **casse-croûte** (kahs-krooht) m

sneakers: **baskets** (bahs-keht) fpl

snow: **neige** (nehzh) f

soap: **savon** (sah-vohN) m

soccer: **football** (fooht-bohl [France]), **soccer** (soh-kehr [Canada]) m

socks: **chaussettes** (shoh-seht) fpl

sofa: **canapé** (kah-nah-pey) m

software: **logiciel** (loh-zhee-syehl) m

soil: **sol** (sohl) m

something: **quelque chose** (kehl-kuh shohz)

son: **fils** (fees) m

sorrel: **oseille** (oh-zehy) f

sorry: **désolé/désolée** (dey-zoh-ley) m/f

south: **sud** (sewd) m

(to) speak/to talk: **parler** (pahr-ley)

special effects: **effets spéciaux** (ey-feh spey-syoh) mpl

special effects: **trucages** (trew-kahzh) mpl

spinach: **épinards** (ey-pee-nahr) mpl

spoon, teaspoon: **cuillère** (kwee-yehr) f

spouse: **époux/épouse** (ey-pooh/ ey-poohz) m/f

spring: **printemps** (praN-tahN) m

spy film: **film d'espionnage** (feelm deh-spee-oh-nahzh) m

stamp: **timbre** (taN-bruh) m

staple: **agrafe** (ah-grahf) f

stapler: **agrafeuse** (ah-grah-fuhz) f

stay: **séjour** (sey-zhoohr) m

(to) stay: **rester** (rehs-tey)

steak: **bifteck** (beef-tehk) m

stop: **arrêt** (ah-reh) m

store window: **vitrine** (vee-treen) f

store: **magasin** (mah-gah-zaN) m

stove: **cuisinière** (kwee-zee-nyehr) f

strawberry: **fraise** (frehz) f

street: **rue** (rew) f

(to) subscribe: **s'abonner** (sah-boh-ney)

sugar: **sucre** (sew-kruh) m

suit: **complet** (kohN-pleh [France]) m

suit: **habit** (ah-bee [Québec]) m

suitcase: **valise** (vah-leez) f

summer: **été** (ey-tey) m

sun: **soleil** (soh-lehy) m

sunglasses: **lunettes de soleil** (lew-neht duh soh-lehy) f pl

supermarket: **supermarché** (sew-pehr-mahr-shey) m

sweatshirt: **sweat** (sweht) m

sweater: **pull** (pewl) m

swimming pool: **piscine** (pee-seen) f

swimming: **natation** (nah-tah-syohN) f

T

(to) take: **prendre** (prahN-druh)

(to) tan: **bronzer** (brohN-zey)

tape: **ruban adhésif** (rew-bahN ahd-ey-zeef) m

tarragon: **estragon** (ehs-trah-gohN) m

tea: **thé** (tey) m

(to) telephone, to call: **téléphoner** (tey-ley-fohh-ney)

ten: **dix** (dees)

tennis: **tennis** (tey-nees) m

thank you: **merci** (mehr-see)

that one: **celui-là/celle-là** (suh-lwee-lah/sehl-lah) m/f

theft: **vol** (vohl) m

then: **puis** (pwee)

there is, there are: **il y a** (eel ee ah)

they: **elles** (ehl) fpl

they: **ils** (eel) mpl

(to) think: **penser** (pahN-sey)

(to be) thirsty: **avoir soif** (ah-vwahr swahf)

thirteen: **treize** (trehz)

this one: **celui-ci/celle-ci** (suh-lwee-see/sehl-see) m/f

thought: **pensée** (pahN-sey) f

thousand: **mille** (meel) m

three: **trois** (twah)

thyme: **thym** (taN) m

ticket window: **guichet** (gee-shey) m

ticket (traffic): **contravention** (kohN-trah-vahN-syohN) f

ticket: **billet** (bee-yeh) m

tie: **cravate** (krah-vaht) f

tip: **pourboire** (poohr-bwahr) m

tire: **pneu** (pnuh) m

tired: **fatigué/fatiguée** (fah-tee-gey) m/f

today: **aujourd'hui** (oh-zhoohr-dwee)

toe: **orteil** (ohr-tehy) m

tomato: **tomate** (toh-maht) f

too bad: **tant pis** (tahN pee)

too much: **trop** (troh)

tooth: **dent** (dahN) f

toothpaste: **dentifrice** (dahN-tee-frees) m

track: **voie** (vwah) f

traffic jam: **embouteillage** (ahN-booh-teh-yahzh) m

train station: **gare** (gahr) f

train: **train** (traN) m

(to) travel: **voyager** (voh-yah-zhey)

trout: **truite** (trweet) f

trunk: **coffre** (koh-fruh) m

tuna: **thon** (tohN) m

turkey: **dinde** (daNd) f

twelve: **douze** (doohz)

twenty: **vingt** (vaN)

two: **deux** (duh)

U

U turn: **demi-tour** (duh-mee-toohr) m

uncle: **oncle** (ohN-kluh) m

under, underneath: **sous** (sooh)

underpants, briefs: **slip** (sleep) m

underwear: **sous-vêtements** (sooh-veht-mahN) m

until: **jusqu'à** (zhews-kah)

username: **pseudo** (psooh-doh) m

V

to validate a ticket: **composter** (kohN-poh-stey)

veal, calf: **veau** (voh) m

vegatable garden: **potager** (poh-tah-zhey) m

vegetables: **légumes** (ley-gewm) mpl

vendor: **marchand/marchande** (mahr-shahN/mahr-shahNd) m/f

victory: **victoire** (veek-twahr) f

violin: **violon** (vyoh-lohN) m

to visit (a place): **visiter** (vee-zee-tey)

to visit (a person): **rendre visite à** (rahN-druh vee-zeet ah)

W

(to) wait: **attendre** (ah-tahN-druh)

waiter, waitress: **serveur/serveuse** (sehr-vuhr/sehr-vuhz) m/f

waiting room: **salle d'attente** (sahl dah-tahNt) f

(to) wake up: **se réveiller** (suh rey-vey-yey)

walk: **promenade** (prohm-nahd) f

wallet: **portefeuille** (pohrt-fuhy) m

(to) want: **vouloir** (vooh-lwahr)

warm/hot: **chaud/chaude** (shoh/shohd) m/f

(to) wash: **laver/se laver** (lah-vey/suh lah-vey)

wastepaper basket: **corbeille à papiers** (kohr-behy ah pah-pyey) m

watch: **montre** (mohN-truh) f

(to) watch: **regarder** (ruh-gahr-dey)

water: **eau** (oh) f

(to) water: **arroser** (ah-roh-zey)

watermelon: **pastèque** (pahs-tehk) f

wave: **vague** (vahg) f

we: **nous** (nooh)

(to) wear, to carry: **porter** (pohr-tey)

web browser: **navigateur** (nah-vee-gah-tuhr) m

week: **semaine** (suh-mehn) f

(to) weigh: **peser** (puh-zey)

weird, bizarre: **bizarre** (beez-ahr)

west: **ouest** (ooh-wehst) m

what: **qu'est-ce que/quoi** (kehs-kuh/kwah)

when: **quand** (kahN)

where: **où** (ooh)

which: **quel/quelle** (kehl) m/f

(to) whistle: **siffler** (see-fley)

white: **blanc/blanche** (blahN/blahNsh) m/f

who: **qui** (kee)

why: **pourquoi** (poohr-kwah)

(to) win: **gagner** (gah-nyey)

window: **fenêtre** (fuh-neh-truh) f

windshield wiper: **essuie-glace** (ey-swee-glahs) m

windshield: **pare-brise** (pahr-breez) m

windsurfing: **planche à voile** (plahNsh ah vwahl) f

wine: **vin** (vaN) m

winter: **hiver** (ee-vehr) m

woman, wife: **femme** (fahm) f

women's suit: **tailleur** (tahy-uhr) m

wool: **laine** (lehn) f

(to) work: **travailler** (trah-vah-yey)

Y

yard, garden: **jardin** (zhahr-daN) m

yellow: **jaune** (zhohn)

you (singular formal, plural): **vous** (vooh)

you (singular informal): **tu** (tew)

you: **toi** (twah)

Z

zip code: **code postal** (kohhd poh-stahl) m

Appendix B

Verb Tables

• •

*N*ote: This appendix shows the conjugation of the present indicative, **passé composé** (past), and simple future tenses. For more on the conjugation of these tenses, refer to Chapters 2, 11, and 13, respectively.

Regular French Verbs

Regular Verbs Ending with –er
For example: parler (to speak)

Past Participle: parlé (spoken); Present participle: parlant (speaking)

	Present	Past	Future
je/j' (I)	parle	ai parlé	parlerai
tu (you, inf.)	parles	as parlé	parleras
il/elle/on (he/she/it/one)	parle	a parlé	parlera
nous (we)	parlons	avons parlé	parlerons
vous (you, form., pl.)	parlez	avez parlé	parlerez
ils/elles (they)	parlent	ont parlé	parleront

Regular Verbs Ending with –ir
For example: finir (to finish)

Past Participle: fini (finished); Present Participle: finissant (finishing)

	Present	Past	Future
je/j' (I)	finis	ai fini	finirai
tu (you, inf.)	finis	as fini	finiras
il/elle/on (he/she/it/one)	finit	a fini	finira
nous (we)	finissons	avons fini	finirons
vous (you, form., pl.)	finissez	avez fini	finirez
ils/elles (they)	finissent	ont fini	finiront

Regular Verbs Ending with –re
For example: vendre (to sell)

Past Participle: vendu (sold); Present Participle: vendant (selling)

	Present	Past	Future
je/j' (I)	vends	ai vendu	vendrai
tu (you, inf.)	vends	as vendu	vendras
il/elle/on (he/she/it/one)	vend	a vendu	vendra
nous (we)	vendons	avons vendu	vendrons
vous (you, form., pl.)	vendez	avez vendu	vendrez
ils/elles (they)	vendent	ont vendu	vendront

Reflexive Verbs
For example: se laver (to wash oneself)

**Past Participle: lavé (washed); Present participle: me/te/se/nous/
vous/ lavant (washing)**

	Present	**Past**	**Future**
je (I)	me lave	me suis lavé/e	me laverai
tu (you, inf.)	te laves	t'es lavé/e	te laveras
il/elle/on (he/she/it/one)	se lave	s'est lavé/e	se lavera
nous (we)	nous lavons	nous sommes lavés/es	nous laverons
vous (you, form., pl.)	vous lavez	vous êtes lavé/e/s/es	vous laverez
ils/elles (they)	se lavent	se sont lavés/es	se laveront

Auxiliary French Verbs

Avoir (ah-vwahr) (*to have*) and **être** (eh-truh) (*to be*) are the two auxiliary verbs used to form all compound past tenses in French.

avoir (to have)
Past Participle: eu (had); Present Participle: ayant (having)

	Present	**Past**	**Future**
je/j' (I)	ai	ai eu	aurai
tu (you, inf.)	as	as eu	auras
il/elle/on (he/she/it/one)	a	a eu	aura
nous (we)	avons	avons eu	aurons
vous (you, form., pl.)	avez	avez eu	aurez
ils/elles (they)	ont	ont eu	auront

être (to be)
Past Participle: été (been); Present Participle: étant (being)

	Present	Past	Future
je/j' (I)	suis	ai été	serai
tu (you, inf.)	es	as été	seras
il/elle/on (he/she/it/one)	est	a été	sera
nous (we)	sommes	avons été	serons
vous (you, form., pl.)	êtes	avez été	serez
ils/elles (they)	sont	ont été	seront

Irregular and Stem-Changing French Verbs

		Present	Past	Future
acheter to buy Past participle: acheté (bought) Present participle: achetant (buying)	*j'*	achète	ai acheté	achèterai
	tu	achètes	as acheté	achèteras
	il/elle/on	achète	a acheté	achètera
	nous	achetons	avons acheté	achèterons
	vous	achetez	avez acheté	achèterez
	ils/elles	achètent	ont acheté	achèteront

		Present	Past	Future
aller	*je/j'*	vais	suis allé/e	irai
to go				
Past participle: allé (went)	*tu*	vas	es allé/e	iras
Present participle: allant (going)	*il/elle/on*	va	est allé/e	ira
	nous	allons	sommes allés/es	irons
	vous	allez	êtes allé/e/s/es	irez
	ils/elles	vont	sont allés/es	iront
appeler	*j'*	appelle	ai appelé	appellerai
to call				
Past participle: appelé (called)	*tu*	appelles	as appelé	appelleras
Present participle: appelant (calling)	*il/elle/on*	appelle	a appelé	appellera
	nous	appelons	avons appelé	appellerons
	vous	appelez	avez appelé	appellerez
	ils/elles	appellent	ont appelé	appelleront
boire	*je/j'*	bois	ai bu	boirai
to drink				
Past participle: bu (drank)	*tu*	bois	as bu	boiras
Present participle: buvant (drinking)	*il/elle/on*	boit	a bu	boira
	nous	buvons	avons bu	boirons
	vous	buvez	avez bu	boirez
	ils/elles	boivent	ont bu	boiront

		Present	Past	Future
commencer to begin Past participle: commencé (began) Present participle: commençant (beginning)	*je/j'*	commence	ai commencé	commencerai
	tu	commences	as commencé	commenceras
	il/elle/on	commence	a commencé	commencera
	nous	commençons	avons commencé	commencerons
	vous	commencez	avez commencé	commencerez
	ils/elles	commencent	ont commencé	commenceront
comprendre to understand Past participle: compris (understood) Present participle: comprenant (understanding)	*je/j'*	comprends	ai compris	comprendrai
	tu	comprends	as compris	comprendras
	il/elle/on	comprend	a compris	comprendra
	nous	comprenons	avons compris	comprendrons
	vous	comprenez	avez compris	comprendrez
	ils/elles	comprennent	ont compris	comprendront
conduire to drive Past participle: conduit (drove) Present participle: conduisant (driving)	*je/j'*	conduis	ai conduit	conduirai
	tu	conduis	as conduit	conduiras
	il/elle/on	conduit	a conduit	conduira
	nous	conduisons	avons conduit	conduirons
	vous	conduisez	avez conduit	conduirez
	ils/elles	conduisent	ont conduit	conduiront

		Present	Past	Future
connaître to know (people and places)	*je/j'*	connais	ai connu	connaîtrai
Past participle: connu (knew)	*tu*	connais	as connu	connaîtras
Present participle: connaissant (knowing)	*il/elle/on*	connaît	a connu	connaîtra
	nous	connaissons	avons connu	connaîtrons
	vous	connaissez	avez connu	connaîtrez
	ils/elles	connaissent	ont connu	connaîtront
devoir to have to	*je/j'*	dois	ai dû	devrai
Past participle: dû (had to)	*tu*	dois	as dû	devras
Present participle: devant (having to)	*il/elle/on*	doit	a dû	devra
	nous	devons	avons dû	devrons
	vous	devez	avez dû	devrez
	ils/elles	doivent	ont dû	devront
dire to say	*je/j'*	dis	ai dit	dirai
Past participle: dit (said)	*tu*	dis	as dit	diras
Present participle: disant (saying)	*il/elle/on*	dit	a dit	dira
	nous	disons	avons dit	dirons
	vous	dites	avez dit	direz
	ils/elles	disent	ont dit	diront

		Present	Past	Future
écrire	j'	écris	ai écrit	écrirai
to write				
Past participle: écrit (wrote)	tu	écris	as écrit	écriras
Present participle: écrivant (writing)	il/elle/on	écrit	a écrit	écrira
	nous	écrivons	avons écrit	écrirons
	vous	écrivez	avez écrit	écrirez
	ils/elles	écrivent	ont écrit	écriront
entendre	j'	entends	ai entendu	entendrai
to hear				
Past participle: entendu (heard)	tu	entends	as entendu	entendras
Present participle: entendant (hearing)	il/elle/on	entend	a entendu	entendra
	nous	entendons	avons entendu	entendrons
	vous	entendez	avez entendu	entendrez
	ils/elles	entendent	ont entendu	entendront
envoyer	j'	envoie	ai envoyé	enverrai
to send				
Past participle: envoyé (sent)	tu	envoies	as envoyé	enverras
Present participle: envoyant (sending)	il/elle/on	envoie	a envoyé	enverra
	nous	envoyons	avons envoyé	enverrons
	vous	envoyez	avez envoyé	enverrez
	ils/elles	envoient	ont envoyé	enverront

		Present	Past	Future
espérer	*j'*	espère	ai espéré	espérerai
to hope				
Past participle: espéré (hoped)	*tu*	espères	as espéré	espéreras
Present participle: espérant (hoping)	*il/elle/on*	espère	a espéré	espérera
	nous	espérons	avons espéré	espérerons
	vous	espérez	avez espéré	espérerez
	ils/elles	espèrent	ont espéré	espéreront
faire	*je/j'*	fais	ai fait	ferai
to do, to make				
Past participle: fait (did, made)	*tu*	fais	as fait	feras
Present participle: faisant (doing, making)	*il/elle/on*	fait	a fait	fera
	nous	faisons	avons fait	ferons
	vous	faites	avez fait	ferez
	ils/elles	font	ont fait	feront
lire	*je/j'*	lis	ai lu	lirai
to read				
Past participle: lu (read)	*tu*	lis	as lu	liras
Present participle: lisant (reading)	*il/elle/on*	lit	a lu	lira
	nous	lisons	avons lu	lirons
	vous	lisez	avez lu	lirez
	ils/elles	lisent	ont lu	liront

		Present	Past	Future
manger to eat Past participle: mangé (ate) Present participle: mangeant (eating)	*je/j'*	mange	ai mangé	mangerai
	tu	manges	as mangé	mangeras
	il/elle/on	mange	a mangé	mangera
	nous	mangeons	avons mangé	mangerons
	vous	mangez	avez mangé	mangerez
	ils/elles	mangent	ont mangé	mangeront
mettre to put, to put on (as with clothes), to place Past participle: mis (put, put on, placed) Present participle: mettant (putting, putting on, placing)	*je/j'*	mets	ai mis	mettrai
	tu	mets	as mis	mettras
	il/elle/on	met	a mis	mettra
	nous	mettons	avons mis	mettrons
	vous	mettez	avez mis	mettrez
	ils/elles	mettent	ont mis	mettront
offrir to offer Past participle: offert (offered) Present participle: offrant (offering)	*j'*	offre	ai offert	offrirai
	tu	offres	as offert	offriras
	il/elle/on	offre	a offert	offrira
	nous	offrons	avons offert	offrirons
	vous	offrez	avez offert	offrirez
	ils/elles	offrent	ont offert	offriront

		Present	Past	Future
partir	*je*	pars	suis parti/e	partirai
to leave				
Past participle: parti (left)	*tu*	pars	es parti/e	partiras
Present participle: partant (leaving)	*il/elle/on*	part	est parti/e	partira
	nous	partons	sommes partis/es	partirons
	vous	partez	êtes parti/e/s/es	partirez
	ils/elles	partent	sont partis/es	partiront
payer	*je/j'*	paie	ai payé	paierai
to pay				
Past participle: payé (paid)	*tu*	paies	as payé	paieras
Present participle: payant (paying)	*il/elle/on*	paie	a payé	paiera
	nous	payons	avons payé	paierons
	vous	payez	avez payé	paierez
	ils/elles	paient	ont payé	paieront
préférer	*je/j'*	préfère	ai préféré	préférerai
to prefer				
Past participle: préféré (preferred)	*tu*	préfères	as préféré	préféreras
Present participle: préférant (prefering)	*il/elle/on*	préfère	a préféré	préférera
	nous	préférons	avons préféré	préférerons
	vous	préférez	avez préféré	préférerez
	ils/elles	préfèrent	ont préféré	préféreront

		Present	Past	Future
pouvoir to be able to (can) Past participle: pu (could) Present participle: pouvant (being able to)	je/j'	peux	ai pu	pourrai
	tu	peux	as pu	pourras
	il/elle/on	peut	a pu	pourra
	nous	pouvons	avons pu	pourrons
	vous	pouvez	avez pu	pourrez
	ils/elles	peuvent	ont pu	pourront
prendre to take (to have [with food and drink] or to have a meal) Past participle: pris (took) Present participle: prenant (taking)	je/j'	prends	ai pris	prendrai
	tu	prends	as pris	prendras
	il/elle/on	prend	a pris	prendra
	nous	prenons	avons pris	prendrons
	vous	prenez	avez pris	prendrez
	ils/elles	prennent	ont pris	prendront
recevoir to receive Past participle: reçu (received) Present participle: recevant (receiving)	je/j'	reçois	ai reçu	recevrai
	tu	reçois	as reçu	recevras
	il/elle/on	reçoit	a reçu	recevra
	nous	recevons	avons reçu	recevrons
	vous	recevez	avez reçu	recevrez
	ils/elles	reçoivent	ont reçu	recevront

		Present	Past	Future
rendre to give back Past participle: rendu (gave back) Present participle: rendant (giving back)	*je/j'*	rends	ai rendu	rendrai
	tu	rends	as rendu	rendras
	il/elle/on	rend	a rendu	rendra
	nous	rendons	avons rendu	rendrons
	vous	rendez	avez rendu	rendrez
	ils/elles	rendent	ont rendu	rendront
rire to laugh Past participle: ri (laughed) Present participle: riant (laughing)	*je/j'*	ris	ai ri	rirai
	tu	ris	as ri	riras
	il/elle/on	rit	a ri	rira
	nous	rions	avons ri	rirons
	vous	riez	avez ri	rirez
	ils/elles	rient	ont ri	riront
savoir to know (facts, information) Past participle: su (knew, discovered, found out) Present participle: sachant (knowing)	*je/j'*	sais	ai su	saurai
	tu	sais	as su	sauras
	il/elle/on	sait	a su	saura
	nous	savons	avons su	saurons
	vous	savez	avez su	saurez
	ils/elles	savent	ont su	sauront

		Present	Past	Future
servir to serve	*je/j'*	sers	ai servi	servirai
Past participle: servi (served)	*tu*	sers	as servi	serviras
Present participle: servant (serving)	*il/elle/on*	sert	a servi	servira
	nous	servons	avons servi	servirons
	vous	servez	avez servi	servirez
	ils/elles	servent	ont servi	serviront
sortir to go out	*je*	sors	suis sorti/e	sortirai
Past participle: sorti (went out)	*tu*	sors	es sorti/e	sortiras
Present participle: sortant (going out)	*il/elle/on*	sort	est sorti/e	sortira
	nous	sortons	sommes sortis/es	sortirons
	vous	sortez	êtes sorti/e/s/es	sortirez
	ils/elles	sortent	sont sortis/es	sortiront
tenir to hold	*je/j'*	tiens	ai tenu	tiendrai
Past participle: tenu (held)	*tu*	tiens	as tenu	tiendras
Present participle: tenant (holding)	*il/elle/on*	tient	a tenu	tiendra
	nous	tenons	avons tenu	tiendrons
	vous	tenez	avez tenu	tiendrez
	ils/elles	tiennent	ont tenu	tiendront

		Present	Past	Future
venir to come Past participle: venu (came) Present participle: venant (coming)	*je*	viens	suis venu/e	viendrai
	tu	viens	es venu/e	viendras
	il/elle/on	vient	est venu/e	viendra
	nous	venons	sommes venus/es	viendrons
	vous	venez	êtes venu/e/s/es	viendrez
	ils/elles	viennent	sont venus/es	viendront
vivre to live Past participle: vécu (lived) Present participle: vivant (living)	*je/j'*	vis	ai vécu	vivrai
	tu	vis	as vécu	vivras
	il/elle/on	vit	a vécu	vivra
	nous	vivons	avons vécu	vivrons
	vous	vivez	avez vécu	vivrez
	ils/elles	vivent	ont vécu	vivront
voir to see Past participle: vu (saw) Present participle: voyant (seeing)	*je/j'*	vois	ai vu	verrai
	tu	vois	as vu	verras
	il/elle/on	voit	a vu	verra
	nous	voyons	avons vu	verrons
	vous	voyez	avez vu	verrez
	ils/elles	voient	ont vu	verront

		Present	**Past**	**Future**
vouloir to want Past participle: voulu (wanted) Present participle: voulant (wanting)	*je/j'*	veux	ai voulu	voudrai
	tu	veux	as voulu	voudras
	il/elle/on	veut	a voulu	voudra
	nous	voulons	avons voulu	voudrons
	vous	voulez	avez voulu	voudrez
	ils/elles	veulent	ont voulu	voudront

Appendix C

Answer Key

• •

*T*he following pages provide you with the answer keys to the Fun & Games activities at the end of the chapters.

Chapter 3: Getting Started with Pronunciation and Basic Expressions

1. m'appelle, 2. je, 3. grande, 4. femme, 5. elle, 6. l'anglais, 7. ça va, 8. toi, 9. voici, 10. parles, 11. bien

Chapter 4: Getting Your Numbers, Dates, and Times Straight

A. Il est dix heures et quart (du matin), Il est dix heures quinze; B. Il est deux heures et demie (de l'après-midi), Il est quatorze heures trente; C. Il est neuf heures moins le quart (du soir), Il est vingt heures quarante-cinq; D. Il est onze heures moins cinq (du soir), Il est vingt-deux heures cinquante-cinq; E. Il est midi, Il est douze heures

Chapter 5: Talking about Your Home, Family, and Daily Routine

A. la salle de bains; 1) la douche 2) la baignoire; B. la chambre 1) le lit 2) la table de nuit; C. le salon, la salle de séjour/le séjour; 1) les rideaux 2) le sofa/ le canapé 3) le fauteuil; D. la cuisine; 1) la cuisinière 2) l'évier 3) la chaise

Chapter 6: Getting to Know You: Making Small Talk

A. l'hiver, B. l'été, C. le printemps, D. l'automne, E. il fait du vent, F. il fait chaud, G. il pleut, H. il neige

Chapter 7: Asking Directions and Finding Your Way

A. Descendez/Prenez, B. Tournez à droite, C. Prenez, D. tournez sud-ouest, E. Tournez à droite, F. Suivez

Chapter 8: Bon Appétit! Dining Out and Going to the Market

A. une baguette, B. des crevettes, C. des haricots verts, D. le poulet, E. des pêches, F. le jambon, G. l'ananas, H. des pommes de terre

Chapter 9: Shopping Made Easy

A. un chapeau, B. une chemise, C. un veston, D. une cravate, E. des chaussures, F. une veste, G. un chemisier, H. une jupe, I. des chaussures à talons, J. une robe, K. un manteau

Chapter 10: Going Out on the Town

A. un musée, B. Une boîte de nuit, C. un cinéma, D. une symphonie, E. une soirée, F. un opéra

Chapter 11: Taking Care of Business and Telecommunicating

Activity 1: A. la lampe, B. les enveloppes, C. le moniteur, D. l'ordinateur, E. la souris, F. les ciseaux, G. le stylo, H. l'agrafeuse, I. le bureau, J. la corbeille à papiers

Activity 2: A. arrivé (e), B. parlé, C. voulu, D. rentrés (es), E. fait, F.choisi, G. eu

Chapter 12: Recreation and the Outdoors

A. faire de la voile, B. faire du surf, C. faire de la plongée libre, D. pêcher, E.faire du ski, F. faire une randonnée, G. faire de la natation, H. faire du vélo, I. faire du tennis, J. faire du golf

Chapter 13: Planning a Trip

A. le Portugal, B l'Espagne, C. l'Angleterre, D. la Belgique, E. les Pays-Bas, F. l'Allemagne, G. l'Italie, H. la Grèce

Chapter 14: Dealing with Money in a Foreign Land

A. vingt centimes – La Semeuse, B. cinq centimes – La Marianne, C. dix centimes – La Semeuse, D. deux centimes – La Marianne, E. deux euros – L'Arbre

Chapter 15: Getting Around: Planes, Trains, Taxis, and More

1. H, 2. F., 3. D, 4. A, 5. B, 6. E, 7. C, 8. G

Chapter 16: Finding a Place to Stay

A. Oui, une chambre avec des lits jumeaux; B. Non. Avec salle de bain/avec baignoire; C. Non, au premier étage ; D. Oui.; E. Non. Pour deux nuits.

Chapter 17: Handling Emergencies

1. la poitrine 2. l'épaule 3. l'oeil 4. la tête 5. le nez 6. la bouche 7. le cou 8. le bras 9. la main 10. l'estomac 11. la jambe 12. le pied 13. la cheville 14. le genou

Appendix D

On the CD

● ●

Track Listing

The following is a list of the tracks that appear on this book's audio CD. Note that this is an audio-only CD — it'll play in any standard CD player or in your computer's CD-ROM drive.

Track 1: Introduction and the French alphabet (Chapter 3)

Track 2: Greeting business associates (Chapter 3)

Track 3: Talking about time (Chapter 4)

Track 4: Discussing an apartment for rent (Chapter 5)

Track 5: Making small talk (Chapter 6)

Track 6: Discussing the weather (Chapter 6)

Track 7: Finding out where Versailles is (Chapter 7)

Track 8: Paying the bill (Chapter 8)

Track 9: Shopping for a dress (Chapter 9)

Track 10: Making plans for the day (Chapter 10)

Track 11: Holding for your party (Chapter 11)

Track 12: Talking about sports (Chapter 12)

Track 13: Going camping (Chapter 12)

Track 14: Booking a trip with a travel agent (Chapter 13)

Track 15: Exchanging money (Chapter 14)

Track 16: Discussing a method of payment (Chapter 14)

Track 17: Discussing the bus schedule (Chapter 15)

Track 18: Buying a train ticket (Chapter 15)

Track 19: Asking about hotel vacancies (Chapter 16)

Track 20: Making arrangements for luggage at check out (Chapter 16)

Track 21: Making a doctor appointment (Chapter 17)

Customer Care

If you have trouble with the CD, please call John Wiley & Sons, Inc. Product Technical Support at 877-762-2974. Outside the United States, call 317-572-3993. You can also contact John Wiley & Sons, Inc. Product Technical Support at `support.wiley.com`. John Wiley & Sons, Inc. will provide technical support only for installation and other general quality control items.

To place additional orders or to request information about other John Wiley & Sons, Inc. products, please call 877-762-2974.

Index

● *D* ●

• F •

• *Q* •